A Bolt from the Blue

and Other Essays

A Bolt from the Blue
and Other Essays

Mary McCarthy

edited and with an introduction by

A. O. SCOTT

NEW YORK REVIEW BOOKS

New York

A BOLT FROM THE BLUE
AND OTHER ESSAYS

by Mary McCarthy

Copyright © 2002 by NYREV, Inc.

This edition published in 2002
in the United States of America by
The New York Review of Books
1755 Broadway
New York, NY 10019
www.nybooks.com

"Introduction to *Theatre Chronicles*," "Class Angles and a Wilder Classic," "Shaw and Chekhov," "Eugene O'Neill—Dry Ice," "A Streetcar Called Success," "A New Word," "The American Realist Playwrights," "Elizabethan Revivals," "The Fact in Fiction," "America the Beautiful: The Humanist in the Bathtub," "Mlle. Gulliver en Amérique," "My Confession," "Up the Ladder from *Charm* to *Vogue*," and "Letter from Portugal" are reprinted by permission of the Mary McCarthy Literary Trust.

"A Bolt from the Blue," "Burroughs's *Naked Lunch*," "J. D. Salinger's Closed Circuit," "On *Madame Bovary*," "Hanging by a Thread," "On Rereading a Favorite Book," "Acts of Love," "*Ideas and the Novel*: Lecture I," "The Home Program," "Philip Rahv (1908–1973)," "F. W. Dupee (1904–1979)," "The Very Unforgettable Miss Brayton," "Notes of a Resident of the Watergate," and "The Moral Certainties of John D. Ehrlichman" are reprinted by permission of Harcourt Inc. and the Mary McCarthy Literary Trust.

Library of Congress Cataloging-in-Publication Data

McCarthy, Mary, 1912–.
A bolt from the blue and other essays / Mary McCarthy; edited and with an introduction by A. O. Scott.
    p. cm.
    ISBN 1-59017-010-5 (alk. paper)
    I. Scott, A. O.   II. Title.
PS3525.A1435 B65 2002
814'.52 — dc21

2002002881

ISBN 1-59017-010-5

Printed in the United States of America on acid-free paper.

May 2002

1 3 5 7 9 10 8 6 4 2

Contents

Introduction

Introducing Mary McCarthy is, in some ways, a superfluous task. In the years since her death, in 1989, her eventful life has been chronicled in two thoughtful biographies. The impressive selection of her work that remains in print—including *Memoirs of a Catholic Girlhood*, a half-dozen novels and story collections, her vivid guides to Venice and Florence—has been augmented by the posthumous publication of her *Intellectual Memoirs* and her correspondence with Hannah Arendt. The passage of time has quieted the clamor of the midcentury New York literary scene in which she flourished, and dulled the thorny debates—about the Moscow show trials, Senator McCarthy, Vietnam, and Watergate—that preoccupied its partisans, but McCarthy herself nonetheless remains a vivid, glamorous, and controversial figure. Still, even as her aura of renown has retained some of its luster, and her reputation as a leading American woman of letters survives her, McCarthy's standing as a writer remains in doubt and in dispute. Her devotees may infer traces of her influence everywhere they look— in the latest campus novels, in proliferating memoirs of unhappy childhood, and even in *Sex and The City*, the popular HBO series about a smart, sexually adventurous New York writer and the company she keeps—but McCarthy's originality and perspicacity, her ability to connect her society's passing fancies with its deepest torments, are not sufficiently acknowledged.

One of the ambitions of this book, which brings together twenty-eight of McCarthy's essays on literature, politics, and culture, is to make a somewhat paradoxical case for her importance as a novelist—one of a handful of indispensable American writers of realist fiction in the immediate postwar era. Her slim, packed book of lectures *Ideas and The Novel*, published when her own novel-writing days were done (and excerpted here), illuminates her desire to put back into fiction everything modernism, starting with James, had seen fit to excise, in other words everything people actually talk about—politics, art, religion, food, furniture, and so on. In an earlier pair of lectures, "The Fact in Fiction" and "Characters in Fiction," delivered in Eastern Europe in 1950, McCarthy looks back on the nineteenth century, when "novels, including James's, carried the news—of crime, high society, politics, industry, finance, and low life." Granting all the complexities of modern life that make old-fashioned realism untenable, she argues for a fiction of persons, objects, and events, of charmed and disenchanted lives viewed—and judged—in their immediate, documentable social surroundings.

The reviews and lectures assembled in the first section of this book can be read as a kind of ad hoc manifesto—a series of inquiries into the aesthetic principles and practices McCarthy was simultaneously exploring in her fiction. Whether addressing contemporaries or old masters, reflecting on the grand scheme of literary history or the minutiae of a particular novel or theatrical production, she holds fast to premises that have as much to do with ethics as with taste. A play that offends our sense of reality, that assaults the ear with sentiment and bad lyricism, is, in her judgment, not only deformed but dishonest. Though most of her literary touchstones lay in the nineteenth century—Tolstoy and Flaubert, Ibsen and Chekhov—there is something Augustan in her love of clarity and her occasionally severe sense of decorum. But this classical rigor coexists with a sometimes exhausting appetite for detail, for fictions as overstuffed and enveloping as the furniture they describe.

This tension—between intellectual precision and a kind of voracious materialism, between the order of thought and the mess of life—is palpable in *The Group*, in *The Company She Keeps*, and in the pieces that comprise the second part of this book. The subjects range from the high political drama of the Committee in Defense of Leon Trotsky and the Watergate hearings to fond, intimate remembrances of old friends, from French Existentialists to women's magazines. The author seems equally at home—and yet also equally at odds with the company and the surroundings—in the bustle of Portugal, the steamy frenzy of Saigon, and the stately calm of Newport. In every passage of description one feels the tug of argument. The world is there to be judged, made sense of, thought about. But it is also, splendidly and absurdly, *there*—a stream of odd facts and curious propositions, a congeries of eccentrics, fast-talkers, and bores, a self-replenishing warehouse stocked with costumes, objects, and *jeux d'esprit*.

Taken together, these essays—from *Partisan Review* and *House and Garden*, from *The New York Review of Books* and *Holiday*, as well as from many other periodicals British and American, thriving and defunct—illuminate the cultural and intellectual history of mid-century America. At the same time, and perhaps more valuably, they reveal an extraordinary literary personality—funny, charming, didactic, intimate, and thoroughly, fundamentally critical. In the course of a career that spanned more than five decades—from the left-wing literary bohemia of the 1930s to the literary celebrity circuit of the 1970s, from the Committee for the Defense of Leon Trotsky to *The Dick Cavett Show*—Mary McCarthy was a protean and prolific author of novels, stories, reminiscences, travelogues, letters, and magazine features. But she was, first of all, a critic. This is in part a matter of chronological accident. Like many young people drawn to the intellectual hothouse of Depression-era New York, McCarthy got her start in the back pages of the opinion journals, loitering with the other ambitious, underemployed aspirants in the offices of *The New Republic* and *The Nation* in the hope of being given a book to review. In 1937, when *Partisan Review*, founded three years earlier, cut its umbilical tie to the Communist Party and relaunched under the editorship of Philip Rahv and William Philips, McCarthy, who was living with Rahv at the time, signed on as theatre critic, a post she would occupy, on and off, for the next twenty-five years.

Later, she would recall the assignment as something of a fluke. Since her name appeared on the magazine's masthead, she needed to be given something to do, and reviewing plays was considered to be a suitably trivial occupation for a woman four years out of Vassar. Besides, McCarthy's first husband, Harold Johnsrud, was an actor and a playwright, so it was assumed that she must have, if not expertise exactly, then at least some affinity for the theatre. But if criticism was something McCarthy took up, by convenience and happenstance, on her way to grander, more durable projects, it was also central to her vocation as a writer. In 1941, when, at the urging of her second husband, Edmund Wilson, she turned to fiction, her efforts—the coolly candid stories that comprised her first book, *The Company She Keeps*—developed a persona already evident in her earliest reviews. Margaret Sargent, McCarthy's alter ego in these tales, is clever and opinionated, fearless sometimes to the point of foolishness, and in possession of an analytical, judgmental temperament at once intimidating and seductive. Margaret marries and divorces, goes to dinner parties, editorial meetings, and her analyst's office, has affairs with pedigreed intellectuals and traveling salesmen, but mainly what she does, in the first, second, and third persons, is think, argue, criticize. The recounting of Margaret's adventures is impelled as much by argumentative logic as by narrative movement, and the stories have the verve and grace, the deft, offhand coherence, of first-rate essays.

What interests McCarthy, whether anatomizing the behavior of an adulterous husband, a feckless divorcee, or, three decades later, a White House aide at the Senate Watergate hearings, is nuances of performance and strategies of storytelling. Her characters—real, fictional, and composite—take their turn on the domestic or the social stage, or give voice to the novels they are composing in their own heads, while the author sits, pencil in hand, making notes for the next scrupulous, unsparing review.

McCarthy's friend Elizabeth Hardwick once wrote that "literature, in her practice, has the elation of an adventure—and of course that elation mitigates and makes aesthetically acceptable to our senses the strictness of her judgment." This may be even truer of McCarthy's essays than it is of her fiction. One may wince at her merciless dissections of J. D. Salinger or *A Streetcar Named Desire*, and still revel in the elegant precision of her scalpel-work. "Pale Diana.... Whose... arrows sing cleaner through the pelt?" asked Hardwick's husband, Robert Lowell, in a sonnet dedicated to McCarthy. The pages that follow echo with the thump of well-aimed shafts—"ninety percent on target," in Lowell's estimate—piercing hides thickened by habitual praise. A review of *The Iceman Cometh* begins with the observation that a new work by O'Neill "is guaranteed to last two-and-a-half hours longer than any other play, with the exception of the uncut *Hamlet*." By the end of the next paragraph, the page is as strewn with dead bodies as the stage at the end of Shakespeare's bloody tragedy: "To audiences accustomed to the oily virtuosity of George Kaufman, George Abbott, Lillian Hellman, Odets, Saroyan, the return of a playwright who—let us be frank—cannot write is a solemn and sentimental occasion."

Of course, to paraphrase Gertrude Stein, unkind remarks are not literary criticism. What is, in the end, most intoxicating about the *Iceman* piece is not its witty savagery but its seriousness, its confident articulation of a coherent point of view. McCarthy's commitment, as a novelist, to realism made her an especially acute critic of its dramatic misappropriation. Her impatience with the American realist playwrights—evident in the essay with that title and also in reviews of Odets, O'Neill, Tennessee Williams, and Arthur Miller—will strike their admirers as unfair, but her case against them is not easily dismissed. It arises from a nearly allergic sensitivity to sentimentality, rhetorical inflation, and unwarranted generalization, vices endemic not only to midcentury American theatre but to the culture that surrounded it.

It is likely that McCarthy developed this aversion to cant, and the ability to hear its tinny resonance at frequencies inaudible to the untrained ear, as a result of her encounter with the Stalinism of the 1930s. Like many of her *Partisan Review* colleagues—and like the anti-Communist left-wing intelligentsia generally—McCarthy discerned a resemblance between the sloganeering kitsch of Thirties Communism and the smiling consumerism of the postwar American mainstream. But just as her recoil from Communism never hardened into reaction, her sense of estrangement from American mass culture largely avoided the traps of snobbery and pessimism. The ambivalence about the character and direction of the national life in the 1940s and 1950s was hardly hers alone—it bubbles up again and again in novels, in symposia, in the pages of the quarterlies—but there is an elegance, a verve, that distinguishes even a somber and anxious essay like "America the Beautiful" from the rather more pompous pronouncements of McCarthy's rivals and friends.

The New York intellectual scene in which McCarthy flourished is regarded today either with nostalgia or ridicule. One of McCarthy's achievements was to reflect the absurdity and the nobility of her time and place in equal measure. The forming of committees and editorial boards, the repudiation of former allies and the reconciliation with erstwhile enemies, the endless position-taking—all of this reflected serious, principled concerns. But the life of the mind was lived in reasonable freedom and comfort, and conducted against a sound-track of love affairs, dinner parties, gossip, and shop talk. Few writers could match McCarthy's ability to attend at once to the clamor and clutter of daily life—she had a Hollywood production designer's eye for contemporaneous period detail—and the deep rumblings of history. Indeed, to be a citizen of politically engaged literary New York at midcentury was to experience big historical dynamics largely through the minute fluctuations of social life. "I too have had a share in the political movements of our day," McCarthy declares in "My Confession," taking issue with the conversion narratives of former Communists like Whittaker Chambers and Elizabeth Bentley, "and my experience cries out against their experience. It is not the facts I balk at—I have never been an espionage agent—but the studio atmosphere of sublimity and purpose that enfolds the facts and the chief actor." She presents her own flirtation with Communism as something of a caprice—not frivolous, exactly, but certainly fun. It's a lark, after all, to imagine yourself on the right side of history, and to feel superior to everyone who isn't. The fun stops abruptly at a cocktail party, when someone asks McCarthy if she thinks Trotsky deserves a fair hearing. Since she's been in Nevada getting divorced, she hasn't been following the Moscow trials, and so she answers, "of course," without really thinking about it, thereby capriciously committing herself to a moral position from which she will not swerve. (The experience is also recounted, a bit more dramatically, in "Portrait of the Intellectual as a Yale Man.") "Most of us who became anti-Communists at the time of the trials," she concludes,

> were drawn in, like me, by accident and almost unwillingly. Looking back, as on a love affair, a man could say that if he had not had lunch in a certain restaurant on a certain day, he might not have been led to ponder the facts of the Moscow trials.... Our anti-Communism came to us neither as the fruit of a special

wisdom nor as a humiliating awakening from a prolonged deception, but as a natural event, the product of chance and propinquity.

Another name for which might be grace. If the story told in "My Confession" suggests a life full of unexpected turns, the manner of its telling is evidence of a character that would remain receptive to the operations of chance. McCarthy's literary aesthetics and her approach to the art of living were not far apart. "The tree of life, said Hegel, is greener than the tree of thought," she wrote in an essay, not reprinted here, called "Settling the Colonel's Hash."

> I have quoted this before but I cannot forebear from citing it again in this context. This is not an incitement to mindlessness or an endorsement of realism ... (there are several kinds of reality, including interior reality); it means only that the writer must be, first of all, a listener and observer, who can pay attention to reality, like an obedient pupil, and who is willing, always, to be surprised by the messages reality is sending though to him.

While this passage represents a rare lapse in erudition—the remark about the trees comes from Goethe's *Faust*, not Hegel—it also identifies the quality that McCarthy's readers will find most apparent, and most appealing, in her work. The openness to surprise is as much the duty of readers as of writers, and it is what separates worthwhile criticism from clever hackwork. McCarthy's skill at deflation is more than matched by the quality of her enthusiasm, and her impatience with the clumsiness of so much American realism is balanced by her amazed appreciation of writers—Nabokov, Burroughs, Calvino—who respond to the pressure of reality by breaking gloriously free of it.

"A Bolt from the Blue" is the title of her rapt, dazzlingly learned review of *Pale Fire*, and it is a phrase that suits nearly every essay in this volume. Readers of McCarthy's novels, and those encountering her for the first time, will find themselves surprised and provoked, instructed and charmed. Her appraisals are skeptical and generous, knowing and curious. She appears, variously, in the guise of teacher and confidant, comrade and scold. As with any strong critic, her judgment can often be questioned, whether on the subject of Vietnam or Tennessee Williams, but her clear, astringent intelligence cannot be doubted any more than her voice can be forgotten.

A. O. SCOTT

PART ONE

I

INTRODUCTION TO
THEATRE CHRONICLES

FOR THE CURRENT reader, the point of view of this book may be hard to locate; where is this criticism coming from? "It is to be hoped that Mr. Young will devote himself to one of Chekhov's more mature plays." So *The Seagull* in a distinguished dramatic critic's adaptation was dismissed by an insufferable little-magazine reviewer—myself, twenty years ago. This probably could not have happened in England, or France or Italy, even during the Thirties; only in America, or rather in a tiny section of New York, could an air of supreme authority be assumed with so few credentials.

In the first fourth of the book the reader will find quite a few such sentences, which make me wince with pain to read over but which I have let stand, in the interests of the record and because I think anyone who could write so foolishly owes a debt to society that cannot be canceled out by the mere process of getting older. But it is not usually the opinions I aired (as in this case) that give me such pain to hear again; it is the tone of voice in which they are pronounced—the voice of a young, earnest, pedantic, pontificating critic, being cocksure and condescending.

"The playwright assumes that his hero's irresolution is of a tragic order, while, as a matter of fact, it is comicopathetic." It is the voice of a period as well as that of a person. The period was 1937—the time of the Spanish Civil War and the Moscow trials. The place was Union Square, New York, where radical demonstrations were always held and which was surrounded by cheap dress shops, cafeterias, subway kiosks, and run-down office buildings, like the one at 22 East 17 Street, a tall, skinny, gray building at the northern end, the first address of the new *Partisan Review,* a magazine that had been "stolen" from the Communists by a group of young people, including me, who were supposed to be Trotskyites. This whole region was Communist territory; "they" were everywhere—in the streets, in the cafeterias; nearly every derelict building contained at least one of their front groups or schools or publications. Later, when the magazine moved to the old Bible House on Astor Place, the *New Masses* had offices on the same floor, and meeting *"them"* in the elevator, riding down in silence, enduring their cold scrutiny, was a prospect often joked about but dreaded. The fact of being surrounded physically, of running a gamut, was a concrete illustration of their power in New York at that time, a power that spread uptown to publishers' offices and to the Broadway theatre and to various cultural agencies of the government, like the WPA Writers' Project and the Federal Theatre. They were strong, and we were weak, and the note of haughty disdain found in the early pieces of this book was, in part, a girl's way of meeting this unequal situation.

The story that we on *Partisan Review* were Trotskyists was an exaggeration. The boys, as we used to call the principal editors because they were always in the back room, powwowing, had been through the Communist discipline, which made them wary of direct political ties. We wanted to be wholly independent in artistic matters, and the daring of our attitude was summed up in the statement that we would print a poem by T. S. Eliot if we could get one (later we did). The "boys" were still committed to Marxism, and so were the other young men who figured on the masthead as editors, except one—the backer. The backer, a young abstract painter from a good old New York family, was so "confused" politically that one day he went into the Workers' Bookshop (Stalinist) and asked for a copy of Trotsky's *The Revolution Betrayed*; he was wearing spats that day, too, and carrying a cane, and the thought of the figure he must have cut made the rest of us blanch. "Did anyone recognize you? Do you think they knew who you were?" we all immediately demanded.

My position was something like the backer's; that is, I was a source of uneasiness and potential embarrassment to the magazine, which had accepted me, unwillingly, as an editor because I had a minute "name" and was the girlfriend of one of the "boys," who had issued a ukase on my behalf. I was not a Marxist; I should have liked, rather, to be one, but I did not know the language, which seemed really like a foreign tongue. At college I had majored in Elizabethan literature and studied the Roman classics, Renaissance and medieval Latin, and Renaissance and medieval French; in contemporary literature I had not got much beyond *The Counterfeiters*, in English, and Aldous Huxley. All my habits of mind were bourgeois, my fellow editors used to tell me. They were always afraid that I was going to do something, in real life or in print, that would "disgrace *Partisan Review*"; this was a fear that worried me even more than it did them. I used to come down to the office on Saturdays (I worked for a publisher during the week) and listen to the men argue, in the inner room, beyond the partition, pounding the table and waving their arms in the air. Once a month, late at night, after the dishes were done, I would write my "Theatre Chronicle," hoping not to sound bourgeois and give the Communists ammunition.

The field assigned me was the theatre, because, just before this, I had been married to an actor. It was often debated whether we should have a theatre column at all. Some of the editors felt that the theatre was not worth bothering with, because it was neither a high art, like Art, nor a mass art, like the movies. But this was also an argument for letting me do it. If I made mistakes, who cared? This argument won out. Being an editor, at least in name, I had to be allowed to do *something*, and the "Theatre Chronicle" (we spelled it "theater") was "made work," like the WPA jobs of the period. I could not fail to see this or to be aware that nobody had much confidence in my powers as a critic. Nevertheless, I was determined to make good. And the column was successful. People liked it, the editors decided. It was "something a little different." A university professor who was also a leading Marxist said that it was "the best theatre criticism he had read since Georg Brandes." Probably the professor had not read any theatre criticism since Georg Brandes, whom, incidentally, I had never heard of, or just barely, but we did not stop to examine the compliment too closely.

At that time (and this is doubtless still the case), *Partisan Review* was unknown to press agents and to theatre people generally; we *paid* for my balcony tickets. Most of our readers never went to the theatre. Out of these two circumstances arose some of the peculiarities of the column. Since we were not on the free list, we did not have to worry about coverage, about reviews coming out on time, or about what anybody in the theatre thought of my judgments, which were mostly unfavorable. In the same way, our readers did not look to my column as a guide or wait to hear from me whether or not to line up for tickets. Consequently, reviews often came out after a play had closed, and nobody minded; there were long hiatuses too during which I lived in the country and did not review at all. That is why this collection has nothing on *The Cocktail Party* or Arthur Miller or William Inge. It was not a checklist but a chronicle, and, like some old chronicle, full of lacunae.

Our readers were young people, college and high school teachers, radicals, and bohemians. Many of them, even if they lived in New York, were too poor to buy theatre tickets. They went to the movies instead. As moviegoers, they had their own aesthetic and were prone to suspect that the theatre was no good; yet they liked to read about it, from a distance, and see it taken to pieces (i.e., analyzed). This accounts for the fact that, though the column was always popular, I almost never received a letter taking issue with my judgments; once, when I reviewed Tennessee Williams, two or three letters did come in, disagreeing, but this was unique. Our readers, an intellectual minority, were ready to take it on assurance that the American theatre was not only bad, but very bad.

This was and remains a closely held national secret. Foreign readers and critics would be astonished to learn that there was, to say the least, a difference of opinion among American intellectuals about the worth of such writers as Clifford Odets, Tennessee Williams, Arthur Miller, or of the Actors Studio style of playing just as the Nobel Prize Committee was probably astonished to learn that in American literary circles Steinbeck was not regarded as a great writer.

The agreement, passive or active, of a group of readers does not, of course, prove anything about the theatre, except that it had failed, as a whole, to interest these people enough to make them go see for themselves. Recently this has changed, owing partly to prosperity, partly to the off-Broadway theatre, with its foreign and avant-garde plays, and partly to the movies themselves, which have made Tennessee Williams and the others available to anyone to judge; today most intellectuals have seen at least one play by Williams, Inge, and Miller, and at least one movie directed by Kazan. Their opinion, so far as I can tell, remains about the same as when they did not have the price of a ticket: they think this theatre is corn, and they are glad when someone says so.

None of the regular critics do, and this, in itself, provides grounds for suspicion. Any concert of opinion, in America, on official levels, creates automatically a swell of discord from below, and it was the function of *Partisan Review* for many years, in all its departments, to express this discord as loudly as possible. We on *Partisan Review* were continually attacking something or somebody—the Right, the

Middle, and the so-called Left, which in the Thirties was hardly distinguishable from the Middle ("Communism is twentieth-century Americanism" was one of the great slogans of the period). The novels of John Steinbeck, the plays of Clifford Odets, the criticism of Van Wyck Brooks, the philosophy of Jacques Maritain, the poetry of Archibald MacLeish (to name some of the main enemies) were all very successful commercially or very much à la mode.

To be continually on the attack is to run the risk of monotony, an effect we tried to counteract by a lively style. A greater risk is that of mechanical intolerance. Aesthetic puritanism, of which we were rampant examples and which, I believe, is absolutely necessary in America, has, like all puritanism, a tendency to hypocrisy—based on a denial of one's own natural tastes and instincts. I remember how uneasy I felt when I found myself liking Thornton Wilder's *Our Town*; I was almost afraid to praise it in the magazine, lest the boys conclude that I was starting to sell out. I am still surprised to discover that a commercial success, like *Come Back, Little Sheba*, is really quite good, even though this no longer makes me wonder, as it once would have, whether my standards are slipping... The American fear of failure, about which so much has been written, has its logical counterpart: the fear of success—of becoming one oneself or of admiring it in others. This was our (or my) besetting phobia, a product of the time, the place, and perhaps the person.

Yet in all honesty it must be said that it was not a question of *looking* for flaws in most of the plays here discussed ("You people are looking for pimples on the great smiling face of the Soviet Union," somebody charged at a meeting of the League of American Writers, the year *Partisan Review* was founded). The flaws, to me, were so evident that I found it hard to believe that others did not notice them. I really hated the kind of theatre the regular critics liked or at any rate treated respectfully. And, going rather frequently to the theatre, in the course of time I learned that many members of the audience and many actors felt the same way; it was an almost invariable law, for instance, that the most glaringly bad performer in any given cast would be the one who "got the notices" in the newspaper criticisms. This strange situation has not changed in twenty years. "America's Greatest Actress," the "First Lady of our Theatre," etc., who is still going strong, is our worst actress, famous as such in the profession. It is as though Toscanini had really been a terrible conductor. These "secrets" of the theatre make it appear, sometimes, as a fantastic conspiracy which can be talked about quite openly without ever reaching the ears of the critics or of the ordinary ticket-buyer. The commonest explanation offered is that the critics are stupid, but they are not more stupid, probably, on the average, than critics of music and books or than the theatre critics of other countries. I have been speaking, just now, about acting, where the mystery is deepest, but the same queer blindness or deafness extends to plays. How often, for example, one reads in the paper or in a weekly magazine that a "dull" play—let us say *Measure for Measure*—has been redeemed (or failed to be redeemed) by a valiant performance. That the exact opposite will prove to be the case can be predicted with certainty without moving from the breakfast table. (All this is only true, by the way, of the "legitimate" theatre; with revues and musical comedies there is a common standard, at least about performers: Ethel Merman, Bobby Clark, Bert Lahr, Mary Martin, Pinza, Fred Astaire, Beatrice Lillie, have been liked by nearly everyone.)

My early reviews lisp the Marxist language; I was trying to tell the reader, in his own words, why he would agree with me. Maxwell Anderson has "no system of intellectual values"; in the Thirties that was the worst thing, short of "fascist," you could say about a person, and not only in left-wing circles—had not T.S. Eliot rated Shakespeare lower than Dante for lack of a "system of thought"? It was a doctrinaire time, and everybody was engaged in "smoking out" the latent tendencies in works of art, like FBI investigators. On *Partisan*

Review we did not call innocent people fascists; that was a Communist trick. But we, or at least I, did use labels and cant terms to beat poor mediocrities like Maxwell Anderson over the head. This begins to disappear from the chronicles toward the end of the war. By that time I had become more skillful at obliging a play to "tell something," but no longer for the sake of incriminating the author; now the play was telling something about the society that was paying to see it.

I had begun to treat Broadway plays as commodities, which is what they are, and to ask what they were being used for, what needs, wishes, and transient moods they satisfied. And here is the interest of the more journalistic part of this collection: it is a kind of social history seen through the theatre of the last two decades. Most of the plays discussed were trivial and have long been forgotten, but in these *ephemeridae*, studied with such care, the America of that time is, for me at any rate, recaptured: the New Deal years, the war years, the years of Truman. The theatre, being sociable by nature, is a more sensitive register of time and its fleeting humors than the movies, which address themselves to the solitary mass man. The difference between the theatre and the movies is illustrated by the intermission and the coming-up of the house lights; the intermission and the discussions that take place during it, the moving about and watching other members of the audience, are a real part of the play. Few people remember the circumstances under which they saw a movie, while most people do with a play; going to the movies alone is a common habit or vice, but going to the theatre alone is a practice, chiefly, of dramatic critics.

Looking through these chronicles, I see that time itself, the lost dimension, figures again and again as the playwright's toy. Fantasies of going backward in time seem to have been popular from *Berkeley Square* to *Brigadoon*, as though a sigh rose from these decades: "If we had it to do over..." There is a great deal, too, about money, always to the same sad tune: money does not bring happiness. Love, as a theme, is scarcely present; it has retreated to the dark temples of the movie houses. But politics and military affairs—"current events"—play a bigger part than I would have thought, which means that the theatre is still close to the newspaper and the pamphlet, a medium for rational discussion, as it was for Beaumarchais and Shaw.

In the early reviews there is evident a naive belief that artistic judgments can be enforced on the reader by a battery of argument. This, I think, is again a mixture of period and person. The notion that abstract reasoning can crush a fact (e.g., a successful play, a political phenomenon), a wholly un-Marxist notion, was nonetheless the principle on which most of our criticism was practiced. I "proved" that the public was being taken in by Playwright x, just as *Partisan Review*'s political analyses proved, issue after issue, that Stalin was bamboozling the working class. Such irrefutable proofs had no power, I fear, to alter a single opinion. Those who were taken in by Stalin or by Playwright x, as I have already suggested, were unlikely to read *Partisan Review* in any case.

What I did not realize was that my own judgments had not been reached by relentless logic and lawyer's points—the methods by which I sought to convince the reader. It was not logic but my ears that told me that most American plays were horribly badly written. This is either heard or it isn't. The false notes continually struck by American playwrights either offend or they don't—you cannot *argue* that a singer is off pitch. The desire to argue dies hard, however, especially in a woman, and I cannot drop the subject of bad writing, here, without trying to get in a last word. "Yes," some people will agree, of a play by Tennessee Williams, "it *is* badly written, but it's good theatre." I have never been able to make out what this expression means, exactly. "Strong" situations? Masochistic groveling? Sexual torture? Is Sophocles "good theatre"? Is Shakespeare? Apparently not, for the term is always used defensively, to justify a kind of shoddiness, which is held to be excusable for the stage. Indeed, the American playwright is always being "excused," as though he were some wretched pupil bringing a note from his parent: "Please excuse Tennessee or Arthur or Clifford; he has a writing difficulty." This started with O'Neill, whose lack of verbal gift was a genuine affliction, from which he suffered just as a stammerer does; he speaks of it in *Long Day's Journey into Night*. "I couldn't touch what I tried to tell you just now," says Edmund, who is the young O'Neill. "I just stammered. That's the best I'll ever do.... Well, it will be faithful realism, at least. Stammering is the native eloquence of us fog people." O'Neill's handicap, however, which made it painful for him to articulate his thoughts, was quite another thing from the bad writing of his successors, which is unconscious and serene and often takes the form of pretentious "fine writing," as in the choruses of Arthur Miller's *A View from a Bridge*. Miller is not just lame; he is what textbooks and grammars call hazy; that is, he does not seem to know what he wants to express.

But what is the use of saying this? It is either well known to the reader or so unsuspected by him that a genuine revelation, an opening of the eyes and ears, as in some biblical miracle, would be required to bring it home to him. A comparison will sometimes do this; the appearance of John Gielgud beside Marlon Brando in the film of *Julius Caesar* made many people, and particularly actors, aware for the first time of something wrong in the very rudiments of American acting. Recently the off-Broadway theatre, with its productions of Molière, Shaw, Chekhov, Turgenev, Ibsen, Montherlant, Strindberg, O'Casey, Hauptmann, Brecht, Genet, at least offers an idea, even though the playing is very amateurish, of what a real articulate theatre can be. It does suggest a standard. And the public has responded by deciding that the off-Broadway theatre is "fun," an adventure to go to, like the speakeasies of the old days.

No wonder there is a general sense of blinking surprise. This lively, witty theatre found in downtown basements and converted lofts is a different world altogether from the Broadway cave-world of the American School playwrights, who have accustomed us to a stage inhabited by apes with complexes. The typical character of the so-called American realist school is a subhuman member of the lower urban middle class. This creature is housed in a living room filled with installment-plan furniture, some of which will be broken before the play is over. The sound of breakage and the sound of heavy breathing will signify "theatre." As directed by Elia Kazan, whip-cracking ring-master of this school of brutes, the hero is found standing with clenched fists, stage left, yelling at some member of his family, stage right, until one of them breaks into hysterical weeping and collapses onto a chair by the stage-center table, his great head buried in his hands. The weeping character is confessing to being alcoholic, homosexual, a failure.

The sight of a strong man or, even better, of two strong men crying uncontrollably is one of the commonest sights on the American stage, uptown, today. I have never seen such a spectacle in real life; perhaps my experience is too limited. I have seen men cry when somebody died and I have seen drunken tears, but I have never seen two men sobbing loudly together—over something one of them has said to the other. Whittaker Chambers said that he and Alger Hiss cried together when he decided to leave the Party. Even if this is true (and Chambers was not very reliable), at least one of these two men was exceptionally histrionic, while the characters who behave this way on the stage are supposed to be average Americans. The characters of Tennessee Williams are supposed to be average *Southern* Americans, fruitier, that is, than the Northern kind.

One thing, however, must be said for Tennessee Williams: his characters do sometimes talk with a local, recognizable accent. They come from a definite place, and their speech shows it. A disturbing aspect of *Death of a Salesman* was that Willy Loman seemed to be Jewish, to judge by his speech cadences, but there was no mention of this on the stage. He could not be Jewish because he had to be "America." All the living rooms, backyards, stoops, and fire escapes of the American School claim to be "America," which is not so much a setting as a big, amorphous idea; the puzzle for the audience, except with Tennessee Williams, is to guess where these living rooms, roughly, are and who is living in them, which might make it possible to measure the plausibility of the action. "Those old Irish actors were exactly like that," the man next to me said of Frederic March's performance in *Long Day's Journey into Night*; this was a real testimonial to the performer and to the (now old-fashioned) solidity of O'Neill's play. On the contrary, the man who was quoted by the *The New Yorker* as saying, after *Death of a Salesman*, "That damned New England territory never was any good" had committed a boner; he had missed the play's "profundity" by trying to localize the trouble.

Still, *Death of a Salesman* is the only play of the new American School that can be said to touch home; *Come Back, Little Sheba*, by William Inge, though good, does not attempt to be more than a genre study of an alcoholic and his wife, which is watched with that same detached fascination exercised by a pair of quarreling neighbors seen through a window or heard in an adjoining flat: "Look! He's beating her up again!" The Salesman, as Arthur Miller calls him, signaling with the capital *S* in the stage directions, is meant to be someone we all know, if not Ourselves. What is the matter with Willy Loman? Why is he so unhappy and why do we feel for him with a pang of recognition? "America" is what is wrong with him, Arthur Miller would answer, and to some extent this is true. The conception of the salesman's home with its installment-plan furniture as a house of shabby lies and competitive boasts is sadly close to our national life; it is in fact precisely a close-up of the "home" depicted in full color by advertisers in the national magazines, with Father, Mother, two fine Kids, and the Product. But the play is wholly conceptualized, like the ads to which it gives a bitter retort. Parents, children, and neighbors are cutout figures, types, in both the advertised dream and the night-mare that closes in on Willy Loman like a mortgage foreclosing. Ideally, the play would be a kind of grim satire, the negative of the positive. *This is the way your pretty picture looks from the inside*, the playwright would be saying to the advertising men. Insofar as the play does this, it is arresting and moving in a sardonic way. "He's liked but not *well* liked," Willy keeps insisting, of a neighbor, and the shrewdness that persists in making this distinction is both funny and horrible. The problem is to convert this into tragedy; that is, to make genuine Universals out of these prefab types, which Arthur Miller can only do by having someone preach about them.

"Attention must be paid," intones the shrill, singsong voice of the mother, ordering her sons to take notice of their father's plight. "Attention, attention, must finally be paid to such a person." She is really admonishing the audience that Willy is, as she says, "a human being." But that is just it; he is a Human Being without being anyone, a sort of suffering Statistic. The mother's voice raised in the old melancholy Jewish rhythms ("Attention must be paid" is not a normal American locution; nor is "finally," placed where it is; nor is "such a person," used as she uses it) seems to have been summoned from some other play that was about particular people. Yet poor Willy is only a composite, like one of those faces in magazine guessing-games with the eyes and forehead of one film star, the nose of another, the mouth and chin of a third; as a composite, he is a subject for the editorial page, which could take note of his working conditions, ask for unemployment benefits and old-age care for him, call "attention," in short, to the problem of the salesman in the Welfare State. No one could write an editorial calling attention to the case of King Lear. Yet some of the same elements are present; there is an old man with thankless children and a grandiose dream of being "well liked"—i.e., of being shown the proofs of love—that ends in isolation, ignominy, and lunacy. Lear, however, has the gift of language, which is not just a class endowment, for the Fool has it too. This gift of language is what makes him human and not just "a human being."

—1963

2

CLASS ANGLES AND
A WILDER CLASSIC

PINS AND NEEDLES at Labor Stage is like a New Deal parade, a union picnic, a college play, a Gilbert and Sullivan operetta, a smart, up-to-date Broadway revue. "It illustrates," the program says, "the concept of working class drama which has guided Labor Stage, Inc. from the beginning: that plays for workers must be entertaining and alive." If Labor Stage, Inc., which is sponsored by the International Ladies Garment Workers Union, is any barometer of the state of mind of the working class, then America must already have achieved a classless society. For what *Pins and Needles* least resembles is the proletarian theatre. Only its actors—cutters, pressers, cloakmakers, and dressmakers of the ILGWU—are proletarian. Its themes, its techniques, its perspectives are bourgeois-Democratic.

In *Pins and Needles* there are, to be sure, certain nostalgic whiffs of revolutionary theatre, certain misleading family likenesses to the old Theatre Union Sunday night potpourris. The ancient enemies, Hitler, Mussolini, the Mikado, are once again summoned up—but with a difference. They have lost the aura of menace that used to attend them, and now appear merely as clowns. The metamorphosis of the dictators, as a matter of fact, gives the key to what estranges *Pins and Needles* from Fourteenth Street and unites it to Broadway. It is simply a question of intention. *Pins and Needles* is designed to divert. All the didactic and hortatory elements of the proletarian drama have been shed, and in their place we get high spirits, merriment, and bounce. Good nature has superseded bitterness. The dictators have turned comedians, and the indictment of capitalism is subdued to a genial spoofing of Macy's, militarism, Americanism (100 percent, not twentieth-century), popular love songs, high-pressure advertising, social snobbery, and etiquette books. Ingratiation is the keynote of the performance. The presence of amateur actors on the stage is in itself disarming, and nothing that might disturb the good feeling between the actors and an ordinary middle-class New York audience has been allowed to creep into the production.

This bonhomie toward capitalism and the world at large is easily explained. Where the revolutionary theatre represented (by proxy) a working class which was irreconcilably hostile to society, the ILGWU players represent (directly) a section of the working class which has made peace with society under the aegis of the New Deal. *Pins and Needles* is the group expression of a large, well-run, relatively contented labor union whose union contracts are signed without much trouble and whose demands on the system do not exceed decent minimum wages, decent maximum hours, the closed shop, and the right to picket. You cannot produce trenchant political satire—at least not in America in this period—if your political horizon is the Wagner Act, and *Pins and Needles* is at its best and most characteristic in the song numbers, where the political satire, such as it is, melts into irresponsible good humor, polysyllabic playfulness, and musical wit. "Sing Me a Song with Social Significance," "Dear Beatrice Fairfax," and "Four Little Angels of Peace," all good, all by Harold J. Rome, are in the pert, worldly, staccato tradition that runs from Gilbert and Sullivan through Cole Porter. The theatregoer, whatever his class allegiance, is likely to go home humming them.

It is interesting that the one jarring note in this symphony of good cheer is struck by Mr. Marc Blitzstein, author of *The Cradle Will*

Rock. In a hysterical sketch called "F. T. P. Plowed Under," Mr. Blitzstein belabors the Federal Theatre, which last June abandoned his play to the mercies of individual enterprise. The sketch is strained and unconvincing even as burlesque: a personal injury has been generalized into a national calamity, and the spleen displayed by the author is manifestly in excess of its cause. Yet it is Mr. Blitzstein's stridency—in *Pins and Needles* so misdirected, so malapropos—that is the special, quintessential quality of *The Cradle Will Rock*. If the function of *Pins and Needles* is to ingratiate, the mission of *The Cradle Will Rock* is to antagonize.

A curious feature of Mr. Blitzstein's play is that, though it has for its subject the class war as exemplified in the steel industry, it is almost totally lacking in internal conflict. The conflict which one ordinarily finds within or between the characters of the drama has been moved out past the proscenium arch into the theatre itself. *The Cradle Will Rock* is a kind of well-drilled assault on the feelings and nerves of its audience. What is presented is not so much the workers versus the bosses in Steeltown, U.S.A., as Mr. Blitzstein versus the ticket-holders in the Mercury Theatre. The prominence of the author in the production—he is actor, commentator, and pianist—gives focus to the sadistic impulses of the script. Mr. Blitzstein's acrid personality is, in fact, the whole show. He, as insolent and sardonic entrepreneur, sits downstage center at the piano; the actors behind him are his marionettes. The timing and precision of the cast's performance have the cold, military perfection of the dance routines of the Radio City Rockettes. *The Cradle Will Rock* is a triumph of theatrical goose-stepping. The drama has become dehumanized; it has been made into a marvelous mechanical monster which begins to operate with great efficiency whenever Mr. Blitzstein pulls the switch.

Mr. Blitzstein's creatures are, of course, abstractions, as their names indicate. That is why they are so easily manipulated. Mr. Mister, the steel magnate, is the biggest abstraction of them all, and his syco-phants, Editor Daily, President Prexy, Doctor Specialist, Reverend Salvation, and the rest, are presented solely in terms of their occupa-tions. This is as true of the proletarians as it is of the bosses, shop-keepers, and petty bourgeois intellectuals, for Mr. Blitzstein's work has a wonderful uniformity. All of the characters are exhibited as specimens of class behavior, and the result is a series of satirical and sentimental grotesques. There is an element of horror in the per-fect predictability of these unicellular creations, and the little, white-faced, class-conscious Columbine of a prostitute is nearly as repellent, consequently, as the oversexed, overdressed, overeffusive Mrs. Mis-ter. Larry Foreman, strike leader and hero, is meant, I suppose, to rep-resent the spirit of joy in the insurgent working class, but he, too, has been stepped up into caricature until he resembles a madcap master of ceremonies in a Broadway nightclub, and his ultimate song of triumph carries an overtone of savage hotcha which considerably detracts from the high seriousness of the play's finale.

It is clear that Mr. Blitzstein's deterministic formula for playwriting rules out the possibility of moral struggle within his characters. What is at first sight more puzzling is that the class struggle itself is barely dramatized. The two groups, workers and bosses, never clash, never indeed really touch each other, until the very end of the play. Then Mr. Mister tries to bribe Larry Foreman to sell out the strike; Larry re-affirms his allegiance to labor; everybody sings a song; and the house lights go up. It is as if two solar systems had been functioning sepa-rately on the stage, and their meeting, which one might have expected to be a major collision, turned out to be a passing and inconclusive contact. Perhaps Mr. Blitzstein was too well aware of the brittleness of his puppet-people to risk them in any head-on encounter. His cau-tion, whether deliberate or accidental, was undoubtedly justified.

The abstract and heartless nature of Mr. Blitzstein's work will, I think, set up an instinctive resistance in any normal American spectator. The pleasure one takes in *The Cradle Will Rock* is the pleasure of feeling one's native sensibilities violated. This play is having much the same kind of vogue, and producing much the same response as the Surrealist and abstract art shows did at the Modern Museum. Though its setting and subject matter are American, it is essentially a nonindigenous plant. Musically, it is very much indebted to the German, Kurt Weill. Dramatically, it shares a certain neo-primitivism with Auden and Isherwood, but it lacks the free play of public-school-boy fancy that one finds in *The Ascent of F6* and *The Dog Beneath the Skin*. Its real kinship is with postwar German Expressionism, which, except for Elmer Rice's *The Adding Machine*, never managed to take root in America.

The fact is that the tendency of American playwrights has always been to particularize rather than to generalize. Even in the revolutionary theatre where the emphasis theoretically should have been on the mass, not the individual, the American playwright's impulse was to write a "problem drama" with proletarian characters, and leave the mass recitatives to the Europeans. The Federal Theatre in its Living Newspaper productions has been working with groups, but these groups have been visibly atomized, each individual being endowed with such little eccentricities as would make him "recognizable" in a sort of neighborly fashion to the audience. That this American method of seeing and translating experience has its dangers and limitations, that it readily drops into mere homeliness and triviality, the present state of the commercial theatre testifies. This method, however, has within itself the power of expansion; Mr. Blitzstein's method can only contract.

Mr. Thornton Wilder's play, *Our Town*, at the Morosco, is the inverse of *The Cradle Will Rock*. Both plays are done without settings or props; both employ a commentator who serves as intermediary between actors and audience; both deal with an American town. But while

Mr. Blitzstein is a sort of public prosecutor of Steeltown of 1937, Mr. Frank Craven, stage manager and spokesman for Mr. Wilder, appears as a kind of indulgent defense attorney for a certain small New England town of thirty years ago. Mr. Blitzstein evokes an industrial town which is abstract and odious; Mr. Craven and Mr. Wilder, a hometown which is concrete and dear. *Our Town*, like *Ah, Wilderness!*, is an exercise in memory, but it differs from the O'Neill work in that it is not a play in the accepted sense of the term. It is essentially lyric, not dramatic. The tragic velocity of life, the elusive nature of experience, which can never be stopped or even truly felt at any given point, are the themes of the play—themes familiar enough in lyric poetry, but never met, except incidentally, in drama. Mr. Wilder, in attempting to give these themes theatrical form, was obliged, paradoxically, to abandon almost all the conventions of the theatre.

In the first place, he has dismissed scenery and props as irrelevant to, and, indeed, incongruous with his purpose. In the second place, he has invented the character of the Stage Manager, an affable, homespun conjurer who holds the power of life and death over the other characters, a local citizen who is in the town and outside of it at the same time. In the third place, he has taken what is accessory to the ordinary play, that is, exposition, and made it the main substance of his. The greater part of the first two acts is devoted to the imparting of information, to situating the town in time, space, politics, sociology, economics, and geology. But where in the conventional play, such pieces of information are insinuated into the plot or sugared over with stage business and repartee, in Mr. Wilder's play they are communicated directly; they take the place of plot, stage business, and repartee. Mr. Craven himself tells the biographies of the townspeople; he calls in an expert from the state college to give a scientific picture of the town, and the editor of the local newspaper to describe its social conditions. The action which is intermittently progressing on the stage merely illustrates Mr. Craven's talk.

Mr. Wilder's fourth innovation is the most striking. In order to dramatize his feelings about life he has literally raised the dead. At the opening of the third act a group of people are discovered sitting in rows on one side of the stage; some of the faces are familiar, some are new. They are speaking quite naturally and calmly, and it is not until one has listened to them for some minutes that one realizes that this is the cemetery and these are the dead. A young woman whom we have seen grow up and marry the boy next door has died in childbirth; a small shabby funeral procession is bringing her to join her relatives and neighbors. Only when she is actually buried does the play proper begin. She has not yet reached the serenity of the long dead, and she yearns to return to the world. With the permission of the Stage Manager and against the advice of the dead, she goes back—to a birthday of her childhood. Hardly a fraction of that day has passed, however, before she retreats gratefully to the cemetery, for she has perceived that the tragedy of life lies in the fragmentary and imperfect awareness of the living.

Mr. Wilder's play is, in a sense, a refutation of its own thesis. *Our Town* is purely and simply an act of awareness, a demonstration of the fact that in a work of art, at least, experience *can* be arrested, imprisoned, and preserved. The perspective of death, which Mr. Wilder has chosen, gives an extra poignancy and intensity to the small-town life whose essence he is trying so urgently to communicate. The little boy delivering papers, for example, becomes more touching, more meaningful and important, when Mr. Craven announces casually that he is going to be killed in the war. The boy's morning round, for the spectator, is transfigured into an absorbing ritual; the unconsciousness of the character has heightened the consciousness of the audience. The perspective is, to be sure, hazardous: it invites bathos and sententiousness. Yet Mr. Wilder has used it honorably. He forbids the spectator to dote on that town of the past. He is concerned only with saying: this is how it was, though then we did not know it. Once in a while, of course, his memory fails him, for young love was never so baldly and tritely gauche as his scene in the soda fountain suggests. This is, however, a deficiency of imagination, not an error of taste; and except in the third act, where the dead give some rather imprecise and inapposite definitions of the nature of the afterlife, the play keeps its balance beautifully. In this feat of equilibrium Mr. Wilder has had the complete cooperation of Mr. Craven, the serene, inexorable matter-of-factness of whose performance acts as a discipline upon the audience. Mr. Craven makes one quite definitely homesick, but pulls one up sharp if one begins to blubber about it.

—April 1938

3

SHAW AND CHEKHOV

IF YOU WANT to make a rational structure of *Heartbreak House* you can say that it is a sort of layer cake of meanings. The top layer is a play about a houseful of unhappy, articulate, rudderless English people of the upper middle class who, while attempting to straighten out their sex relations, are surprised by the air raid of a foreign power. The second layer is an allegory of the moral and political bankruptcy of the European leisure class. The mad but profound old sea captain signifies the spirit of Old England. The captain's two daughters exemplify the class that was born to govern but that abdicated its responsibility in favor of the new forces of finance capitalism, represented by the practical businessman. In the one daughter we see the upper-class escape into the strong-arm philistinism of colonial government; in the other, the retreat into the dream world of dilettante cultivation. The air raid is the war which that class has unwittingly prepared for its own destruction. The third layer is a dramatic exposition of the protean character of human nature. It is this third layer on which the play rests; yet it is a foundation neither fixed nor solid, and it keeps the other elements, superimposed upon it, in a kind of dizzying perpetual motion.

None of the characters can keep his shape; none is consistent. The captain is wise, but he is also crazy; he is the only strong person on the stage, but he gets his strength from rum. The powerful capitalist has no capital; he lives on traveling expenses and commissions. He is a hard bargainer, but his heart is pitifully vulnerable. The braggart and liar is a courageous man. The worldly diplomat is a lady's lapdog. The ingenue is a materialistic schemer. The burglar is no burglar. The churchy old reformer is a shrewd observer. The conventional snob is a troubled and intelligent woman. The great beauty has no power over her husband. These contradictory traits of character, revealed one by one as the play goes on, succeed but do not permanently displace one another. They ebb and flow through the characters, and it is no accident, I think, that *Heartbreak House* is a ship, its owner and philosopher a captain, and the play's most poetic imagery predominantly marine.

The nightmarish fluidity of the characters inundates the play's schematism. Since the people will not stay put, since good people will not be good or bad people bad, the plot misses a point and the allegory a moral. Yet the failure of the plot, the blurring of the allegory, introduce into *Heartbreak House* the extra dimension which is so often lacking in Shaw's work. The third element, by unsettling the other two—the comedy of morals, and the political allegory—has given the drama an interior tension, a sense of dubiety and disquietude. The brightness of the comedy and the grandeur of the allegory intensify this final, anxious uncertainty and raise it to the level of tragic doubt. To the pathos of the play's lost people is added the terror of the play's lost author, who could not, in conscience, make his story come out right, or, indeed, come out at all. For the author as well as for the characters the apocalyptic air raid that finishes the play appears to come as a merciful release from striving. Like a nervous and abstracted conversationalist, he had already begun to repeat himself before it happened.

Of the three elements discussed, the first is most conspicuously present in Orson Welles's production. The Mercury Theatre company act out *Heartbreak House* as if it were one of those weekend comedies by Rachel Crothers or Frederick Lonsdale. Mady Christians, as the captain's emancipated daughter, gives a fair imitation of Ina Claire. With the exception of George Coulouris, whose Boss Mangan is a genuinely strident, strangled, unhappy, self-made man, the captain's guests appear to be the poised, self-confident, ineffably impertinent loungers that we meet so often at theatrical house parties, though they lack a good deal of the style and speed to which we are accustomed. So far as possible, neuroticism and anxiety have been banished from the stage. The set, as well as the characters, has been brightened up into cheerful conventionality: the captain's psychically malodorous house seems to have been carefully air-conditioned. Since this is a play which, as Shaw himself said, "began with an atmosphere and does not contain one word that was foreseen before it was written," a play which draws its life from the ominous thickness of its atmosphere, the effect of Mr. Welles's housecleaning is obvious. Under such circumstances, the serious parts of the play lose almost all meaning, and *Heartbreak House* seems a sentimental misnomer for the gay if languid world in which the Mercury Theatre Shavians dwell.

The failure of Mr. Welles's production to expose the contradictions that corrode Shaw's people is most damaging in the key cases of Hector Hushabye, played by Vincent Price, and Captain Shotover, played by Mr. Welles. Hector Hushabye, as written, is a real fantastico, a commedia dell'arte clown with a touch of nobility, an extravagant rhetorician who can be a poet, a ham actor who is tortured by sincerity. Mr. Price, who was Prince Albert in *Victoria Regina*, plays Hector as if the two characters had a good deal in common. This erratic personage, who is of all the captain's relatives his most sympathetic listener, is bleached into a good-looking, wooden Englishman with a stolid interest in routine infidelity.

The captain undergoes an even more startling transformation. Mr. Welles as an actor has always seemed to secrete a kind of viscous holy oil with which he sprays the rough surfaces of his roles. He has this time applied so thick a coat that the real Captain Shotover is practically invisible. Where the real captain is brisk and peppery, Mr. Welles is slow and sibylline. The real captain is a retired man of action; Mr. Welles is a retired armchair prophet. The funereal deliberation of Mr. Welles's performance obliterates the distinction made by the playwright between the vigor and enterprise of the old England and the decadent lassitude of the new, a distinction which is the mainspring of the play's political allegory. The contradictions within the captain himself, the drunkenness and madness that deflect the old man's will and discolor his vision, are likewise suppressed. Mr. Welles's captain exudes an odor of unmitigated sanctity, and the play's ultimate and most grotesque irony, which reveals its wise man as a besotted crank, goes by unperceived.

The sentimentality of Mr. Welles's acting, the nervelessness of his direction, the bare, mechanical competence of the majority of his supporting cast combine to act as a steamroller on Shaw's *Heartbreak House*. The density of the original structure is lost; the play is flattened out until it looks like a sketchy blueprint of itself. Mr. Welles's production can only serve to remind the public that the original still exists in the library.

Shaw described his own play as a "Fantasia in the Russian manner on English themes," and in his preface to the published version, he notes that Chekhov "had produced four fascinating dramatic studies of *Heartbreak House*." One of these was *The Seagull*, which has recently been done by the Theatre Guild in association with the Lunts. The resemblances between the two plays are only superficial. They have in common the "futility" which is supposed to be Chekhov's special property. Both show the disintegration of a cultured, leisured class. Both emphasize the perverse contradictions of human nature. Both use the "confession" as a method of revealing character. Shaw's play, however, deals in generalizations; Chekhov's in particularities. Shaw's people are thought of as symbols of abstract social ideas; Chekhov's people are observed concretely, and only in the aggregate become symbolic of a social order. Shaw's conception of character is inorganic;

Chekhov's organic. The dramatic quick-changes to which the characters of *Heartbreak House* are subjected proceed not from the characters themselves but from a generalization about human beings in the mind of the playwright. Even the most complex of the *Heartbreak House* people are literary fabrications, wound together skein by skein. The antithetical traits of Chekhov's people, on the contrary, have grown together in such a way that it is often impossible to disentangle a single strand. Even in the treatment of the "confession" one sees the artificiality of Shaw and the simple naturalness of Chekhov. Chekhov's confession seems to arise from an artless preoccupation with the self which runs throughout Russian life and literature. Shaw's confessions are displays of an impudent and self-conscious exhibitionism which is certainly characteristic of the playwright but can hardly be said to be typical of the class and nation he writes about.

There is a certain coldness and poverty—witness the last act of *Heartbreak House*—even in Shaw's best work which prevent him from equaling the best of Chekhov. Yet *Heartbreak House*, one of his greatest plays, compares very well, I think, with *The Seagull*, one of Chekhov's worst. In *Heartbreak House* the vastness and nobility of the conception, the eloquence of the style, redeem the occasional thinness of the characterization, while the sentimental triviality of Chekhov's theme tends to debase the value of his most acute and poignant observations. The older people in *The Seagull*, the successful writer, the actress, the unhappy spinster who drinks, the invalid landowner, are among the best shabby-genteel portraits in Chekhov's gallery, but the young people, with whom the plot is really concerned, are melodramatic figures seen at a distance through a mist of tears. The commonplace character of the plot, which tells of a young girl's "ruin" at the hands of a vain and selfish older man, and of her young lover's consequent suicide, is not improved by the "poetic" analogy drawn between the girl and a seagull shot by a bored sportsman. The difficulty is that the girl's degradation is not directly observed but summed up in its tritest outlines by one of the characters, and the inner motivation for the boy's collapse is never given. The real story takes place offstage. It is not properly incorporated in the play, and the playwright, consequently, is demanding sympathy for his characters on what are artistically false pretenses. The final irony by which Chekhov makes the novelist forget both the significance he himself had attributed to the seagull and the fact that he had ordered it to be stuffed is an extremely vulgar concession to the conventional demands for neatness in playwriting, a concession which Chekhov in his later plays would never have made.

The acting of the Guild company was such as to draw a clean line between what is meretricious and what is good in the play. Both of the young people were bad. The girl was merely pallid, but Richard Whorf's Constantine was a kind of museum of horrors, containing all the clichés and curiosities of juvenile acting. The older people were, on the whole, good, ranging from the excellence of Margaret Webster as the ironic Masha, through the skill and frequent insight of Alfred Lunt's Trigorin, the solidity of Sydney Greenstreet's Peter Sorin, down to the slick overacting of Lynn Fontanne's Arkadina.

Stark Young's sharp and unaffected translation cleared away a great many of the cobwebs which one had previously thought to be part of Chekhov, but which prove merely to have clung to the styles of his earlier translators. It is to be hoped that Mr. Young will next devote himself to one of Chekhov's more mature plays.

—June 1938

Footnote, 1956. It was Lunt's performance, actually, that made the play seem "meretricious." He played the novelist as an aging roué who seduced the young girl out of sheer idle depravity. But the novelist in Chekhov is a decent enough fellow in his late thirties (sometimes thought to be a self-portrait) who reluctantly lets himself be seduced by the young girl. The reason he forgets the seagull is that he is preoccupied with his writing; he is a vocational study of the literary man—that is why he is defenseless against a fresh young admirer.

4

EUGENE O'NEILL—DRY ICE

THE CRUCIAL FIGURE of O'Neill's new play is a mad hardware salesman. Consonantly, the play itself is like some stern piece of hardware
in one of those dusty old-fashioned stores into which no Pyrex dish or
herb shelf or French provincial earthenware had yet penetrated, which
dealt in iron-colored enamel, galvanized tin, lengths of pipe and
wrenches, staples, saws, and nails, and knew nothing more sophisticated than the double boiler. Ugly, durable, mysteriously utilitarian,
this work gives the assurance that it has been manufactured by a reliable company; it is guaranteed to last two and a half hours longer
than any other play, with the exception of the uncut *Hamlet*.

The Iceman Cometh is indeed made of ice or iron; it is full of will
and fanatic determination; it appears to have hardened at some extreme
temperature of the mind. In the theatre today, it is attractive positively because of its defects. To audiences accustomed to the oily virtuosity of George Kaufman, George Abbott, Lillian Hellman, Odets,
Saroyan, the return of a playwright who—to be frank—cannot write
is a solemn and sentimental occasion. O'Neill belongs to that group
of American authors, which includes Farrell and Dreiser, whose choice
of vocation was a kind of triumphant catastrophe; none of these men
possessed the slightest ear for the word, the sentence, the speech, the
paragraph; all of them, however, have, so to speak, enforced the career

they decreed for themselves by a relentless policing of their beat. What they produce is hard to praise or to condemn; how is one to judge the great, logical symphony of a tone-deaf musician? Pulpy in detail, their work has nevertheless a fine solidity of structure; they drive an idea or a theme step by step to its brutal conclusion with the same terrible force they have brought to bear on their profession. They are among the few contemporary American writers who know how to exhaust a subject; that is, alas, their trouble. Their logical, graceless works can find no reason for stopping, but go on and on, like elephants pacing in a zoo. In their last acts and chapters, they arrive not at despair but at a strange, blank nihilism. Their heroes are all searchers; like so many nonverbal, inarticulate people, they are looking for a final Word that will explain everything. These writers are, naturally, masters of suspense.

O'Neill has neither the phenomenal memory which serves Farrell as a substitute for observation, nor the documentary habits which, for Dreiser, performed the same service. In *The Iceman Cometh*, the scene is a cheap bar somewhere in downtown New York in the year 1912; the characters are the derelict habitués of the back room—a realist's paradise, one would think. But it needs only a short walk along Third Avenue today (or the armchair method of inquiry) to solidify the suspicion that, unless drinking *moeurs* have changed in the last thirty-five years, O'Neill is an incompetent reporter. In the day and a half that elapses on the stage of the Martin Beck, none of the characters is visibly drunk, nobody has a hangover, and, with a single brief exception, nobody has the shakes; there are none of those rancorous, semi-schizoid silences, no obscurity of thought, no dark innuendos, no flashes of hatred; there is, in short, none of the terror of drink, which, after all, in the stage that Harry Hope's customers have presumably reached, is a form of insanity. What is missing is precisely the thing that is most immediately striking and most horrifying in any human drunkard, the sense of the destruction of personality. Each of

O'Neill's people is in perfect possession of the little bit of character the author has given him. The Boer is Boerish, the Englishman English, the philosopher philosophizes, and the sentimental grouch who runs the establishment grouches and sentimentalizes in orderly alternation. So obedient indeed are these supposed incorrigibles to the play's thematic dictation, so well behaved in speech and in silence, that one might imagine, if one shut one's eyes, that one was attending the Christmas exercises in some respectable school ("I am Wind, I blow and blow," says little Aeolus with his bag).

And the didactic tone is, in fact, the play's natural mode. The "realistic" scene that stretches, rather Moscow Art–style and frieze-like, across the stage is no more than mood or décor. The play quickly calls itself to order, the drunkards awake and embark on an elementary study of the nature of reality and illusion. Each drunkard, it seems, has his "pipe dream": he imagines that tomorrow he will get a job, take a walk, marry, see the anarchist millennium, go home to England or South Africa. A hardware salesman, beloved of all, who is expected to arrive for one of his periodical benders, finally does appear on the dot of the dramatist's excellent schedule; he is changed, sober, exhilarated, he has a mission to perform; he will cure Harry Hope and his customers of the illusions that are making them unhappy. In the course of the play, he obliges each of the characters to test himself. All fail to carry out the actions projected in the pipe dream, but self-knowledge, the recognition of failure, does not bring them the freedom the salesman promised. On the contrary, it kills whatever life was left in them; disgruntled, despairing, demoralized, they cannot even get drunk, though they are full of red-eye whiskey. Fortunately, it turns out that the salesman had attained his own state of freedom and euphoria by killing his wife; the police come for him, and Harry Hope and his clients, perceiving that he is mad, can dismiss the truths he has taught them and feel their liquor again (though this statement must be taken on faith, since here, as in the rest of the play, alcoholism does not have its customary sour breath, and the characters, like the actors who are impersonating them, seem to have been swallowing ponies of tea). As the happy derelicts carouse, one character who is without illusions, the boy who has betrayed his anarchist mother to the police, goes out and commits suicide, and another character, the philosopher, who is also capable of facing truth, indicates that he will soon join him in a plunge from the fire escape. Life, then, consists of illusion, and if death is reality, reality is also death.

The odd thing about *The Iceman Cometh* is that this rather bony synopsis does it perfect justice; in fact, it improves it by substituting, whenever possible, the word "illusion" for the word "pipe dream," which recurs with a crankish and verbally impoverished tastelessness about two hundred times during the play. What shreds of naturalism cling to this work are attached to and encumber the dialogue; the language has the wooden verisimilitude, the flat, dead, echoless sound of stale slang that make Farrell's novels and the later works of Sinclair Lewis so stilted. O'Neill here has not even the justification of sociological pedantry, which these other writers might bring forward. His intention is symbolic and philosophical, but unfortunately you cannot write a Platonic dialogue in the style of *Casey at the Bat*. O'Neill might have studied the nature of illusion through the separate relations to illusion of a group of characters (*The Three Sisters*), but his people are given but a single trait each, and they act and react, in the loss and recapture of illusion, not individually but in a body. Bare and plain, this play has the structure of an argument; its linguistic deficiencies make it maudlin. How is your wife getting along with the iceman, the characters roar, over and over again, and though death is the iceman, the joke is not appreciably refined by this symbolic treatment; rather, it is death that is coarsened.

Yet it must be said for O'Neill that he is probably the only man in the world who is still laughing at the iceman joke or pondering its implications. He is certainly the only writer who would have the courage or the lack of judgment to build a well-made play around it. This sense of one man's isolation is what, above all, gives *The Iceman Cometh* its salient look. Though it is full of reminders of Saroyan (the barroom, the loose-witted philosophical talk, the appearance of the Redeemer at the middle table), of O'Casey (again the drunkards, and the tense, frightened young man who has betrayed the Cause), of Ibsen, Thornton Wilder, and even of Maxwell Anderson (the ripples of the Mooney and Sacco-Vanzetti cases which lap at the edges of a distant slum, and again the homemade philosophy) *The Iceman Cometh* seems nevertheless estranged from all influences and impressions. Its solitariness inside its rigid structure suggests the prison or the asylum or the sound of a man laughing in a square, empty room.

—November–December 1946

(The following article appeared in the book section of *The New York Times* for Sunday, August 31, 1952.)

In the mid-1940s *A Moon for the Misbegotten* was tried out on the road by the Theatre Guild but never brought to New York. "Casting difficulties" were spoken of, which is generally a theatrical euphemism for loss of interest in a property. Yet the play, as it appears in book form, seems very much like the New England farm plays of the O'Neill apogee, and in particular like *Desire Under the Elms*, which was revived last winter in New York. The spectacle of a mature play by a renowned dramatist vainly haunting the managers' offices while revivals of his early successes close and open has a certain sardonic pathos, a note of *Enoch Arden*.

A Moon for the Misbegotten is *Desire Under the Elms* grown old and hoarse and randy. There is the familiar puritan triad of greed, land, and sexual repression. There are a demonic old man, a stony unrewarding farm, a vital Demeter of a woman. The finale is lit by an apocalyptic dawn, and the whole play is reddened by whiskey, like a bloodshot eye. There is an opening which is really a prologue, with the cunning son (two in *Desire Under the Elms*) deserting the farm with a sum of money stolen from the miser father. This opening imparts to both plays a curious, desolate aspect, as if normal self-interest, in the person of the departing sons, had stealthily forsaken the vicinity; those who are left are survivors in a waste.

A Moon for the Misbegotten, however, is not laid in the period-past of the gold rush but in the golden bootleg Twenties, on a Connecticut tenant farm, an old box of a house raised up on blocks of timber. The characters are not New Englanders of the original stock but Irish supplanters. The heroine is a gigantic young woman, 180 pounds broad and tall, who carries a club to defend herself; as the daughter of a bootlegger and shifty, shiftless farmer, she is known throughout the neighborhood for her herculean sexual prowess. A sort of Olympian knockdown comedy is enacted between the trickster father and the virago daughter, but this comedy is at bottom sad, for the daughter is in actuality a virgin with a strong maternal heart and the father a grimy cupid with benevolent matrimonial plans for her.

These plans center on a middle-aged alcoholic of educated pretensions, the son of a well-known Thespian who owned farm property. Here the theme of puritanism suddenly appears, like an elemental blight. Behind the pagan façade of Irish boasting, drinking, and ribaldry is revealed a wheyey sentimentality and retching hatred of sex. With the nuptial couch all readied in the tar-papered lean-to, James Tyrone Jr., man of the world and Broadway rake-hell, makes his true confession: he is a man who, like Stephen Dedalus, has wronged his dying mother, and wronged her again, a thousand times over, when, escorting her body home on the train, he entertained a prostitute in his drawing room while Mama was in the baggage car ahead. In his moment of opportunity, he sobs himself chastely to sleep, a guilt-sickened altar boy.

This moment, in which the bootlegger's daughter discovers that this middle-aged man is really "dead," emotionally speaking—an exhausted mummified child—is a moment of considerable poignancy. The defeat of all human plans and contrivances is suddenly shaped in the picture of the titaness sitting staring at a stage moon with a shriveled male infant drunkenly asleep at her side. The image of the survivors takes on a certain grotesque epic form; the woman, stage center, like a gentle beached whale, appears for an instant as the last survivor of the world.

What disturbs one here, however, as in so many of O'Neill's plays, is the question of how far the author himself is a victim of the same sentimentality and self-pity that is exhibited clinically in the characters; how far, specifically, O'Neill himself is taken in by the "tragic" figure of James Tyrone Jr., who is merely a pitiable wreck. My impression is that O'Neill himself does not know, that he puts the character forward like a question, which he hopes may be answered favorably. The crudity of the technique makes it hard to descry intention. Nevertheless, despite this, despite the tone of barbershop harmony that enters into all O'Neill's work, this play exacts homage for its mythic powers, for the element of transcendence jutting up woodenly in it like a great homemade Trojan horse.

5

A STREETCAR CALLED SUCCESS

YOU ARE AN ordinary guy and your wife's sister comes to stay with you. Whenever you want to go to the toilet, there she is in the bathroom, primping or having a bath or giving herself a shampoo and taking her time about it. You go and hammer on the door ("For Christ's sake, aren't you through yet?"), and your wife shushes you frowningly: Blanche is very sensitive and you must be careful of her feelings. You get sore at your wife; your kidneys are sensitive too. My God, you yell, loud enough so that Blanche can hear you, can't a man pee in his own house, when is she getting out of here? You are pretty sick too of feeling her criticize your table manners, and does she have to turn on the radio when you have a poker game going, who does she think she is? Finally you and your wife have a fight (you knew all along that She was turning the little woman against you), you decide to put your foot down, Blanche will have to go. Your wife reluctantly gives in—anything for peace, don't think it's been a treat for *her* ("But let me handle it, Stanley; after all, she's my own *sister!*"). One way or another (God knows what your wife told her) Blanche gets the idea. You buy her a ticket home. But then right at the end, when you're carrying her bags downstairs for her, you feel sort of funny; maybe you were too hard; but that's the way the world is, and, boy, isn't it great to be alone?

This variation on the mother-in-law theme is the one solid piece of theatrical furniture that *A Streetcar Named Desire* can show; the rest is antimacassars. Acrimony and umbrage, tears, door-slamming, broken dishes, jeers, cold silences, whispers, raised eyebrows, the determination to take no notice, the whole classic paraphernalia of insult and injury is Tennessee Williams's hope chest. That the domestic dirty linen it contains is generally associated with the comic strip and the radio sketch should not invalidate it for him as subject matter; it has nobler antecedents. The cook, one may recall, is leaving on the opening page of *Anna Karenina*, and Hamlet at the court of Denmark is really playing the part of the wife's unwelcome relation. Dickens, Dostoevsky, Farrell rattle the skeleton of family life; there is no limit, apparently, to what people will do to each other in the family; nothing is too grotesque or shameful; all laws are suspended, including the law of probability. Mr. Williams, at his best, is an *outrageous* writer in this category; at his worst, he is outrageous in another.

Had he been content in *A Streetcar Named Desire* with the exasperating trivia of the in-law story, he might have produced a wonderful little comic epic, The Struggle for the Bathroom, an epic ribald and poignant, a *comédie larmoyante* which would not have been deficient either in those larger implications to which his talent presumes, for the bathroom might have figured as the last fortress of the individual, the poor man's club, the working girl's temple of beauty; and the bathtub and the toilet, symbol of illusion and symbol of fact, the prone and the upright, the female and the male, might have faced each other eternally in blank, porcelain contradiction as the area for self-expression contracted to the limits of this windowless cell. Mr. Williams, however, like the Southern women he writes about, appears to have been mortified by the literary poverty of such material, by the pettiness of the arena which is in fact its grandeur. Like Blanche DuBois in *A Streetcar Named Desire* and the mother in *The Glass Menagerie*, he is addicted to the embroidering lie, and though his taste in fancywork differs from these ladies', inclining more to the modernistic, the stark contrast, the jagged scene, the jungle motifs ("Then they come together with low, animal moans"), the tourist Mexican ("*Flores para los muertos, corones para los muertos*"), to clarinet music, suicide, homosexuality, rape, and insanity, his work creates in the end that very effect of painful falsity which is imparted to the Kowalski household by Blanche's pink lampshades and couch covers.

To illustrate with a single instance, take the character of Blanche. In her Mr. Williams has caught a flickering glimpse of the faded essence of the sister-in-law; thin, vapid, neurasthenic, romancing, genteel, pathetic, a collector of cheap finery and of the words of old popular songs, fearful and fluttery and awkward, fond of admiration and overeager to obtain it, a refined pushover and perennial and frigid spinster, this is the woman who inevitably comes to stay and who evokes pity because of her very emptiness, because nothing can ever happen to her since her life is a shoddy magazine story she tells herself in a daydream. But the thin, sleazy stuff of this character must be embellished by Mr. Williams with all sorts of arty decorations. It is not enough that she should be a drunkard (this in itself is plausible); she must also be a notorious libertine who has been run out of a small town like a prostitute, a thing absolutely inconceivable for a woman to whom conventionality is the end of existence; she must have an "interesting" biography, a homosexual husband who has shot himself shortly after their marriage, a story so patently untrue that the audience thinks the character must have invented it; and finally she must be a symbol of art and beauty, this poor flimsy creature to whom truth is mortal, who hates the feel of experience with a pathologic aversion—she must not only be a symbol but she must be given a poetic moment of self-definition; she who has never spoken an honest word in her life is allowed, indeed encouraged, to present her life to the audience as a vocational decision, an artist's election of the beautiful, an act of supreme courage, the choice of the thorny way.

In the same manner, Stanley Kowalski, the husband, who has been all too enthusiastically characterized as the man who wants to pee, the realist of the bladder and the genitals, the monosyllabic cynic, is made to apostrophize sexual intercourse in a kind of Odetsian or Tin Pan Alley poetry. Dr. Kinsey would be interested in a semiskilled male who spoke of the four-letter act as "getting those colored lights going."

If art, as Mr. Williams appears to believe, is a lie, then anything goes, but Mr. Williams's lies, like Blanche's, are so old and shopworn that the very truth upon which he rests them becomes garish and ugly, just as the Kowalskis' apartment becomes the more squalid for Blanche's attempts at decoration. His work reeks of literary ambition as the apartment reeks of cheap perfume; it is impossible to witness one of Mr. Williams's plays without being aware of the pervading smell of careerism. Over and above their subject matter, the plays seem to emanate an ever-growing confidence in their author's success. It is this perhaps which is responsible for Mr. Williams's box-office draw: there is a curious elation in this work which its subject matter could not engender. Whatever happens to the characters, Mr. Williams will come out rich and famous, and the play is merely an episode in Mr. Williams's career. And this career in itself has the tinny quality of a musical romance, from movie usher to Broadway lights, like *Alexander's Ragtime Band* or *The Jolson Story*. Pacing up and down a Murray Hill apartment, he tells of his early struggles to a sympathetic reporter. He remembers his "first break." He writes his life story for a Sunday supplement. He takes his work seriously; he does not want success to spoil him; he recognizes the dangers; he would be glad to have advice. His definition of his literary approach is a triumph of boyish simplicity: "I have always had a deep feeling for the mystery in life." This "Hello Mom" note in Mr. Williams's personality is the real, indigenous thing. He is the Aldrich Family and Andy Hardy and possibly Gene Tunney and bride's biscuits and the mother-in-law joke. The cant of the intelligentsia (the jargon, that is, of failure) comes from his lips like an ill-learned recitation: he became, at one point, so he says, "that most common American phenomenon, the rootless, wandering writer"—is this a wholly fitting description of a talent which is as rooted in the American pay dirt as a stout and tenacious carrot?

—March 1948

6

A NEW WORD

AT FIRST GLANCE, the main actors in *Look Back in Anger* appear to be three newspapers and an ironing board. When the curtain goes up, on a cheap one-room flat, the audience sees a pair of Sunday papers, a cloud of pipe smoke, and some men's feet and legs protruding; more papers are scattered on the floor, and, off to one side, a woman is silently ironing a shirt. "Why do I do this every Sunday?" exclaims Jimmy Porter, throwing his paper down. "Even the book reviews seem to be the same as last week's. Different books—same reviews." At the rise of the third-act curtain, months later, the two male figures are still enveloped in the Sunday papers, while a woman is silently ironing a shirt. Same scene—different girl. Nothing really changes; nothing can change. That is the horror of Sunday. Jimmy's wife, Alison, a colonel's daughter, has finally left him, but her girlfriend, Helena, has stepped into her shoes. Jimmy, a working-class intellectual, still has a hostage from the ruling class doing the washing and the cooking, and his friend, Cliff, an uneducated Welsh boy, who boards with them, is still looking on. There has been a swap of upper-class women, like the swap of posh newspapers: you put down *The Observer* and pick up *The Sunday Times*—same contents, different makeup. A blonde is replaced by a brunette, and there is a different set of makeup on the dressing table. The two "class" newspapers, one Liberal, one Tory, are interchangeable, and the mass newspaper, *The News of the World*, is a weekly Psychopathia Sexualis. Other fixtures in the cast of characters are some church bells outside, the unseen landlady downstairs, and a storage tank in the middle of the flat that represents Jimmy Porter's mother-in-law—in the third act, the new girl at the ironing board, a homemaker, has put a slipcover on "Mummy," which does not alter the fact that Mummy is still present, built in to the apartment, as she is built in to English life.

The stagnant boredom of Sundays in a provincial town, with the pubs closed and nothing to do but read the papers, is a travesty of the day of rest—the day which officially belongs to the private person, who is here seen as half an inert object and half a restless phantom staring through the bars of his prison. Nobody can deny that this feeling of being pent-up is characteristic of Sunday, perhaps for the majority of people in Anglo-Saxon countries. Jimmy Porter is still young enough to feel that something *ought* to happen, something a little different, to break the monotony. He believes that Sunday has a duty to be interesting. John Osborne's critics, on the contrary, believe that Jimmy has a duty not to be bored or at least not to show it, not to keep talking about it. As Helena, who marches into the play waving the standard of criticism, tells her friend Alison, Jimmy will have to learn to behave like everybody else.

"Why can't you be like other people?" This extreme demand, which always rises to the surface in quarrels between married couples, leaps from behind the footlights to confront Jimmy Porter; the play alerts a kind of intimate antagonism in its audiences, as though audience and hero were a wedded pair, headed straight for the divorce court, recriminations, lawyers, ugly charges. Criticism has picked the play to pieces, as though it were a trumped-up story; imagined discrepancies or improbabilities are pounced on ("The play is not true to life; people do their ironing on Mondays," or "They would have finished reading the papers by four o'clock in the afternoon"). One critic, writing in *The*

New Republic, thinks he knows why Jimmy Porter can't be like other people: homosexual tendencies. Nor would Jimmy Porter, if he could reply, change a single feature of his conduct to avoid the drawing of this inference. The play almost asks to be misunderstood, like an infuriated, wounded person; out of bravado, it coldly refuses to justify itself.

Jimmy Porter's boredom is a badge of freedom, and he will not be passive about it; for him, boredom is a positive activity, a proclamation. To be actively, angrily, militantly bored is one of the few forms of protest open to him that do not compromise his independence and honesty. At the same time it is one of the few forms of recreation he can afford; his boredom becomes an instrument on which he plays variations, as he does on his trumpet in the next room. But other people suffer, it is said. He ought not to make other people suffer because *he* is unhappy and out of sorts. No doubt, but this is unfortunately the way unhappy people are; they are driven to distribute the suffering.

For Jimmy Porter, moreover, there is a principle involved. He is determined to stay alive, which means that he must struggle against the soporific substitutes for real life that make up the Sunday program: the steady soft thud of the iron and the regular rustle of newsprint. His friend, Cliff, keeps telling him to shut up; his badgered wife, Alison, only wants peace, a little peace, but that is what Jimmy, or a part of Jimmy, his needling, cruel voice, has decided that she shall not have. He is fighting to keep her awake, to keep himself and his friend awake, as though all three were in the grip of a deathly coma or narcosis that had been spread over all of England by the gases emanating from the press, the clergy, the political parties, the BBC. Jimmy Porter's gibes are a therapeutic method designed to keep a few people alive, whether they like it or not, and patterned on the violent procedures used with patients who have taken an overdose of drugs and whose muttered plea, like Alison's, is always to be left alone.

This, at any rate, is what Jimmy thinks he is doing. His voice is a calculated irritant that prevents the other characters from lapsing into torpor. For his own part he is tired of listening to himself and would be glad to tune in on another station, where something was really happening, where there was a little enthusiasm; he would like, sometime, just once, to hear "a warm, thrilling voice cry out Hallelujah!" Instead, there is only the deadly static provided by the Sunday weeklies, the Bishop of Bromley blessing the hydrogen bomb, and the church bells ringing outside. He thinks he would like to listen to a concert of Vaughan Williams's music, but the ironing interferes with the reception, and he irritably shuts the radio off.

"Interference" is what Jimmy detests, whether it comes from the iron, his mother-in-law, his wife's girlfriend, or the church bells. He is morbidly suspicious in any case and morbidly sensitive to "foreign" noises. At the same time, he is unnerved by silence. The only sound he really trusts is the sound of his own voice, which he keeps turned on mechanically, almost absently, as other people keep a phonograph going. This voice is very droll and funny, which is how it placates censure; it is "as good as a show." But the other characters sometimes plead with Jimmy to be quiet; they cannot "hear themselves think" or read the papers in peace or go on with the ironing because of that voice. And if it stops talking, it moves into the next room and starts blowing on a trumpet. It never runs down and when it seems to flag for a moment, it is only to gather fresh energy, like a phonograph that pauses to let the record turn over. Jimmy demands an undivided attention, even when he is absent, and he is quick to know when no one is listening. "I'm sorry; I wasn't listening properly," says Alison at the beginning of the play. "You bet you weren't listening," he retorts. "Old Porter talks and everyone turns over and goes to sleep. And Mrs. Porter gets 'em going with the first yawn."

Behind all this is more than egotism or a childish insistence on being the center of the stage. Jimmy Porter is a completely isolated person whose profoundest, quickest, most natural instinct is mistrust. This is the automatic, animal wariness of a creature that feels itself surrounded. Solidarity, a working-class virtue, is for him the only virtue that is real; he exacts complete allegiance and fealty from anyone who enters his life. His women appear, so to speak, wearing his colors; both girls, while they *are* his, are seen wearing one of his old shirts over their regular clothes. When Alison is found in a slip, dressing to go out, in the second act, this is proof that she is about to revert, away from him, back to her own kind. Jimmy would make his women into men if he could, *not* because he is a covert homosexual, but because, if they were men, he could trust them. Women do not have that natural quality of solidarity that exists between men, and they have always been suspected by men for precisely this reason; women live in the artificial realm of the social and are adepts at transferring allegiances ("making new friends") and at all the arts of deception and camouflage of which the dressing table, stage left, is the visible sign. Alison lets Jimmy down at the crucial moment of the play—a thing he finds unthinkable, as does Alison's father, Colonel Redfern. This is followed, appropriately, by another betrayal: Alison's girlfriend, Helena, seizes Jimmy for herself.

The story of *Look Back in Anger* has, from this point of view, a great deal in common with *Hamlet*. Cliff, the working-class Welsh boy, is Jimmy Porter's Horatio, who sticks to him without understanding all the fine points of Jimmy's philosophy; and the scenes Jimmy makes with Alison have the same candid brutality that Hamlet showed to Ophelia. In both cases, the frenzied mockery springs from an expectation of betrayal. Ophelia is felt to be the ally of the corrupt court with the murderer-king at its head, of her dull brother, Laertes, and her father, that ass Polonius. In *Look Back in Anger*, brother Nigel is Laertes and Alison's mother is cast in the role of Polonius, lurking behind the arras. The fact that Alison is secretly exchanging letters with her means that she is in communication with the enemy, like that other docile daughter, Ophelia. Women cannot be trusted because they do not understand that such an act is treachery; they do it "in all innocence." Apart from anything else, they do not take in the meaning of a declaration of war.

Both Hamlet and Jimmy Porter have declared war on a rotten society; both have been unfitted by a higher education from accepting their normal place in the world. They think too much and criticize too freely. Jimmy, like Hamlet, might have become a species of courtier or social sycophant; that is, he might have "got ahead." Critics complain that he ought to have found a job at a provincial university, instead of torturing himself and his nice wife by running a sweet stall. Hamlet, too, might have settled down to a soft berth in the court of Denmark, married Ophelia, and waited for the succession. Hamlet's tirades and asides are plainly calculated to disturb and annoy the court. He too cannot stop talking and, like Jimmy Porter, who practices vaudeville routines, he turns to the players for relief from the "real" world of craft, cunning, and stupidity. Both heroes are naturally histrionic, and in both cases the estrangement, marked by histrionics, is close at moments to insanity. Both have no fixed purpose beyond that of awakening the people around them from their trance of acceptance and obliging them to be conscious of the horror and baseness of the world. Both (though this is clearer in Hamlet's case) suffer from a horrible self-doubt that alternates with wild flashes of conviction, and neither wholly wills the events he himself is causing. Yet neither wants to repent whatever it is that is driving him to destroy everything in sight, and both repel pity. "He wouldn't *let* me pity him," said a young woman, sadly, coming out of *Look Back in Anger*. That is just the concession the play refuses to make; if the audience pitied Jimmy Porter, this would be interference.

The Entertainer is a softer play than *Look Back in Anger*. The enemy here is identified with the "men of Suez" and the right wing generally; this, being a political grievance, is easier for the audience to sympathize with. To be angry about politics is conventional. The Suez crisis is somewhat arbitrarily linked with a family of music hall performers whose contact with the invasion is so remote, theatrically, that the fact that they have a son "out there," fighting, is only mentioned, like an afterthought, at the end of the third scene. On the surface, this play has far more plot than *Look Back in Anger*: Archie Rice, a down-and-out music hall comedian, is pursued by bankruptcy and the figure of the Income Tax man; he wants to leave his old, sodden, moronic wife and marry a young girl; his daughter goes to the Trafalgar Square protest meeting against Suez and breaks her engagement; his father dies; his other son and probably his wife are going off to Canada to join some relations, while he is slated for jail. Yet much of this plot is clumsily messengered in, by telegrams, newspaper stories, straight narration, so that it seems a kind of dubious hearsay—the daughter's engagement to someone called "Graham"; the young girl they say Archie wants to marry; even the two deaths. The relations in Canada come to life, if life it can be called, in the letter that is read from them describing their TV set and their new Chevrolet Bel Air. This is enough to tell Archie that he would rather go to jail, and it is enough for the audience to get the picture in a flash. But, with this exception, nothing that occurs on the periphery carries much conviction; the center is Archie Rice, lit by a spot, standing before a curtain gamely doing his act, while beyond him, in the wings, there is only an empty blackness, a void of shadows. Somewhere in that void there is the Man with the Hook—death and taxes.

Jimmy Porter is "as good as a show," and Archie, with his tipped hat and bow tie and gloves and cane and blackened eyebrows, is the grisly show itself. He is the eternal performer who enters before the variety queens and who has to hold the audience or else be jerked off the stage. His function is to keep the show going, no matter what—if a fire breaks out or the bombs start falling or somebody dies. Like Jimmy, Archie cannot stop talking; this is his professional misfortune —the commitment he has made to the management. Silence, for this old pro, is the ultimate terror; he listens intently, head cocked, for the laugh or the patter of applause rising from the darkness of the pit, to assure him that he is still there, in the spotlight, in short that he still exists. If his own voice falters, if he dries up, he is done for; the orchestra will strike up to cover the silence, and the hook will come out to claim him. All the clichés of the stage, of the old trouper who "never missed a performance," take on in this play a quality of sheer horror.

The actor and the soldier have the same mythology; timing, coordination, a cool nerve, resourcefulness, are essential to the discipline. A vaudevillian like Archie Rice looks on the stage as a fort he is holding, until relief in the form of the next turn will appear. Before a performance every actor experiences a slight case of battle nerves, and actors, like soldiers, are superstitious. In *The Entertainer* this equation between the actor and the soldier is instinctively caught and exploited for an effect of tragic pathos. The link with Suez seems strained in terms of stage-plotting, while the characters are merely talking and drinking gin, like other people. But when Archie, in costume, is revealed with a tall nude behind him, like a recruiting poster, who wears the helmet of Britannia and holds a bulldog and a trident, the grotesque relation becomes real. His fading personal fortunes are eerily identified with the fading of the Empire. His personal hollowness echoes the present hollowness of the Empire idea, and the proposed retreat to Canada signifies the shift of power. The old growling bulldog England is represented by Archie's father, an old trouper and veteran who went through the Dardanelles without a scratch and who reenlists, as it were, when summoned by Archie to save the family's collective life; he dies at his post, performing, and his coffin is draped in the Union Jack. The old man's sacrifice, to save a "no-good, washed-up, tatty show," is a useless expenditure. The silence that Archie fears closes in at the end; it is the death of old England. The actor is finished, and it is the audience's turn to "have a go."

"Don't clap too hard, we're all in a very old building"—this grim antique vaudeville wheeze which is part of Archie's stock of gags evokes another play, written at another crisis of the declining Empire, during the First World War: Shaw's *Heartbreak House*. Shaw's drafty old country house, England, which is run by a mad, drunken sea captain, has gone down still another step with John Osborne, and become a drafty old vaudeville house at a run-down coastal resort, with an alcoholic comedian introducing a girl show. Shaw was a man of sixty when he wrote *Heartbreak House*, and Osborne was twenty-eight, last year, when *The Entertainer* was first produced. Both men had received a bitter education in the school of poverty that made the protected assumptions of well-to-do people appear to them as a kind of ludicrous insanity. Shaw's father was a drunkard; Osborne's mother was a barmaid. Shaw got his training for the stage as a speaker at street corners and socialist meetings; Osborne got his as an actor, often unemployed. Bravado, impatience of cant, and a gift of gab are the product of these experiences. Shaw, to the day of his death, was obsessed with waking people up, rubbing their noses in the raw facts of life, of which they seemed so incredibly ignorant; Osborne is the same, though somewhat more savage, having come from lower down in the social scale. Shaw was, of course, an inveterate entertainer; that was his calamity, like Archie Rice's. And, like Jimmy Porter, he could never give his public a rest, leave them in peace to read the paper; he was always "at" them, telling them their faults, just as he did with his friends. The audience, toward the end, got a little tired of him, and he, no doubt, got a little tired of himself, coming on to do his turn, in his grizzled stage eyebrows and beard. More and more, as he grew older, he had the feeling that he was talking sense and no one was listening.

Throughout both John Osborne's plays there is a longing for a message, a "new word"—for purification, simplification. Personally, like Shaw, he is a vegetarian and does not drink alcohol. Shaw thought he had a message, if he could only get people to hear it. Osborne is in a more radical fix. Shaw could not sell him simplified spelling or an easy way to socialism. There is no new word, and, if there were, nobody would listen. One of Archie Rice's sons is a conscientious objector, but he has no hope of converting anyone and does not try; being a CO is his way of being an oddball, in a family of oddballs, and he accepts it for that, as one accepts one's face. Archie Rice's daughter has been giving art lessons to a gang of tough kids in a London Youth Club; she does not expect any good to come of it. Yet she has been moved by the Trafalgar Square meeting to the point where she feels that something *might* happen, something in fact *must* happen, some change or redemption. Hence she comes home and starts trying to redeem Archie. But Archie is way ahead of her—a nice man, friendly, but far beyond recall, off in lunar space, where no new word could reach him. The transparent gauzes and dissolving walls of the stage set explain what has happened to the home the girl has come back to and which she takes for solid. It is a transparent deception; you can see straight through it, out into the blackness. This ectoplasm of a home is inhabited by monologists; nobody listens, as the girl and the old man protest; everyone tells the same story, airs the same objections, like a collection of tired phonographs. The voices are slurred and they forget what they started to say; there was a point to be made, long ago, but it has been forgotten.

Archie, the head of this dissolving household, has been dead a long time and floated off into filmy unreal distances, beyond the pull of gravity, with the spotlight still playing on him, picking him out, like some powerful telescope. Nothing can happen to Archie anymore because he is a spook, dead, as he says, behind the eyes. Archie is in eternity, steadily doing his routine, grinding out his grinning patter, like the salt mill that fell into the sea ("You wouldn't think I was sexy to look at me, would you? No, honestly, would you, lady?"). He has heard something once (the "warm, thrilling voice"), an old Negress singing, but he was half-slewed at the time, so that his account of the message is garbled. Now he half-listens to his daughter, politely, warily, trying to get her point of view, that is, to fix the remote point in space where this new sound is coming from. Archie is not always certain when he is onstage and when he is at home; it is all a cover-up anyway. He may be dead, but he is not taken in. The last story he tells, in his final stage appearance, is a story about a little man who finds himself in eternity, in paradise, and when a saint on the welcoming committee asks him what he thinks of it, he looks around the upper regions and answers with a four-letter word. After a moment's consternation, the saint throws his arms around the little man and kisses him. He has been waiting to hear that word ever since he came there —that is, for all eternity.

What is that word, exactly? And what has John Osborne got against heaven? The answer is very simple. The word is hell (h-e-l-l), and that is what John Osborne has to say about this other-Eden, demi-paradise, the Welfare State, where, as Archie observes ironically, "nobody wants, and nobody goes without, all are provided for." The anger of John Osborne, which has angered so many people, is total and uncompromising; these two plays are nothing more or less than lively descriptions of hell. Those who want to be told what is biting the playwright have only to look around them, at the general fatuity and emptiness which is so much taken for granted that it appears as normal and almost no one hopes or wishes for anything better. A good deal has been made of the fact that Osborne, in an essay published in a volume called *Declaration*, attacked the Queen and the Tories; but the Queen, as admirers of royalty are fond of pointing out, is only a symbol anyway, a symbol of the universal cover-up in which the Tories cooperate, but not the Tories alone. Osborne is no Labour Party canvasser, offering false teeth and nationalized steel to the masses; the changes which might be effected, under present conditions, by a return of Labour to power would be minute, and Osborne knows this. To have Labour in power would make a tiny difference, a break in the monotony; a *little* reality might filter in. Osborne is a socialist who prefers working-class people to people who have never seen a flat with an outside toilet for the same reason that Shaw did: because, on the whole, they are more real; because, like Candida's father and Eliza Doolittle's father, they are shameless and unregenerate observers of what goes on around them. Sixty or seventy years ago, when Shaw began writing, such a preference appeared less shocking and mystifying than it does today, which itself is a proof that it was time someone spoke out again, plainly, and let the sound of a human voice, now evidently so unfamiliar, rattle the old building.

—*London, 1956–1958*

7

THE AMERICAN
REALIST PLAYWRIGHTS

AS SOON AS this title is announced for a lecture or an article, a question pops up: Who are they? Is there, as is assumed abroad, a school of realists in the American theatre or is this notion a critical figment? The question is legitimate and will remain, I hope, in the air long after I have finished. Nevertheless, for purposes of discussion, I am going to take for granted that there is such a group, if not a school, and name its members: Arthur Miller, Tennessee Williams, William Inge, Paddy Chayefsky, the Elmer Rice of *Street Scene*. Behind them, casting them in the shadow, stands the great figure of O'Neill, and opposite them, making them seem more homogeneous, are writers like George Kelly, Wilder, Odets, Saroyan. Their counterparts in the novel are Dreiser, Sherwood Anderson, James T. Farrell, the early Thomas Wolfe—which illustrates, by the way, the backwardness of the theatre in comparison with the novel. The theatre seems to be chronically twenty years behind, regardless of realism, as the relation of Beckett to Joyce, for example, shows. The theatre feeds on the novel; never vice versa: think of the hundreds of dramatizations of novels, and then try to think of a book that was "novelized" from a play. There is not even a word for it. The only actual case I can call to mind is *The Other House* by Henry James—a minor novel he salvaged from a play of his own that failed. To return to the main subject, one characteristic of American realism in the theatre is that none of its practitioners currently—except Chayefsky—wants to call himself a realist. Tennessee Williams is known to his admirers as a "poetic realist," while Arthur Miller declares that he is an exponent of the "social play" and identifies himself with the Greek playwrights, whom he describes as social playwrights also. This delusion was dramatized, if that is the word, in *A View from the Bridge*.

The fact that hardly a one of these playwrights cares to be regarded as a realist without some qualifying or mitigating adjective's being attached to the term invites a definition of realism. What does it mean in common parlance? I have looked the word "realist" up in the *Oxford English Dictionary*. Here is what they say. "...In reference to art and literature, sometimes used as a term of commendation, when precision and vividness of detail are regarded as a merit, and sometimes unfavorably contrasted with idealized description or representation. In recent use it has often been used with the implication that the details are of an unpleasant or sordid character." This strikes me as a very fair account of the historical fate of the notion of realism, but I shall try to particularize a little, in the hope of finding out why and how this happened. And I shall not be condemning realism but only noting what people seem to think it is.

When we say that a novel or a play is realistic, we mean, certainly, that it gives a picture of ordinary life. Its characters will be drawn from the middle class, the lower middle class, occasionally the working class. You cannot write realistic drama about upper-class life; at least, no one ever has. Aristocracy does not lend itself to realistic treatment, but to one or another kind of stylization: romantic drama, romantic comedy, comedy of manners, satire, tragedy. This fact in itself is a realistic criticism of the aristocratic idea, which cannot afford, apparently, to live in the glass house of the realistic stage. Kings and noble men, said Aristotle, are the protagonists of tragedy—not women or slaves. The same is true of nobility of character or intellect. The exceptional man, whether he be Oedipus or King Lear or one of the romantic revolutionary heroes of Hugo or Musset, is fitted to be the protagonist of a tragedy, but just this tragic fitness disqualifies him from taking a leading role in a realist drama. Such figures as Othello or Hernani can never be the subject of realistic treatment, unless it is with the object of deflating them, showing how *ordinary*—petty or squalid—they are. But then the hero is no longer Othello but an impostor posing as Othello. Cut down to size, he is just like everybody else but worse, because he is a fraud into the bargain. This abrupt foreshortening is why realistic treatment of upper-class life always takes the harsh plunge into satire. No man is a hero to his valet, and Beaumarchais's Figaro is the spokesman of social satire—not of realism; his personal and private realism turns his master into a clown. Realism deals with ordinary men and women or, in extreme forms, with sub-ordinary men, men on the level of beasts or of blind conditioned reflexes (*La Bête Humaine, The Hairy Ape*). This tendency is usually identified with naturalism, but I am regarding naturalism as simply a variety of realism.

Realism, historically, is associated with two relatively modern inventions, i.e., with journalism and with photography. "Photographic realism" is a pejorative term, and enemies of realistic literature often dismissed it as "no more than journalism," implying that journalism was a sordid, seamy affair—a daily photographic close-up, as it were, of the clogged pores of society. The author as sheer observer likened himself to a camera (Dos Passos, Christopher Isherwood, Wright Morris), and insofar as the realistic novel was vowed to be a reflector of ordinary life, the newspapers inevitably became a prime source of material. Newspaper accounts impressed the nineteenth century with their quality of "stark objectivity," and newspapers, which appeared every day, seemed to be the repositories of everydayness and to give a multiple image of the little tragedies and vicissitudes of daily life. In America, in the early part of this century, the realistic novel was a partner of what was called "muckraking" journalism, and both were linked with populism and crusades for political reform.

Hence, perhaps, in part, the unsavory associations in common speech of the word "realistic," even when applied in nonliterary contexts. Take the phrase "a realistic decision." If someone tells you he is going to make "a realistic decision," you immediately understand that he has resolved to do something bad. The same with "Realpolitik." A "realistic politics" is a euphemism for a politics of harsh opportunism; if you hear someone say that it is time for a government to follow a realistic line, you can interpret this as meaning that it is time for principles to be abandoned. A politician or a political thinker who calls himself a political realist is usually boasting that he sees politics, so to speak, in the raw; he is generally a proclaimed cynic and pessimist who makes it his business to look behind words and fine speeches for the motive. This motive is always low.

Whatever the field, whenever you hear that a subject is to be treated "realistically," you expect that its unpleasant aspects are to be brought forward. So it is with the play and the novel. A delicate play like Turgenev's *A Month in the Country*, though perfectly truthful to life, seems deficient in realism in comparison with the stronger medicine of Gorki's *The Lower Depths*. This is true of Turgenev's novels as well and of such English writers as Mrs. Gaskell. And of the peaceful parts of *War and Peace*. Ordinary life treated in its uneventful aspects tends to turn into an idyll. We think of Turgenev and Mrs. Gaskell almost as pastoral writers, despite the fact that their faithful sketches have nothing in common with the artificial convention of the true pastoral. We suspect that there is something Arcadian here— something "unrealistic."

If realism deals with the ordinary man embedded in ordinary life, which for the most part is uneventful, what then is the criterion that makes us forget Turgenev or Mrs. Gaskell when we name off the realists? I think it is this: what we call realism, and particularly dramatic realism, tends to single out the ordinary man at the moment he might get into the newspaper. The criterion, in other words, is drawn from journalism. The ordinary man must become "news" before he qualifies to be the protagonist of a realistic play or novel. The exceptional man is news at all times, but how can the ordinary man get into the paper? By committing a crime. Or, more rarely, by getting involved in a spectacular accident. Since accidents, in general, are barred from the drama, this leaves crime—murder or suicide or embezzlement. And we find that the protagonists of realistic drama, by and large, are the protagonists of newspaper stories—"little men" who have shot their wives or killed themselves in the garage or gone to jail for fraud or embezzlement. Now drama has always had an affinity for crime; long before realism was known, Oedipus and Clytemnestra and Macbeth and Othello were famous for their deeds of blood. But the crimes of tragedy are the crimes of heroes, while the crimes of realistic drama are the crimes of the nondescript person, the crimes that are, in a sense, all alike. The individual in the realistic drama is regarded as a cog or a statistic; he commits the uniform crime that sociologically he might be expected to commit. That is, supposing that 1,031 book-keepers in the state of New York are destined to tamper with the accounts, and 304 policemen are destined to shoot their wives, and 1,115 householders to do away with themselves in the garage, each individual bookkeeper, cop, and householder has been holding a ticket in this statistical lottery, like the fourteen Athenian youths and maidens sent off yearly to the Minotaur's labyrinth, and he acquires interest for the realist theatre only when his "number" comes up. To put it as simply as possible, the cop in *Street Scene* commits his crime—wife-murder—without having the moral freedom to choose to commit it, just as Willy Loman in *Death of a Salesman* commits suicide—under sociological pressure. The hero of tragedy, on the contrary, is a morally free being who identifies himself with his crime (i.e., elects it), and this is true even where he is fated, like Oedipus, to commit it and can be said to have no personal choice in the matter. Oedipus both rejects and accepts his deeds, embraces them in free will at last as *his*. It is the same with Othello or Hamlet. The distinction will be clear if you ask yourself what tragedy of Shakespeare is closest to the realistic theatre. The answer, surely, is *Macbeth*. And why? Because of Lady Macbeth. Macbeth really doesn't choose to murder the sleeping Duncan; Lady Macbeth chooses for him; he is like a middle-class husband, nagged on by his ambitious wife, the way the second vice-president of a bank is nagged on by his Mrs. Macbeth, who wants him to become first vice-president. The end of the tragedy, however, reverses all this; Macbeth becomes a hero only late in the drama, when he pushes Lady Macbeth aside and takes all his deeds on himself. Paradoxically, the conspicuous tragic hero is never free *not* to do his deed; he cannot escape it, as Hamlet found. But the mute hero or protagonist of a realistic play is always free, at least seemingly, not to emerge from obscurity and get his picture in the paper. There is always the chance that not he but some other nondescript bookkeeper or policeman will answer the statistical call.

The heroes of realistic plays are clerks, bookkeepers, policemen, housewives, salesmen, schoolteachers, small and middling businessmen. They commit crimes but they cannot be professional criminals (unlike the heroes of Genet or the characters in *The Beggar's Opera*), for professional criminals, like kings and noble men, are a race apart. The settings of realistic plays are offices, drab dining rooms or living rooms, or the backyard, which might be defined as a place where some grass has once been planted and failed to grow. The backyard is a favorite locus for American realist plays, but no realist play takes place in a garden. Nature is excluded from the realist play, as it has been from the realistic novel. The presence of Nature in Turgenev (and in Chekhov) denotes, as I have suggested, a pastoral intrusion. If a realist play does not take place in the backyard, where Nature has been eroded by clothespoles, garbage cans, bottled-gas tanks, and so on, it takes place indoors, where the only plant, generally, is a rubber plant. Even with Ibsen, the action is confined to a room or pair of rooms until the late plays like *A Lady from the Sea*, *The Master Builder*, *John Gabriel Borkman*, when the realistic style has been abandoned for symbolism and the doors are swung open to the garden, mountains, the sea. Ibsen, however, is an exception to the general rule that the indoor scene must be unattractive: his middle-class Scandinavians own some handsome furniture; Nora's house, like any doll's house, must have been charmingly appointed. But Ibsen is an exception to another rule that seems to govern realistic drama (and the novel too, for that matter)—the rule that it must not be well written. (Thanks to William Archer's wooden translations, his work now falls into line in English.) This rule in America has the force, almost, of a law, one of those iron laws that work from within necessity itself, apparently, and without conscious human aid. Our American realists do not *try* to write badly. Many, like Arthur Miller, strive to write "well," i.e., pretentiously, but like Dreiser in the novel they are cursed with inarticulateness. They "grope." They are, as O'Neill said of himself, "fogbound."

The heroes are petty or colorless; the settings are drab; the language is lame. Thus the ugliness of the form is complete. I am not saying this as a criticism, only observing that when a play or a novel fails to meet these norms, we cease to think of it as realistic. Flaubert, known to be a "stylist," ceases to count for us as a realist, and even in the last century, Matthew Arnold, hailing Tolstoy as a realist, was blinded by categorical thinking—with perhaps a little help from the translations—into calling his novels raw "slices of life," sprawling, formless, and so on. But it is these clichés, in the long run, that have won out. The realistic novel today is more like what Arnold thought Tolstoy was than it is like Tolstoy or any of the early realists. This question of the beauty of form also touches the actor. An actor formerly was supposed to be a good-looking man, with a handsome figure, beautiful movements, and a noble diction. These attributes are no longer necessary for a stage career; indeed, in America they are a positive handicap. A good-looking young man who moves well and speaks well is becoming almost unemployable in American "legit" theatre; his best hope today is to look for work in musical comedy. Or posing for advertisements. On the English stage, where realism until recently never got a foothold, the good-looking actor still rules the roost, but the English actor cannot play American realist parts, while the American actor cannot play Shakespeare or Shaw. A pretty girl in America may still hope to be an actress, though even here there are signs of a change: the heroine of O'Neill's late play, *A Moon for the Misbegotten*, was a freckled giantess five feet eleven inches tall and weighing 180 pounds.

Eisenstein and the Italian neo-realists used people off the street for actors—a logical inference from premises which, being egalitarian and documentary, are essentially hostile to professional elites, including Cossacks, Swiss Guards, and actors. The professional actor in his greasepaint is the antithesis of the pallid man on the street. But film and stage realism are not so democratic in their principles as may at first appear. To begin with, the director and a small corps of professionals—electricians and cameramen—assume absolute power over the masses, i.e., over the untrained actors picked from the crowd; no resistance is encountered, as it would be with professional actors, in molding the human material to the director-dictator's will. And even with stars and all-professional casts, the same tendency is found in the modern realist or neo-realist director. Hence the whispered stories of stars deliberately broken by a director: James Dean and Brigitte Bardot. Similar stories of brainwashing are heard backstage. This is not surprising if realism, as we now know it, rejects as nonaverage whatever is noble, beautiful, or seemly, whatever is capable of "gesture," whatever in fact is free. Everything I have been saying up till now can be summed up in a sentence. Realism is a depreciation of the real. It is a gloomy puritan doctrine that has flourished chiefly in puritan countries—America, Ireland, Scandinavia, northern France, nonconformist England—chilly, chilblained countries, where the daily world is ugly and everything is done to keep it so, as if as a punishment for sin. The doctrine is spreading with industrialization, the growth of ugly cities, and the erosion of Nature. It came late to the English stage, long after it had appeared in the novel, because those puritan elements with which it is naturally allied have, up until now, considered the theatre to be wicked.

At the same time, in defense of realism, it must be said that its great enemy has been just that puritan life whose gray color it has taken. The original realists—Ibsen in the theatre, Flaubert in the novel—regarded themselves as "pagans," in opposition to their puritan contemporaries, and adhered to a religion of Beauty or Nature; they dreamed of freedom and hedonistic license (Flaubert) and exalted (Ibsen) the autonomy of the individual will. Much of this "paganism" is still found in O'Casey and in the early O'Neill, a curdled puritan of Irish-American stock. The original realists were half Dionysian aesthetes ("The vine-leaves in his hair") and their heroes and heroines were usually rebels, protesting the drabness and meanness of the common life. Ibsen's characters complain that they are "stifling"; in the airless hypocrisy of the puritan middle-class parlor, people were being poisoned by the dead gas of lies. Hypocrisy is the cardinal sin of the middle class, and the exposure of a lie is at the center of all Ibsen's plots. The strength and passion of realism is its resolve to tell the whole truth; this explains why the realist in his indictment of society avoids the old method of satire with its delighted exaggeration. The realist drama at its highest is an implacable exposé. Ibsen rips off the curtain and shows his audiences to themselves, and there is something inescapable in the manner of the confrontation, like a case slowly being built. The pillars of society who sit in the best seats are, bit by bit, informed that they are rotten and that the commerce they live on is a commerce of "coffin ships." The action on the Ibsen stage is too close for comfort to the lives of the audience; only the invisible "fourth wall" divides them. "This is the way we live now!" Moral examination, self-examination are practical as a duty, a Protestant stock-taking, in the realist mission hall.

For this, it is essential that the audience accept the picture as true; it cannot be permitted to feel that it is watching something "made up" or embellished. Hence the stripping down of the form and the elimination of effects that might be recognized as literary. For the first time too, in the realist drama, the accessories of the action are described at length by the playwright. The details must strike home and convince. The audience must be able to place the furniture, the carpets, the ornaments, the napery and glassware as "just what these people would have." This accounts for the importance of the stage set. Many critics who scornfully dismiss the "boxlike set" of the realistic drama, with its careful disposition of furniture, do not understand its function. This box is the box or "coffin" of average middle-class life opened at one end to reveal the corpse within, looking, as all embalmed corpses are said to do, "just as if it were alive." Inside the realist drama, whenever it is genuine and serious, there is a kind of double illusion, a false bottom: everything appears to be lifelike but this appearance of life is death. The stage set remains a central element in all true realism; it cannot be replaced by scrim or platforms. In *Long Day's Journey into Night*, surely the greatest realist drama since Ibsen, the family living room, with its central overhead lighting fixture, is as solid and eternal as oak and as sad as wicker, and O'Neill in the text tells the stage designer what books must be in the glassed-in bookcase on the left and what books in the other by the entrance. The tenement of Elmer Rice's *Street Scene* (in the opera version) was a magnificent piece of characterization; so was the Bronx living room of Odets's *Awake and Sing!*—his sole (and successful) experiment with realism. I can still see the bowl of fruit on the table, slightly to the left of stage center, and hear the Jewish mother interrupting whoever happened to be talking, to say,

"Have a piece of fruit." That bowl of fruit, which *was* the Jewish Bronx, remains more memorable as a character than many of the people in the drama. This gift of characterization through props and stage set is shared by Paddy Chayefsky in *Middle of the Night* and by William Inge in *Come Back, Little Sheba*, where an unseen prop or accessory, the housewife's terrible frowsty little dog, is a masterstroke of realist illusionism and, more than that, a kind of ghostly totem. All these plays, incidentally, are stories of death-in-life.

This urgent correspondence with a familiar reality, down to the last circumstantial detail, is what makes realism so gripping, like a trial in court. The dramatist is witnessing or testifying, on an oath never sworn before in a work of art, not to leave out anything and to tell the truth to the best of his ability. And yet the realistic dramatist, beginning with Ibsen, is aware of a missing element. The realist mode seems to generate a dissatisfaction with itself, even in the greatest masters: Tolstoy, for example, came to feel that his novels, up to *Resurrection*, were inconsequential trifling; the vital truth had been left out. In short, as a novelist, he began to feel like a hypocrite. This dissatisfaction with realism was evidently suffered also by Ibsen; halfway through his realist period, you see him start to look for another dimension. Hardly had he discovered or invented the new dramatic mode than he showed signs of being cramped by it; he experienced, if his plays are an index, that same sense of confinement, of being stifled, within the walls of realism that his characters experience within the walls of middle-class life. Something was missing: air. This is already plain in *The Wild Duck*, a strange piece of auto-criticism and probably his finest play; chafing, restless, mordant, he is searching for something else, for a poetic element, which he represents, finally, in the wild duck itself, a dramatic symbol for that cherished wild freedom that neither Ibsen nor his characters can maintain, without harming it, in a shut-in space. But to resort to symbols to make good the missing element becomes a kind of forcing, like trying to raise a wild bird in an attic, and the strain of this is felt in *Rosmersholm*, where symbols play a larger part and are charged with a more oppressive weight of meaning. In *The Lady from the Sea*, *The Master Builder*, and other late plays, the symbols have broken through the thin fence or framework of realism; poetry has spread its crippled wings, but the price has been heavy.

The whole history of dramatic realism is encapsulated in Ibsen. First, the renunciation of verse and of historical and philosophical subjects in the interests of prose and the present time; then the dissatisfaction and the attempt to restore the lost element through a recourse to symbols; then, or at the same time, a forcing of the action at the climaxes to heighten the drama; finally, the renunciation of realism in favor of a mixed mode or hodgepodge. The reaching for tragedy at the climaxes is evident in *Hedda Gabler* and still more so in *Rosmersholm*, where, to me at any rate, the climactic shriek "To the millrace!" is absurdly like a bad film. Many of Ibsen's big moments, even as early as *A Doll's House*, strike me as false and grandiose, that is, precisely, as stagey. Nor is it only in the context of realism that they appear so. It is not just that one objects that people do not act or talk like that—Tolstoy's criticism of King Lear on the heath. If you compare the millrace scene in *Rosmersholm* with the climax of a Shakespearean tragedy, you will see that the Shakespearean heroes are far less histrionic, more natural and *ordinary*; there is always a stillness at the center of the Shakespearean storm. It is as if the realist, in reaching for tragedy, were punished for his hubris by a ludicrous fall into bathos. Tragedy is impossible by definition in the quotidian realist mode, since (quite aside from the question of the hero) tragedy is the exceptional action one of whose signs is beauty.

In America the desire to supply the missing element (usually identified as poetry or "beauty") seems to grow stronger and stronger exactly in proportion to the author's awkwardness with language. The less a playwright can write prose, the more he wishes to write poetry and to raise his plays by their bootstraps to a higher realm. You find these applications of "beauty" in Arthur Miller and Tennessee Williams; they stand out like rouge on a pitted complexion; it is as though the author first wrote the play naturalistically and then gave it a beauty treatment or face lift. Before them, O'Neill, who was too honest and too philosophically inclined to be satisfied by a surface solution, kept looking methodically for a way of representing the missing element in dramas that would still be realistic at the core. He experimented with masks (*The Great God Brown*), with the aside and the soliloquy (*Strange Interlude*), with a story and pattern borrowed from Greek classic drama (*Mourning Becomes Electra*). In other words, he imported into the American home or farm the machinery of tragedy. But his purpose was always a greater realism. His use of the aside, for example, was very different from the traditional use of the aside (a kind of nudge to the audience, usually on the part of the villain, to let them in on his true intent or motive); in *Strange Interlude* O'Neill was trying, through the aside, to make available to the realistic drama the discoveries of modern psychology, to represent on the stage the unconscious selves of his characters, at cross-purposes with their conscious selves but just as real if not realer, at least according to the psychoanalysts. He was trying, in short, to give a more complete picture of ordinary people in their daily lives. It was the same with his use of masks in *The Great God Brown*; he was appropriating the mask of Athenian drama, a ritual means of putting a distance between the human actor and the audience, to bring his own audience closer to the inner humanity of his character—the man behind the mask of conformity. The fact that these devices were clumsy is beside the point. O'Neill's sincerity usually involved him in clumsiness. In the end, he came back to the straight realism of his beginnings: *The Long Voyage Home*, the title of his young Caribbean series, could also be the title of the great play of his old age: *Long Day's Journey into Night*. He has sailed beyond the horizon and back into port; the circle is complete. In this late play, the quest for the missing element, as such, is renounced; poetry is held to be finally unattainable by the author. "I couldn't touch what I tried to tell you just now," says the character who is supposed to be the young O'Neill. "I just stammered. That's the best I'll ever do. I mean, if I live. Well, it will be faithful realism, at least. Stammering is the native eloquence of us fog people." In this brave acknowledgment or advance acceptance of failure, there is something very moving. Moreover, the acceptance of defeat was in fact the signal of a victory. *Long Day's Journey into Night*, sheer dogged prose from beginning to end, achieves in fact a peculiar poetry, and the relentless amassing of particulars takes on, eventually, some of the crushing force of inexorable logic that we find in Racine or in a Greek play. The weight of circumstance itself becomes a fate or nemesis. This is the closest, probably, that realism can get to tragedy.

The "stammering" of O'Neill was what made his later plays so long, and the stammering, which irritated some audiences, impatient for the next syllable to fall, was a sign of the author's agonized determination to be truthful. If O'Neill succeeded, at last, in deepening the character of his realism, it was because the missing element he strove to represent was not, in the end, "poetry" or "beauty" or "philosophy" (though he sometimes seems to have felt that it was) but simply meaning—the total significance of an action. What he came to conclude, rather wearily, in his last plays was that the total significance of an action lay in the accumulated minutiae of that action and could not be abstracted from it, at least not by him. There was no truth or meaning beyond the event itself; anything more (or less) would be a lie. This pun or tautology, this conundrum, committed him to a cycle of repetition, and memory, the mother of the Muses, became his only muse.

The younger American playwrights—Miller, Williams, Inge, Chayefsky—now all middle-aged, are pledged, like O'Neill, to verisimilitude. They purport to offer a "slice of life," in Tennessee Williams's case a rich, spicy slab of Southern fruitcake, but still a slice of life. The locus of their plays is the American porch or backyard or living room or parlor or bus station, presented as typical, authentic as home-fried potatoes or "real Vermont maple syrup." This authenticity may be regional, as with Williams and Paddy Chayefsky (the Jewish Upper West Side; a Brooklyn synagogue), or it may claim to be as broad as the nation, as with Arthur Miller, or somewhere rather central, in between the two, as with William Inge. But in any case, the promise of these playwrights is to show an ordinary home, an ordinary group of bus passengers, a typical manufacturer, and so on, and the dramatis personae tend to resemble a small-town, non-blue-ribbon jury: housewife, lawyer, salesman, chiropractor, working man, schoolteacher... Though Tennessee Williams's characters are more exotic, they too are offered as samples to the audience's somewhat voyeuristic eye; when Williams's film, *Baby Doll*, was attacked by Cardinal Spellman, the director (Elia Kazan) defended it on the grounds that it was true to life that he and Williams had observed, on location, in Mississippi. If the people in Tennessee Williams were regarded as products of the author's imagination, his plays would lose all their interest. There is always a point in any one of Williams's dramas where recognition gives way to a feeling of shocked incredulity; this shock technique is the source of his sensational popularity. But the audience would not be electrified if it had not been persuaded earlier that it was witnessing something the author vouched for as a common, ordinary occurrence in the Deep South.

Unlike the other playwrights, who make a journalistic claim to neutral recording, Arthur Miller admittedly has a message. His first-produced play, *All My Sons*, was a social indictment taken, almost directly, from Ibsen's *Pillars of Society*. The coffin ships, rotten, unseaworthy vessels caulked over to give an appearance of soundness, become defective airplanes sold to the government by a corner-cutting manufacturer during the Second World War; like the coffin ships, the airplanes are a symbol of the inner rottenness of bourgeois society, and the sins of the father, as *almost* in Ibsen, are visited on the son, a pilot who cracks up in the Pacific theatre (in Ibsen, the ship-owner's boy is saved at the last minute from sailing on *The Indian Girl*). The insistence of this symbol and the vagueness or absence of concrete detail express Miller's impatience with the particular and his feeling that his play ought to say "more" than it appears to be saying. Ibsen, even in his later, symbolic works, was always specific about the where, when, and how of his histories (the biographies of his central charac-ters are related with almost too much circumstantiality), but Miller has always regarded the specific as trivial and has sought, from the very outset, a hollow, reverberant universality. The reluctance to awaken a specific recognition, for fear that a larger meaning might go unrecog-nized by the public, grew on Miller with *Death of a Salesman*—a strong and original conception that was enfeebled by its creator's insistence on universality and by a too-hortatory excitement, i.e., an eagerness to preach, which is really another form of the same thing. Miller was bent on making his Salesman (as he calls him) a parable of Everyman, exactly as in a clergyman's sermon, so that the drama has only the quality—and something of the canting tone—of an illustrative moral example. The thirst for universality becomes even more imperious in *A View from the Bridge*, where the account of a waterfront killing that Miller read in a newspaper is accessorized with Greek architec-ture, "archetypes," and, from time to time, intoned passages of verse, and Miller announces in a preface that he is not interested in his hero's "psychology." Miller does not understand that you cannot turn a newspaper item about Italian longshoremen and illegal immigration into a Greek play by adding a chorus and the pediment of a temple. Throughout Miller's long practice as a realist, there is not only a naive searching for another dimension but an evident hatred of and con-tempt for reality—as not good enough to make plays out of.

It is natural, therefore, that he should never have any interest in how people talk; his characters all talk the same way—somewhat funereally, through their noses. A live sense of speech differences (think of Shaw's *Pygmalion*) is rare in American playwrights; O'Neill tried to cultivate it ("dat ol davil sea"), but he could never do more than write perfunctory dialect, rather like that of somebody telling a Pat and Mike story or a mountaineer joke. The only American realist with an ear for speech, aside from Chayefsky, whose range is narrow, is Tennessee Williams. He does really hear his characters, especially his female characters; he has studied their speech patterns and, like Professor Higgins, he can tell where they come from; Williams too is the only realist who places his characters in social history. Of all the realists, after O'Neill, he has probably the greatest native gift for the theatre; he is a natural performer and comedian, and it is too bad that he suffers from the inferiority complex that is the curse of the recent American realists—the sense that a play must be bigger than its characters. This is really a social disease—a fear of being underrated—rather than the claustrophobia of the medium itself, which tormented Ibsen and O'Neill. But it goes back to the same source: the depreciation of the real. Real speech, for example, is not good enough for Williams and from time to time he silences his characters to put on a phonograph record of his special poetic long-play prose.

All dramatic realism is somewhat sadistic; an audience is persuaded to watch something that makes it uncomfortable and from which no relief is offered—no laughter, no tears, no purgation. This sadism had a moral justification, so long as there was the question of the exposure of a lie. But Williams is fascinated by the refinements of cruelty, which with him becomes a form of aestheticism, and his plays, far from baring a lie that society is trying to cover up, titillate society like a peepshow. The curtain is ripped off, to disclose, not a drab scene of ordinary life, but a sadistic exhibition of the kind certain rather specialized tourists pay to see in big cities like New Orleans. With Williams, it is always a case of watching some mangy cat on a hot tin roof. The ungratified sexual organ of an old maid, a young wife married to a homosexual, a subnormal poor white farmer is proffered to the audience as a curiosity. The withholding of sexual gratification from a creature or "critter" in heat for three long acts is Williams's central device; other forms of torture to which these poor critters are subjected are hysterectomy and castration. Nobody, not even the SPCA, would argue that it was a good thing to show the prolonged torture of a dumb animal on the stage, even though the torture were only simulated and animals, in the end, would profit from such cases being brought to light. Yet this, on a human level, is Tennessee Williams's realism—a cat, to repeat, on a hot tin roof. And, in a milder version, it is found again in William Inge's *Picnic*. No one could have prophesied, a hundred years ago, that the moral doctrine of realism would narrow to the point of becoming pornography, yet something like that seems to be happening with such realistic novels as *Peyton Place* and the later John O'Hara and with one branch of the realist theatre. Realism seems to be a highly unstable mode, attracted on the one hand to the higher, on the other to the lower elements in the human scale, tending always to proceed toward its opposite, that is, to irreality, tracing a vicious circle from which it can escape only by repudiating itself. Realism, in short, is forever begging the question— the question of reality. To find the ideal realist, you would first have to find reality. And if no dramatist today, except O'Neill, can accept being a realist in its full implications, this is perhaps because of lack of courage. Ibsen and O'Neill, with all their dissatisfaction, produce major works in the full realist vein; the recent realists get discouraged after a single effort. *Street Scene*; *All My Sons*; *The Glass Menagerie*; *Come Back, Little Sheba*; *Middle of the Night*; perhaps *Awake and Sing!* are the only convincing evidence that exists of an American realist school—not counting O'Neill. If I add *Death of a Salesman* and *A Streetcar Named Desire*, it is only because I do not know where else to put them.

—*July 1961*

74

8

ELIZABETHAN REVIVALS

THE AMERICAN THEATRE, unable to produce a renaissance of its own, has imported an old one. With the withering away of the American playwright, the Elizabethan playwright has been called in to understudy. During the 1920s, the most energetic years of the American theatre, a few old stagers with repertory companies of confirmed Shakespearean hams were, as if by common consent, appointed official caretakers of the Bard, and an occasional revival of *Hamlet* or *Romeo and Juliet* on the part of a recognized star was no more than a duty call paid to the grave of an honored but distant relative. Today the best and liveliest young talent has been turned full blast on Shakespeare and his colleagues. The last two seasons have seen nine high-powered Elizabethan revivals, with three more promised before the season's end. Since both American and British acting seem to be temporarily in crescendo, and the Elizabethan plays are admittedly good, the result has been two quite stimulating theatrical seasons.

The current phenomenon of a theatre without playwrights suggests that classic plays have an additional function beyond those generally assigned to them. Classics, in general, are supposed (a) to please readers and (b) to instruct writers. The present Elizabethan façade of Broadway makes one think that classics, by their very nature, are also meant to fill a cultural interregnum, to tide over an art medium which, without them, would collapse. In a literal sense, this can only be true of the interpretative arts—music, stage production, and criticism—and, obviously, such use of the classics is most observable in these fields. I am totally ignorant of music, so of that I cannot speak, but it is painfully clear that in American literary criticism the tendency is to reexamine the great works of the past, since practically no creative literary work is being done in the present. However, in a more obscure and less explicable manner, the classics can, it seems to me, act as a lifeline to the primary arts themselves. This is because the relationship between the primary and the interpretative arts is not one-sided but reciprocal, and the classics, by keeping the interpretative arts alive and perhaps even fermenting them a little, can vicariously succor the primary arts. Thus the interest in problems of acting and production which this regime of revivals has imposed upon theatre people can hardly fail, if properly handled, to introduce new techniques, which will evoke new playwrights who will be anxious to use them. So simplified, this sounds a bit too much like the-house-that-Jack-built to have any but a fairy-tale truth, and, of course, an art so carefully inbred would become too attenuated to be worth preserving. This recipe for the fertilization of the arts is but one of several with which it must be applied jointly; it cannot be taken as a panacea.

At any rate, on Broadway today the process is only in its fetal stage. No serious new techniques are yet being evolved from Shakespearean productions; rather, tricks are being played on them. A spirit of carnival excitement possesses these revivals, and an annual Shakespearean World Series seems to have been written into the rules of the game. Last year it was John Gielgud versus Leslie Howard with *Hamlet* as the ballpark; this year it will be Orson Welles versus Maurice Evans with *Henry IV, Part I*. (Mr. Evans on tour is doing an occasional matinee with himself as Falstaff, and expects to bring the play into town in the fall. Mr. Welles anticipates a spring production with himself in the same role.) In these ostentatious rivalries one can see the exploitation of Elizabethan plays in its most blatant and harmless form. In the actual productions of Gielgud's *Hamlet* and Welles's *Caesar*, the exploiter, that is, the stunt artist, wears a more successful disguise.

The two productions were poles apart in theory and in performance, but they met on common ground in their attitude toward the material. In both cases there was a preoccupation with the forms of the play at the expense, of course, of its meanings. Mr. Gielgud was obsessed with the acting traditions of *Hamlet*, and a book recently published by the Oxford University Press, *John Gielgud's Hamlet*, by Rosamond Gilder, makes this very clear. Mr. Gielgud himself has a chapter on "Costumes, Scenery, and Stage Business," in which he appears to have set up a virtual barricade of stage props between himself and the lines of the play. He seems always more interested in his differences or agreements with, say, Sir Henry Irving, as to whether or not a sword should be worn at a certain point, than in any less conspicuously physical feature of the production. His connoisseurship of the fine points of past productions of *Hamlet* seduced him also into a rather desperate hunt for new readings, new inflections in familiar speeches. These were sometimes illuminating, more often tortured and distracting. I do not mean to imply that Mr. Gielgud had no conception of Hamlet. He did, but it was muffled by his precious, strained, almost dandified manipulation of the baggage of the production. His own performance was so decorated, so crammed with minutiae of gesture, pause, and movement that its general outline was imperceptible to an audience.

The rococo style is of all styles probably the most inappropriate to a production of Shakespeare, and Mr. Gielgud's *Hamlet*, with all its refinements, was a kind of climax of the rococo. Indeed, I think it impossible to do a good production of Shakespeare in terms of the tradition of the eighteenth and nineteenth centuries. Whether actor and producer swallow that tradition whole, or whether they deviate from it in much or in little, as long as their thinking is bounded by that tradition the result will be a more or less competent theatrical barbarism. It is strange that Mr. Gielgud's interest in the stage history of Shakespeare should not have carried him back to Shakespeare's own day. If any style of presentation is relevant to Shakespeare's plays it is surely the style of Shakespeare's period, the style to whose terms he adapted those plays. Yet Mr. Gielgud, speaking of the first scene of *Hamlet*, where the Ghost appears on the sentinel's platform, is full of pity and condescension for the Elizabethans. "One wonders," he says, "how this scene can have been played effectively when it was originally written. A noisy, fidgeting, mostly standing audience, no darkness, afternoon sunshine streaming on to a tidy little platform." The point is that the plays were written with these conditions, consciously or unconsciously, in mind. There being no stage paraphernalia to create the "illusion," the lines themselves had to do the work of scenery, careful costuming, and props. It is therefore a tautology to add externally to Shakespeare what exists already in the very fiber of his plays, and the heaviness one feels in most traditional presentations of Shakespeare is the heaviness of repetition, of underscoring. Moreover, it seems as if Shakespeare were intended to be played fast; in fact, I can think of no other way in which blank verse can be read effectively. The caressive attention Mr. Gielgud gave his lines, the pregnant pauses, the judiciously interlarded stage business, all interfered with the sweep of the verse, and the dramatic sweep of the play. This kind of acting (which is and has been, by the way, the prevailing style for Shakespeare) tends to atomize the plays, to reduce them to collections of small and (again) quite heavy nuggets.

If Mr. Gielgud's production was a sort of ornamental appliqué imposed on the original, Mr. Welles's *Caesar* was a piece of plastic surgery. Mr. Welles, to judge from his interpretations of *Macbeth*, *Dr. Faustus*, and *Caesar*, has the idea an Elizabethan play is a liability which only by the most strenuous showmanship, by cutting, doctoring, and modernizing, can be converted into an asset. Mr. Welles's method is to find a modern formula into which a classic can somehow be squeezed. In the case of *Macbeth*, the formula was *The Emperor Jones*; for *Dr. Faustus* it was a Punch and Judy show; for *Caesar* it was the proletarian play. Now of these three it seems to me only *Dr. Faustus* was truly successful, for here the formula actually corresponded in a way to the spirit and construction of the original, and one saw a play that was modern and that was, at the same time, *Dr. Faustus*. The other two have been what people call "interesting"; they have not been good.

The Harlem *Macbeth* is now far enough in the past so that even those who enjoyed it can see that it was at best a pleasant bit of legerdemain. *Caesar*, however, is still thought of as an important production. This is not the first play of Shakespeare's to have been done in modern dress, and superficially, therefore, Mr. Welles's stunt of taking the Romans out of their togas does not sound as novel as on the stage it seems. What is novel about the production is Mr. Welles's motive for putting it in modern dress. In the past, when *Hamlet*, for example, was done by Basil Sydney in a dinner jacket, the motive was, apparently, to say something about Hamlet, to show how modern a character he is. The purpose of the Mercury Theatre *Caesar*, on the contrary, was to say something about the modern world, to use Shakespeare's characters to drive home the horrors and inanities of present-day fascism. *Caesar*, in fact, was Mr. Welles's personal acknowledgment of the bankruptcy of contemporary playwriting, for in *Caesar* Mr. Welles as director tried to construct a modern play of his own: an antifascist melodrama in which Caesar figures as a proto-Mussolini and Brutus as a fighting Progressive.

Only a very superficial understanding of Shakespeare's play could have permitted Mr. Welles to entertain this notion for long. *Julius Caesar* is about the tragic consequences that befall idealism when it attempts to enter the sphere of action. It is perhaps also a comment on the futility and dangerousness of action in general. In a nonpolitical sense it is a "liberal" play, for it has three heroes, Caesar, Antony, and Brutus, of whom Brutus is the most large-souled and sympathetic. Shakespeare's "liberal" formula, which insists on playing fair with all its characters, is obviously in fearful discord with Mr. Welles's anti-fascist formula, which must have heroes and villains at all costs. The production of *Caesar*, consequently, turns into a battleground between Mr. Welles's play and Shakespeare's play. Mr. Welles has cut the play to pieces; he has very nearly eliminated the whole sordid tragic business of the degeneration and impotence of the republican forces; he has turned the rather shady Cassius into a shrewd and jovial comedian whose heart is in the right place; he has made Caesar, whose political stature gave the play dignity and significance, into a mechanical, expressionless robot; he has transformed the showy, romantic, buccaneering Antony into a repulsive and sinister demagogue. If he could do all this and still come out with a play that was consistent and uniformly forceful, the experiment might be forgivable. There were some things, however, which could not be cut or distorted, and these by their very incongruous presence destroyed the totality of the play's effect. The most prominent of these unassimilated chunks of Shakespeare was Antony's final speech ("This was the noblest Roman of them all"—too famous, doubtless, to be cut), which in the mouth of the black-shirt monster of the Welles production seemed an unconvincing and even tasteless tribute to the memory of Brutus.

The Mercury Theatre *Caesar*, it goes without saying, had virtues that are lacking in the ordinary Shakespearean revival. The simplicity of the mounting, the calm, conversational tone of the players, an excellent if wrongheaded performance by George Coulouris as Antony, were all new and commendable. There were, on the other hand, certain vulgarities of playing that arose from the oversimplification of a complex work. Orson Welles's Brutus was cloying and monotonous: his performance seemed to be based on the single theory that if you drop your voice two registers below the voices of the other actors you will give an impression of innocent saintliness.

Yet whatever the technical virtues or faults of the Mercury Theatre company, its energies, like the energies of Mr. Gielgud, seem to me to be misapplied. If the classics are to play any important role in the American theatre, their contents ought at least to be examined. To encrust them with traditional ornament or chop them into newspaper headlines is to shut them off from the world and the theatre. Acting as an art cannot exist by itself; it must feed on the material of plays. Both Mr. Welles and Mr. Gielgud, who in a peculiar way are trying "to lead their own lives," to make themselves independent of plays, are the potential victims of a sterile cleverness, which can readily lead them to a very dead end.

Mr. Gielgud and Mr. Welles, unfortunately, represent the dominant trends in the production of revivals. Only Maurice Evans, who stands outside both the old school and the new, has given a Shakespearean performance in which the actor was in harmonious relation with the play. Yet Mr. Evans has so carefully eschewed eccentricities and mannerisms of style that he will not easily attract imitators. Mr. Welles's forthcoming Falstaff will probably create a greater stir; my money is on Mr. Evans.

—*February 1938*

Footnote, 1956. I was wrong, I now see, in overestimating Mr. Evans. It is Mr. Gielgud who has become a fine Shakespearean—witness his performance of Cassius in the James Mason–Marlon Brando film. But I was right, I think, about Orson Welles, who is still up to his old tricks, in his London *Moby Dick*, another "adaptation" of a classic that is not unlike the comic-book version. In seventeen years, Mr. Evans has faded. Mr. Welles has remained the same, and Mr. Gielgud has grown, partly, I suppose, because of that attention to detail, to the physical aspect of the production, which I mistakenly reprehended in this review.

9

A BOLT FROM THE BLUE

PALE FIRE IS a jack-in-the-box, a Fabergé gem, a clockwork toy, a chess problem, an infernal machine, a trap to catch reviewers, a cat-and-mouse game, a do-it-yourself kit. This new work by Vladimir Nabokov consists of a 999-line poem of four cantos in heroic couplets together with an editor's preface, notes, index, and proof corrections. When the separate parts are assembled, according to the manufacturer's directions, and fitted together with the help of clues and cross-references, which must be hunted down as in a paper chase, a novel on several levels is revealed, and these "levels" are not the customary "levels of meaning" of modernist criticism but planes in a fictive space, rather like those houses of memory in medieval mnemonic science, where words, facts, and numbers were stored till wanted in various rooms and attics, or like the Houses of astrology into which the heavens are divided.

The poem has been written by a sixty-one-year-old American poet of the homely, deceptively homely, Robert Frost type who teaches at Wordsmith College in New Wye, Appalachia; his name is John Shade, his wife is called Sybil, née Irondell or Swallow; his parents were ornithologists; he and his wife had a fat, plain daughter, Hazel, who killed herself young by drowning in a lake near the campus. Shade's academic "field" is Pope, and his poem, *Pale Fire*, is in Pope's heroic measure; in content, it is closer to Wordsworthian pastures—rambling, autobiographical, full of childhood memories, gleanings from Nature, interrogations of the universe: a kind of American *Prelude*. The commentator is Shade's colleague, a refugee professor from Zembla, a mythical country north of Russia. His name is Charles Kinbote; he lives next door to Shade in a house he has rented from Judge Goldsworth, of the law faculty, absent on sabbatical leave. (If, as the commentator points out, you recombine the syllables of "Wordsmith" and "Goldsworth," you get Goldsmith and Wordsworth, two masters of the heroic couplet.) At the moment of writing, Kinbote has fled Appalachia and is living in a log cabin in a motor court at Cedarn in the Southwest; Shade has been murdered, fortuitously, by a killer calling himself Jack Grey, and Kinbote, with the widow's permission, has taken his manuscript to edit in hiding, far from the machinations of two rival Shadians on the faculty. Kinbote, known on the campus as the Great Beaver, is a bearded vegetarian pederast, who has had bad luck with his youthful "ping-pong partners"; a lonely philologue and longstanding admirer of the poet (he has translated him into Zemblan), he has the unfortunate habit of "dropping in" on the Shades, spying on them (they don't draw theirs) with binoculars from a post at a window or in the shrubbery; jealous of Mrs. Shade, he is always available for a game of chess or a "good ramble" with the tolerant poet, whom he tirelessly entertains with his Zemblan reminiscences. "I fail to see how John and Sybil can stand you," a faculty wife hisses at him in the grocery store. "What's more, you are insane."

That is the plot's ground floor. Then comes the *piano nobile*. Kinbote believes that he has inspired his friend with his tales of his native Zembla, of its exiled king, Charles the Beloved, and the Revolution that started in the Glass Works; indeed, he has convinced himself that the poem is *his* poem—the occupational mania of commentators— and cannot be properly understood without his gloss, which narrates Zemblan events paralleling the poet's composition. What at once irresistibly peeps out from Kinbote's notes is that he himself is none other than Charles the Beloved, disguised in a beaver as an academic; he escaped from Zembla in a motorboat and flew to America after a short stay on the Côte d'Azur; an American sympathizer, a trustee of Wordsmith, Mrs. Sylvia O'Donnell, has found him a post on the language faculty. His colleagues (read "mortal enemies") include—besides burly Professor Hurley, head of the department and an adherent of "*engazhay*" literature—Professor C., a literary Freudian and owner of an ultramodern villa, a certain Professor Pnin, and an instructor, Mr. Gerald Emerald, a young man in a bow tie and green velvet jacket. Meanwhile the Shadows, the Secret Police of Zembla, have hired a gunman, Jakob Gradus, alias Jacques d'Argus, alias Jacques Degré, alias Jack Grey, to do away with the royal exile. Gradus's slow descent on Wordsmith synchronizes, move by move, with Shade's composition of *Pale Fire*; the thug, wearing a brown suit, a trilby, and carrying a Browning, alights on the campus the day the poem is finished. In the library he converges with Mr. Gerald Emerald, who obligingly gives him a lift to Professor Kinbote's house. There, firing at the king, he kills the poet; when the police take him, he masks his real purpose and identity by claiming to be a lunatic escaped from a local asylum.

This second story, the *piano nobile*, is the "real" story as it appears to Kinbote of the events leading to the poet's death. But the real, real story, the story underneath, has been transpiring gradually, by degrees, to the reader. Kinbote is mad. He is a harmless refugee pedant named Botkin who teaches in the Russian department and who fancies himself to be the exiled king of Zembla. This delusion, which he supposes to be his secret, is known to the poet, who pities him, and to the campus at large, which does not—the insensate woman in the grocery store was expressing the general opinion. The killer is just what he claims to be—Jack Grey, an escaped criminal lunatic, who has been sent to the State Asylum for the Insane by, precisely, Judge Goldsworth, Botkin's landlord. It is Judge Goldsworth that the madman intended to murder, not Botkin, alias Kinbote, alias Charles the

Beloved; the slain poet was the victim of a case of double mistaken identity (his poem, too, is murdered by its editor, who mistakes it for something else). The clue to Gradus-Grey, moreover, was in Botkin's hands when, early in the narrative, he leafed through a sentimental album kept by the judge containing photographs of the killers he had sent to prison or condemned to death: "...a strangler's quite ordinary-looking hands, a self-made widow, the close-set merciless eyes of a homicidal maniac (somewhat resembling, I admit, the late Jacques d'Argus), a bright little parricide aged seven...." He got, as it were, a preview of the coming film—a frequent occurrence in this kind of case. Projected onto Zembla, in fact, are the daily events of the campus. Gradus's boss, Uzumrudov, one of the higher Shadows, met on the Riviera in a green velvet jacket, is slowly recognized to be "little Mr. Anon.," alias Gerald Emerald, alias Reginald Emerald, a teacher of freshman English, who has made advances to (read in reverse "had advances made to him by") Professor Botkin, and who is also the author of a rude anonymous note suggesting that Professor Botkin has halitosis. The paranoid political structure called Zembla in Botkin's exiled fantasy—with its Extremist government and secret agents—is a transliteration of a pederast's persecution complex, complicated by the "normal" conspiracy-mania of a faculty common room.

But there is in fact a "Zembla," behind the Iron Curtain. The real, real story, the plane of ordinary sanity and common sense, the reader's presumed plane, cannot be accepted as final. The explanation that Botkin is mad will totally satisfy only Professors H. and C. and their consorts, who can put aside *Pale Fire* as a detective story, with the reader racing the author to the solution. *Pale Fire* is not a detective story, though it includes one. Each plane or level in its shadow box proves to be a false bottom; there is an infinite perspective regression, for the book is a book of mirrors.

Shade's poem begins with a very beautiful image, of a bird that has flown against a window and smashed itself, mistaking the reflected sky in the glass for the true azure. "I was the shadow of the waxwing slain / By the false azure in the windowpane." This image is followed by another, still more beautiful and poignant, a picture of that trick of optics whereby a room at night, when the shades have not been drawn, is reflected in the dark landscape outside.

> *Uncurtaining the night, I'd let dark glass*
> *Hang all the furniture above the grass,*
> *And how delightful when a fall of snow*
> *Covered my glimpse of lawn and reached up so*
> *As to make chair and bed exactly stand*
> *Upon that snow, out in that crystal land!*

"That crystal land," notes the commentator, loony Professor Botkin. "Perhaps an allusion to Zembla, my dear country." On the plane of everyday sanity, he errs. But on the plane of poetry and magic, he is speaking the simple truth, for Zembla is Semblance, Appearance, the mirror-realm, the Looking-Glass of Alice. This is the first clue in the treasure hunt, pointing the reader to the dual or punning nature of the whole work's composition. *Pale Fire*, a reflective poem, is also a prism of reflections. Zembla, the land of seeming, now governed by the Extremists, is the antipodes of Appalachia, in real homespun democratic America, but it is also the *semblable*, the twin, as seen in a distorting glass. Semblance becomes resemblance. John Shade and Gradus have the same birthday—July 5.

The word "Zembla" can be found in Pope's *Essay on Man* (Epistle 2, v); there it signifies the fabulous extreme north, the land of the polar star.

> *But where the Extreme of Vice was ne'er agreed.*
> *Ask where's the North? At York, 'tis on the Tweed;*
> *In Scotland, at the Oroades, and there,*

> *At Greenland, Zembla, or the Lord knows where;*
> *No creature owns it in the first degree,*
> *But thinks his neighbor farther gone than he.*

Pope is saying that vice, when you start to look for it, is always some-where else—a will-o'-the-wisp. This somewhere else is Zembla, but it is also next door, at your neighbor's. Now Botkin is Shade's neighbor and vice versa; moreover, people who live in glass houses... Shade has a vice, the bottle, the festive glass, and Botkin's vice is that he is an *invert*, i.e., turned upside down, as the antipodes are, relative to each other. Further, the reader will notice that the word "Extreme," with a capital (Zemblan Extremists), and the word "degree" (*gradus* is "degree" in Russian) both occur in these verses of Pope, in the neigh-borhood of Zembla, pre-mirroring *Pale Fire*, as though by second sight. Reading on, you find (lines 267–268), the following couplet quoted by John Shade in a discarded variant of his own manuscript:

> *See the blind beggar dance, the cripple sing,*
> *The sot a hero, lunatic a king....*

The second line is *Pale Fire* in a nutshell. Pope continues (lines 269–270):

> *The starving chemist in his golden views*
> *Supremely blest, the poet in his muse.*

Supremely Blest is the title of John Shade's book on Pope. In this sec-tion of the poem, Pope is playing on the light-and-shade antithesis and on what an editor calls the "pattern of paradoxical attitudes" to which man's dual nature is subject. The lunatic Botkin incidentally, playing king, *inverts* his name.

To leave Pope momentarily and return to Zembla, there is an

actual Nova Zembla, a group of islands in the Arctic Ocean, north of Archangel. The name is derived from the Russian *Novaya Zemlya*, which means "new land." Or *Terre Neuve*, Newfoundland, the New World. Therefore Appalachia = Zembla. But since for Pope Zembla was roughly equal to Greenland, then Zembla must be a green land, an Arcadia. Arcady is a name often bestowed by Professor Botkin on New Wye, Appalachia, which also gets the epithet "green," and he quotes "*Et in Arcadia ego*," for Death has come to Arcady in the shape of Gradus, ex-glazier and killer, the emissary of Zembla on the other side of the world. Green-jacketed Gerald Emerald gives Death a lift in his car.

The complementary color to green is red. Zembla has turned red after the Revolution that began in the Glass Factory. Green and red flash on and off in the narrative like traffic signals and sometimes reverse their message. Green appears to be the color of death, and red the color of life; red is the king's color and green the color of his enemies. Green is preeminently the color of seeming (the theatrical greenroom), the color, too, of camouflage, for Nature, being green at least in summer, can hide a green-clad figure in her verdure. But red is a color that is dangerous to a wearer who is trying to melt into the surroundings. The king escapes from his royal prison wearing a red wool cap and sweater (donned in the dark) and he is only saved by the fact that forty loyal Karlists, his supporters, put on red wool caps and sweaters, too (red wool yarn—"yarn" comes from Latin "sooth-sayer"—is protective Russian folk magic) and confuse the Shadows with a multitude of false kings. Yet when the king arrives in America he floats down with a green silk parachute (because he is in disguise?), and his gardener at New Wye, a Negro whom he calls Balthasar (the black king of the three Magi), has a green thumb, a red sweater, and is seen on a green ladder; it is the gardener who saves the king's life when Gradus, alias Grey, appears.

Now when Alice went through the looking glass she entered a

chess game as a white pawn. There is surely a chess game or chess problem in *Pale Fire*, played on a board of green and red squares. The poet describes his residence as "the frame house between Goldsworth and Wordsmith on its square of green"; the Rose Court in the royal palace in Onhava (Far Away), the Zemblan capital, is a sectile mosaic with rose petals cut out of red stone and large thorns cut out of green marble. There is much stress, in place descriptions, on framing, and reference is made to chess problems of "the solus rex type." The royal fugitive may be likened to a lone king running away on the board. But in problems of the solus rex type, the king, though outnumbered, is, curiously enough, not always at a disadvantage; for example, a king and two knights cannot checkmate a lone king—the game is stalemated or drawn. All the chess games played by characters in the story are draws. The plot of the novel ends in a kind of draw, if not a stalemate. The king's escape from the castle is doubtless castling.

Chess is the perfect mirror-game, with the pieces drawn up confronting each other as in a looking glass; moreover, castles, knights, and bishops have their twins as well as their opposite numbers. The piece, by the way, called the bishop in English in French is *le fou* or madman. In the book there are two opposed lunatics at large: Gradus and Kinbote. The moves made by Gradus from the Zemblan capital to Wordsmith in New Wye parallel spatially the moves made in time by the poet toward the completion of his poem; at the zero hour, there is a convergence of space and time. What is shadowed forth here may be a game of three-dimensional chess—three simultaneous games played by a pair of chess wizards on three transparent boards arranged vertically. A framed crystal land, the depth-echo of the bedroom projected onto the snow.

The moves of Gradus also hint some astrological progression. Botkin reached Judge Goldsworth's "chateau" on February 5, 1959; on Monday, February 16, he was introduced to the poet at lunch at the Faculty Club; on March 14, he dined at the Shades', etc. The magnum opus of old John Shade is begun July 1; under the sign of Cancer, he walks sideways, like a crab. The poem is completed (except for the last line) the day of Gradus's arrival, July 21, on the cusp between Cancer and Leo. As the poet walks to his death, the sound of horseshoes is heard from a neighboring yard (horseshoe crabs?). The fateful conjunction of three planets seems to be indicated, and the old astrological notion of events on earth mirroring the movements of the stars in the sky.

The twinning and doubling proliferate; the multiplication of levels casts a prismatic, opaline light on Faculty Row. Zembla is not just land but earth—"Terra the Fair, an orbicle of jasp," as John Shade names the globe; a Zemblan feuilletonist had fancifully dubbed its capital Uranograd—"Sky City." The fate of Charles the Beloved is a rippling reflection of the fate of Charles II of England on his travels, of Bonnie Prince Charlie, and of the deposed Shakespearean rulers for whom streets are named in Onhava—Coriolanus Lane, Timon Alley. Prospero of *The Tempest* pops in and out of the commentary, like a Fata Morgana, to mislead the reader into looking for "pale fire" in Shakespeare's swan song. It is not there, but *The Tempest* is in *Pale Fire*: Prospero's emerald isle, called the Ile of Divels, in the New World, Iris, and Juno's peacock, sea caves, the chess game of Ferdinand and Miranda, Prospero's enchantments, his lost kingdom, and Caliban, whom he taught language, that supreme miracle of mirroring.

Nature's imitations of Nature are also evoked—echo, the mockingbird perched on a television aerial ("TV's huge paperclip"), the iridescent eyes of the peacock's fan, the cicada's emerald case, a poplar tree's rabbit-foot—all the "natural shams" of protective mimicry by which, as Shade says in his poem, "The reed becomes a bird, the knobby twig/ An inchworm, and the cobra head, a big/Wickedly folded moth." These disguises are not different from the exiled king's red cap and sweater (like the markings of a bird) or the impersonation of an actor. Not only Nature's shams but Nature's freaks dance in and out of the lines: rings around the moon, rainbows and sun dogs (bright spots of light, often colored, sometimes seen on the ring of the solar halo), the heliotrope or sun-turner, which, by a trick of language, is also the bloodstone, Muscovy glass (mica), phosphorescence (named for Venus, the Morning Star), mirages, the roundlet of pale light called the ignis fatuus, fireflies, everything speckled, freckled, curiously patterned, dappled, quaint (as in Hopkins's poem "Pied Beauty"). The arrowy tracks of the pheasant, the red heraldic barrings of the Vanessa butterfly, snow crystals. And the imitation of natural effects in manufactures: stained glass, paperweights containing snowstorms and mountain views, glass eyes. Not to mention curios like the bull's-eye lantern, glass giraffes, Cartesian devils. Botkin, the bearded urning, is himself a prime "freak of Nature," like Humbert Humbert. And freakish puns of language ("Red Sox Beat Yanks 5/4 on Chapman's Homer"), "muscat" (a cat-and-mouse game), anagrams, mirror-writing, such words as "versipel." The author loves the ampersand and dainty diminutives ending in "let" or "et" (nymphet). Rugged John Shade is addicted to "word-golf," which he induces Botkin to play with him. Botkin's best scores are hate-love in three (late-lave-love), lass-male in four (last-mast-malt-male), live-dead in five. If you play word-golf with the title words, you can get pale-hate in two and fire-love in three. Or pale-love in three and fire-hate in three.

The misunderstandings of scholarship, cases of mistaken word-identity, also enchant this dear author. E.g., "alderwood" and "alderking" keep cropping up in the gloss with overtones of northern forest magic. What can an alderking be, excluding chief or ruler, which would give king-king, a redundancy? *Erle* is the German word for alder, and the alder tree, which grows in wet places, has the curious property of not rotting under water. Hence it is a kind of magic tree, very useful for piles supporting bridges. And John Shade, writing of the loss of his daughter, echoes Goethe's "The Erl-King."

Who rides so late in the night and the wind?
It is the writer's grief. It is the wild
March wind. It is the father with his child.

Now the German scholar Herder, in translating the elf-king story from the Danish, mistook the word for elf (*elle*) for the word for alder. So it is not really the alderking but the elf- or goblin-king, but the word "alder" touched by the enchanted word "elf" becomes enchanted itself and dangerous. Goethe's erl-king, notes Kinbote, fell in love with the traveler's little boy. Therefore alderking means an eerie, dangerous invert found in northern forest-countries. Similar sorcerers' tricks are played with the word "stone." The king in his red cap escaping through the Zemblan mountains is compared to a *Steinmann*, which, as Kinbote explains, is a pile of stones erected by alpinists to commemorate an ascent; these stone men, apparently, like snowmen, were finished off with a red cap and scarf. The *Steinmann*, then, becomes a synonym for one of the king's disguised followers in red cap and sweater (e.g., Julius Steinmann, Zemblan patriot). But the *Steinmann* has another meaning, not divulged by Kinbote; it is the *homme de pierre* or *homme de St. Pierre* of Pushkin's poem about Don Giovanni, in short the stone statue, the Commendatore of the opera. Anyone who sups with the stone man, St. Peter's deputy, will be carried off to hell. The mountain that the *Steinmann*-king has to cross is wooded by Mandevil Forest; toward the end of his journey he meets a disguised figure, Baron Mandevil, man of fashion, catamite, and Zemblan patriot. Read man-devil, but read also Sir John Mandeville, medieval impostor and author of a book of voyages who posed as an English knight (perhaps a chess move is indicated?). Finally the stone (glancing by glass houses) is simply the stone thrown into a pool or lake and starting the tremulous magic of widening ripples that distort the clear mirroring of the image—as the word "stone" itself, cast into the pool of this paragraph, has sent out wavelets in a widening circle.

Lakes—the original mirrors of primeval man—play an important part in the story. There are three lakes near the campus, Omega, Ozero, and Zero (Indian names, notes Botkin, garbled by early settlers); the king sees his consort, Disa, Duchess of Payn (sadism; theirs was a "white" marriage) mirrored in an Italian lake. The poet's daughter has drowned herself in Lake Omega; her name ("...in lone Glenartney's hazel shade") is taken from *The Lady of the Lake*. But a hazel wand is also a divining rod, used to find water; in her girlhood, the poor child, witch Hazel, was a poltergeist.

Trees, lakes, butterflies, stones, peacocks—there is also the waxwing, the poet's alter ego, which appears in the first line of the poem (duplicated in the last, unwritten line). If you look up the waxwing in the OED, you will find that it is "a passerine bird of the genus *Ampelis*, esp. *A. garrulus*, the Bohemian waxwing. Detached from the chatterers by Monsieur Vieillot." The poet, a Bohemian, is detached from the chatterers with whom he is easily confused. The waxwing (belonging to the king's party) has red-tipped quills like sealing wax. Another kind of waxwing is the Cedar Waxwing. Botkin has fled to Cedarn. The anagram of "Cedarn" is "nacred."

More suggestively (in the popular sense), the anal canal or "back door" or "*porte étroite*" is linked with a secret passage leading by green-carpeted stairs to a green door (which in turn leads to the greenroom of the Onhava National Theatre), discovered by the king and a boyhood bedfellow. It is through this secret passage (made for Iris Acht, a leading actress) that the king makes his escape from the castle. Elsewhere a "throne," in the child's sense of "the toilet," is identified naughtily with the king. When gluttonous Gradus arrives in Appalachia, he is suffering from a severe case of diarrhea, induced by a conflict of "French" fries, consumed in a Broadway restaurant, with a genuine French ham sandwich, which he had saved from his Nice–Paris railway trip. The discharge of his bowels is horribly paralleled with the discharge of the automatic pistol he is carrying; he is the modern automatic man. In discharging the chamber of his pistol he is exercising what to him is a "natural" function; earlier the slight sensory pleasure he will derive from the act of murder is compared to the pleasure a man gets from squeezing a blackhead.

This is no giggling, high-pitched, literary camp. The repetitions, reflections, misprints, and quirks of Nature are the stamp or watermark of a god or supreme intelligence. There is a web of sense in creation, old John Shade decides—not text but texture, the warp and woof of coincidence. He hopes to find "some kind / Of correlated pattern in the game, / Plexed artistry, and something of the same / Pleasure in it as they who played it found." The world is a sportive work of art, a mosaic, an iridescent tissue. Appearance and "reality" are interchangeable; all appearance, however deceptive, is real. Indeed it is just this faculty of deceptiveness (natural mimicry, trompe l'oeil, imposture), this power of imitation, that provides the key to Nature's cipher. Nature has "the artistic temperament"; the galaxies, if scanned, will be an iambic line.

Kinbote and Shade (and the author) agree in a detestation of symbols, except those of typography and, no doubt, natural science ("H_2O is a symbol for water"). They are believers in signs, pointers, blazes, notches, all of which point into a forest of associations, a forest in which other woodmen have left half-obliterated traces. All genuine works contain precognitions of other works or reminiscences of them (and in curved time the two are the same), just as the flying lizard already possessed a parachute, a fold of skin enabling it to glide through the air.

Shade, as an American, is an agnostic, and Kinbote, a European, is a vague sort of Christian who speaks of accepting "God's presence—a faint phosphorescence at first, a pale light in the dimness of bodily life, and a dazzling radiance after it." Or, more concessive, "Somehow Mind is involved as a main factor in the making of the universe." This Mind of Kinbote's seems to express itself most lucidly in dualities, pairs, twins, puns, couplets, like the plots of Shakespeare's early comedies. But this is only to be expected if one recalls that to make a cutout heart or lacy design for Valentine's Day all a child needs is a scissors and a folded piece of paper—the fold makes the pattern, which, unfolded, appears as a miracle. It is the quaint principle of the butterfly. Similarly, Renaissance artificers used to make wondrous "natural" patterns by bisecting a veined stone, an agate or a carnelian, as you would bisect an orange. Another kind of magic is the child's trick of putting a piece of paper on the cover of a schoolbook and shading it with a pencil; wonderfully, the stamped title, *Caesar's Gallic Wars*, emerges, as though embossed, in white letters. This, upside down, is the principle of the pheasant's hieroglyph in the snow or the ripple marks on the sand, to which we cry "How beautiful!" There is no doubt that duplication, stamping, printing (children's transfers), is one of the chief forms of magic, a magic we also see in Jack Frost's writing on the window, in jet trails in the sky—an intelligent spirit seems to have signed them. But it is not only in symmetry and reproduction that the magic signature of Mind is discerned, but in the very imperfections of Nature's work, which appear as guarantees of authentic, hand-knit manufacture. That is, in those blemishes and freckles and streakings and moles already mentioned that are the sports of creation, and what is a vice but a mole?

Nabokov's tenderness for human eccentricity, for the freak, the "deviate," is partly the naturalist's taste for the curious. But his fond, wry compassion for the lone black piece on the board goes deeper than classificatory science or the collector's chop-licking. Love is the burden of *Pale Fire*, love and loss. Love is felt as a kind of homesickness, that yearning for union described by Plato, the pining for the other half of a once-whole body, the straining of the soul's black horse to unite with the white. The sense of loss in love, of separation (the room *beyond*, projected onto the snow, the phantom moves of the chess knight, that deviate piece, *off* the board's edge onto ghostly squares), binds mortal men in a common pattern—the elderly couple watching TV in a lighted room, and the "queer" neighbor watching *them* from his window. But it is most poignant in the outsider: the homely daughter stood up by her date, the refugee, the "queen," the bird smashed on the windowpane.

Pity is the password, says Shade, in a philosophical discussion with Kinbote; for the agnostic poet, there are only two sins, murder and the deliberate infliction of pain. In the exuberant high spirits, the wild laughter of the book, there is a cry of pure pain. The compassion of Nabokov stops violently short of Gradus, that grey, degraded being, the shadow of a Shade. The modern, mass-produced, jet-propelled, newspaper-digesting killer is described with a fury of intimate hatred; he is Death on the prowl. Unnatural Death is the natural enemy of the delicate, gauzy ephemerids who are Nabokov's special love. Kinbote makes an "anti-Darwinian" aphorism: "The one who kills is *always* his victim's inferior."

Gradus in his broad-brimmed hat, with his umbrella and black traveling bag, figures as a kind of Batman out of children's comic books, whirring darkly through space; yet he is also Mercury (the mercury stands at so many *degrees* in the thermometer; there is a headless statue of Mercury in the secret passage leading from the palace to the theatre), conductor of souls to the underworld, Zeus's undercover agent, god of commerce, travel, manual skill, and thievery. In short, a "Jack of small trades and a killer," as Kinbote calls Jacques d'Argus, who was a pharmacology student at one time (the caduceus) and a messenger boy for a firm of cardboard-box manufacturers; Mercury or Hermes was the slayer of the giant Argus put to watch on Io by Juno-Hera; the hundred eyes of Argus were set in the tail of the peacock, Juno's familiar. Hermes, born and worshiped in Arcady, is simply a stone or herm; he is thought to have been in early times the daimon that haunted a heap of stones (the *Steinmann* or grave-ghost), also the place-spirit of a roadside marker or milestone;

as a road god, he was the obvious patron of traders and robbers. He was often represented as a rudimentary stock or stone with a human head carved on top and a phallus halfway up. The beheaded Gradus-d'Argus has reverted to a rudimentary state of insentient stoniness—a sex-hater, he once tried to castrate himself.

Not only Hermes-Mercury, most of the nymphs of Arcady and gods of Olympus are glimpsed in *Pale Fire*, transformed, metamorphosed into animal or human shapes. Botkin is identified by Sybil Shade with the botfly, a kind of parasitic horsefly that infests sheep and cattle. Io, in cow form, was tormented by a gadfly sent by Hera; one of the Vanessa butterflies is the Io, marked with peacock eyes. Another is the *Limenitis Sibylla*, the White Admiral, and the Red Admiral is the *Vanessa Atalanta*, which feeds on wounded tree stems, like the scarred hickory in Shade's bosky garden. Atalanta was another Arcadian. The sibyls, on the other hand, are connected with Apollo, and Shade with his laurel trees is an Apollonian figure. But Sibyl was born Swallow; the land of Arcady was drained by swallow-holes, and the first sibyl was daughter of Dardanus, ancestor of the Trojans, an Arcadian king. The Hyperboreans (read Zemblans) were a legendary people sacred to Apollo living behind the north wind in a land of perpetual sunshine—a counter-Arcadia. Zeus, the sky-king, is heard in the thunderstorms that occur at crucial moments in the Zemblan story—at the arrival of Gradus in America and in Mandevil Forest, on Mount Mandevil, when the king is making his escape; Zeus's thunderbolts, in classical times, were stones too, by which oaths were sworn.

The Arcadians and Olympians of *Pale Fire* are meteoric fugitives, like the deposed Kinbote, fitfully apprehended in a name, a passing allusion. Shade's ornithologist mother was called Caroline Lukin—a triple reference to the Carolina waxwing, to Apollo Lukeios, and to the sacred wood, *lucus* in Latin, full of singing birds? A reference to the Pléiade edition of Proust conjures up the Pleiades, daughters of

Atlas, who were turned into stars and set in the constellation Taurus. One of the seven Pleiades is Electra, "the shining one"; the word "electricity" in Greek was the word for amber, which was sent to Delphian Apollo by his Hyperboreans in the north. Shade has written a poem about electricity. But the Pleiad was also a group of seven poets who sought to revive tragedy at the court of Ptolemy Philadelphus in Alexandria, one of whom, Lykophron, was the author of a curious riddling poem, like *Pale Fire* one of the hermetic puzzles of its time, called the *Alexandra*—another name for Cassandra, Priam's daughter, who was loved by Apollo.

Amid such myriads of micalike references to gods, nymphs, and demons there is hardly a glance at Christian myth and legend. I have found only two: the oblique allusion to St. Peter as gatekeeper of Heaven and the chess-jesting one to the Black King of the Magi. The book is adamantly classical, magical, and scientific. The author's attitude toward the mystery of the universe is nearer to the old herborist's charmed wonder than to the modern physicist's "faith." His practical morality is not far from Kant's, while his practical pantheism contains Platonic gleams: Kinbote's "phosphorescence" recalls the cave myth. Kinbote reverts to this notion when he concedes in his final remarks that Shade's *Pale Fire*, for all its deficiencies, has "echoes and wavelets of fire and pale phosphorescent hints" of the real Zemblan magic. This madman's concession may also be taken as the author's apology for his own work, in relation to the fiery Beyond of the pure imagination—the sphere of pure light or fire. But Plato's empyrean is finished, a celestial storehouse or vault of models from which the forms of earthly life are copied. In Nabokov's view (see Shade's couplet, "*Man's life as commentary to abstruse Unfinished poem*. Note for future use"), the celestial Poem itself is incomplete.

The source of "pale fire" is *Timon of Athens*, Act IV, Scene 3, Timon speaking to the thieves:

> *... I'll example you with thievery:*
> *The sun's a thief, and with his great attraction*
> *Robs the vast sea; the moon's an arrant thief,*
> *And her pale fire she snatches from the sun;*
> *The sea's a thief....*

This idea of natural thievery is bound up with the mirror-theme, for a mirror is held by primitive people to "steal" the image of the man it reflects, and all reflection, including poetic mimesis, can be regarded as a theft from reality, which in turn is always stealing ideas and plagiarizing from itself. It is only appropriate that thieving Mercury, patron of letters, "that transcendental tramp," as Kinbote calls Gradus, should be one of the work's principal characters. Botkin, in effect, has stolen Shade's poem. The moon, shining with her borrowed rays, appears in the luna moth; Io, the cow, was originally a moon goddess, as is shown by her crescent horns. Shade's Aunt Maud had a verse book kept open at the index ("Moon, Moonrise, Moor, Moral"), and Shade's *Webster's* is open at M. The sky-god Zeus's love affairs with various moon goddesses—e.g., Europa as well as Io—are hinted at. Finally, the Red Admiral Vanessa butterfly, which accompanies the poet Shade like a herald of death into Botkin's garden, is often seen, as on that fatal day, at sunset; it has the unusual habit of flying at night, looking for its home—commonly a hollow tree; in other words, the Red Admiral is a butterfly that acts like its nocturnal double, a moth.

Pale Fire itself circles like a moth, or a moon, around Shakespeare's mighty flame. Hiding in the lines, there are many allusions to Shakespeare's plays, to his biography, to the trees mentioned in Shakespeare, and the treacherous color green may betray the presence of Shakespeare's enemy, the poet Robert Greene, who described the Bard as an upstart crow dressed in others' feathers; the crow, of course, is a thief. It is also the southernmost constellation, at the other pole from Zembla.

The pale fire of the title spreads beyond its original Shakespearean source and beacons toward a number of odd corners. In the commentary there is an account of the poet burning his rejected drafts in "the pale fire of the incinerator." An amusing sidelight is provided by the word "ingle," used by Kinbote to mean a catamite or boy favorite, but which also means blaze, from the Gaelic word for fire. I think too of the pale fire of opals and of Shelley, whose "incandescent soul" is mentioned in Shade's poem:

> *Life like a dome of many-colored glass*
> *Stains the white radiance of eternity.*

Whether the visible world, for Nabokov, is a prismatic reflection of eternity or the other way around is a central question that begs itself but that remains, for that very reason, moot and troubling. In the game of signaling back and forth with mirrors, which may be man's relation with the cosmos, there is perhaps no before or after, first or second, only distance—separation, exile—and across it, the agitated flashing of the semaphore.

In any case, this centaur-work of Nabokov's, half-poem, half-prose, this merman of the deep, is a creature of perfect beauty, symmetry, strangeness, originality, and moral truth. Pretending to be a curio, it cannot disguise the fact that it is one of the very great works of art of this century, the modern novel that everyone thought was dead and that was only playing possum.

—June 1962

10

BURROUGHS'S *NAKED LUNCH*

LAST SUMMER AT the International Writers' Conference in Edinburgh, I said I thought the national novel, like the nation-state, was dying and that a new kind of novel, based on statelessness, was beginning to be written. This novel had a high, aerial point of view and a plot of perpetual motion. Two experiences, that of exile and that of jet-propelled mass tourism, provided the subject matter for a new kind of story. There is no novel, yet, that I know of, about mass tourism, but somebody will certainly write it. Of the novel based on statelessness, I gave as examples William Burroughs's *The Naked Lunch*, Vladimir Nabokov's *Pale Fire* and *Lolita*. Burroughs, I explained, is not literally a political exile, but the drug addicts he describes are continually on the move, and life in the United States, with its present narcotics laws, is untenable for the addict if he does not want to spend it in jail (in the same way, the confirmed homosexual is a chronic refugee, ordered to move on by the Venetian police, the Capri police, the mayor of Provincetown, the mayor of Nantucket). Had I read it at the time, I might have added Günter Grass's *The Tin Drum* to the list: here the point of view, instead of being high, is very low—that of a dwarf; the hero and narrator is a displaced person, born in the Free City of Danzig, of a Polish mother (who is not really a Pole but a member of a minority within Poland) and an uncertain father, who may be a German grocer or a Polish postal employee. In any case, I said that in thinking over the novels of the last few years, I was struck by the fact that the only ones that had not simply given me pleasure but interested me had been those of Burroughs and Nabokov. The others, even when well done (Compton-Burnett), seemed almost regional.

This statement, to judge by the British press, was a shot heard round the world. I still pick up its reverberations in Paris and read about them in the American press. I am quoted as saying that *The Naked Lunch* is the most important novel of the age, of the epoch, of the century. The only truthful report of what I said about Burroughs was given by Stephen Spender in *Encounter*, October 1962. But nobody seems to have paid attention to Spender any more than anyone paid attention to what I said on the spot. When I chided Malcolm Muggeridge in person with having terribly misquoted me in the *New Statesman*, he appeared to think that there was not much difference between saying that a book was one of two or three that had interested you in the last few years and saying that it was one of the "outstanding novels of the age." According to me, the age is still Proust, Joyce, Kafka, Lawrence, Faulkner, to mention only the "big names," but to others evidently the age is shrinking to the length of a publishing season, just as a literary speaker is turned into a publisher's tout. The result, of course, is a disparagement of Burroughs, because if *The Naked Lunch* is proclaimed as the masterpiece of the century, then it is easily found wanting. Indeed, I wonder whether the inflation of my remarks was not at bottom malicious; it is not usually those who admire Burroughs who come up to me at parties to announce: "I *read* what you said at Edinburgh." This is true, I think, of all such publicity; it is malicious in effect whatever the intention and permits the reader to dismiss works of art and public figures as "not what they are cracked up to be." A similar thing happened with *Dr. Zhivago*, a wonderful book, which attracted much hatred and venom because it was not Tolstoy. Very few critics said it was Tolstoyan, but the impression got around that

they had. Actually, as I recall, the critics who mentioned Tolstoy in connection with Pasternak were those bent on destroying Pasternak's book.

As for me, I was left in an uncomfortable situation. I did not want
to write to the editors of British newspapers and magazines, denying
that I had said whatever incontinent thing they had quoted me as saying. This would have been ungracious to Burroughs, who was the
innocent party in the affair and who must have felt more and more
like the groom in a shotgun literary wedding, seeing my name yoked
with his as it were indissolubly. And the monstrousness of the union,
doubtless, was what kept the story hot. In the end, it became clear to
me that the only way I could put an end to this embarrassment was by
writing at length what I thought about *The Naked Lunch*—something I was reluctant to do because I was busy finishing a book of my
own and reluctant, also, because the whole thing had assumed the
proportions of a cause célèbre and I felt like a witness called to the
stand and obliged to tell the truth and nothing but the truth under
oath. This is not a normal critical position. Of course the critic normally tries to be truthful, but he does not feel that his review is some
sort of payoff or eternal reckoning, that the eye of God or the world
press is staring into his heart as he writes. Now that I have written the
present review, I am glad, as always happens, to have made a clean
breast of it. This is what I think about Burroughs.

"You can cut into *The Naked Lunch* at any intersection point,"
says Burroughs, suiting the action to the word, in "an atrophied preface" he appends as a tailpiece. His book, he means, is like a neigh-
borhood movie with continuous showings that you can drop into
whenever you please—you don't have to wait for the beginning of
the feature picture. Or like a worm that you can chop up into sections
each of which wriggles off as an independent worm. Or a nine-lived
cat. Or a cancer. He is fond of the word "mosaic," especially in its
scientific sense of a plant-mottling caused by a virus, and his muse
(see etymology of "mosaic") is interested in organic processes of

multiplication and duplication. The literary notion of time as simultaneous, a montage, is not original with Burroughs; what is original is the scientific bent he gives it and a view of the world that combines biochemistry, anthropology, and politics. It is as though *Finnegans Wake* were cut loose from history and adapted for a Cinerama circus titled "One World." *The Naked Lunch* has no use for history, which is all "ancient history"—sloughed-off skin; from its planetary perspective, there are only geography and customs. Seen in terms of space, history shrivels into a mere wrinkling or furrowing of the surface as in an aerial relief map or one of those pieced-together aerial photographs known in the trade as (again) mosaics. The oldest memory in *The Naked Lunch* is of jacking off in boyhood latrines, a memory recaptured through pederasty. This must be the first space novel, the first serious piece of science fiction—the others are entertainment.

The action of *The Naked Lunch* takes place in the consciousness of One Man, William Lee, who is taking a drug cure. The principal characters, besides Lee, are his friend, Bill Gains (who seems momentarily to turn into a woman called Jane); various members of the Narcotics Squad, especially one Bradley the Buyer; Dr. Benway, a charlatan medico who is treating Lee; two vaudevillians, Clem and Jody; A. J., a carnival con man, the last of the Big Spenders; a sailor; an Arab called Ahmed; an archetypal Southern druggist, Doc Parker ("a man don't have no secrets from God and his druggist"); and various boys with whining voices. Among the minor characters are a number of automobiles, each with its specific complaint, like the oil-burning Ford v-8; a film executive; the Party Leader; the Vigilante; John and Mary, the sex acrobats; and a puzzled American housewife who is heard complaining because the Mixmaster keeps trying to climb up under her dress. The scene shifts about, from New York to Chicago to St. Louis to New Orleans to Mexico to Malmö, Tangier, Venice, and the human identities shift about too, for all these modern places and modern individuals (if that is the right word) have interchangeable parts. Burroughs is fond too of the word "ectoplasm," and the beings that surround Lee, particularly the inimical ones, seem ectoplasmic phantoms projected on the wide screen of his consciousness from a mass séance. But the haunting is less visual than auditory. These "characters," in the colloquial sense, are ventriloquial voices produced, as it were, against the will of the ventriloquist, who has become their dummy. Passages of dialogue and description keep recurring in different contexts with slight variations, as though they possessed ubiquity.

The best comparison for the book, with its aerial sex acts performed on a high trapeze, its con men and barkers, its arenalike form, is in fact with a circus. A circus travels but it is always the same, and this is Burroughs's sardonic image of modern life. The Barnum of the show is the mass-manipulator, who appears in a series of disguises. *Control,* as Burroughs says, underlining it, *can never be a means to anything but more control—like drugs,* and the vicious circle of addiction is reenacted, worldwide, with sideshows in the political and "social" sphere—the "social" here has vanished, except in quotation marks, like the historical, for everything has become automatized. Everyone is an addict of one kind or another, as people indeed are wont to say of themselves, complacently: "I'm a crossword puzzle addict, a hi-fi addict," etc. The South is addicted to lynching and nigger-hating, and the Southern folk custom of burning a Negro recurs throughout the book as a sort of Fourth of July carnival with fireworks. Circuses, with their cages of wild animals, are also dangerous, like Burroughs's human circus; an accident may occur, as when the electronic brain in Dr. Benway's laboratory goes on the rampage, and the freaks escape to mingle with the controlled citizens of Freeland in a general riot, or in the scene where the hogs are let loose in the gourmet restaurant.

On a level usually thought to be "harmless," addiction to platitudes and commonplaces is global. To Burroughs's ear, the Bore, lurking in the hotel lobby, is literally deadly ("'You look to me like a man of intelligence.' Always ominous opening words, my boy!"). The same for Doc Parker with his captive customer in the back room of his pharmacy ("...so long as you got a legitimate condition and an Rx from a certified bona feedy M.D., I'm honored to serve you"), the professor in the classroom ("Hehe hehe he"), the attorney in court ("Hehe hehe he," likewise). The complacent sound of snickering laughter is an alarm signal, like the suave bell-tones of the psychiatrist and the emphatic drone of the Party Leader ("You see men and women. *Ordinary* men and women going about their ordinary every-day tasks. Leading their ordinary lives. That's what we need...").

Cut to ordinary men and women, going about their ordinary every-day tasks. The whine of the put-upon boy hustler: "All kinda awful sex acts." "Why cancha just get physical like a human?" "So I guess he come to some kinda awful climax." "You think I am innarested to hear about your horrible old condition? I am not innarested at all." "But he comes to a climax and turns into some kinda awful crab." This aggrieved tone merges with the malingering sighs of the American housewife, opening a box of Lux: "I got the most awful cold, and my intestines is all constipated." And the clarion of the Salesman: "When the Priority numbers are called up yonder I'll be there." These average folks are addicts of the science page of the Sunday supplements; they like to talk about their diseases and about vile practices that paralyze the practitioner from the waist down or about a worm that gets into your kidney and grows to enormous size or about the "horrible" result of marijuana addiction—it makes you turn black and your legs drop off. The superstitious scientific vocabulary is diffused from the laboratory and the mental hospital into the general population. Overheard at a lynching: "Don't crowd too close, boys. His intestines is subject to explode in the fire." The same diffusion of culture takes place with modern physics. A lieutenant to his general: "But chief, can't we get them started and they imitate each other like a chained reaction?"

The phenomenon of repetition, of course, gives rise to boredom; many readers complain that they cannot get through *The Naked Lunch*.

And/or that they find it disgusting. It *is* disgusting and sometimes tiresome, often in the same places. The prominence of the anus, of feces, and of all sorts of "horrible" discharges, as the characters would say, from the body's orifices, becomes too much of a bad thing, like the sadomasochistic sex performances—the autoejaculation of a hanged man is not everybody's cantharides. A reader whose erogenous zones are more temperate than the author's begins to feel either that he is a square (a guilty sentiment he should not yield to) or that he is the captive of a joyless addict.

In defense, Swift could be cited, and indeed between Burroughs and Swift there are many points of comparison; not only the obsession with excrement and the horror of female genitalia but a disgust with politics and the whole body politic. Like Swift, Burroughs has irritable nerves and something of the crafty temperament of the inventor. There is a great deal of Laputa in the countries Burroughs calls Interzone and Freeland, and Swift's solution for the Irish problem would appeal to the American's dry logic. As Gulliver, Swift posed as an anthropologist (though the study was not known by that name then) among savage people; Burroughs parodies the anthropologist in his descriptions of the American heartland: "...the Interior a vast subdivision, antennae of television to the meaningless sky... Illinois and Missouri, miasma of mound-building peoples, groveling worship of the Food Source, cruel and ugly festivals." The style here is more emotive than Swift's, but in his deadpan explanatory notes ("This is a rural English custom designed to eliminate aged and bedfast dependents"), there is a Swiftian laconic factuality. The "factual" appearance of the whole narrative, with its battery of notes and citations, some straight, some loaded, its extracts from a diary, like a ship's log, its pharmacopoeia, has the flavor of eighteenth-century satire. He calls himself a "Factualist" and belongs, all alone, to an Age of Reason, which he locates in the future. In him, as in Swift, there is a kind of soured utopianism.

Yet what saves *The Naked Lunch* is not a literary ancestor but humor. Burroughs's humor is peculiarly American, at once broad and sly. It is the humor of a comedian, a vaudeville performer playing in "One," in front of the asbestos curtain of some Keith Circuit or Pantages house long since converted to movies. The same jokes reappear, slightly refurbished, to suit the circumstances, the way a vaudeville artist used to change Yonkers to Renton when he was playing Seattle. For example, the Saniflush joke, which is always good for a laugh: somebody is cutting the cocaine/the morphine/the penicillin with Saniflush. Some of the jokes are verbal ("Stop me if you've heard this atomic secret" or Dr. Benway's "A simopath . . . is a citizen convinced he is an ape or other simian. It is a disorder peculiar to the army and discharge cures it"). Some are "black" parody (Dr. Benway, in his last appearance, dreamily, his voice fading out: "Cancer, my first love"). Some are whole vaudeville "numbers," as when the hoofers, Clem and Jody, are hired by the Russians to give Americans a bad name abroad: they appear in Liberia wearing black Stetsons and red galluses and talking loudly about burning niggers back home. A skit like this may rise to a frenzy, as if in a Marx Brothers or a Clayton, Jackson, and Durante act, when all the actors pitch in. E.g., the very funny scene in Chez Robert, "where a huge icy gourmet broods over the greatest cuisine in the world": A. J. appears, the last of the Big Spenders, and orders a bottle of ketchup; immediate pandemonium; A. J. gives his hog call, and the shocked gourmet diners are all devoured by famished hogs. The effect of pandemonium, all hell breaking loose, is one of Burroughs's favorites and an equivalent of the old vaudeville finale, with the acrobats, the jugglers, the magician, the hoofers, the lady-who-was-sawed-in-two, the piano player, the comedians, all pushing into the act.

Another favorite effect, with Burroughs, is the metamorphosis. A citizen is turned into animal form, a crab or a huge centipede, or into some unspeakable monstrosity, like Bradley the Narcotics Agent who turns into an unidentifiable carnivore. These metamorphoses, of course, are punishments. The Hellzapoppin effect of orgies and riots and the metamorphosis effect, rapid or creeping, are really cancerous on-slaughts—matter on the rampage multiplying itself and "building" as a revue scene "builds" to a climax. Growth and deterioration are the same thing: a human being "deteriorates" or grows into a one-man jungle. What you think of it depends on your point of view; from the junky's angle, Bradley is better as a carnivore eating the Narcotics Commissioner than he was as "fuzz"—junky slang for the police.

The Naked Lunch contains messages that unluckily for the ordinary reader are somewhat arcane. Despite his irony, Burroughs is a prescriptive writer. He means what he says to be taken and used literally, like an Rx prescription. Unsentimental and factual, he writes as though his thoughts had the quality of self-evidence. In a special sense, *The Naked Lunch* is coterie literature. It was not intended, surely, for the general public, but for addicts and former addicts, with the object of imparting information. Like a classical satirist, Burroughs is dead serious—a reformer. Yet, as often happened with the classical satirists, a wild hilarity and savage pessimism carry him beyond his therapeutic purpose and defeat it. The book is alive, like a basketful of crabs, and common sense cannot get hold of it to extract a moral.

On the one hand, control is evil; on the other, escape from control is mass slaughter or reduction to a state of proliferating cellular matter. The police are the enemy, but as Burroughs shrewdly observes in one passage: "A *functioning* police state needs no police." The policeman is internalized in the robotized citizen. From a libertarian point of view, nothing could be worse. This would seem to be Burroughs's position, but it is not consistent with his picture of sex. To be a libertarian in politics implies a faith in Nature and the natural, that is, in the life principle itself, commonly identified with sex. But there is little affection for the life principle in *The Naked Lunch*, and sex, while magnified—a common trait of homosexual literature—is a kind of mechanical man-trap baited with fresh meat. The sexual climax, the jet of sperm, accompanied by a whistling scream, is often a death spasm, and the "perfect" orgasm would seem to be the posthumous orgasm of the hanged man, shooting his jism into pure space.

It is true that Nature and sex are two-faced, and that growth is death-oriented. But if Nature is not seen as far more good than evil, then a need for control is posited. And, strangely, this seems to be Burroughs's position too. *The human virus can now be treated*, he says with emphasis, meaning the species itself. By scientific methods, he implies. Yet the laboratory of *The Naked Lunch* is a musical-comedy inferno, and Dr. Benway's assistant is a female chimpanzee. As Burroughs knows, the Men in White, when not simple con men, are the fuzz in another uniform.

The Naked Lunch, Burroughs says, is "a blueprint, a How-To Book.... How-To extend levels of experience by opening the door at the end of a long hall." Thus the act of writing resembles and substitutes for drug-taking, which in Burroughs's case must have begun as an experiment in the extension of consciousness. It does not sound as if pleasure had ever been his motive. He was testing the controls of his own mechanism to adjust the feed-in of data, noting with care the effects obtained from heroin, morphine, opium, Demerol, Yage, cannabis, and so on. These experiments, aiming at freedom, "opening a door," resulted in addiction. He kicked the imprisoning habit by what used to be known as willpower, supplemented by a nonaddictive drug, apomorphine, to whose efficacy he now writes testimonials. It seems clear that what was involved and continues to be involved for Burroughs is a Faustian compact: knowledge-as-power, total control of the self, which is experienced as sovereign in respect to the immediate environment and neutral in respect to others.

At present he is interested in Scientology, which offers its initiates the promise of becoming "clears"—free from all hang-ups. For the novel he has invented his cut-out and fold-in techniques, which he is convinced can rationalize the manufacture of fictions by applying modern factory methods to the old "writer's craft." A text may be put together by two or three interested and moderately skilled persons equipped with scissors and the raw material of a typescript. Independence from the vile body and its "algebra of need," freedom of movement across national and psychic frontiers, efficiency of work and production, by means of short cuts, suppression of connectives, and other labor-saving devices, would be Uncle Bill Burroughs's patent for successful living. But if such a universal passkey can really be devised, what is its purpose? It cannot be enjoyment of the world, for this would only begin the addictive process all over again by creating dependency. Action, the reverse of enjoyment, has no appeal either for the author of *The Naked Lunch*. What Burroughs wants is out, which explains the dry, crankish amusement given him by space, interplanetary distances, where, however, he finds the old mob still at work. In fact, his reasoning, like the form of his novel, is circular. Liberation leads to new forms of subjugation. If the human virus can be treated, this can only be under conditions of asepsis: the Nova police. Yet Burroughs is unwilling, politically, to play the dread game of eugenics or euthenics, outside his private fantasy, which, since his intelligence is aware of the circularity of its utopian reasoning, invariably turns sardonic. *Quis custodet custodes ipsos?*

—*March 1963*

11

J. D. SALINGER'S
CLOSED CIRCUIT

WHO IS TO inherit the mantle of Papa Hemingway? Who if not J. D. Salinger? Holden Caulfield in *The Catcher in the Rye* has a brother in Hollywood who thinks *A Farewell to Arms* is terrific. Holden does not see how his brother, who is *his* favorite writer, can like a phony book like that. But the very image of the hero as pitiless phony-detector comes from Hemingway. In *Across the River and into the Trees*, the colonel gets a message on his private radar that a pockmarked writer he darkly spies across the room at Harry's Bar in Venice has "outlived his talents"—apparently some sort of crime. "I think he has the same pits on his heart and in his soul," confides the heroine, in her careful foreign English. That was Sinclair Lewis.

Like Hemingway, Salinger sees the world in terms of allies and enemies. He has a good deal of natural style, a cruel ear, a dislike of ideas (the enemy's intelligence system), and a ventriloquist's knack of disguising his voice. The artless dialect written by Holden is an artful ventriloquial trick of Salinger's, like the deliberate, halting English of Hemingway's waiters, fishermen, and peasants—anyone who speaks it is a good guy, a friend of the author's, to be trusted.

The Catcher in the Rye, like Hemingway's books, is based on a scheme of exclusiveness. The characters are divided into those who belong to the club and those who don't—the clean marlin, on the one hand, and the scavenger sharks on the other. Those who don't belong are "born that way"—headmasters, philanthropists, roommates, teachers of history and English, football coaches, girls who like the Lunts. They cannot help the way they are, the way they talk: they are obeying a law of species—even the pimping elevator operator, the greedy prostitute, the bisexual teacher of English who makes an approach to Holden in the dark.

It is not anybody's fault if just about everybody is excluded from the club in the long run—everybody but Ring Lardner, Thomas Hardy, Gatsby, Isak Dinesen, and Holden's little sister, Phoebe. In fact it is a pretty sad situation, and there is a real adolescent sadness and lonely desperation in *The Catcher in the Rye*; the passages where Holden, drunk and wild with grief, wanders like an errant pinball through New York at night are very good.

But did Salinger sympathize with Holden or vice versa? Stephen Dedalus in a similar situation met Mr. Bloom, but the only "good" person Holden meets is his little sister—himself in miniature or in glory, riding a big brown horse on a carousel and reaching for the gold ring. There is something false and sentimental here. Holden is supposed to be an outsider in his school, in the middle-class world, but he is really an insider with the track all to himself.

And now, ten years after *The Catcher in the Rye* we have *Franny and Zooey*. The book has been a best seller since *before* publication.

Again the theme is the good people against the stupid phonies, and the good is still all in the family, like the shares in a family-owned "closed" corporation. The heroes are or were seven children (two are dead), the wonderful Glass kids of a radio quiz show called *It's a Wise Child*, half-Jewish, half-Irish, whose parents were a team of vaude-villians. These prodigies, nationally known and the subjects of many psychological studies, are now grown up: one is a writer-in-residence in a girls' junior college; one is a Jesuit priest; one is a housewife; one is a television actor (Zooey); and one is a student (Franny). They are all geniuses, but the greatest genius of them all was Seymour, who committed suicide on vacation in an early story of Salinger's called "A Perfect Day for Bananafish." Unlike the average genius, the Glass kids are good guys; they love each other and their parents and their cat and their goldfish, and they are expert phony-detectors. The dead sage Seymour has initiated them into Zen and other mystical cults.

During the course of the story, Franny has a little nervous break-down, brought on by reading a small green religious book titled *The Way of a Pilgrim*, relating the quest for prayer of a simple Russian peasant. She is cured by her brother Zooey in two short séances between his professional television appointments; he recognizes the book (it was in Seymour's library, of course) and, on his own inspiration, without help from their older brother Buddy or from the Jesuit, teaches her that Jesus, whom she has been sweating to find via the Jesus Prayer, is not some fishy guru but just the Fat Lady in the audience, plain ordinary humanity with varicose veins, the you and me the performer has to reach if the show is going to click.

This democratic commercial is "sincere" in the style of an advertising man's necktie. The Jesus Zooey sells his sister is the old Bruce Barton Jesus—the word made flesh, Madison Avenue style. The Fat Lady is not quite everybody, despite Zooey's fast sales patter. She is the kind of everybody the wonderful Glass kids tolerantly accept. Jesus may be a television sponsor or a housewife or a television play-wright or your Mother and Dad, but He (he?) cannot be an intellectual like Franny's horrible boyfriend, Lane, who has written a paper on Flaubert and talks about Flaubert's "testicularity," or like his friend Wally, who, as Franny says plaintively, "looks like somebody who spent the summer in Italy or someplace."

These fakes and phonies are the outsiders who ruin everything. Zooey feels the same way. "I hate any kind of so-called creative type who gets on any kind of ship. I don't give a goddam what his reasons are." Zooey likes it here. He likes people, as he says, who wear horrible neckties and funny, padded suits, but he does not mind a man who dresses well and owns a two-cabin cruiser so long as he belongs to the real, native, video-viewing America. The wonderful Glass family has three radios, four portable phonographs, and a TV in their wonderful living room, and their wonderful, awesome medicine cabinet in the bathroom is full of sponsored products all of which have been loved by someone in the family.

The world of insiders, it would appear, has grown infinitely larger and more accommodating as Salinger has "matured." Where Holden Caulfield's club excluded just about everybody but his kid sister, Zooey and Franny's secret society includes just about everybody but creative types and students and professors. Here exception is made, obviously, for the Glass family: Seymour, the poet and thinker, Buddy, the writer, and so on. They all have college degrees; the family book-shelves indicate a wide, democratic culture:

> *Dracula* now stood next to *Elementary Pali*, *The Boy Allies at the Somme* stood next to *Bolts of Melody*, *The Scarab Murder Case* and *The Idiot* were together, *Nancy Drew and the Hidden Staircase* lay on top of *Fear and Trembling*.

The Glass family librarian does not discriminate, in keeping with the times, and books are encouraged to "mix." In Seymour's old bedroom, however, which is kept as a sort of temple to his memory, quotations, hand-lettered, from a select group of authors are displayed on the door: Marcus Aurelius, Issa, Tolstoy, Ring Lardner, Kafka, St. Francis de Sales, Mu Mon Kwan, etc. This honor roll is extremely institutional.

The broadening of the admissions policy—which is the text of Zooey's sermon—is more a propaganda aim, though, than an accomplishment. No doubt the author and his mouthpiece (who is smoking a panatela) would like to spread a message of charity. "Indiscrimination," as Seymour says in another Salinger story, "...leads to health and a kind of very real, enviable happiness." But this remark itself exhales an ineffable breath of gentle superiority. The club, for all its pep talks, remains a closed corporation, since the function of the Fat Lady, when you come down to it, is to be what?—an audience for the Glass kids, while the function of the Great Teachers is to act as their coaches and prompters. And who are these wonder kids but Salinger himself, splitting and multiplying like the original amoeba?

In Hemingway's work there was hardly anybody but Hemingway in a series of disguises, but at least there was only one Papa per book. To be confronted with the seven faces of Salinger, all wise and lovable and simple, is to gaze into a terrifying narcissus pool. Salinger's world contains nothing but Salinger, his teachers, and his tolerantly cherished audience—humanity. Outside are the phonies vainly signaling to be let in. They do not have the key, unlike the kids' Irish mother, Bessie, a home version of the Fat Lady, who keeps invading the bathroom while her handsome son Zooey is in the tub or shaving.

Sixty-eight pages of "Zooey" are laid in the family bathroom, the "throne" room, the holy of holies, the temple of the cult of self-worship. What methodical attention Salinger pays to Zooey's routines of shaving and bathing and nail-cleaning, as though these were priestly rituals performed by a god on himself. A numinous vapor, an aura, surrounds the mother, seated on the toilet, smoking and soliloquizing, while her son behind the figured shower curtain reads, smokes, bathes, answers. We have the sense of being present at a mystery: ablution, purification, catharsis. It is worth noting that this closet drama has a pendant in a shorter scene in a public toilet in the story "Franny" which misled many *New Yorker* readers into thinking that Franny was pregnant—why else, having left her boyfriend at the table, was she shutting herself up in a toilet in the ladies' room, hanging her head and feeling sick?

Those readers were not "in" on the fact that Franny was having a mystical experience. Sex, which commonly takes two, not related by blood, is an experience that does not seem to possess erotic interest (phonies do it) for Salinger, and Zooey behind the shower curtain is taboo even to the mother who bore him. He is separated from her, as in a temple, by a veil. The reader, however, is allowed an extended look.

A great deal of attention is paid too to the rituals of cigarette lighting and of drinking from a glass, as though these oral acts were sacred —epiphanies. In the same way, the family writings are treated by Salinger as sacred scriptures or the droppings of holy birds, to be studied with care by the augurs: letters from Seymour, citations from his diary, a letter from Buddy, a letter from Franny, a letter from Boo Boo, a note written by Boo Boo in soap on a bathroom mirror (the last two are from another story, "Raise High the Roof Beam, Carpenters").

These imprints of the Glass collective personality are preserved as though they were Veronica's veil in a relic case of well-wrought prose. And the eerie thing is, speaking of Veronica's veil—a popular subject for those paintings in which Christ's eyes are supposed to follow the spectator with a doubtless reproachful gaze—the reader has the sensation in this latest work of Salinger's that the author is sadly watching him or listening to him read. That is, the ordinary relation is reversed, and instead of the reader reading Salinger, Salinger, that Man of Sorrows, is reading the reader.

At the same time, this quasi-religious volume is full of Broadway humor. The Glass family is like a Jewish family in a radio serial. Everyone is a "character." Mr. Glass with his tangerine is a character; Mrs. Glass in her hairnet and commodious wrapper with her cups of chicken broth is a character. The shower curtain, scarlet nylon with a design of canary-yellow sharps, clefs, and flats, is a character; the teeming medicine cabinet is a character. Every phonograph, every chair is a character. The family relationship, rough, genial, insulting, is a character.

In short, every single object possessed by the Glass communal ego is bent on lovably expressing the Glass personality—eccentric, homey, good-hearted. Not unlike *Abie's Irish Rose*. And the family is its own best audience. Like Hemingway stooges, they have the disturbing faculty of laughing delightedly or smiling discreetly at each other's jokes. Again a closed circuit: the Glass family is the Fat Lady, who is Jesus. The mirrored Glass medicine cabinet is Jesus, and Seymour is his prophet.

Yet below this self-loving barbershop harmony a chord of terror is struck from time to time, like a judgment. Seymour's suicide suggests that Salinger guesses intermittently or fears intermittently that there may be something wrong somewhere. Why did he kill himself? Because he had married a phony, whom he worshiped for her "simplicity, her terrible honesty"? Or because he was so happy and the Fat Lady's world was so wonderful?

Or because he had been lying, his author had been lying, and it was all terrible, and he was a fake?

—October 1962

12

ON *MADAME BOVARY*

WHEN FLAUBERT MADE his famous statement—"Madame Bovary is me"—he was echoing one of his favorite authors, Cervantes. Cervantes, on his deathbed, so the story goes, was asked whom he meant to depict in Don Quixote. "Myself," he answered. In Cervantes's case, this must have been true, quite simply and terribly, whether or not he ever said it. In Flaubert's, the answer was an evasion. He was tired of being asked about the "real-life original" of his heroine. According to tradition, there *was* one; in fact, there may have been two or even three. First and most important was Delphine Delamare, née Couturier, the wife of a public health officer in the Bray region of Normandy, not far from where Flaubert lived. In 1848, aged twenty-seven, she killed herself, leaving behind her a little girl, Alice-Delphine. Among her effects, it was said, was an unpaid bill from a circulating library in Rouen. Flaubert's friends had suggested her case to him as the subject for a novel, on the writing-course principle of "Write about what you know." What better source than a mother-in-law? Old Madame Delamare, the doctor's widowed mother, used to come to see old Madame Flaubert and lament his marital unhappiness, his untimely death; Flaubert's niece remembered her well and was convinced that the old lady's complaints about her daughter-in-law's misconduct were the basis for *Madame Bovary*. In an inventory of Delamare's property and papers, made on his decease, an IOU of three hundred francs to "Madame Flaubert" has recently been found.

Dr. Delamare had died, presumably of grief, like Charles Bovary, long before *Madame Bovary* appeared, in 1857; he survived his wife by only twenty-one months. But other principals in the Delamare drama (rumor gave her many lovers) and a chorus of commentators were still living. And many years later, in the village of Ry—which advertises itself as the original of Yonville l'Abbaye—Delphine Delamare's smart double curtains, yellow and black, were still talked about by her neighbors, like her blue-and-silver wallpaper. Today her house is gone (two different houses have competed for that title), her tombstone has been lost or stolen, but her garden is there, the property of the village pharmacist, who displays in his shop what purports to be Monsieur Homais's counter.

The real Monsieur Homais was probably legion. Flaubert is said to have spent a month at Forges-les-Eaux studying the local pharmacist, a red-hot anticlerical and diehard republican, whom he had already spotted and banded, but he is also thought to have had his eye on other atheistical druggists, birds of the same feather, in the neighborhood.

In short, *Madame Bovary* revived and spread a scandal (a second suspected Rodolphe was uncovered at Neufchâtel-en-Bray) that had been a nine-days' wonder in the locality, and Flaubert was no doubt sick of the gossip and somewhat remorseful, like most authors, for what he had started, tired too maybe of hearing his mother tax him with what he had "done" to poor Delamare's memory. At the same time, as an author, he must have resented the cheapening efforts of real life to claim for itself material he had transmuted with such pain in his study; even in her name, "Delphine Delamare" sounds like a hack's alias for Emma Bovary.

The gossip was not silenced by his denials. Indeed, it proliferated, breeding on the novel itself—impossible to know how much elderly witnesses, interviewed in Ry forty years later, had had their memories refreshed by contact with the novel. Was the Delamares' elegant furniture really sold at auction to satisfy her creditors? And the unfortunate doctor's "two hundred rose stocks *de belle variété*"? What about the "mahogany Gothic prie-dieu embroidered in subdued blue and yellow gros point" by Delphine Delamare? In 1890, on the word of one authority, it could be seen in Rouen, the cushion considerably faded. In 1905, the servant Félicité (her real name was Augustine), aged seventy-nine, was still talking to visitors about her mistress, differing stoutly with others who remembered her on the color of her hair. "No. Not blond. Chestnut." After *Madame Bovary*, figures in the Delamare story, real or fancied, must have spent their lives as marked men. The rumored "Rodolphe," a veritable Cain, was said to have emigrated to America, then come back and shot himself on a Parisian boulevard. If that happened to an actual country gentleman of the vicinity named Louis Campion (and there is no record of such a suicide), it cannot have been part of Flaubert's intention. And the gossip, as always, must have been wrong quite a bit of the time. Even given Flaubert's passion for documentation, he cannot have set out to make an exact copy of the village of Ry and its inhabitants. How well, in fact, he could have known it, except as the site of the Delamare drama, is a matter of doubt.

He must have passed through it, on his way from Rouen, and certainly the village, even now, shows correspondences with the décor of the novel, though, as in a dream, nothing is in quite its right place: the church, the cemetery, the marketplace, Monsieur Homais's pharmacy, the Lion d'Or. The "river" behind Madame Delamare's garden has shrunk to a feeble stream, more of a ditch or drain, really, and the real river runs past the village, not through it. But there are the outlying meadows, the poplars, the long single street, which is an extended *place* in the novel; "Rodolphe's château" is pointed out on a nearby road, and along the river there are many cow-crossings made of old planks reminiscent of the one Emma used, at the foot of her garden, going by the wet nurse's house to meet her lover. In the courtyard of the Hôtel de Rouen, identified by a marker as the "Lion d'Or," a suggestible person can believe himself to be in the setting of *Madame Bovary*.

Human suggestibility, obviously, has magnified and multiplied correspondences in a way no doubt undreamed of by Flaubert. The fame of the novel caused dubious and even false claimants to be presented or present themselves as the genuine originals. A notary in the Oise named Louis Bottais (or Léon Bottet; there is some confusion) pretended to have served as the model for Léon; he was unmasked as an impostor. The progressive pharmacist at Ry, toward the end of the century, modeled *himself* on Monsieur Homais, who he insisted had been drawn from his father—as though this were reason for family pride.

The net has been cast wider. A second—or third—model for Emma has been found in the wife of Flaubert's friend the sculptor Pradier, who made the pretty ladies, Lille and Strasbourg, that sit on pedestals like halted patriotic floats on the Place de la Concorde. A "memoir" of this woman, written out in an illiterate script by her confidante, a carpenter's wife, had fallen into Flaubert's hands. Did he use it? Louise Pradier was good-looking, silly, extremely unfaithful to her husband, and up to her neck in debt. In the "memoir," where she is called "Ludovica," she is being driven to suicide by her debts and adulterous anxieties; her husband, like Charles Bovary, dies of the shock dealt him by the discovery of his wife's infidelities and the bills she had run up. In reality, Pradier long outlived his separation from Louise, and Louise herself, though she may have talked of it, never threw herself in the Seine. She was living when *Madame Bovary* came out and she and her bohemian friends may have been persuaded, whatever the truth was, that she had "sat for" Flaubert.

This endless conjecturing on the part of the public is the price paid by the realistic novelist for "writing about what he knows." With *Salammbô* and *The Temptation of Saint Anthony*, there was no occasion for Flaubert to issue denials. But *Madame Bovary* was fraught with embarrassment for its author, who foresaw, while still writing it, the offense he was going to give his neighbors by the heavy dosage of Norman "local color" he had put in. And as often happens, whatever he did to change, combine, disguise, invent, probably made matters worse, purely fictive episodes being taken as the literal truth.

There may also have been correspondences with reality invisible to ordinary provincial readers but suspiciously visible to his immediate family: "I know where you got *that!*" an author's relations cry, in amusement or reproach. Take the following, as a guess. Dr. Delamare studied under Flaubert's father, a well-known surgeon, at the Hôtel-Dieu in Rouen; whether he was a poor student or not is uncertain. In any case, being dead, he could not be hurt by the book. But there was someone else who conceivably could be: Flaubert's brother, Achille, also a doctor, highly regarded in local medical circles. He operated on their father; gangrene developed, and Dr. Flaubert died. It is thought that he may have had a diabetic condition, always dangerous for a surgical patient. In any case, the outcome was fatal. A little later, Flaubert's sister Caroline died of puerperal fever. Whether Achille was in attendance is not clear. But the two deaths, coming so close together, greatly affected Flaubert. In a letter, he described sitting up with Caroline's body while her husband and a priest snored. Just like Emma's wake. Flaubert remembered those snores. Did he remember the operation performed on his father when he wrote about Charles's operation on the clubfooted inn boy—the most villainous folly in the book? Or did he fear that Achille remembered and would draw a parallel, where none had been intended? A novelist is an elephant, but an elephant who must claim to forget.*

---

*This account of the sources of *Madame Bovary* has been revised, thanks to criticism administered by Francis Steegmuller when the essay first appeared. As far as the Delamares are concerned, my present documentation comes mainly from Géraud Venzac, *Au pays de Madame Bovary*.

On the one hand, Flaubert declared *he* was Emma. On the other, he wrote to a lady: "There's nothing in *Madame Bovary* that's drawn from life. It's a *completely invented* story. None of my own feelings or experiences are in it." So help him God. Of course, he was fibbing, and contradicting himself as well. Like all novelists, he drew on his own experiences, and, more than most novelists, he was frightened by the need to invent. When he came to do the ball at Vaubyessard, he lamented, "It's so long since I've been to a ball." If memory failed, he documented himself, as he did for Emma's school reading, going back over the children's stories he had read as a little boy and the picture books he had colored. If he had not had an experience the story required, he sought it out. Before writing the chapter about the agricultural fair, he went to one; he consulted his brother about clubfoot and, disappointed by the ignorance manifest in Achille's answers, procured textbooks. There is hardly a page in the novel that he had not "lived," and he constantly drew on his own feelings to render Emma's.

All novelists do this, but Flaubert went beyond the usual call of duty. Madame Bovary was not Flaubert, certainly; yet he became Madame Bovary and all the accessories to her story, her lovers, her husband, her little greyhound, the corset lace that hissed around her hips like a slithery grass snake as she undressed in the hotel room in Rouen, the blinds of the cab that hid her and Léon as they made love. In a letter he made clear the state of mind in which he wrote. That day he had been doing the scene of the horseback ride, when Rodolphe seduces Emma in the woods. "What a delicious thing writing is—not to be you any more but to move through the whole universe you're talking about. Take me today, for instance: I was man and woman, lover and mistress; I went riding in a forest on a fall afternoon beneath the yellow leaves, and I was the horses, the leaves, the wind, the words he and she spoke, and the red sun beating on their half-closed eyelids, which were already heavy with passion." It is hard to imagine another great novelist—Stendhal, Tolstoy, Jane Austen,

Dickens, Dostoevsky, Balzac—who would conceive of the act of writing as a rapturous loss of identity. Poets have often expressed the wish for otherness, for fusion—to be their mistress's sparrow or her girdle or the breeze that caressed her temples and wantoned with her ribbons, but Flaubert was the first to realize this wish in prose, in the disguise of a realistic story. The climax of the horseback ride was, of course, a coupling, in which all of Nature joined in a gigantic, throbbing *partouze* while Flaubert's pen flew. He was writing a book, and yet from his account you would think he was *reading* one. "What a delicious thing reading is—not to be you any more but to flow through the whole universe you're reading about . . . " etc., etc.

Compare this, in fact, to the rapt exchange of platitudes between Léon and Emma on the night of their first meeting, at dinner at the Lion d'Or. "'. . . Is there anything better, really, than sitting by the fire with a book while the wind beats on your window panes and the lamp is burning?' 'Isn't it so?' she said, fixing him with her large black eyes wide open. 'One forgets everything,' he continued. 'The hours go by. Without leaving your chair you stroll through imagined landscapes as if they were real, and your thoughts interweave with the story, lingering over details or leaping ahead with the plot. Your imagination confuses itself with the characters, and it seems as if it were your own heart beating inside their clothes.' 'How true! How true!' she said."

The threadbare magic carpet, evidently, is shared by author and reader, who are both escaping from the mean provincial life close at hand. Yet *Madame Bovary* is one of a series of novels—including *Don Quixote* and *Northanger Abbey*—that illustrate the evil effects of reading. *All* reading, in the case of *Madame Bovary*, not simply the reading of romances. The books Emma fed on were not pure trash, by any means; in the convent she had read Châteaubriand; as a girl on the farm, she read *Paul et Virginie*. The best sellers she liked were of varying quality: Eugène Sue, Balzac, George Sand, and Walter Scott.

She tried to improve her mind with history and philosophy, starting one "deep" book after another and leaving them all unfinished. Reading was undermining her health, according to her mother-in-law, who thought the thing to do was to stop her subscription to the lending library in Rouen. It ought to be against the law, declared the old lady, for circulating libraries to supply people with novels and books against religion, that mock at priests in speeches taken from Voltaire. Flaubert is making fun of Madame Bovary, Senior, and yet he too felt that Emma's reading was unhealthy. And for the kind of reason her mother-in-law would give: books put ideas in Emma's head. It is characteristic of Flaubert that his own notions, in the mouths of his characters, are turned into desolate echoes—into clichés.

Léon too is addicted to books, as the passage cited shows. *He* prefers poetry. But it is not only the young people in *Madame Bovary* who are glamorized by the printed page. Monsieur Homais is another illustration of the evil effects of reading. He offers Emma the use of his library, which contains, as he says, "the best authors, Voltaire, Rousseau, Delille, Walter Scott, the *Echo des Feuilletons*." These authors have addled his head with ideas. And Monsieur Homais's ideas are dangerous, literally so; not just in the sense Madame Bovary, Senior, meant. An idea invading Monsieur Homais's brain is responsible for Charles's operation on the deformed Hippolyte. Monsieur Homais had read an article on a new method for curing clubfoot and he was immediately eager that Charles should try it; in his druggist mind there was a typical confusion between humanitarian motives and a Chamber of Commerce zeal. The operation is guaranteed to put Yonville l'Abbaye on the map. He will write it up himself for a Rouen paper. As he tells Charles, "An article in the paper gets around. People talk about it. It ends by snowballing." This snowballing is precisely what is happening, with horrible consequences yet to come. Thanks to an article in the press, Hippolyte will lose his leg.

The diffusion of ideas in the innocent countryside is the plot of

Madame Bovary. When the book ran serially, Flaubert's editors, who were extremely stupid, wanted to cut the clubfoot episode: it was unpleasant, they said, and contributed nothing to the story. Flaubert insisted; he regarded it as essential to the book. As it is. This is the point where Monsieur Homais interlocks with Emma and her story; elsewhere he only talks and appears busy. True, Emma gets the arsenic from his "Capernaum"—a ridiculous name for his inner sanctum based on the transubstantiation controversy—but this is not really the druggist's fault. He is only an accessory. But when it comes to the operation Monsieur Homais is the creative genius; it is his hideous brainchild, and Charles is his instrument. Up to the time of the operation, Monsieur Homais could appear as mere comic relief or prosaic contrast. But with the operation the affinity between apparent opposites—the romantic dreamer and the "man of science"—becomes clear. Monsieur Homais is not just Emma's foil; he is her alter ego.

For the first time, they see eye to eye; they are a team pulling together to persuade Charles to do the operation, and for the same reason: a thirst for fame. And both, in their infatuation with a dream, have lost sight of the reality in front of them, which is Charles. He surrenders to the dazzling temptation they hold out to him. What is it, exactly? The temptation to be something other than what he is, a slow, cautious, uncertain practitioner who is terrified to set a simple fracture. Charles has got *nothing* out of books; he cannot even stay awake after dinner to peruse a medical text. He accepts his ignorance innocently as his lot in life and takes precautions to do as little harm as possible; his pathos as a doctor is that he is aware of being a potential hazard to his patients. Yet when Hippolyte's clubfoot is offered him, he falls, like Adam, urged on by the woman and the serpent. After the operation, Charles's limitations are made public, and the touching hope he had, of securing Emma's love by being different from what he is, is lost to both of them. This is the turning point of the book. Emma has met resistance in Charles, the resistance of inert reality to her desire to make it over, as she can change the paper in her parlor. In furious disgust she resumes her relations with Rodolphe, and from then on her extravagances have a hysterical aim—revenge on Charles for his inability to be papered over.

Both Emma and Monsieur Homais regard themselves as confined to a sphere too small for their endowments—hers in sensibility, his in sense. Emma takes flight into the country, where the château is, into the town, with its shops and "culture." Monsieur Homais's solution is to inflate the village he lives in by his own self-importance and by judicious publicity. It must be remembered that if Emma is a reader, Monsieur Homais is not only a reader but a *writer*—the local correspondent of the *Fanal de Rouen*. That is, they represent the passive and the active side of the same vice. No local event has *happened* for Monsieur Homais till he has cast it into an epic fiction to be sent off to his paper; for Emma, less fertile, nothing happens in Yonville l'Abbaye by definition.

Emma surely felt that she had nothing in common with the grotesque pockmarked druggist in his velvet cap with the gold tassel; he was the antithesis of refinement. But Monsieur Homais was attracted to her and sensed a kindred spirit. He expressed this in his own way: "She's a woman of great parts who wouldn't be out of place in a subprefecture." Homais is a textbook case of the Art of Sinking in prose, and this is the comic side of his hobbled ambitions: he would like to be a modern Hippocrates, but he is a druggist—halfway between a cook and a doctor. He is bursting with recipes; he has a recipe for everything. At the same time, he would like to turn his laboratory, which is a kind of kitchen, into a consulting room; he has been in trouble with the authorities for playing doctor—practicing medicine without a license.

Emma's voluptuous dreams in coarser form have tickled the druggist's thoughts. He takes a fatherly interest in Léon, his lodger, seeing the notary's clerk as a younger self and imagining on his behalf a wild student life in Paris, with actresses, masked balls, champagne, and possibly a love affair with a great lady of the Faubourg St. Germain. He is dreaming à la Emma, but aloud, and he lends his dream, as it were, with a show of philanthropy to Léon. This is double vicariousness. In practice, Monsieur Homais's dissipations are more thrifty. When he goes to Rouen for an outing, he insists that Léon accompany him to visit a certain Bridoux, an apothecary who has a remarkable dog that goes into convulsions at the sight of a snuffbox. The unwilling clerk is seduced by Monsieur Homais's excitement into witnessing this performance, which is evidently the pharmacist's equivalent for a visit to a house of ill fame; and Léon, having yielded like a voyeur to his curiosity, knows he is committing an infidelity to Emma, who is waiting impatiently in "their" hotel room for him. In fact, between Emma and Homais, there has always been a subtle rivalry for Léon, and this betrayal is the first sign that she is losing. Léon is turning into a bourgeois; soon he will give up the flute and poetry, get a promotion, and settle down. As Léon is swallowed by the middle class, Monsieur Homais emerges. By the end of the novel, he has published a book, taken up smoking, like an artist, and bought two Pompadour statuettes for his drawing room.

Bridoux's dog is an evil portent for Emma; he has been heard before, offstage, at another critical juncture, when Emma falls ill of brain fever, having received the "fatal" note from Rodolphe in a basket of apricots. Homais, to whom love is unknown, blames the smell of the apricots and is reminded of Bridoux's dog, another allergic subject. For Yonville l'Abbaye grief and loss only release a spate of anecdotes; similar instances are recalled, to reduce whatever has happened to its lowest common denominator. This occurs on the very first night the Bovarys arrive in Yonville; Emma's little greyhound has jumped out of the coach coming from Tostes, and Lheureux, the draper, her nemesis-to-be, tries to console her with examples of lost and strayed dogs who found their masters after a lapse of years. Why, he has heard of one that came all the way back from Constantinople to Paris. And another that did fifty leagues as the crow flies and swam four rivers. And his own father had a poodle that jumped up on him one night on the street, after twelve years' absence. These wondrous animals, almost human, you might say, are a yipping chorus of welcome to Yonville l'Abbaye, where everything has a parallel that befell someone's cousin, and there is nothing new under the sun.

Emma's boredom and her recklessness distinguish her from Monsieur Homais, who is a coward and who creates boredom around him without suffering it himself. Yet Emma is tiresome too, at least to her lovers, and she would have been tiresome to Flaubert in real life, as he well knew, because her boredom is a silly copy of his own, and she is never more conventional and tedious than when she is decrying convention. She and Léon agree that membership in a circulating library is a necessity if you have to live in the provinces (he also has a music subscription), and they are both wholly dependent on this typical bourgeois institution. The lending library is a central metaphor of *Madame Bovary* because it is the inexhaustible source of *idées reçues*—borrowed ideas and stock sentiments which circulate tritely among the population.

But for Flaubert all ideas become trite as soon as somebody expresses them. This applies indifferently to good ideas and bad. He makes no distinction. For him, the lending library is an image of civilization itself. Ideas and feelings as well get more and more soiled and grubby, like library books, as they pass from hand to hand. The curé's greasy thumbprint on Christian doctrine is just as repulsive as Monsieur Homais's coffee stain on the philosophy of the Enlightenment. The pursuit of originality is as pathetic as Emma's decorating efforts. Similarly with the quality called sincerity. If it exists, it is inarticulate, pre-verbal, dumb as an ox or as the old peasant woman who is awarded a medal at the agricultural fair for fifty years of meritorious service. The speech of presentation annihilates fifty years of merit—a life—in a flash by turning it into *words*.

From his own point of view, this renders Flaubert's efforts in his study as unavailing as Emma's quest for a love that will live up to her solitary dreams. Words, like lovers, have the power of lying, and they also, like lovers, have a habit of repeating themselves, since language is finite. Flaubert's horror of repetition in writing (which has been converted into the dogma that you must never use the same word, above all the same adjective, twice on a page) reflects his horror of repetition in life. Involuntary repetition is banality. What remains doubtful, though, is whether banality is a property of life or a property of language or both. In Emma's eyes, it is life that is impoverished and reality that is banal, reality being symbolized for her by Charles. But Charles is not banal; Rodolphe and Léon are banal, and it is exactly their banality that attracts her.

Rodolphe is superior to Léon, in that his triteness is a calculation. An accomplished comedian, he is not disturbed, at the agricultural fair, by the drone of the voice awarding money prizes for animal flesh, manure, and flax, while he pours his passionate platitudes into Emma's fluttered ears. "Tell me, why have we known each other, we two? What chance has willed it?" His view of Emma is the same as the judge's view of a merino ram. She is flesh, with all its frailties, and he is putting her through her paces, noting her points. Yet Rodolphe is trite beyond his intention. He is wedded to a stock idea of himself as a sensual brute that prevents him from noticing that he actually cares for Emma. His recipes for seduction, like the pomade he uses on his hair, might have been made for him by a pharmacist's formula, and the fact that they work provides him with a ready-made disillusionment. Since he knows that "eternal love" is a cliché, he is prepared to break with Emma as a matter of course and he drops a manufactured tear on his letter of adieu, annoyed by a vague sensation that he does not recognize as grief. As for Léon, he is too cowardly to let himself see that his fine sentiments are platitudes; he deceives himself in the opposite way from Rodolphe: Rodolphe feels something and convinces himself that it is nothing, while Léon feels nothing and dares not acknowledge it, even in secrecy. His very sensuality is timid and short-lived; his clerkly nature passively takes Emma's dictation.

Emma does not see the difference. She is disappointed in both her lovers and in "love" itself. Her principal emotions are jealousy and possessiveness, which represent the strong, almost angry movement of her will. In other words, she is a very ordinary middle-class woman, with banal expectations of life and an urge to dominate her surroundings. Her character is only remarkable for an unusual deficiency of natural feeling. Emma is trite; what happens to her is trite. Her story does not hold a single surprise for the reader, who can say at every stage, "I felt it coming." Her end is inevitable, but not as a classic doom, which is perceived as inexorable only when it is complete. It is inevitable because it is ordinary. *Anyone* could have prophesied what would become of Emma—her mother-in-law, for instance. It did not need a Tiresias. If you compare her story with that of Anna Karenina, you are aware of the pathos of Emma's. Anna is never pathetic; she is tragic, and what happens to her, up to the very end, is always surprising, for real passions and moral strivings are at work, which have the power of "making it new." In this her story is distinct from an ordinary society scandal of the period. Nor could any ordinary society Cassandra have forecast Anna's fate. "He will get tired of her and leave her. You wait," they would have said, of Vronsky. He did not. But Rodolphe could have been counted on to drop Emma, and Léon to grow frightened of her and bored.

Where destiny is no more than average probability, it appears inescapable in a peculiarly depressing way. This is because any element in it can be replaced by a substitute without changing the outcome; e.g., if Rodolphe had not materialized, Emma would have found someone else. But if Anna had not met Vronsky on the train, she might still be married to Karenin. Vronsky is *necessary*, while Rodolphe and Léon are interchangeable parts in a machine that is engaged in mass production of human fates. *Madame Bovary* is often called the first modern novel, and this is true, not because of any technical innovations Flaubert made (his counterpoint, his *style indirect libre*) but because it is the first novel to deal with what is now called mass culture. Emma did not have television, and Félicité did not read comic books in the kitchen, but the phenomenon of seepage from the "media" was already present in every Yonville l'Abbaye, and Flaubert was the first to note it.

Mass culture in *Madame Bovary* means the circulating library and the *Fanal de Rouen* and the cactus plants Léon and Emma tend at opposite windows, having read about them in a novel that has made cactuses all the rage. It means poor Charles's phrenological head—a thoughtful attention paid him by Léon—and the pious reading matter the curé gives Emma as a substitute for "bad" books. It means the neoclassic town hall, with its peristyle, and the tax collector at his lathe, an early form of do-it-yourself. One of the last visions Emma has of the world she is leaving is the tax collector in his garret pursuing his senseless hobby, turning out little wooden imitations of ivory curios, themselves no doubt imitations produced in series in the Orient for export. She has run to Binet's attic from the notary's dining room, which has simulated-oak wallpaper, stained-glass insets in the windowpanes, a huge cactus, a "niche," and reproductions of Steuben's *Esmeralda* and Schopin's *Potiphar*. Alas, it is like Emma to stop, in her last hours of life, to *envy* the notary. "That's the dining-room *I* ought to have," she says to herself. To her, this horrible room is the height of good taste, but the blunder does not just prove she had *bad* taste. If the notary had had reproductions of the *Sistine Madonna* and the *Mona Lisa*, she would have been smitten with envy too. And she would have been right not to distinguish, for in the notary's interior any reproduction would have the same value, that of a trophy, like a stuffed stag's head. This is the achievement of mass-produced and mass-marketed culture.

In Emma's day, mass-produced culture had not yet reached the masses; it was still a bourgeois affair and mixed up, characteristically, with a notion of taste and discrimination—a notion that persists in advertising. Rodolphe in his château would be a perfect photographic model for whiskey or tobacco. Emma's "tragedy" from her own point of view is her lack of purchasing power, and a critical observer might say that the notary's dining room simply spelled out the word "money" to her. Yet it is not as simple as that; if it were, Emma's head would be set straighter on her shoulders. What has happened to her and her spiritual sisters is that simulated-oak wallpaper has become itself a kind of money inexpressible in terms of its actual cost per roll. Worse, ideas and sentiments, like wallpaper, have become a kind of money too and they share with money the quality of abstractness, which allows them to be exchanged. It is their use as coins that has made them trite—worn and rubbed—and at the same time indistinguishable from each other except in terms of currency fluctuation. The banalities exchanged between Léon and Emma at their first meeting ("And what music do you prefer?" "Oh, German music, which makes you dream") are simply coins; money in the usual sense is not at issue here, since both these young people are poor; they are alluding, through those coins, to their inner riches.

The same with Rodolphe and Emma; the same with nearly the whole cast of characters. A meeting between strangers in *Madame Bovary* inevitably produces a golden shower of platitudes. This shower of platitudes is as mechanical as the droning action of the tax collector's lathe. It appears to be beyond human control; no one is responsible and no one can stop it. There is a terrible scene in the middle of the novel where Emma appeals to God, in the person of the curé, to put an end to the repetitive meaninglessness of her life. God is preoccupied and inattentive, and as she moves away from the church, she hears the village boys reciting their catechism. "What is a Christian?" "He who being baptized . . . baptized . . . baptized. . . ."

The answer is lost in an echo that reverberates emptily through the village. Yet the question, although intoned by rote, is a genuine one—the fundamental question of the book—for a Christian means simply a soul here. It is Emma's demand—"What am I?"—coming back at her in ontological form, and there is no reply.

If this were all, *Madame Bovary* would be a nihilistic satire or howl of despair emanating from the novelist's study. But there *is* a sort of tongue-tied answer. That is Charles Bovary. Without Charles, Emma would be the moral void that her fatuous conversation and actions disclose. Charles, in a novelistic sense, is her redeemer. To her husband, she is sacred, and this profound and simple emotion is contagious.

He is stupid, a peasant, as she calls him, almost a devoted animal, clumsy, a dupe. His broad back looks to her like a platitude. He has small eyes; he snores. Until she reformed him, he used to wear a night-cap. Weeping beneath the phrenological head, he is nearly ridiculous. He is nearly ridiculous at the opera (she has taken him to hear *Lucia di Lammermoor*) when he complains that the music is keeping him from hearing the words. "I like to know where I am," he explains, though he, of all people, does not know where he is, in the worldly way of knowing what is going on under his nose. His next blunder, at the opera, is to spill a glass of orgeat down the back of a cotton spinner's wife. He has no imagination, Emma thinks, no "soul." When they find the green silk cigar case that must belong to the vicomte, on the way home from the ball at Vaubyessard, Charles's only reaction is to note that it contains two smokable cigars.

Yet this provincial, this philistine is the only real romantic in the novel—he and the boy Justin, Monsieur Homais's downtrodden apprentice, who dreams over Emma's fichus and underdrawers while Félicité irons in the kitchen. These two, the man and the boy, despised and rejected, are capable of "eternal love." Justin lets Emma have her death (the arsenic) because he cannot refuse her, just as Charles lets her have her every desire. The boy's passion drives him to books, instead of the other way around: Monsieur Homais catches him read-ing a book on "Married Love," with illustrations. Justin is only a child and he weeps like a child on Emma's grave. Charles is a man, a provider, and he has a true man's solicitude for the weaker creature. He sheds tears when he sees Emma eat her first bread and jam after her brain fever. This heavy, maladroit man is a person of the utmost delicacy of feeling. If he is easy to deceive, it is because his mind is pure. It never enters his head that Emma can be anything but good.

He first meets her in the kitchen of her father's farmhouse. He has been waked up at night to go set Farmer Rouault's leg, in a scene reminiscent of a genre painting: *Fetching the Doctor*. A succession of genre scenes follows that evoke the Dutch masters of light—Vermeer and Pieter de Hooch: Emma making the bandage, pricking her fingers with the needle and putting them into her mouth to suck while the doctor watches; Emma in the kitchen sewing a white stocking, dart-ing her tongue into a liqueur glass of curaçao; Emma in the farmyard under a silk parasol. In the big kitchen Charles's senses are heated as she cools her cheek against her palm and her palm against the great andirons, and his mind is buzzing, like the flies crawling up the empty cider glasses, as he looks at her bare shoulders with little drops of sweat on them. He is a man, and she is a young lady; his bewilderment and bewitchment arise from this fusion of the sensual and the sacred. For him, marriage with Emma is a sacrament, and the reader never sees him in the act of love with her, as though Charles, ever tactful, rever-ently drew the bed curtains.

Why did she marry him? Flaubert does not really say. "To get away from the farm" is not enough. Would she have married Monsieur Homais if he had come courting? There are a number of questions about Emma's inner life that Flaubert does not ask. But thanks to Charles, the answer does not matter, because to him the whole thing is a mystery, and like the mysteries of faith to be accepted with holy joy and not puzzled over. For Charles, Emma is a mystery from start to finish. The fact that she ministers to his comfort, prepares charming little dishes, takes care of his house and his patients' accounts, is part of the ineffable mystery of her sharing his bed. The reader is persuaded by Charles's unquestioning faith, to the point where Emma's little gewgaws—her watch charms, her monocle, her ivory workbox, the blue glass vases on her mantelpiece, her silver-gilt thimble—partake of her seductiveness. More than that, these acquisitions, seen through Charles's vision, do just what an advertiser would promise: they give Emma *value*. Thus Charles is not only Emma's dupe but also the dupe of commerce. And yet it works; the reader is convinced that Emma is somehow *better* than, say, Madame Homais—which is not true.

Through Charles, Emma acquires poetry. But he could not possibly put into words what she means to him, and if he could have articulated a thought on the subject, would have declared that *she* had brought poetry into his life. This is so. There was no poetry with his first wife, the widow. Emma's beauty, of course, is a fact of her nature, and Charles has responded to it with worship, which is what beauty —a mystery—deserves. This explains why Charles, though quite deceived by Emma's character, is not a fool; he has recognized something in her about which he *cannot* be deceived.

Charles, like Farmer Rouault, is dumbly rooted in the organic world, where things speak in a simple sign language. A turkey delivered to the doctor says "Thank you" every year for a cure, like a votive offering in church, and two horses in the stable say that business is doing well. Flaubert is not sentimental about the peasantry, yet he prefers Nature and those who live with her and come to resemble her—as old couples come to resemble each other—to the commercial people of the town and the vulgar aristocrats of the châteaux, toward whose condition the tradespeople are aspiring. The peasants still have the virtue of concreteness, and their association with the soil and its products guarantees that they are largely, so to speak, homemade. Emma brings her freshness from the cider-presses of the farm, which she hates.

The country people in general are at a kind of halfway stage in the process of evolution from the animal kingdom to Monsieur Homais. The farm men who come to Emma's wedding are seen by the author as collections of strange, out-of-date clothes hung on frames of flesh and bones—tailcoats and shooting jackets and cutaways and stiff shirts, reeking of history and doubtless of camphor, that have been kept in the wardrobe all year round and issue forth only to go to weddings and funerals, as if by themselves. These grotesque animated garments, each with a strong personality, have as absurd a relation to their owners as the queer cap Charles wears on his first day at school. The new cap, which is like a recapitulation of the history of headgear, is an uncomfortable ill-fitting false self donned for a special occasion—Charles's introduction to civilization, learning, book culture. The country boy does not know what to do with the terrible cap, any more than how to give his full name, which he pronounces in a queer way, as though it too were extraneous to him, a humiliation that has been stuck to him and that he cannot get rid of, just as he cannot put the cap down. A name is a label. Witness the penmanship flourishes of Monsieur Homais's names for his children: Napoleon, Franklin, Athalie...

Many novels begin with the hero's first day in school, and Charles is the hero of the book that, characteristically for him, bears someone else's name. *Madame Bovary* starts with his appearance among his jeering schoolfellows and ends with his death. Charles is docile. It does not occur to him to rebel. His mother, his teachers, his schoolmates, and finally the widow make a citizen of him. They equip him with a profession, for which he is totally unfitted but which he wears, like the cap he has been given, mildly and without protest. He did not choose to be a doctor; he did not choose his name; he did not choose the widow. The only thing in life he chooses is Emma. She is his first and last piece of self-expression. Or not quite the last. When she is taken away from him, his reverence and gratitude to the universe turn to blasphemy. "I hate your God!" he bursts out to the curé, who is trying to console him with commonplaces. "Still the spirit of rebellion," the priest answers, with an ecclesiastical sigh.

Now at first glance this appears to be an irony, since Charles has never rebelled until that moment against anything, let alone God. But Flaubert's ironies are deceptive, and what sounds like an irony is often the simple truth, making a double irony. The priest is right. From the very beginning, Charles has been an obstinate example of passive resistance to the forces of the time and the milieu. A proof of this is that, in all his days, he pronounces only one platitude. His love for Emma is the deepest sign of that obstination. He loves her in the teeth of circumstance, opinion, prudent self-interest, in the teeth even of Emma herself.

This passive resistance of Charles's, taking the form of a love of beauty, seems to come from nowhere. There is nothing in Charles's history to explain it: a drunken father, a dissatisfied mother, a poor education, broken off for lack of money. Add to this a very middling IQ. No program for human improvement could be predicated on Charles's mute revolt against organized society. He is a sheer accident, nothing less than a placid miracle occurring among the notaries and tradesmen, the dyers and spinners of the textile city of Rouen, where he hankers, uncomplaining, for his country home, which was no Arcadia either. He is a revelation, and at the same time his whole effort is to escape notice, to hide in his fleshly envelope like an animal in its burrow. Moreover, his goodness (for that is what it amounts to) has no practical utility and will leave no trace behind it. As a husband, he is a social handicap to Emma, and his mild deference probably contributes to her downfall; a harsher man might have curbed her extravagances, so that she would not have felt obliged to commit suicide. After his death his little girl is sent to work as a child laborer in a cotton mill; he has not even been able to protect his young. His predecessor, a Pole (perhaps another romantic; he "decamped" to avoid his creditors), whose practice and house he moved into, at least left behind the bower he constructed to drink beer in on summer evenings, which in Emma's day was shaded by clematis and climbing nasturtiums. But the only reminder of himself Charles leaves in Yonville l'Abbaye is Hippolyte's stump and two artificial legs, one for best—bought by Emma—and one for everyday. Was he drawn from life? A little of him, including his first wife, the widow, may have been borrowed from Eugène Delamare. There may be reminiscences of a schoolmate, especially the cap. All that can be said is that Charles Bovary, wherever he came from, dawning in a vision or patiently constructed out of treasured bits and pieces of reality, was cherished by his creator as a stubborn possibility that cannot be ruled out even from a pessimistic view of the march of events.

—*Spring 1964*

13

HANGING BY A THREAD

IF YOU CAN imagine an auditory pantomime, you will be in the peculiar world of Nathalie Sarraute. A pantomime in reverse, where instead of tiptoeing action and gesture, you have vocables, so to speak, with their fingers to their mouths. In pantomime, the spectator "understands" a dialogue or soliloquy from the signs made by the performer ("He is afraid," "He is arguing," "His feelings are hurt"); in the mime of Nathalie Sarraute, an invisible action or plot—that is, a relation—is understood from snatches of overheard speech, the word in some way reverting to its primitive function of sign or indicator. And just as an "Ouch!" or a "Pow!" in a silent movie has a greater sonority than any "Ouch!" or "Pow!" recorded on the soundtrack of a talkie, so the action in Nathalie Sarraute emerges from the murk that conceals it with a degree of visibility that is almost immodest.

The action is simplified, conventional, classic—a Punch-and-Judy show, Keystone comedy, or Pearl White cliffhanger—having to do with the seesawing of power in a human group, which can be as large as a mob or as small as a single integer. Some creature is being chased; he makes a narrow escape; they are after him again; he tries to hide, flattens himself against a wall, melts into a crowd, puts on a disguise; they catch him, tear off his false whiskers; he begs for mercy, uttering pathetic squeals. It is always the One and the Many, even and most emphatically when the delicate power balance trembles and oscillates within a palpitating individual heart. In the outer world, alliances and ententes, protective networks, more or less durable, can be made, but within the individual heart there is a continuous division and multiplication. What counts statistically as one person is a turmoil of constant side-changing, treachery, surrender, appeasement; in that sanctum nobody can be safe even long enough to get his breath.

At the outset, Mme. Sarraute's reader, finding himself in this strange and unquiet territory, may be somewhat bewildered. He hears voices talking but cannot assign them to bodies with names, hair color, eye color, identifying marks. It is like listening to a conversation—or a quarrel—on the other side of the thin partition of a hotel room; you long to rush down and consult the register. But there is no register in this hotel; no telltale shoes are put out at night in the corridor, and the occupants of the room next to you keep changing just as you think you have them placed.

At the opening of *The Golden Fruits*, a couple were reviewing an evening out: "You're terrible. You could make an effort just once. I was so embarrassed." Husband and wife, obviously. You knew it was the wife talking because in French the endings of adjectives and past participles make the sex of the speaker clear. More important than their difference of gender, which only indicated that they belonged to the great majority of couples (nothing "queer" about them), was the evidence that here was a pair who kept up with the latest cultural currents—currents which would soon turn into a veritable maelstrom engulfing the newly launched novel "everybody" was talking about.

At the opening of *Between Life and Death*, we are again in a literary milieu, but now it is not the novel but the novelist we find. In person. The voice we hear is male, of course—we can gather that right away—and it is describing its methods of work. "'I always write on the typewriter. Never in longhand.'" At once the reader is aware of a familiar smell—the incense of fame. That man is not just talking to himself. He is on an imaginary stage of some sort, a confident projection of his own ego into the world. Obligingly and doubtless not for the first time, he "acts out" the process of creation. It is a demonstration, like glassblowing. There he is at his desk, frowning, pursing his lips, shaking his head, screwing up his eyes (to get perspective); he tears the sheet of paper out of the machine, crumples it into a ball, throws it on the floor ("No, it won't do"), puts in a fresh sheet of paper, starts over. Over and over. As often as ten times in a sitting. It goes on like this day after day: "I reread. I tear out the page. I crumple it. I toss it aside." Suiting the gesture to the word, his arm rises and falls, folds and unfolds, like the "arm" of a machine, illustrating the mechanics of production. And his wife adds her voice: Yes, that's the way he works. His study is a mass of waste paper. He throws the rejects on the floor. Some days he comes out reeling. He doesn't hear you when you speak to him.

No doubt remains. He *has* to be a successful writer. If he were a failure, nobody would be interested to hear how he worked, whether he wrote by hand or on the typewriter, how much he revised, what he did with his first drafts, and so on. And the wife's two bits' worth clinches it. When you live with a great man, a perfectionist, you are inured to his precious litter, his bouts of inattention. Her dulled voice implies a public, not just the immediate listeners who constitute a silence around him, but what is known as an audience. The form, then, taking shape in the first chapter, is the interview. Not a single interview, with a sympathetic critic or TV host, such as you would find described in a realistic novel, but dozens, hundreds, *all* interviews boiled down to their purest essence.

Such interrogatories are the modern index to fame, above all in Europe, where the publication of a book is the signal alerting a mass of professional questioners with pencils and notebooks, tape recorders, microphones, cameras. A factory whistle has blown in the communications industry. Amateur questioners too, rising from behind a palm in a hotel lobby, approaching after a lecture, concealed in trains, behind the white coat of the family doctor, the starched uniform of the nurse: "Where do you find your ideas?" "How did you get your start?" "So you make your corrections with a ballpoint? You have a 'thing' about fountain pens? How interesting." If it is true that every citizen today believes he has one book in him (the story of his life), then the legion of interviewers, eager for the recipe, the trade secret, is potentially equal to the whole of humanity. The situation in its automatism and inherent repetitiousness is comical, and the author who takes it seriously, swells with its importance, is a fool, like this poor clown onstage talking about the final "mystery" of creation.

Yet already in the opening chapter there is a fly in the ointment. A small voice detaches itself from the reverential silence. It belongs to a woman, and that woman is a writer herself. A budding writer, apparently, because she is so timid. But she too knows what it is to suffer and doubt, tear sheets of paper off the typewriter, crumple them into balls, start over, to lie awake at night. *Of course* there can be no comparison; *she* is not famous; nobody could want to know, except in mockery, about *her* habits of work. Frightened by her own daring, she shrinks back into the circle of the others. A second budding writer, an "I" this time, is pushed forward, struggling; denying any literary ambitions, he flees to safety in the crowd, refusing to listen to the encouragements of the famous man, who remains in the center alone.

In Mme. Sarraute's work, you often find a circle surrounding a single figure, an "it" in the middle, as in a children's game. To be chosen "it," however, is not as enviable as it looks at first. Isolated, you can become the butt of tormentors before you know what has happened; the rules of the game have been changed without a word of warning. You have been betrayed by the "ring" around you who have led you on, maneuvered you into the spotlight by flattery and now start closing in, abetted by your own need of praise and reassurance, the inner traitor, always seeking to join them. This encirclement befell the eponymous hero of *The Golden Fruits,* but we were not privy to the novel's sufferings as it was bounced about like a pinball in the game of taste-making, unable to escape or come to rest on a fixed point, its own selfhood or identity. It was mute, like the medallioned oak door of *The Planetarium,* which could not disclose whether it was beautiful or ugly or so-so. But in the present novel, although we start as onlookers, amused or repelled by a comic spectacle, we are eventually precipitated into the tragic arena of a consciousness, where the "it" stands alone.

The famous man of the first pages, not unaware of his danger, believes he can beat the game by splitting into two, one part remaining in the center bathed in a soft light while his other part, the common man, denying any special talent (it's just a dreary industriousness, he claims; application of the seat of the pants to the seat of the chair), seeks to find a place in the dark of the auditorium. That simple half of himself would like to know, just as much as they, what it was that made him a writer, set him apart. Well, he says modestly, resuming the interrupted "interview," maybe some of it was hereditary. In the genes. He had a Breton grandfather who was a tombstone-cutter in his youth—quite a character; you could almost call him creative, the way he improved on people's epitaphs with inventions of his own. On the other side, he had Italian blood; that grandfather was a shepherd. And as a child he himself had a passion for words. Yes, it went that far back; as long as he could remember, he was playing by himself with words.

Then (a new chapter is starting) the reader is aware of a sort of air turbulence: a disconcerting shift has taken place. Of time, place, persons? He cannot yet make out. The voices are using some of the same words and expressions but they no longer sound the same. Now it is a "she" who is large and famous, and "he" has become youthful, humble, small. He has sent her his manuscript, and she has replied with a letter—such an astounding, generous letter. Reading him, she has discovered that they speak the same language; it is she, not he, who should be grateful—for the pleasure he has given her. A fellow spirit! At last someone he can talk to without the usual precautions. He can tell her *anything*. As a child, she too must have played with words. He is sure of it. Just like him, in his little crib, with the bars on the sides, pronouncing words to himself at night. They were his first toys. And when he was a little older, there was one word in particular... Too late he recognizes the trap; her pale eyes are mocking him. She is not a fellow spirit but one of the others, disguised, sent out to disarm him.

Here the novel begins to unfold its complexities. Who exactly *are* the others? Instead of the audience the deluded creature thought was out there, it is a ferocious jury of writers that is confronting him and disqualifying his claim to "belong." An inner circle has replaced the outer circle, and now, rudely manhandled, his words echoed with jeers, he finds himself on the perimeter, unable to gain admittance except on strict and contemptuous probation. Yet these persons who are hustling him into a uniform, thrusting him into the lowest class of aspirants, are not simply writers more securely established than himself. They seem to have some connection with the public, whose judicial arm they are. Or the public is *their* judicial arm. Maybe they are critics—an unnatural hybrid of writer and reader.

It is not only the others drawn into a circle who have undergone this alarming metamorphosis. He himself is changed to the point where you would barely recognize him. If he did not hark back to the old business about his childhood and what predetermined his "election" to write, he could pass for a simple unpretentious being. It is they who have twisted his words, to use against him. He has only answered the questions they asked him as honestly as he could. He does tear out and crumple and start over. It was true about his Breton grandfather and his unhappy childhood and the game he played with *"héros, héraut, hérault, erre haut."* Truth is no defense. By their fruits you shall know them. Most people have had an unhappy childhood, an erratic ancestor. Who does he think he is?

That naturally is the central question, which the book's central figure is the last to be able to answer. If he says he is nobody, it is a lie. False modesty. If he says he is "somebody," they will laugh at him. No one, when the searchlight has picked him out, can wriggle out of that dilemma or rise above it. The egregious clown of the first chapter loses his outlines, multiplies, subdivides, becomes all writers, bad, good, and indifferent. His fatuity is seen to be merely an aspect of fame. Insofar as we are famous, we are fools, and fame is something we cannot exactly help but which is done to us with or without our eager cooperation. The fame which makes a writer stand out in high relief from the crowd *exposes* him; hence his protests about being no different from anybody else, untalented, a drudge. These protests are usually sincere, though never believed, and if a writer has the folly to complain of his fame, he is smiled at, like a rich person talking about the "curse" of having money. The writer wanted it, did he not? He worked for it. Probably what he really wanted was glory, which, unlike fame, is not a market commodity.

Still it seems to be a fact that the writer is like everybody else—only more anxious, more preoccupied with himself and with the state of health of that alien part of him which is his talent, the part that has the least to do with *him*, and that is, alas, the most in view. Yet something of the sort is true for everyone. The important part of ourselves that constitutes our definition, our outline, cannot be seen from the inside, even if it can be *felt* occasionally in what we think of as our best moments, when we are "in form." The experiencing subject is unsure of his identity, which is objectified for him by others, though in a fragmentary and unreliable way. I cannot trust the mirror for instance to tell me whether I am beautiful or ugly; nor can I altogether trust the compliments—or the reverse—of friends and family, which send me running back to the mirror for confirmation. This ceaseless back-and-forth, commonest among people known as "sensitive" but universal at least in youth, is epitomized in the ordeal of the writer, whose existence, as writer, must be repeatedly confirmed by a public, so that, to quote Mme. Sarraute's title, he is always hanging between life and death.

That it is a life-and-death struggle is evident from the metaphors used in literary journalism. "I murdered it," says a reviewer complacently of the latest novel. "Lethal," say his admiring friends. "Slaughter. A massacre." "Vitriolic." An author, reading over a passage he has finished, sighs to himself: "Dead. Dead. Dead." That in fact is the sole criterion an author employs to judge his own work, as though he was holding a mirror up to the mouth of an unconscious patient. "Fine result," comments the alter ego of Mme. Sarraute's writer-hero. "It's dead. Not a breath of life." "How do you mean, no life?" cries the anguished hero, who imagines he has given his best, all his treasures, to this text. "Why?" "Oh, you know me," the other replies. "I'm quite simple. Very primitive...between ourselves two words suffice. As coarse as these two: It's dead. It's alive. And it's dead. Nothing comes through."

For the writer it is not a mere question of success or failure. He hangs by a thread over nothingness, annihilation. He has put, as they say, so much of himself into his book. And there is no one he can rely on entirely, not the public, his publisher, his literary sponsors, not even his alter ego, that faithful companion who is called into consultation whenever a chapter or a passage is "ready to show." He cannot be totally sure of the objectivity of the *fidus Achates*. Maybe there is not enough distance between them. The other may be partial to him on account of their old relationship. Or he may be infected by his masochism, his sickly doubts, and be oversevere with him. Maybe there is too much distance. What if the other is too conscious of the reviewers out there, lying in wait? The interior critic has to keep a foot in that camp as well; otherwise he would be of no use to him.

But wholly trust him or not, this friend, second self, arbiter, is all he has in the world, and he clings to him, damp and trembling, readying himself for the verdict. It is what he feared, "knew all along" was coming. A death sentence. Can there be no reprieve? At first the other is final—no hope. Junk it. But at length he is persuaded to take a second look. Together they assess the damage. Right here is where it goes wrong; back there, yes, possibly, there is a part that can be saved. Reanimated, resurrected by these crumbs of comfort, the writer thinks he has the strength to start over. But first he sends the other out of the room. He has to be alone. The other knows him too well. He cannot have him always bending over his shoulder, trying to be helpful.

Before he was able to divide himself into two and establish this "working relationship," his judge was out there, unfathomable, unpredictable, promoting him and demoting him according to some grading system which he himself can never get the hang of. We return, like a team of journalists, to those who knew him when. His mother, his teachers, his schoolmates spotted him from way back as one of "those." They recognized the signs: brooding in corners, taking an undue interest in words, having bizarre aversions to some of the most harmless ones, talking to himself, "awkwardness, shyness, the feeling of being different, superiority." Back then, though they forget it, these were black marks against him in the Book of Life, pointing to a misfit. How can he say such a thing? Now that he is a literary discovery, what he ignorantly thought were black marks turn out to have been gold stars, and claims to have been his original discoverer are inserted in the record. His mother "knew" from birth, when they brought him in to her: "your high forehead, your look of concentration." His teacher has never forgotten his school composition—"My First Sorrow"—on the death of his little dog, run over by a train. An amazing sense of language for a child.

When his first book is taken, the editor employed to "handle" him is familiar with the signs: arrogance, false humility, childishness, unwillingness to rewrite. They are all alike, authors; he knows them like the inside of his pocket. The more in fact the neophyte-hero inches forward in achieving recognition, the more he is treated as a specimen of an already familiar category of persons, as though there were nothing special about him except his having entered that category, whose laws are now found to govern his slightest movement, even his movements of rebellion, whether he is conscious of it or not.

Readers are sure they know where he got this or that detail in his book. These are Mme. Jacquet's fingers. "Don't worry. Nobody's going to tell her." It's no use trying to fool them. They have heard those disclaimers before. There is nothing in the book whose sources they cannot sniff out: "Your entire childhood. I saw it...camouflaged, of course." And his secret motivations for writing, all plain as a pikestaff: "a defense reaction," "an unconscious need for revenge."

If he serves tea to visitors, an ordinary teakettle turns in the telling and retelling into a samovar, the tea turns into a rare sophisticated blend, and his nervous gestures are "slow, almost solemn," like a priest lifting a chalice. "You seemed to be officiating," reports his mother. His father is confident that he has his number too. When the hero bursts happily in to tell him that his book has been accepted, the father, barely looking up from something he is writing: "How much did they take to publish that?"

Being neither "somebody" nor nobody, like a defective syllogism, the debutant novelist is reduced to an absurdity. His struggles against claims to know him, pin a label on him, file him, are the purest comedy. What is involved is possession, property, the little tickets that are stuck on his work: "Symbolism. Surrealism. Impressionism.... Comic. Tragic. Ontological. Drama. Psychodrama." One of the funniest passages, a little masterpiece written by an angel on the head of a pin (found in Chapter 12), has to do with a false claim check. An elder pontifical critic has discovered what he calls the main axis of the book, "the point around which the whole work is organized.... That

scene is the empty railway station.... It's a pause. A destroyed center."
But there is no scene in a railway station. The efforts of the hero to
retrieve the horrible situation caused by this blunder (which of course
nullifies in a flash the critic's very valuable endorsement) amount to
a sort of negotiated surrender. They compromise on a room full of
empty benches, in fact a ministry. In an early short story there was a
railway station...

Yet the hero, though outnumbered, is still a force to reckon with.
The others fear him as a spy concealed among them, pretending to be
minding his own business while covertly taking notes. Nor is their
surmise mistaken, even if they are usually barking up the wrong tree,
as with Mme. Jacquet's fingers, which really belonged to a friend of
his grandmother's. Knowledge, they think, is power, and in their view,
this note-taking is a power play: he has got them where he wants
them, in a book, appropriated them for his own purposes. And the
criminal may actually be paid royalties for the stolen property he
vends. That is why his attempts to hide must be foiled. He must be
brought out into the open, expelled from the circle into the middle. A
woman pounces: "You know he too is one." That is also why he must
be enrolled in the regiment of his fellow writers, who can keep a
watch on him if he tries to desert.

All this belongs to the social comedy of the literary life, recognizable to anybody who has ever taken part in it. The humiliations and
vicissitudes of the hero are not very important in the final analysis,
except as furnishing merriment. They are just occupational hazards
the little fellows have to put up with—at least in outward appearance
the great are not subject to them.

But *Between Life and Death* has another dimension, beyond the
social, always the cruel playground of comedy: the games people play.
In Chapter 8, a book finally begins to write itself, and at once we are
on another scale, an immense staircase, as the hero, conquering his
fear, ascends from life toward death, and as usual in death he is alone.

He is going into the temple, like the child Virgin Mary, climbing the steep steps in Titian's famous *Presentation*, leaving behind the street crowd and the old woman selling eggs on the bottom stair. For the duration of this chapter, we have left the circle; we no longer hear the desperate pitter-patter of running feet, the thud of ignominious falls on banana peels. Instead, we are in a realm of music. It is a ballet of words, which, as force gathers, turns into a march, a triumphal march, with brass winds blowing in the orchestra. Then, suddenly, at the height of exultation, there is silence, Total. The tragic hero is dividing into two, to face his alter ego.

Nothing of the sort—a rending of the veil—has been attempted before, and one would have said in advance that it was impossible, short of demonstration, to show how an author composes, that is, to create with words a sort of program music imitating the action of other words as they assemble on a page. It is all very well for a piano to imitate raindrops or paint to imitate foliage, but how can a medium imitate itself? Mme. Sarraute has done it; she does it twice in the novel—again and even more tremendously in the desperate final chapter, where the writer, older, is uncertain of his music, which often sounds to him now like a player piano with him pumping the pedals but which nevertheless swells out with a greater resonance and more complex harmony until it breaks off.

Of course he is writing *Between Life and Death*. "Take this one to start with, this tiny fragment...that arm like the arm of a jointed puppet, which stretches out, folds, drops, that fist that opens...."

This device, of the novel enclosed within the novel (the Quaker Oats box), might have seemed a mere form, not new either, of literary op art, if the force of it here at the finale did not close on us like Nemesis. We had half felt it coming, we were "prepared," yet we were not sure. So there is only one author, as we suspected, one book, which they all were writing: *this* book, fabricated in solitude, imperfect, conscious of its blemishes, modest, gigantically boastful, daring to enter the arena, expose itself, and contest its right to survival. Just as the encircled hero stands or falls, finally, by his work, his salient into the world and his redoubt, his last point of retreat, so his creator elects to stand *by* him, taking him by the hand, ready to fall *with* him, naked both, saying "We."

The infinite regress of the Quaker Oats box expresses also the "mystery" of creation, for the nearer you draw to that process, the less you understand it. "Mystery" in ironic quotation marks, yet it *is* a mystery, despite the fact that ignorant people are content to call it that, knowledgeably—as though in pronouncing the word they had somehow taken possession of the thing itself and were jumping all over it shouting its name—"It's a mystery, that's all there is to it. We're in the presence of a mystery." The force of repetition kills eternal truths; that conviction obsessed Flaubert, whose *taedium vitae* took the form of a horror of banality. In this literally double-faced novel, facing inward and outward, like the year god, mischievous, sly, glinting occasionally with malice, but also somber, tragic, heart-shaking in its directness, Mme. Sarraute has undertaken something very bold—the rescue of banality from itself.

Every bromide uttered by her hero and his sycophants proves to be true—specious but true. Whether you feel it as truth or imposture depends a good deal on the tone of voice. Is he preening himself on tearing out and crumpling or is he confessing it, confiding it, mentioning it? There is a whole slithery gamut of nuances. "I have to admit I'm a perfectionist"—what is false about that sentence? Working very carefully, with a pair of tweezers, we may be able to detach the inverted commas from that "confession." It is rare that we find a direct lie when they have been removed—i.e., that the speaker is a shiftless loafer. Usually the inverted commas have sprung up there as the result of mirror-rehearsal or repetition.

In the next-to-the-last chapter, the self-important novelist of the first chapter is back again, older and more munificent with his clichés and precepts. With a shudder, the reader recognizes that voice. "'We should pay attention to no one. To no one. And to nothing. Except to this.' He lays his hand flat on his chest." Of course he is right, insofar as what he recommends is possible. Everyone would agree. But, more than being right, this old whore has somehow become rather sympathetic. He too has a deflating, puncturing double, though you would never have imagined it, to hear him talk. *She* knows that he is finished as a writer, ready for the funeral parlor. He sees her sitting out there in the circle, who all know it too. She may even be his self-effacing consort. They think he has not guessed it himself but they are wrong. How could he not guess when he senses her *here*, in his plump chest, where he has just reverently laid his hand?

Having kept company with a succession of other, shyer novelists, we are no longer deceived by the façade he showed us when we first met him. At present we see how it is for him, inside, and there no differences exist: all are alike.

In fact for Mme. Sarraute's hero banality is the irritant that gives rise to the work of art, whose worst enemy, by the way (as we saw in *The Golden Fruits*), is good taste. The banal, the "common," which offend the connoisseur, excite in the artist a morbid sort of itch that fatally asks to be scratched. A vulgar, drawling pronunciation. Such overheard sentences as "If you keep on like that, your father will like your sister better than you." Tiny parcels of living substance around which words begin to dance their ballet or mobilize like iron filings in the presence of a magnet. With a little guidance from the author, a current is made to run from the living substance (which may first appear as an effluvium oozing from a crack in the wall that separates each of us from others) through the dancing, wheeling words, which come out faster and faster, in a jet. He watches them perform, moves them about slightly, withdraws one very gently, like somebody playing jackstraws, so as not to upset the structure, and substitutes another. By preference they should be ordinary words (farewell *héros, hérault, erre haut*), in working clothes; an unfamiliar word in Mme. Sarraute's own novels is likely to be found in the dictionary marked "*Fam.*" (familiar). A local irritation caused by vulgarity produces an excretion, as with the oyster and the pearl, but the stream or spray of words that come from it (the metaphors keep changing) must retain some of the insipidity, flatness, of the original sickly substance.

The name given to the particle of living substance, the germ of the novelist's novel, is simply *la petite chose*. If other people try to assign a more precise name to her ("A vulgar accent, that's all; you mustn't let it get under your skin"), he is furious; they are taking her away from him, but she is his. As the book progresses, this humble creature, a sort of Cinderella, assumes a more and more important role. Now there are three in the novelist's workroom: himself, his double, and *la petite chose*. It is almost a crowd.

By the final chapter, success has altered the relations between them. His double is no longer his plain old friend; he talks in a new stylish way, betraying the time he has been spending in literary circles. "Alive" and "dead" aren't good enough for him anymore. He has his nose in a big grammar—the one critics use to trip up an author. Sometimes his voice cannot be heard over the voice of the crowd. The worst, the most alarming sign is that he is no longer as critical as he used to be. Don't worry; just publish it, he says. Everything between them is upside down. Now it is the "I" who is suddenly captious, wants to improve, rewrite, but the "You" brusquely stops him. You're crazy. Leave it alone. How cynical he now is about the public! "They'll never notice the difference" is his attitude. Or doesn't he care any more himself?

Evidently he is lost to the hero, who has no one to turn to in his extremity. All he can hear is the other writers out there, sneering at him for the enormity of his ambition to join some of them on their pedestals. The wider public seems to have disappeared. It is dark. But he is not utterly alone. *La petite chose* has stuck by him, after all, despite the mistakes he has made with her, painting her up, sending her to the great dressmakers. In fact, they have become closer, since the double has been unfaithful. *She* has not changed; she still has that stale, musty smell he has a perverse liking for. Feeling her there, he takes heart again. He dares another look at the chapter. And lo, as though recalled, reassured, by the nearness of *la petite chose*, his double is once more at his side. Not too close, says the author, but not too far off either. They look together at the chapter, examine it for signs of life. It seems to be faintly breathing. Is it the hero's imagination or does his old friend observe too a fine mist on the pocket mirror placed before its mouth?

The book, naturally, ends on a question, the question asked by all books: Am I alive or dead? The answer, if by that is meant the reception, is material for *The Golden Fruits*. Indeed, the hero of the present work in his most aghast moments could not have foreseen what happened. Did it get bad reviews? Good? Mixed? It got no reviews. It came out in the month of May during the Paris general strike, when there were no newspapers or magazines, no television, and radio that consisted of news bulletins. By the time the media were back in service, the spring publishing season was over. Everyone went away for the summer, and when they came back, it was the fall publishing season. Nobody was talking anymore about the books of last spring.

What happened to *Between Life and Death* was a common fate. Democratic. Covered by the act-of-God clause in the contract. Any book published in May was killed instantly, without suffering. A good way to go. Some lingered as a memory, in a few bookstore windows; a few people bought them, probably. A brief notice or so may have followed, in the fall or winter—not reviews but oversights remedied. Perhaps there has been somewhere a real review of *Between Life and Death* that I missed. All that is sad but funny. It belongs to the comedy of the literary life. What is important is that the book was written. It exists, compact in itself, independently of the sum of its readers and having a kind of self-evidence like a theorem in geometry.

Soon somebody will find it, in a train or a hotel or even a bookstore: "I never knew she wrote that." Though it is less a "born" classic than *The Golden Fruits*, it is more original, more complex, larger, deeper. Its greatest originality, more striking than its bewitching technical resources but leaning on them for support, is its egalitarian view of its subject. Hence the strange appropriateness of its being killed during the May–June revolutionary events; it would not have minded that. In any case it is a heroic book, as much a deed as an imitation of one, and therefore merits not fame but glory.

—July 1969

14

ON REREADING
A FAVORITE BOOK

REOPENING *ANNA KARENINA* after more than thirty years, I find that I know it virtually by heart. Every episode, just about every incident, every observation is as I remember it and *where* I remember it. Other favorite books suffer alteration during an interval of being unread. Coming back to them, you see that you have totally forgotten a whole subplot; secondary characters have become complete strangers— does the name Raffles in *Middlemarch* ring a bell? Or else episodes that have stuck in the memory do not seem to be there at all or have shrunk to a phrase or a paragraph—needles in a haystack. One's feelings toward the main characters may have altered with the onset of "maturity": now we prefer Pierre to Prince Andrei and Hector to Achilles. Recently I had the mortifying experience of meeting once again the wise youth Adrian (*The Ordeal of Richard Feverel*), like a childhood crush grown unrecognizable—what could have been the attraction? The return to a favorite novel is generally tied up with changes in oneself that must be counted as improvements but have the feel of losses. It is like going back to a favorite house, country, person; nothing is where it belongs, including one's heart.

But in *Anna Karenina*, oddly, the only big thing I have forgotten is one I would expect to remember: that Levin's older brother, the consumptive, is a Communist. Add to that a little thing: that Vronsky has whiskers and a mustache with tips that he twirls. Otherwise all is in its place: Anna's swift resolute step, Karenin's ears, Vronsky's white, strong, even teeth, which, when we have our last sight of him near the end of the novel, after Anna has killed herself, are making his jaw twitch impatiently with an incessant gnawing toothache. Yes, it is in a train station, like Anna's death and their first meeting, and he is going off to fight as a volunteer in the Serbian war against the Turks (taking along a whole squadron at his own expense), and there are ladies with bouquets to see the brave volunteers off. And whom does he meet at the first stop, on the platform, but Levin's other brother, the writer, who commends him for his public spirit. And Vronsky tersely answers. "'Yes, as a weapon I may be of some use. But as a man, I'm a wreck,' he jerked out. He could hardly speak for the throbbing ache in his strong teeth, that were like rows of ivory in his mouth." Then, on the station platform, a different sensation, "that set his whole being in anguish," causes him for an instant to forget his toothache; the sight of a tender gliding smoothly along the rails has reminded him of Anna's still-warm mangled body and lovely intact head as he had found her laid out on a table in the railway shed. Remorse overwhelms him, and his face works with sobs.

The somatology, the harsh reduction to bedrock, is pure Tolstoy. Yet it would be wrong to sense a sarcasm and think that Vronsky is "shown up" by having a toothache—the most untragical, because most everyday, of human ills—at such an inappropriate moment. Rather, the "lowly" origin of the agony he suffers raises him, as if on a cross. In that moment he is redeemed from his creator's scorn. The reproach of Anna's memory has been powerful enough to anesthetize the ache "for an instant," which is as much as can be expected of a man. A bite of remorse that is sharper than the gnawing of a toothache is the mark of a strong nature. Indeed, as a man of feeling, Vronsky has passed a final exam here that many or most of us would fail. Tolstoy has judged him, ultimately, as a human animal, and, measured by that standard, Vronsky's "points" stand out.

The inappropriate, in fact, the utterly inconsonant, is Tolstoy's peculiar stamping ground: Pierre's white hat and green swallowtail coat at the Battle of Borodino; Levin's search for a dress shirt on his wedding morning. The story of Levin and Kitty—and of Vronsky and Anna—has begun on that note, with the foolish, totally unsuitable smile on Anna's brother's face when his wife confronts him with proof of his adultery. Since that unforgivable smile Dolly has refused to see Stiva, which is why Anna has had to come from Petersburg to reconcile them. Stiva's smile is both a dreadful giveaway and it is not. As with Vronsky's aching big tooth, Stiva is not diminished by an irrepressible surfacing of his animal nature. On the contrary, that involuntary movement of the lips, a reflex as he tells himself, somehow bestows credit on him, where the appropriate gestures—denying everything, justifying himself, begging forgiveness—would not have. The smile is proof of both his "bestial" guilt and his bestial innocence, i.e., his simplicity. His inconsequence is a sign of the good in him, as, I think, it always is for Tolstoy. It is of the same family as Levin's absurd remark—utterly out of keeping with his feelings, which are wholly bent on Kitty—toward the beginning of the novel when Stiva, who has invited him to lunch, asks him whether he likes turbot: "What? . . . Turbot? Yes, I am *awfully* fond of turbot." No doubt Levin, hearing himself, could have bitten off his tongue, and this too is a sign of election.

The two men—one in the raptures of undeclared love, one (when he remembers) in a state of marital apprehensiveness—lunch on three dozen oysters, champagne, Parmesan, soup, turbot, chablis, roast of beef, capons, finishing off with a fruit salad. Even Levin, who would have preferred cabbage soup and kasha, does not lack appetite. This is a book of the body, and Stiva, though he is a procurer only of nourishment (perch brought live to the kitchen, asparagus, and a joint are what he gives Karenin for dinner), is a sort of Pandarus-by-example. Like Criseyde's uncle, he is a joyful advertisement for the flesh and its claims—a sympathetic figure, more sympathetic, certainly, than he ought to be, given Tolstoy's morality. Those three dozen oysters stick to him like a classical attribute or like the manner of his martyrdom (Saint Lawrence's gridiron, Saint Apollonia's teeth) to a pictured saint.

Meanwhile his incongruous friend and boyhood comrade, Constantine Levin, is trying to live for his soul, but his soul, having become incarnate in Kitty (Stiva's wife's sister), turns out to be obstinately practical, boiling raspberry jam on a charcoal stove on the terrace in the Shcherbatsky way (no water), matchmaking, knowing how to make people comfortable. The thing that astonishes him in Kitty, who is barely grown up, is her tranquil power of handling death, that strange, unnatural rupture with the body.

Sacramental moments, where the spiritual infuses the physical with an overpowering sweetness, are rare in this novel; I think chiefly of the Sunday scene where Dolly's children, having taken Communion at the peasant church in their freshly washed and let-out best clothes, are then, as if to be cleansed a second time, piled into the wagonette to go mushrooming and have a bathing party naked in the river. Here, by a miracle, body and soul are not pulling apart, like an ill-matched team of horses. They can hardly be separated, and when the smallest child, after taking the sacrament, says in English "Please, some more," she of course is right to ask for seconds, as though the Eucharist were a particularly nice dinner.

All this materiality helps account, no doubt, for the fact that *Anna* stays so unchanged in the memory. There is little in it that could be subject to erosion or blurring. Each scene *says* something clearly and distinctly, like an illustration to a child's alphabet book; each figure has its emblem or emblems, which acts as a fixative. We get something of the kind in *War and Peace* (the Princess Marya's heavy tread, Prince Andrei's small white hands) but haphazardly by comparison with *Anna*, where not a sparrow can fall without a special providence. Karenin's protruding ears, his habit of cracking his knuckles, and high shrill voice are truly damning details, condemning him in perpetuity.

No matter how old one gets, if one lives to be a hundred, one's preferences among the people in this novel will never alter. Impossible to like Karenin, and, between honest-hearted Dolly and her unfaithful husband, one still cannot help siding with him, perhaps for being so incorrigible. This trait, seldom endearing in real life, is a prime virtue in a fictional character—Falstaff, Mr. Micawber. Like them, the delinquent Stiva wears well. He surprises in a predictable way, reminding you at once of himself. Of course there is another side to such figures: the pleasure we take in them is somebody else's pain. Dolly's children's patched and gusseted clothes point a telling finger at their father's wayward habits. And yet we do not mind too much on their behalf. Those let-out seams and pieced childish dresses are intrinsic (naturally!) to his spendthrift makeup; we are not judges in Children's Court. As readers, we have other standards. Is it proof of false values if we prefer life-enhancing people (Stiva, the old Prince Shcherbatsky, Anna, Vronsky) to life-diminishing ones (Karenin, the Countess Lidia Ivanovna and her pious circle, Mme. Stahl, even Kitty's sacrificial friend, Varenka)? At any rate Tolstoy agrees. The most unpleasant characters in the novel are the paragons; in comparison, the triflers and worldlings are unoffending—they merely are what they are.

In fact, none of the characters in *Anna Karenina* is corrigible. The changes they go through, sometimes quite surprising, "utterly out of character," like the metamorphosis of Karenin at Anna's sickbed, in the end do not change anything. True, they bear witness to a capacity for change in human nature, and the glimpses we are given of that capacity make the pessimistic *Anna* far more exhilarating than the optimistic *Resurrection*, which succeeded it. Karenin *is* reborn at what he takes to be Anna's deathbed; in the act of pardon he rises from the bureaucratic death-in-life that is his normal state of being.

But these wonderful changes do not last. The character reverts to its previous "set." There is no place in the world for a metamorphosed Karenin. Vronsky turned painter is still Vronsky in an artist's hat and cloak. That is a fact; that is the way it is, and not exactly anybody's fault. An inborn capacity for change is, as it were, corrected by the contrary force of inertia.

Nor does that always work out so badly. Take the chapter where Vronsky adds up his debts—does his *lessive*, as he calls it. The normal fictional expectation is that he will never be able to pay all those bills, especially with Anna on his hands (which we are sure she soon will be). Here is the gun hanging on the wall that must go off in the last chapter; only ruin can lie ahead for him. Yet to our relief and bewilderment this is the last we hear of the subject. Since he and Anna are soon traveling in Italy and then back in Russia living in great style while he plunges into costly farming experiments, we might assume that someone (his mother doubtless) has died and resolved his difficulties. But nothing of the sort; after Anna is dead, his mother is again in the station, to see him off for the Serbian war and ride part of the way in the compartment with him. In short (as happens with countries), his monetary crisis, which seemed so desperate, somehow does not come to a head. Life goes on as before. That is the way it is: we add up our debts, shove the heaps of bills we have no way of paying back into the drawer, and worry along pretty much as before. "Ruin" is just a word. The gun on the wall shoots blanks.

It is terrible that it should be so, almost as terrible as that Karenin is unable to taste for long the pure joy of forgiveness. Anna would seem to be the exception to that bleak rule; she is punished for her "sin," and at least this *looks* like something decisive. It is clear that she kills herself to be free of the force of inertia at work in her circumstance. Nothing so very dreadful has happened: Vronsky has not left her; he has not even ceased to love her despite the provocation she gives him. The cruel alteration is not in him but in herself: the gradual coarsening of her face and body—allegoric, as always in Tolstoy. "She had broadened out all over." Suicide for her is an act of rebellion against the indeterminateness, lack of clarity, imposed on her like a privation of freedom. By throwing herself at an oncoming train, shaking off the encumbering little red handbag, surely a symbol of her worldly position, she violently writes *Finis*—at last a definition.

For me, *Anna Karenina* is terribly true, almost truer than any novel ought to be. No illusions are permitted to survive in its rigorous climate; *War and Peace* is softer, more clement. Levin ends *Anna* with the admission of his own incorrigibility; he has not changed, as he always dreamed he would, and now he knows that he never will be different. Still that is not quite the end; he tells himself at once that there *is* a difference, even though it is imperceptible—an *inner* difference that he owes to the rediscovery of the Christian truths he has known as a child. True, nothing outwardly will change, but he has lost the inner feeling of meaninglessness. Now every minute of his life has a "positive meaning of goodness with which I have the power to invest it." These are the last words of the novel and a kind of consolation. But since, precisely, by Tolstoyan standards the proof should be visible and palpable, there is no reason to believe that this too is not an illusion, of a very common kind, created by need.

Everyone needs the good, hankers for it, as Plato says, because of the lack of it in the self. This greatly craved goodness is meaning, which is absent from the world, outside the chain of cause and effect and incommensurable with reason. Yet Levin's intimations of it owe a great deal, surely, to Kitty, to the unaccustomed delights of fatherhood and new-married life, i.e., to material factors, so that the conviction we are left with as we close the novel may be just as time-determined as Vronsky's feeling of pureness on leaving the Shcherbatskys', which is partly due to his not having smoked for several hours. The hero of *Anna* is Anna, after all, not Levin. She is the tragic sacrifice, and if the novel is a tragedy, of templelike Greek logic (the only novel in history to achieve this stature), it is because the power of suffering in Anna imposes meaning by the drastic act of autodestruction. The excruciating ache of Vronsky's strong, even teeth, the twitching of his jaw are a restatement of the theme in his limited corporeal language.

—*March 22, 1981*

15

ACTS OF LOVE

CALVINO IS A wizard. His last work of fiction, *The Castle of Crossed Destinies*, was inspired by two packs of tarot cards. The hero of the latest, *If on a winter's night a traveler*, is "the new Calvino"—in other words, itself. The novel the reader has opened is the same novel a Reader inside the cover has gone to a bookstore to procure, having seen an item in a newspaper announcing that a book by this author, the first in several years, has appeared. Everything fairly normal so far. Calvino's Reader—the one inside the story—is a reasonable updating of the "dear reader" of the old fictioneers. As we might expect, relations with him have become more informal, positively familiar: right away the author is calling him "you" ("*tu*," "*ti*," "*te*," in the original), which is like getting on a first-name basis at the first handshake. "Calvino," a hospitable figure, is concerned that the new owner of his book should have optimum conditions for the enjoyment of it: good light, a comfortable position, no distractions ("No, I don't want to watch TV!"), cigarettes and an ashtray if he smokes.

What may strike the reader (small *r*, you or me, not Him) as possibly a bit odd is the insistence on the Reader's anticipation, as though this were an *ars amoris* and the whole first chapter, in which we meet author and reader but not yet the book, were the foreplay, stimulation of erectile tissue prior to the act of reading as recommended by a rather permissive sex manual. The Reader is instructed to "Relax," "Concentrate"; we watch him, alone at last with the desired object, sensuously postpone his pleasure, turning the volume over in his hands, glancing through the jacket copy, while the author, also watching, approves, *up to a point*: "Of course, this circling of the book... this reading around it before reading inside it, is a part of the pleasure... but like all preliminary pleasures, it has its optimum duration if you want it to serve as a thrust toward the more substantial pleasure of the consummation of the act, namely the reading of the book." This should be a hint of what is to follow: consummation withheld— a series of beginnings, ten to be exact, ten novels that break off just as they are getting interesting, ten cunningly regulated instances of coitus interruptus in the art and practice of fiction.

From the start, from the very first lines, like a barely heard alarm bell, "the new Calvino" induces slight anxiety in the Reader preparing himself to recognize the "unmistakable tone" of the author—one of the small initial sensations, highly pleasurable, of opening a volume by an author one already knows. But now the awaited sensation fails to materialize: this new one does not read like a Calvino. There seems to be no connection with any of his others. Nonetheless the Reader persists, swallowing his first disappointment. In one who is hooked on the potent old drug, the urge to read is greater than the urge to read a Calvino.

In fact, as our marvelous storyteller fully demonstrates, the addict can no longer be choosy; we behold him at the mercy of his habit, suffering withdrawal symptoms when the supply is abruptly cut off, unable to break himself of the solitary practice, so easily fallen into, of letting his eyes run from left to right, then right to left on a swift diagonal, dropping down a line, and again left to right, back and forth across any bound sheets of printed white paper so long as order and serial pagination have been respected. And how little it takes, for example, to compel reader identification with the pronoun "I" in a first-person narrative, no matter where it is supposed to be happening and amid what company—more and more, these days, no introductions are necessary. In the course of this short book "You" will identify yourself with a series of complete strangers, some of whom, like the fellow with the suitcase in the first novel, never even let you know their name and occupation.

As my reader has surely heard if he is tuned in to literary events, *If on a winter's night a traveler* keeps turning into other novels, into, finally, nine successive polymorphs that break off at the point where the reader starts to feel real suspense as to what will happen next, the point where in an old movie serial the heroine is tied to the railroad tracks and the engine is coming steadily toward the viewer, who has to wait patiently for next week's installment not to be sure of the worst. Ten short cliffhangers (though in some cases the drop is modest), ten contemporary authors (counting the false Calvino), ten titles, ten manners somehow familiar to the ear but by no means parodistic. The confusion begins with a rather common binder's error, always maddening to the innocent purchaser. By a duplication of "signatures" —as printer's folded sheets of multiples of four are called—after page 32 the bound copy of *If on a winter's nigh*t, instead of going on to page 33, jumps back to page 17, repeating the sequence 17–32, and then, as really can happen, does it *again*, with the awful effect of eternity or of a stuck phonograph needle.

With the second chapter it is the next morning and we are back in the bookstore; the Reader cannot wait to return his defective copy and have it replaced so that he can get on with the story. There, between two rows of bookshelves, among the Penguin Modern Classics, he meets the Other Reader, by name Ludmilla, who has come on the same errand. The bookseller has been telling her, and now he tells the Reader, that unfortunately the signatures of the Calvino book got mixed up at the binder's with those of a Polish book, *Outside the town of Malbork*, by Tazio Bazakbal, so that the Calvino is being withdrawn temporarily from circulation with the publisher's apologies. By luck, though, the bookseller, having checked his stock, finds he has a few sound copies of If on a winter's night, which he can offer the two disappointed readers. But on the joint realization that it was the Polish book they had started on the previous night, they decline the Calvino. It is the Bazakbal they are now eager to finish.

The Reader goes home with the fresh volume, exhilarated by the thought that he will have a companion in his reading, with whom he can compare notes: he has taken her telephone number. The pages this time are uncut, and he arms himself with a paper knife to hack his way through the new obstacle to his impatience. But he has not advanced a page before it is evident that this is not the book he began yesterday. That one took place in a railroad station, and this one is on a farm, seemingly in Central Europe. The style is quite different too: the other was foggy; this is clear-cut and precise, each character being promptly defined by an attribute, such as gnawed nails, or an implement, like a butter curler, that he is handling.

It is the wrong book but it is a book. The Reader reads on. Soon the story begins to absorb him, even though the names of places and people do not sound particularly Polish, which is odd. And then, as his knife goes ahead mechanically cutting, far more swiftly than he is able to read, his eyes suddenly come upon two blank sheets. Then two printed pages. That is how the book continues: an alternation of blank pages and printed pages. Those binders again. And that is not all. The more he considers the bit he has read of Outside the town of Malbork, the more he is persuaded that it has nothing to do with Poland. The names of a river and a town and the consultation of an atlas suggest that it is set in a locality called Cimmeria, identified by Homer (Odyssey XI, 12–19) as a region of perpetual mist and darkness. And, as if this were not enough, when he telephones the Other Reader to hear whether her copy is the same, the voice that answers is different from hers. It is her sister speaking, a left-winger and feminist, named Lotaria.

There is no halting these metamorphoses; the book has taken on the extensible form of a telescope, with one part sliding into the next. Cimmerian, a modern language which has the distinction of being a dead language at the same time, is guarded by a mild dragon, Professor Uzzi-Tuzii, from infiltration by Cimbrian, spoken by a neighboring people who after the Second World War annexed Cimmeria and became the Cimbric People's Republic. *Outside the town of Malbork* proves to really be *Leaning from the steep slope*, the masterpiece of Ukko Ahti, a Cimmerian author of the first quarter of the century. The fragment Professor Uzzi-Tuzii is reading aloud to the two Readers, translating from the original as he goes, is unfortunately all we possess of Ahti's fictional work, so highly representative of Cimmerian literature. Upon finishing the first pages, the writer went into a deep depression and succeeded in taking his own life.

Now Professor Uzzi-Tuzii's little sanctum, already overcrowded with books, is invaded by Lotaria, insisting that the writing is not Cimmerian but Cimbrian. Moreover it is not unfinished. The title was later changed, and it was signed with a different pseudonym, that of Vorts Viljandi, a "complex personality" who wrote in both tongues. At this very moment the entire work is scheduled for analysis and debate by Lotaria's seminar on the feminist revolution, led by Uzzi-Tuzii's rival, Professor Galligani. As Ludmilla and the Reader take their places at a classroom table, Lotaria is holding a bundle of manuscript, *Without fear of wind or vertigo* (the true, post-revolutionary title), from which she will read aloud to the study group in a German translation.

Like each earlier attempt, the session with Lotaria's study group ends unsatisfactorily; as she cuts the reading short, to open the floor for discussion, she dismisses the Reader's plea to look at the rest. "The rest? . . . Oh, there's enough material here to discuss for a month. Aren't you satisfied?" Giving up on the University, the Reader decides to resort to the publisher of the initial defective volumes. There he is turned over to a Mr. Cavedagna, the house's pacifier and problem solver, a little man shrunken and bent, familiar with the complaints of the trade, who leaps to the natural conclusion that the Reader is a writer, whose problem he knows: "You've come about your manuscript?"

In his relief at finding a Reader, so rare nowadays, where he had feared a writer, more and more a drug on the market, the small Dickensian being, himself an escapee from a library shelf, becomes genuinely expansive; for once he can be an open book. Behind the unhappy mixup of the signatures, he explains, lay a villain of a translator, a certain Ermes Marana, doubling as a literary agent, who has been selling the firm a succession of specious foreign novels which he purports to have translated, covering his tracks when suspicion arises by a bewildering series of substitutions.

Thus the Cimbrian or possibly Cimmerian novel by Ukko Ahti was really the so-called Polish novel or can it be vice versa? This impudent sleight of hand, these brazen impostures might have gone on till infinity had it not finally appeared that the swindler did not know a word of those languages; he had merely inserted some appropriate proper names in a trashy text entitled *Looks down in the gathering shadow* that he had plagiarized from a little-known Belgian author, Bertrand Vandervelde. As a proof of confidence, Mr. Cavedagna offers the Reader photocopies of the opening pages of the real French text to look through in the office. It is a gangland story, a novel of the *milieu*; the "I" or reader-surrogate is a retired mobster who has gone into the tropical fish business in the Parisian *banlieue* and is at present having a hard time disposing of the dead body of "Jojo," a former associate.

We are now at the sixth chapter, almost halfway through. These numbered chapters, which at first seemed to be mere bridges leading to the narratives proper, are growing longer and more substantial, generating a suspense of their own, spinning their own plot. Around the Reader and the Other Reader, an independent cast of characters has been assembling: the two professors, Lotaria and her Amazons, Mr. Cavedagna, and now, just when he was needed, a villain, the *traduttore-traditore* of ancient ill repute, Ermes Marana, whose first name seems to link him with the god of thieves. And in the wake of the villain, coolly introduced by him in a series of letters to the publishing house, appears the mythic hero, a Celt of superhuman stature.

Meet Silas Flannery, author of innumerable best sellers that girdle the globe; a Zeus of the realm of book production; legitimate successor to the old titan, creator of James Bond; at present residing on a mountaintop in Switzerland while in the grip of a majestic writing block, on a scale suitable to his fame and his royalties as well as the Alpine scenery. This sunlike figure's momentary (it is hoped) eclipse is spreading grief and terror among publishers, agents, banks, advertising firms, sponsors of the brands of liquor to be drunk by his characters, the fashions they are to wear, the tourist spots they are to visit, all stipulated by contract and now in jeopardy. Not solely the powerful corporate giants of the West but the infant economies of small developing countries expecting to be "put on the map" by a brief stopover of the old Irish author's imaginative progeny on their beaches or coral reefs. As in the case of Demeter grieving for Persephone, a whole world or, rather, industry is in mourning for the stricken creator who does nothing but write in a diary and observe through a spyglass a young woman in a deck chair on a terrace at the bottom of the valley who is reading a book.

Our first acquaintance with Silas Flannery (other than the gossip relayed by Ermes) is made through a text, *In a network of lines that enlace*. The "I" of the narrative is an elderly jogger, a visiting professor at an unnamed university who, if I am not mistaken, has some of the lineaments of Nabokov's Kinbote. It is only a shadow, though, as one might say "Shades of Charles Kinbote," or, as the words "Belgian," "Bernadette," "Jojo," in conjunction with the previous narrative, make one wonder whether a cloud called Simenon has not passed overhead. There is no question, I repeat, of parodies here. There are faint resemblances, delicate reminders, some so evanescent that they

cannot be pinned down to any one author or even school (why do I
sense that Ukko Ahti has something to do with Hungarian literature
or just with the way Hungarians *talk* about Hungarian literature?),
while others, for instance the Japanese novel, *On the carpet of leaves
illuminated by the moon*, do seem to represent a whole distinct class
of book. That "magic" effect, however, as Calvino (the real one)
modestly lets us see, is produced by the manipulation of certain key
words such as ginkgo tree, moon, water lily, leaves, and certain stage
properties such as sukiyaki and the kimono.

In general, though, what we are offered is ten volatile distillations
of the novelistic essence bottled in ten diverse scent containers. The
little narratives are evocative in the same way as the white butterfly
that flies across the valley from the book page the young woman is
reading to alight on the page Silas Flannery is writing. What makes
the white butterfly so poignant? What does it evoke? Literature, I
suppose, because it is softly telling us that it is an author's device, a
symbol; we are given an almost stolen glimpse of the author putting
in a symbol. But, beyond symbolizing a symbol, it also evokes the
errant, fluttery nature of communication, the perishability of message
and messenger (it is an ephemerid), and conceivably the old lepi-
dopterist, Nabokov, still haunting the Swiss peaks and valleys where
he spent his last years. Yet if there is such an allusion it is less an
omaggio dell'autore than a smiling acknowledgment of a presence.

A presence that in my opinion is wrongly evoked in connection
with Italo Calvino, even though I have just been guilty of doing so, led
on by the white butterfly. In the first place, I cannot escape the feeling
that Calvino is no admirer of Nabokov, who likes to treat the reader
as an adversary in a one-way hide-and-seek game. In the second
place, I can see no influences at all at work on "the new Calvino,"
even of writers he has quoted admiringly in his critical prose, no literary genetic imprint, no trace of Borges, for example; if there is a
hereditary line to be found, it winds back, surely, to the Orient, where

all tales come from. There is an overall congeniality with Queneau, but that is a matter of a shared playfulness, on the one hand, and a shared interest, on the other, in the possibility of literature as a semi-mathematical science, with laws to be detected.

In any case, we get to know Silas Flannery through the narrative of the old jogger, and, when we get to know him in person in Chapter 8, which is composed of extracts from his diary, we can distinguish autobiographical elements, quite recent ones, in *In a network of lines that enlace* having to do with "forgetting himself" in the presence of young women. And this in turn allows us to distinguish the real Silas Flannery from the false one; there are *two* sets of pages signed with his name, the second, *In a network of lines that intersect*, being the handiwork of his devilish counterfeiter, Ermes Marana.

When we examine the counterfeit, a curious literary phenomenon comes to light. If embarrassing autobiographical elements, creeping into the first fragment, seem to vouch for its authenticity, the counter-feit reveals itself as such in a not dissimilar fashion: the personality of its true author has "bled" into the work, which is volubly preoccu-pied with kaleidoscopes, with the "polydyptic theatre" (in which numerous small mirrors lining a large box turn a bough into a forest, a lead soldier into an army, and so on), and finally with a financial empire based on catoptrics, i.e., done with mirrors. In these involun-tary revelations we are encountering the phenomenon known to medicine as ecchymosis (to use a Calvino-like word): an oozing of blood into the tissues as the result of a bruise. In other words, the wound and the bow. Ermes Marana's obsession with the dark arts of imitation, seeping into *In a network of lines that intersect*, betrays it as a forgery, just as in the old jogger's fragment a misfired pass made at a girl student proves (unless we have to do with a very clever and knowledgeable copyist) that it is a genuine Flannery. Thus a work can be "read" as an Identikit portrait of the author lurking inside it, unaware of giving himself away.

Of course there is nothing really new here. This kind of literary detection was initiated many years ago by Miss Caroline Spurgeon, who was the first to count the images in Shakespeare's plays, paving the way for a deconstruction of Shakespeare's own image ("Others abide our question,/Thou smilest and art still") as a deep, fathomless person. And it was early in the century when Freud induced Leonardo to betray his secret. These are all modes of "reading" that many of our contemporaries vastly prefer to the older, "passive" kind. Lotaria, as a matter of fact, is still working the Spurgeon territory, drawing up lists of words used in a given novel or group of novels in the order of the frequency of their occurrence; her computer has proved invaluable to her in her labors, whose purpose is to catalog novels in terms of atmosphere, mood, social background, and so on, thereby eliminating the wastefulness inherent in traditional reading habits. She is writing her thesis on Flannery, who finds himself unnerved by the prospect, unable to write a word in case it be "counted" against him by the electronic brain.

Meanwhile, in the seventh chapter, we have come upon a fresh kind of reading. The Reader, invited by Ludmilla to wait for her at her apartment, is seen "reading" the apartment in order to read Ludmilla. Nothing of course is more common. Who has not "read" a house, a set of bookshelves, a medicine cabinet, in the owner's absence? It is true that the objects in Ludmilla's house—or anyone else's—are "elements of a discourse." But with this reading of Ludmilla's house something different is starting to happen. This is at once felt by the pronouns, which suddenly shift places. Here at Ludmilla's, the "You" familiarly addressed is no longer the Reader; it is Ludmilla. "Calvino" is now speaking to her directly, over the head of the Reader, who has become a "he," that is, almost an intruder. And this reversal of the pronouns presages another, sweeter event. Before you can say Jack Robinson, they are in bed together, having metamorphosed into a "You," second-person plural, a single two-headed "*Voi*," two young heads on a pillow. And now half this plural is "reading" Ludmilla's body, her fleshly envelope, as, before she came home, for want of better, he was reading every crevice of the container that is her apartment. And Ludmilla is reviewing *his* body but more cursorily "as if skimming the index." The plot has thickened.

Separation, naturally, follows. He travels to Switzerland to find Silas Flannery. We learn of his visit from entries in Flannery's diary—another mold in which the traditional novel may be cast; we have already had the epistolary form in Marana's letters to the publisher. From the diary too, we learn of another of Marana's diabolical machinations—his arrangement with a Japanese combine to pirate Silas Flannery's complete works. Not exactly pirate, though—copy the model, using native workmanship. As Marana has explained to the old writer, "the great skill of the Japanese in manufacturing perfect facsimiles of Western products has spread to literature." Without revealing his own part in the fraud, he shows Flannery a book signed "Flannery" that Flannery has never written; a firm in Osaka has managed to get hold of the formula. Now the flood of imitations retranslated—or, rather, translated—into English will be indistinguishable from his personal output.

It is a nice touch that the Japanese novel that takes up the next pages should be, if not a perfect facsimile, at least a fair imitation of one, plausible enough to pass inspection in a drugstore paperback rack. Only two more samples remain to be exhibited. The Reader and the Other Reader after a number of vicissitudes are about to be reunited. We readers have seen pass in review, like a series of floats, to our cries of delight and recognition, a parade of the types and varieties of narrative experience, many of them in native costume with flags borne by persons having names like Ponko and Arkadian Porphyrich.

It is better than a parade. It is a *summa fictionis* of scholastic rigor and, like all glorious codifications of divine mysteries, it has to do with love. The act of reading, when finally consummated, is seen to be parallel to the act of love. And at the same time, lest the foregoing seem too awesome for a book so sweet-natured and shyly merry, there is something here suggestive of an old-fashioned small-town garage (maybe an old Fiat place) with a car inside that has the hood up and a jack or so underneath. An inventor in a white coat, the top mechanic, is lovingly tinkering with it, tuning the engine and listening like a doctor. Just about every part of it is worn out and begging for replacement. It is a lovely piece of junk. And yet when the inventor shuts down the hood and takes his place at the wheel of the contraption, removing his white coat (or maybe he is wearing a white short-sleeved jumpsuit), it actually moves, responding to the slightest touch of the accelerator pedal. And what does it run *on*? I think it must run on suspense, an organic natural product that nobody, not even (so far) our inventor, can tell us much about. If I can try to read his mind, I will say that, in the formula for suspense tentatively set out there, one should find at least three parts sex.

—*June 25, 1981*

16

THE FACT IN FICTION

I AM SCHEDULED, I find, to talk to you about "Problems of Writing a Novel." Where this title originated no one seems to know—doubtless in the same bureau that supplies titles for schoolchildren's compositions: "How I Spent My Summer Vacation" or "Adventures of a Penny" or simply "Why?" The problems of writing a novel, to those who do not write, can be reduced to the following questions: "Do you write in longhand or on the typewriter?" "Do you use an outline or do you invent as you go along?" "Do you draw your characters from real life or do you make them up or are they composites?" "Do you start with an idea, a situation, or a character?" "How many hours a day do you spend at your desk?" "Do you write on Sundays?" "Do you revise as you go along or finish a whole draft first?" And, finally, "Do you use a literary agent or do you market your stuff yourself?" Here curiosity fades; the manufacture and marketing of the product complete the story of a process, which is not essentially different from the "story" of flour as demonstrated to a class of boys and girls on an educational trip through a flour mill (from the grain of wheat to the sack on the grocer's shelf) or the "story" of a bottle of claret or of a

---

This is a paraphrase of a talk or talks given to Polish, Yugoslav, and British audiences in the winter of 1960.

brass safety pin. This is the craft of fiction, insofar as it interests the outsider, who may line up, after a lecture like this, to get the author's autograph, in lieu of a free sample—a miniature bottle of wine or a card of "baby" safety pins.

Now I am not going to talk about the problems of the novel in this sense at all but rather to confront the fact that the writing of a novel has become problematic today. Is it still possible to write novels—in longhand or on the typewriter, standing or sitting, on Sundays or weekdays, with or without an outline? The answer, it seems to me, is certainly not yes and perhaps, tentatively, no. I mean real novels—not fairy tales or fables or romances or *contes philosophiques*, and I mean novels of a high order, like *War and Peace* or *Middlemarch* or *Ulysses* or the novels of Dickens, Dostoevsky, or Proust. The manufacture of second-rate novels, or, rather, of facsimiles of the novel, is in no state of crisis; nor is there a difficulty in marketing them, with or without an agent. But almost no writer in the West of any consequence, let us say since the death of Thomas Mann, has been able to write a true novel; the exception is Faulkner, who is now an old man. What was the last novel, not counting Faulkner, that was written in our day? *Ulysses? Man's Fate?* Camus's *The Stranger?* Someone might say *Lolita*, and perhaps it is a novel, a freak, though, a sport or wild mutation, which everyone approaches with suspicion, as if it were a dangerous conundrum, a Sphinx's riddle.

What do I mean by a "novel"? A prose book of a certain thickness that tells a story of real life. No one could disagree with that, and yet many will disagree with much that I am going to say before I am through, so I shall try to be more specific. The words "prose" and "real" are crucial to my conception of the novel. The distinctive mark of the novel is its concern with the actual world, the world of fact, of the verifiable, of figures, even, and statistics. If I point to Jane Austen, Dickens, Balzac, George Eliot, Tolstoy, Dostoevsky, the Melville of *Moby Dick*, Proust, the Joyce of *Ulysses*, Dreiser, Faulkner, it will be admitted that they are all novelists and that, different as they are from a formal point of view, they have one thing in common: a deep love of fact, of the empiric element in experience. I am not interested in making a formal definition of the novel (it is really a very loose affair, a grab bag or portmanteau, as someone has said) but in finding its *quidditas* or whatness, the essence or binder that distinguishes it from other species of prose fiction: the tale, the fable, the romance. The staple ingredient present in all novels in various mixtures and proportions but always in fairly heavy dosage is fact.

If a criterion is wanted for telling a novel from a fable or a tale or a romance (or a drama), a simple rule of thumb would be the absence of the supernatural. In fables and fairy tales, as everyone knows, birds and beasts talk. In novels, they don't; if you find birds and beasts talking in a book you are reading you can be sure it is not a novel. That takes care, for example, of *Animal Farm*. Men in novels may behave like beasts, but beasts in novels may not behave like men. That takes care of *Gulliver's Travels*, in case anyone were to mistake it for a novel. The characters in a novel must obey the laws of nature. They cannot blow up or fly or rise from the dead, as they can in plays, and if they talk to the devil, like Ivan Karamazov, the devil, though he speaks French, is not real like Faust's Mephistopheles, but a product of Ivan's derangement or fissionization. The devil is a part of Ivan. In the same way, in Mann's *Dr. Faustus*, the devil is no longer a member of the cast of characters but resident, you might say, in the fatal spirochete or syphilis germ. This is not a difference in period; Goethe did not believe in real devils either, but he could put one on the stage, because the stage accepts devils and even has a trapdoor ready for them to disappear through, with a flash of brimstone, just as it used to have a machine, up in the flies, for the gods to descend from. There are no gods in the novel and no machinery for them; to speak, even metaphorically, of a *deus ex machina* in a novel—that is, of the entrance of a providential figure from above—is to imply a shortcoming; Dickens is always criticized on this score. But a tale almost requires the appearance of a *deus ex machina* or magic helper. The devil can appear in person in a tale of Hawthorne's like "Young Goodman Brown," but not in Hawthorne's novel *The Scarlet Letter*, though he may be there in spirit.

The novel does not permit occurrences outside the order of nature —miracles. Mr. Krook's going up in spontaneous combustion in his junkshop is a queer Punch-and-Judy note in *Bleak House*. Actually, Dickens thought science had found out that people could explode of their own force, but now it seems that they can't, that Mr. Krook couldn't; it would be all right in a fantasy or a pantomime but not in a novel. You remember how in *The Brothers Karamazov* when Father Zossima dies, his faction (most of the sympathetic characters in the book) expects a miracle: that his body will stay sweet and fresh because he died "in the odor of sanctity." But instead he begins to stink. The stink of Father Zossima is the natural, generic smell of the novel.

By the same law, a novel cannot be laid in the future, since the future, until it happens, is outside the order of nature; no prophecy or cautionary tale like *1984* is a novel. It is the same with public events in the past that never happened, for example the mutiny at the end of World War I led by a Christ-like corporal in Faulkner's *A Fable*; the title is Faulkner's warning to his readers that this volume, unlike his "regular" books, is not to be considered a novel but something quite different. Because the past appears, through recession, to be outside the order of nature (think how improbable and ghostly old photographs look), most historical novels, so-called, are romances, not novels: George Eliot's *Romola* in contrast to *Middlemarch*. This rule is broken by Tolstoy's *War and Peace*, a novel if there ever was one, and the reason for this is that history, as it were, has been purged by Tolstoy's harsh and critical realism of all "historical" elements—the flummery of costume, makeup, and accessories and the myths and lies of historians. The time, moreover (his grandfather's day), was not very remote from Tolstoy's own. When he experimented with writing a novel about the days of Ivan the Terrible, he found he could not do it. A borderline case is Stendhal's *The Charterhouse of Parma*, where actual history (Napoleon's entry into Milan; the Battle of Waterloo, so much admired by Tolstoy) is succeeded by mock history—the spurious history of Parma, complete with numbered despots, prisons, and paid assassins, a travesty invented by Stendhal to correspond with the (literally) travestied Fabrizio in his violet stockings and with the mock heroics of this section of the book. The book is a novel that turns into parody at the moment that history, in Stendhal's opinion, ceased to make sense and turned into a parody of the past. That moment was the triumph of reaction in Europe after 1815.

I ought to make it clear that these distinctions are in no way pejorative; I do not mean "Novel good, fable bad," merely "Novel novel; fable fable." *Candide* is not a novel, but to say so is not a criticism of *Candide*. Indeed, there are certain masterpieces—*Rameau's Nephew*, Gogol's *Dead Souls*, *The Charterhouse of Parma* itself—so quicksilver in their behavior that it is impossible to catch them in a category; these are usually "destructive" books, like *Candide*, where the author's aim is, among other things, to elude the authorities' grasp. When people nowadays tell you something is "not a novel," as they are fond of saying, for instance, about *Dr. Zhivago*, it is always in a querulous tone, as though someone had tried to put something over on them, sell them the Empire State Building or Trajan's Monument or the Palace of Culture, when *they* know better; they were not born yesterday. That is not my intention; I am not speaking as an aggrieved consumer of modern literature (and I admire *Dr. Zhivago* too passionately to demand its identity papers before I will let it pass); I am only trying to see why a special kind of literature, a relatively new kind, what we call the novel, is disappearing from view. To do that, I must know what the novel is; it is like advertising for a missing person; first you need a description of what he looked like when last seen.

Let me begin with the birthmarks. The word "novel" goes back to the word "new," and in the plural it used to mean news—the news of the day or the year. Literary historians find the seed or the germ of the novel in Boccaccio's *Decameron*, a collection of tales set in a frame of actual life. This frame of actual life was the Great Plague of 1348 as it affected the city of Florence, where more than a hundred thousand people died between March and August. The figures and dates come from *The Decameron*, along with a great deal of other factual information about the Black Death: its origin in the East, some years before; its primary and secondary symptoms, differing from those in the East; the time between the appearance of the first symptoms—the tumors or buboes in the groin or armpits, some the size of a common apple, some of an egg, some larger, some smaller—and the onset of death; the means of contagion; the sanitary precautions taken; the medical theories current as to the proper diet and mode of life to stave off infection; the modes of nursing; the rites and methods of burial; and, finally, the moral behavior (very bad) of the citizens of Florence during the scourge. Boccaccio's account is supposed to be a pioneer contribution to descriptive medicine; it is also a piece of eyewitness journalism, not unlike the Younger Pliny's account of the eruption of Mount Vesuvius; the difference is that Pliny wrote his report in a letter (a classic literary form) and that Boccaccio's report is used in a new way, as a setting for a collection of fictions. The "realism," also new, of the separate tales, is grounded, so to speak, in the journalistic frame, with the dateline of a certain Tuesday morning, of the year 1348, when seven young ladies, between the ages of eighteen and twenty-eight, and three young men, the youngest twenty-five, met in the Church of Santa Maria Novella.

If Boccaccio is the ancestor, the "father of the modern novel" is supposed to be Defoe, a Grub Street journalist, and the author of *Robinson Crusoe, Moll Flanders*, and many other works, including *A Journal of the Plague Year* (not Boccaccio's; another one—1664–1665).

Robinson Crusoe was based on "a real-life story," of a round-the-world voyage, which he heard described by the returned traveler and which he pieced out with another, a written account. Not only was the "father of the modern novel" a journalist, but he did not distinguish, at least to his readers, between journalism and fiction. All his stories pretend to be factual reports, documents, and one perhaps is— the life of a famous criminal "as told to Daniel Defoe," i.e., ghost-written. This pretense, which might be called the reverse of plagiarism, the disclaiming, that is, of authorship rather than the claiming of it, was not a special pathological kink of Defoe's. The novel in its early stages almost always purports to be true. Where a fairy tale begins, "Once upon a time, in a certain kingdom," a tale of Boccaccio (chosen at random) begins: "You must know that after the death of Emperor Frederick II, the crown of Sicily passed to Manfred, whose favor was enjoyed to the highest degree by a gentleman of Naples, Arrighetto Capece by name, who had to wife Madonna Beritola Caracciola, a fair and gracious lady, likewise a Neapolitan. Now when Manfred was conquered and slain by King Charles I at Benevento . . . Arrighetto, etc., etc. . . . ." The effect of this naming and placing makes of every story of Boccaccio's a sort of deposition, and this is even truer when the sphere is less exalted and the place is a neighboring village and the hero a well-known lecherous priest.

Many of the great novelists were newspaper reporters or journalists. Dickens had been a parliamentary reporter as a young man; in middle age, he became a magazine editor, and the scent of a "news story" is keen in all his novels. Dostoevsky, with his brother, edited two different magazines, one of which was called *Time* (*Vremya*); he supplied them with fiction and feature stories, and his specialty, you might say, was police reporting—he visited suspects (usually female) in prison, interviewed them, and wrote up his impressions; he also reported trials. Victor Hugo too was a confirmed prison-visitor; his "impressions" of prisons and of current political events—demonstrations, tumults, street fighting—are collected in *Choses vues*. Tolstoy first became widely known through his reports from Sebastopol, where he was serving as a young officer in the Crimean War; he was telling the news, the true, uncensored story of the Siege of Sebastopol, to the civilians back home, and throughout Tolstoy's work, most noticeably in *War and Peace* but in fact everywhere, there is heard the scathing directness of the young officer's tone, calling attention to the real facts behind the official dispatches—the real facts of war, sex, family life, glory, love, death. As he wrote in his second sketch from Sebastopol (which was immediately suppressed by the tsar), "The hero of my story...is—the Truth." Coming to the twentieth century, you meet the American novelist as newspaperman: Dreiser, Sinclair Lewis, Hemingway, O'Hara, Faulkner himself. The American novelist as newspaperman, in the Twenties, became a stock figure in the American myth, so much so that the terms could be inverted and every obscure newspaperman, according to popular belief, had in his desk drawer, besides a pint of whiskey, the great American novel he was writing in his spare time.

There is another kind of "fact" literature closely related to the novel, and that is the travel book, which tells the news of the exotic. Melville's first book, *Typee*, was a book of travel, and you find something of the travelogue in Conrad, Kipling, and a good deal of D. H. Lawrence: *Aaron's Rod*, *The Plumed Serpent*, *Kangaroo*, "The Woman Who Rode Away." There is very little difference, really, between *Kangaroo*, a novel about Australia, and *Sea and Sardinia*, a travel book about Lawrence himself and Frieda in Sardinia. Hemingway remains half a war correspondent and half an explorer; *The Green Hills of Africa* is his "straight" travel book. The type seems to go back to *Robinson Crusoe*; most of Conrad's heroes, one could say, are stranded Robinson Crusoes, demoralized by consciousness. In a more conventional way, Dickens, Stendhal, Henry James all published journals of travel—"impressions." Mark Twain, Henry Miller, George Orwell (*Down and Out in Paris and London*, *Shooting an Elephant*)

—the list is even more arresting if you consider the theatre and try to imagine Ibsen, Shaw, or O'Neill as the authors of travel books. Yet Ibsen spent years abroad, in Italy and Germany, and O'Neill, like Melville and Conrad, went to sea as a young man.

The passion for fact in a raw state is a peculiarity of the novelist. Most of the great novels contain blocks and lumps of fact—refractory lumps in the porridge of the story. Students often complain of this in the old novels. They skip these "boring parts" to get on with the story, and in America a branch of publishing specializes in shortened versions of novels—"cut for greater reading speed." Descriptions and facts are eliminated, and only the pure story, as it were the scenario, is left. But a novel that was only a scenario would not be a novel at all.

Everyone knows that Balzac was a lover of fact. He delighted in catalogs of objects, inventories, explanations of the way institutions and industries work, how art is collected, political office is bought, fortunes are amassed or hoarded. One of his novels, *Les Illusions perdues*, has a chapter which simply describes the way paper is made. The chapter has nothing to do with the action of the novel (it comes in because the hero has inherited a paper factory); Balzac put it in because he happened at the time to know something about the paper business. He loved facts of every kind indiscriminately—straight facts, curious facts, quirks, oddities, aberrations of fact, figures, statistics. He collected them and stored them, like one of his own misers, intending to house them in that huge structure, *The Human Comedy*, which is at once a scale model of the real world and a museum of curios left to mankind as though by a crazy hermit who could never throw anything away.

This fetishism of fact is generally treated as a sort of disease of realism of which Balzac was the prime clinical exhibit. But this is not the case. You find the splendid sickness in realists and nonrealists alike. *Moby Dick*, among other things, is a compendium of everything that was to be known about whaling. The chapters on the whale and on whiteness, which are filled with curious lore, truths that are "stranger than fiction," interrupt and "slow down" the narrative, like the excursus on paper. Yet they cannot be taken away (as the excursus on paper certainly could be) without damaging the novel; *Moby Dick* without these chapters (in the stage and screen versions) is not *Moby Dick*. Or think of the long chapter on the Russian monk in *The Brothers Karamazov*. Father Zossima is about to enter the scene, and, before introducing him, Dostoevsky simply stops and writes a history of the role of the elder in Russian monasticism. In the same way, in *War and Peace*, when Pierre gets interested in Freemasonry, Tolstoy stops and writes an account of the Masonic movement, for which he had been boning up in the library. Everyone who has read *War and Peace* remembers the Battle of Borodino, the capture and firing of Moscow, the analysis of the character of Napoleon, the analysis of the causes of war, and the great chapter on Freedom and Necessity, all of which are nonfiction and which constitute the very terrain of the novel; indeed, it could be said that the real plot of *War and Peace* is the struggle of the characters not to be immersed, engulfed, swallowed up by the landscape of fact and "history" in which they, like all human beings, have been placed: freedom (the subjective) is in the fiction, and necessity is in the fact. I have already mentioned the first chapter of *The Charterhouse of Parma* describing Napoleon's entry into Milan. In *The Magic Mountain*, there are the famous passages on tuberculosis, recalling Boccaccio's description of the plague, and the famous chapter on time, a philosophical excursus like the chapter on whiteness in *Moby Dick* and the chapter on Freedom and Necessity in Tolstoy. Closer to Balzac is Dreiser's picture of the hotel business in *An American Tragedy*; when Clyde becomes a bellhop, Dreiser (though this is not "important" to the story) stops and shows the reader how a hotel, behind the scenes, works.

In newspaper jargon, you might call all this the boilerplate of the novel—durable informative matter set up in stereotype and sold to country newspapers as filler to eke out a scarcity of local news, i.e., of "plot." And the novel, like newspaper boilerplate, contains not only a miscellany of odd facts but household hints and how-to-do-it instructions (you can learn how to make strawberry jam from *Anna Karenina* and how to reap a field and hunt ducks).

The novel, to repeat, has or had many of the functions of a newspaper. Dickens's novels can be imagined in terms of headlines: "Antique Dealer Dies by Spontaneous Combustion in Shop," "Financial Wizard Falls, Panic Among Speculators," "Blackleg Miner Found Dead in Quarry." Henry James, who did his best to exclude every bit of boilerplate from his books and who may have killed the novel, perhaps with kindness (consider the unmentionable small article manufactured by the Newsomes in *The Ambassadors*; what was it? Garters? Safety pins?), even James has the smell of newsprint about him, the smell of the Sunday supplement. His international plots recall the magazine section of the old Hearst newspaper chain, in which every Sunday, after church, Americans used to read about some international marriage between an American heiress and a titled fortune-hunter: Anna Gould and Count Boni de Castellane.

Novels, including James's, carried the news—of crime, high society, politics, industry, finance, and low life. In Dickens you find a journalistic coverage of the news on all fronts and a survey of all the professions from pickpocket to banker, from lawyer to grave-robber. His books tell the whole story of Victorian society, from the front page to the financial section. This ideal of coverage requires him, in fairness, to print, as it were, corrections; a bad Jew is followed by a good Jew, a bad lawyer by a good one, a bad school by a good one, and so on. Or, to put it another way, it is as though he were launching a great roomy Noah's ark with two of each species of creation aboard. In a single book, *Middlemarch*, George Eliot "covers" English life and institutions, as found at their median point—a middling provincial town. The notion of coverage by professions was taken up, somewhat mechanically, by the American novelists Dreiser and Sinclair Lewis. You can hear it in Dreiser's titles: *The Titan*, *The Financier*, *The Genius*, *Twelve Men*. Lewis ticked off the housewife (*Main Street*), the realtor (*Babbitt*), the scientist (*Arrowsmith*), the preacher (*Elmer Gantry*), the social worker (*Ann Vickers*), the retired businessman (*Dodsworth*). A similar census, though of more mobile social types, is seen in Dos Passos. It is Faulkner, however, the most "mythic" of recent American novelists, who has documented a society more completely than any of the realists. Like Dickens, he has set himself the task of a Second Creation. Yoknapatawpha County (capital, Jefferson), Mississippi, is presided over by its courthouse (*Requiem for a Nun*), where its history and vital statistics are on file; we know its population of lawyers, storekeepers, businessmen, farmers, black and white, and their forebears and how they made or lost their money; we know its idiots and criminals and maniacs, its geology and geography, flora and fauna (the bear of that story and the cow of *The Hamlet*); some editions of Faulkner include a map of Yoknapatawpha County, and a letter addressed to Faulkner at Jefferson, Mississippi, would almost certainly reach him, although there is no such place.

The more poetic a novel, the more it has the air of being a factual document. I exaggerate when I say this, but if you think of Faulkner, of *Moby Dick*, of *Madame Bovary* or Proust, you will see there is something in it. Joyce's *Ulysses* is a case in point. There is no doubt that Joyce intended to reconstruct, almost scientifically, twenty-four hours of a certain day in Dublin; the book, among other things, is an exercise in mnemonics. Stephen and Mr. Bloom, in their itineraries, cover certain key points in the life of the city—the beach, the library, the graveyard, the cabman's stand, Nighttown—and a guide to Joyce's Dublin has been published, with maps and a key. Nor is it by chance that the peripatetic Mr. Bloom is an advertising *canvasser*. He travels back and forth and up and down in society like Ulysses, who explored the four corners of the known world. The epic, I might put in here, is the form of all literary forms closest to the novel; it has the "boiler-plate," the lists and catalogs, the circumstantiality, the concern with numbers and dimensions. The epic geography, like that of the novel, can be *mapped*, in both the physical and the social sense.

This clear locative sense is present in all true novels. Take Jane Austen. *Emma* and *Pride and Prejudice* contain few facts of the kind I have been speaking of—nothing like the paper business or the history of the Russian monk. Yet there are facts of a different sort, documents like Mr. Collins's letters, charades, riddles, menus, dance programs ("'Then the two third he danced with Miss King, and the two fourth with Maria Lucas, and the two fifth with Jane again, and the two sixth with Lizzy, and the *Boulanger*—'")—feminine facts, so to speak—and a very painstaking census-taking of a genteel class within the confines of a certain income range, marked off, like a frontier. One difference between Jane Austen and Henry James is that the reader of *Pride and Prejudice* knows exactly how much money the characters have: Mr. Bingley has four or five thousand a year (with a capital of nearly one hundred thousand); Mr. Bennet has two thousand a year, ENTAILED, while Mrs. Bennet brought him a capital of four thousand from her father, an attorney at Meryton; Mr. Darcy has ten thousand a year; his sister, Georgiana, has a capital of thirty thousand. The same with distances, ages, and time. Mr. and Mrs. Bennet have been married twenty-three years; Mrs. Weston, in *Emma*, has been Emma's governess for sixteen years; Mr. Knightley is about seven or eight and thirty; Emma is nearly twenty-one; Jane and Elizabeth, when they are finally married, live thirty miles apart; Highbury is about a mile from Mr. Knightley's property. Whenever the chance arises, Jane Austen supplies a figure. Everything is lucid and perspicuous in her well-charted world, except the weather, which is often unsettled, and this fact too is always noted ("The shower was heavy but short, and it had not been over five minutes when..."). The names of persons who are never seen in the story, like that of "Miss King" just now, are dropped as if artlessly to attest the veracity of the narrative—inviting the reader to clothe these names himself with the common identities of real life.

This air of veracity is very important to the novel. We do really (I think) expect a novel to be true, not only true to itself, like a poem, or a statue, but true to actual life, which is right around the corner, like the figure of "Miss King." We not only make believe we believe a novel, but we do substantially believe it, as being continuous with real life, made of the same stuff, and the presence of fact in fiction, of dates and times and distances, is a kind of reassurance—a guarantee of credibility. If we read a novel, say, about conditions in postwar Germany, we expect it to be an accurate report of conditions in post-war Germany; if we find out that it is not, the novel is discredited. This is not the case with a play or a poem. Dante can be wrong in *The Divine Comedy*; it does not matter, with Shakespeare, that Bohemia has no seacoast, but if Tolstoy was all wrong about the Battle of Borodino or the character of Napoleon, *War and Peace* would suffer.

The presence of a narrator, writing in the first person, is another guarantee of veracity. The narrator is, precisely, an eyewitness, testifying to the reader that these things really happened, even though the reader knows of course that they did not. This is the function of the man called Marlow in Conrad's books; he is there to promise the reader that these faraway stories are true, and, as if Marlow himself were not enough, the author appears as a kind of character witness for Marlow, testifying to having met him in reliable company, over cigars, claret, a polished mahogany table, and so on. The same function is served by the narrator in Dostoevsky's *The Possessed,* who writes in the excited manner of a small-town gossip ("Then I rushed to Varvara Petrovna's") telling you everything that went on in that extraordinary period, which everybody in town is still talking about, that began when young Stavrogin bit the governor's ear. He tells what he saw himself and what he had on hearsay and pretends to sift the collective evidence as to what exactly happened and in what order. Faulkner's favorite narrator is Gavin Stevens, the lawyer, chosen obviously because the town lawyer, accustomed to weighing evidence, would be the most reliable witness—one of the first sources a newspaper reporter sent to do a story on Yoknapatawpha County would be likely to consult.

There is the shadow of an "I" in *The Brothers Karamazov*, but *The Possessed* is the only important novel of Dostoevsky's that is told straight through in the first person, i.e., by a local busybody who seems to have seized the pen. *The Possessed* (in Russian *The Devils*) is the most demonic of all Dostoevsky's novels—the most "unnatural," unfilial, "Gothic." It would seem that the device of the narrator, the eyewitness "I," like Esther Summerson in *Bleak House* (not the autobiographical "I" of *David Copperfield* or of Proust's Marcel, who is something more than a witness), is more often used in novels whose material is exotic or improbable than in the plain novel of ordinary life, like *Middlemarch* or *Emma* or any of Trollope. These novels of ordinary life put no strain on the reader's credulity; he believes without the testimony of witnesses. The first-person narrator is found in Conrad, in Melville, and in *Wuthering Heights*, *Bleak House*, *Jane Eyre*, all of which center around drafty, spooky old houses and are related to the ghost story. In the same way James, who rarely used the first-person narrator, does so with the governess in his ghost story, *The Turn of the Screw*. In other words, on the periphery of the novel, on the borderline of the tale or the adventure story you find a host of narrators. And you arrive, finally, at *Lolita* and meet Humbert Humbert, telling his own story (which you might not have believed otherwise), having been first introduced by another narrator, his "editor," who authenticates his manuscript; Humbert himself has been executed. In short, you are back with Defoe and his "true biographies" of great criminals who were hanged, back at the birth of the novel, before it could stand without support.

Even when it is most serious, the novel's characteristic tone is one of gossip and tittle-tattle. You can hear it in the second sentence (originally the first sentence) of *Anna Karenina*: "Everything was upset at the Oblonskys'." The cook, it seemed, had left; the underservants had given notice; the mistress was shut up in her bedroom because the master had been sleeping with the former French governess. This (I think) is a classic beginning, and yet some person who had never read a novel, coming on those sentences, so full of blunt malice, might conclude that Tolstoy was simply a common scandalmonger. The same might be thought of Dostoevsky, of Flaubert, Stendhal, and (obviously) of Proust, of the earnest George Eliot and the lively Jane Austen and the manly Charles Dickens. Most of these writers were people of high principle; their books, without exception, had a moral, ethical, or educational purpose. But the voice we overhear in their narratives, if we stop to listen for a minute, putting aside preconceptions, is the voice of a neighbor relating the latest gossip. "You will hardly believe what happened next," the novelists from Jane Austen to Kafka (yes indeed) seem to be exclaiming. "Wait and I'll tell you." The whole narrative method of Dostoevsky could be summed up in those two sentences. In Conrad, more ruminative, there can be heard the creaking of chairs as the men around the table settle down to listen to the indefatigable Marlow, who only halts to wet his whistle: "Pass the bottle." The scandals the novelists are primed with are the scandals of a village, a town, or a province—Highbury or Jefferson, Mississippi, or the Province of O——; the scandals of a clique—the Faubourg St. Germain; of a city—Dublin or Middlemarch; or of a nation—Dickens's England; or of the ports and hiring offices—London or Nantucket, where news of the high seas is exchanged and a black mark put against a man's name or a vessel's. Here is another criterion: if the breath of scandal has not touched it, the book is not a novel. That is the trouble with the art novel (most of Virginia Woolf, for instance); it does not stoop to gossip.

The scandals of a village or a province, the scandals of a nation or of the high seas feed on facts and breed speculation. But it is of the essence of a scandal that it be finite, for all its repercussions and successive enlargements. Indeed, its repercussions are like the echo produced in an enclosed space, a chambered world. That is why institutions ("closed corporations") are particularly prone to scandal; they attempt to keep the news in, contain it, and in doing so they magnify it, and then, as people say, "the lid is off." It is impossible, except for theologians, to conceive of a worldwide scandal or a universewide scandal; the proof of this is the way people have settled down to living with nuclear fission, radiation poisoning, hydrogen bombs, satellites, and space rockets. Nobody can get them excited about or even greatly interested in what-will-happen-next to the world; the plot does not thicken. In the same way, Hiroshima, despite the well-meant efforts of journalists and editors, probably caused less stir than the appearance of comets in the past; the magnitude of the event killed even curiosity. This was true, to some extent, of Buchenwald and Auschwitz too.

Yet these "scandals," in the theological sense, of the large world and the universe have dwarfed the finite scandals of the village and the province; who cares any more what happens in Highbury or the Province of O——? If the novelist cares, he blushes for it; that is, he blushes for his parochialism. *Middlemarch* becomes *Middletown* and *Middletown in Transition*, the haunt of social scientists, whose factual findings, even in the face of Auschwitz or a space satellite, have a certain cachet because they are supposed to be "science"; in science, all facts, no matter how trivial or banal, enjoy democratic equality. Among novelists, it is only Faulkner who does not seem to feel an itch of dissatisfaction with his sphere, and there are signs of this even in him—*A Fable*, for example.

But it is not only that the novelist of today, in "our expanding universe," is embarrassed by the insignificance (or lack of "significance") of his finite world. A greater problem is that he cannot quite believe in it. That is, the existence of Highbury or the Province of O—— is rendered improbable, unveracious, by Buchenwald and Auschwitz, the population curve of China, and the hydrogen bomb. Improbable when "you stop to think"; this is the experience of everybody and not only of the novelist; if we stop to think for one second, arrested by some newspaper story or general reflection, our daily life becomes incredible to us. I remember reading the news of Hiroshima in a little general store on Cape Cod in Massachusetts and saying to myself as I moved up to the counter, "What am I doing buying a loaf of bread?" The coexistence of the great world and us, when contemplated, appears impossible.

It works both ways. The other side of the picture is that Buchenwald and Auschwitz are and were unbelievable, and not just to the German people, whom we criticize for forgetting them; we all forget them, as we forget the hydrogen bomb, because their special quality is to stagger belief. And here is the dilemma of the novelist, which is only a kind of professional sub-case of the dilemma of everyone: if he writes about his province, he feels its inverisimilitude; if he tries, on the other hand, to write about people who make lampshades of human skin, like the infamous Ilse Koch, he feels still more the inverisimilitude of what he is asserting. His love of truth revolts. And yet this love of truth, ordinary common truth recognizable to everyone, is the ruling passion of the novel. Putting two and two together, then, it would seem that the novel, with its common sense, is of all forms the least adapted to encompass the modern world, whose leading characteristic is irreality. And that, so far as I can understand, is why the novel is dying. The souped-up novels that are being written today, with injections of myth and symbols to heighten or "deepen" the material, are simply evasions and forms of self-flattery.

I spoke just now of common sense—the prose of the novel. We are all supposed to be born with it, in some degree, but we are also supposed to add to it by experience and observation. But if the world today has become inaccessible to common sense, common sense in terms of broad experience simultaneously has become inaccessible to the writer. The novelists of the nineteenth century had, both as public persons and private figures, great social range; they "knew everybody," whether because of their fame in the great capitals of London, Paris, St. Petersburg, or in their village, province, or county, where everybody knows everybody as a matter of course. Today the writer has become specialized, like the worker on an assembly line whose task is to perform a single action several hundred times a day or the doctor whose task is to service a single organ of the human body. The writer today is turning into a *machine à écrire*, a sort of human typewriter with a standardized mechanical output: hence the meaning of those questions ("How many hours a day?" "How long does it take you?" "Have you ever thought of using a Dictaphone?"). This standardization and specialization is not only a feature of his working hours but of his social existence. The writer today—and especially the young American writer—sees only other writers; he does not know anyone else. His social circle comprises other writers and his girlfriends, but his girlfriends, usually, are hoping to be writers too. The writer today who has a painter for a friend is regarded as a broad-ranging adventurer, a real man of the world. If he teaches in a university, his colleagues are writers or at any rate they "publish," and his students, like his girlfriends, are hoping to write themselves. This explains the phenomenon, often regarded as puzzling, of the "one-book" American writer, the writer who starts out with promise and afterward can only repeat himself or fade away. There is nothing puzzling about it; he wrote that first book before he became a writer, while he was still an ordinary person. The worst thing, I would say, that can happen to a writer today is to become a writer. And it is most fatal of all for the novelist; the poet can survive it, for he does not need social range for his verse, and poets have always clubbed together with other poets in exclusive coteries, which is perhaps why Plato wanted them banned from the Republic.

The isolation of the modern writer is a social fact, and not just the writer's own willful fault. He cannot help being "bookish," which cuts him off from society, since practically the only people left who read are writers, their wives and girlfriends, teachers of literature, and students hoping to become writers. The writer has "nothing in common" with the businessman or the worker, and this is almost literally true; there is no common world left in which they share. The businessman who does not read is just as specialized as the writer who writes.

To throw off this straitjacket is the recurrent dream of the modern novelist, after the age, say, of thirty or thirty-five; before that, his dream was the opposite: to come to New York (or Paris or London) to meet other writers. Various ways out are tried: moving to the country, travel, "action" (some form of politics), the resolute cultivation of side interests—music, art, sport, gardening; sport is very popular with American men novelists, who hold on to an interest in baseball or a tennis racket or a fishing rod as a relic of the "complete man" or complete boy they once were. But if these steps are sufficiently radical, their effect may be the reverse of what was intended. This is what seems to have happened to Gide, D. H. Lawrence, Malraux, Camus, George Orwell. Starting as novelists, they fled, as it were, in all directions from the tyranny of the novelist's specialization: into politics, diary-keeping, travel and travel-writing, war, art history, journalism, "engagement." Nor did they ever really come back to the novel, assuming that was what they wanted to do. Gide stopped with *The Counterfeiters*; Lawrence with *Women in Love*; Malraux with *Man's Fate*; Orwell with his first book, *Burmese Days*; Camus with *The Stranger*. Their later books are not novels, even if they are called so, but fables of various kinds, tracts, and parables. But they did not settle down to a single form or mode, and this perpetual restlessness which they have in common seems a sign of an unrequited, uncon-summated love for the novel, as though in the middle of their *oeuvre* there were a void, a blank space reserved for the novel they failed to be able to write. We think of them as among the principal "novelists" of our time, but they were hardly novelists at all, and in each case their work as a whole has an air of being unfinished, dangling.

They are certainly key modern figures. Allowing for differences in talent, their situation is everybody's; mine too. We are all in flight from the novel and yet drawn back to it, as to some unfinished and problematic relationship. The novel seems to be dissolving into its component parts: the essay, the travel book, reporting, on the one hand, and the "pure" fiction of the tale, on the other. The center will not hold. No structure (except Faulkner's) has been strong enough to keep in suspension the diverse elements of which the novel is made. You can call this, if you want, a failure of imagination. We know that the real world exists, but we can no longer imagine it.

Yet despite all I have been saying, I cannot, being human, help feeling that the novel is not finished yet. Tomorrow is another day. Someone, somewhere, even now may be dictating into a Dictaphone: "At five o'clock in the afternoon, in the capital of the Province of Y——, a tall man with an umbrella was knocking at the door of the governor's residence." In short, someone may be able to believe again in the reality, the factuality, of the world.

—*Summer 1960*

17

IDEAS AND THE NOVEL:
LECTURE I

"HE HAD A *mind so fine that no idea could violate it.*"
T. S. Eliot writing of Henry James in *The Little Review* of August
1918. I offer it to you as a motto or, rather, countermotto for the
reflections that follow, which will take exception, not to the truth of
Eliot's pronouncement (he was right about James), but to the set of
lofty assumptions calmly towering behind it.

The young Eliot's epigram summed up with cutting brevity a creed
that for modernists appeared beyond dispute. Implicit in it is the snub-
bing notion, radical at the time but by now canon doctrine, of the novel
as a fine art and of the novelist as an intelligence superior to mere
intellect. In this patronizing view, the intellect's crude apparatus was
capable only of formulating concepts, which then underwent the process of diffusion, so that by dint of repetition they fell within anybody's
reach. The final, cruel fate of an idea was to turn into an *idée reçue.*
The power of the novelist insofar as he was a supreme intelligence was
to free himself from the workload of commentary and simply, awe-
somely, to show: his creation was beyond paraphrase or reduction. As
pure work of art, it stood beautifully apart, impervious to the dry rot
affecting the brain's constructions and to the welter of factuality.

Thus the separation was perceived as twofold. The reform program for the novel—soon to be promulgated in a position paper like

Jacob's Room (1922)—aimed at correcting not only the errors of the old practitioners, who were prone to philosophize in their works, but also the Victorian "slice of life" theory still admitted by Matthew Arnold and later, permissive notions of the novel as a "spongy tract" (Forster) or large loose bag into which anything would fit. Obviously novels of the old, discredited schools—the historical novel, the novel of adventure, the soapbox or pulpit novel—continued and continue to be written despite the lesson of the Master. Indeed they make up a majority, now as before, but having no recognized aesthetic willing to claim them, they tend to be treated by our critical authorities as marginal—examples of backwardness if they come from the East (Solzhenitsyn) or of deliberate archaizing if they come from the West (say, Iris Murdoch). The pure novel, the quintessential novel, does not acknowledge any family relation with these distant branches. It is a formal, priestly exercise whose first great celebrant was James. The fact that there are no Jamesian novels being produced any more—if there ever were, apart from the Master's own—does not alter the perspective. The Jamesian model remains a standard, an archetype, against which contemporary impurities and laxities are measured.

The importance of James lies not so much in his achievements as in the queerness of them. He did not broaden a way for his successors but closed nearly every exit as with hermetic sealing tape. It is undeniable that this American author, almost single-handed, invented a peculiar new kind of fiction, more refined, more stately, than anything known before, purged, to the limit of possibility, of the gross traditional elements of suspense, physical action, inventory, description of places and persons, apostrophe, moral teaching. When you think of James in the light of his predecessors, you are suddenly conscious of what is not there: battles, riots, tempests, sunrises, the sewers of Paris, crime, hunger, the plague, the scaffold, the clergy, but also minute particulars such as you find in Jane Austen—poor Miss Bates's twice-baked apples, Mr. Collins's "Collins," the comedy of the infinitely small. It cannot have been simply a class limitation or a limitation of experience that intimidated his pen. It was a resolve, very American, to scrape his sacred texts clean of the material factor. And it was no small task he laid on himself, since his novels, even more than most maybe, dealt with material concerns—property and money—and unrolled almost exclusively in the realm of the social, mundane by definition. Nevertheless, he succeeded, this American prodigy. He etherealized the novel beyond its wildest dreams and perhaps etherized it as well.

To take a pleasant example, he managed in *The Spoils of Poynton* to relate a story of a contest for possession of some furniture in immense detail without ever indicating except in the vaguest way what the desirable stuff was. We gather that quite a lot is French—Louis Quinze and Louis Seize are mentioned once each ("the sweetest Louis Seize")—but we also hear of Venetian velvet and of "a great Italian cabinet" in the red room, though with no specifics of place, period, inlays, embossment, and of a little Spanish ivory crucifix. When you think of what Balzac would have made of the opportunity...! Actually *The Spoils of Poynton* is a Balzacian drama done with the merest hints of props and stage setting. James's strategy was to abstract the general noun, furniture, from the particulars of the individual pieces, also referred to as "things." He gives us a universal which we can upholster according to our own taste and antiquarian knowledge. In short, he gives us an Idea. *The Spoils of Poynton* is not a novel about material tables and chairs; it is a novel about the possession and enjoyment of an immaterial Idea, which could be *any* old furniture, *all* old furniture, beautiful, ugly, or neither—it makes no difference, except that if it is ugly the struggle over it will be more ironic. James, however, is not an ironist; no puritan can be. And the fact that with this novel we can supply "real" tables and chairs from our own imagination makes *The Spoils of Poynton*, to my mind, more true to our common experience, hence more classic, than most of his fictions.

But that, for the moment, is beside the point. What I should like to bring out now is another peculiarity: that though James's people end-lessly discuss and analyze, they never discuss the subjects that people in society usually do. Above all, politics. It is not true that well-bred people avoid talk of politics. They cannot stay away from it. Outrage over public events that menace, or threaten to menace, their property and privilege has devolved on them by birthright (though it can also be acquired), and they cannot help sharing it when more than two meet, even in the presence of outsiders, which in fact seems to act as a stimulant. This has surely been so from earliest times, and James's time was no exception, as we know from other sources. But from his fictions (forgetting *The Princess Casamassima*, where he mildly ven-tured into the arena), you could never guess that whispers—or shouts—ever burst out over the tea table regarding the need for a firm hand, for making an example of the ringleaders, what are things coming to, and so on. Dickens's Mr. Bounderby, although no gentleman, put the position in a nutshell with "the turtle soup and the gold spoon," his own blunt résumé of the trade unionist's unmistakable goals. As James's people are constantly telling each other how intelligent they are, more subtlety than this might be expected of them, but we can only hope it. What were Adam Verver's views on the great Free Trade debate, on woman suffrage, on child labor? We do not know. It is almost as if James wanted to protect his cherished creations from our knowledge of the banalities they would utter if he once let us overhear them speak freely.

Or let us try art. These people are traveled and worldly and often in a state of rapture over the museums and galleries they visit, the noble façades of mansions and dear quaint crockets of cathedrals. Yet they rarely come away from a morning of sightseeing with as much as a half-formed thought. They never dispute about what they have looked at, prefer one artist to another, hazard generalizations. In real life, they would certainly have had their ideas about the revolutions that were occurring in painting and sculpture. In Paris, if only out of curiosity, they would have rushed to see the Salon des Indépendants. Wild horses could not have kept them away. A bold pair, armed with a letter from Lady Sackville or Isabella Stewart Gardner, might have penetrated Rodin's studio. His bronze statue of Balzac in a dressing gown, shown at the Salon des Beaux Arts, would already have led the travelers to take sides, some finding it disgusting and incomprehensible while others were calling it a "breakthrough." What would they have made of the nude Victor Hugo in plaster in the Luxembourg Gardens? Or *The Kiss* ("Rather *too* suggestive"?) in marble? Unfailingly one would have heard judgments as to what was permissible and impermissible in art.

James himself, however unversed in politics he might have been, had no deficiency of art appreciation. He wrote well and copiously about painting, sculpture, and architecture. But not in his novels. There all is allusion and murmurous, indistinct evocation of objects and vistas, in comparison with which Whistler's *Nocturne* is a sharp-edge photograph.

In the novels, a taboo is operating—a taboo that enjoins him, like Psyche in the myth or Pandora or Mother Eve, to steer clear of forbidden areas on pain of losing his god-sent gift. The areas on which neither he nor his characters may touch are defined by the proximity of thought to their surface—thought visible, almost palpable, in nuggets or globules readily picked up by the vulgar. Art in other hands might have been such an area, but James took the risk—after all, it was his own great interest—and he actually dared make it the ruling passion of several of his figures, at the price, however, of treating it always by indirection, as a motive but never as a topic in itself. If you think of Proust, you will see the difference.

With religion and philosophy, though, James is as circumspect as he is with politics. As son and brother, he must often have heard these subjects earnestly discussed, which perhaps accounts for his dislike of ideas in general. Or was this only a sense, which grew on him as he sought to find his own way, that he must not trespass on father's and brother's hunting preserve? In any case, with the exception of *The Bostonians*—a middle-period extravagant comedy, which he came almost to disavow, full of cranks, cults, emancipated women, do-gooders, religious charlatanry—neither he nor his characters have a word to say on these matters, nor—it should go without saying—on science. With so much of the stuff of ordinary social intercourse ruled out, the Jamesian people by and large are reduced to a single theme: each other. As beings not given to long silences, who are virtually never seen reading, not even a guidebook, that is what they are condemned to. Whenever a pair or a trio draws apart from the rest, it is to discuss and analyze and exclaim over an absent one—Milly or Maggie or Isabel. Yet here too there is a curious shortage of ideas of the kind you or I might formulate in discussing a friend. In their place are hints, soft wonderings, head-shakings, sentences hanging in the air; communication takes place between slow implication and swift inference: "Oh! Oh! Oh!" The word "Wonderful!" returns over and over as the best that can be said by way of a summing-up.

As James aged, his reticence or the reticence he imposed on his surrogates grew more "wonderful" indeed. With *The Wings of the Dove*, we arrive at a heroine of whom we know only three things: that she is rich, red-haired, and sick. She is clearly meant to be admirable, as we infer from the gasps and cries of the satellite figures around her—"Isn't she superb?," "Everything about you is a beauty," "beautiful," "a dove," "Oh you exquisite thing!" But vulgar particulars are never supplied. As James himself observed in his preface, "...I go but a little way with the direct—that is with the straight exhibition of Milly; it resorts to relief, this process, whenever it can, to some kinder, some merciful indirection: all as if to approach her circuitously, deal with her at second hand, as an unspotted princess is ever dealt with...." And he continues: "All of which proceeds, obviously, from her painter's tenderness of imagination about her, which reduces him to watching her, as it were, through the successive windows of other people's interest in her."

It is an extension of the method, of course, that worked so successfully in *The Spoils of Poynton*. There the "treasures" had only to be called by that name two or three times, the astonished words "rare," "precious," "splendid," to drop one by one from soft young lips, to convince the reader that "the nice old things" were worth squabbling over at least to those engaged in the squabble. But the moral splendor of a human being needs more demonstration than the museum quality of mobile property, at any rate in a novel. One can decide that the fuss being made about furniture is ridiculous or justified or a little of both, and, as I have been saying, it does not greatly matter which. It is unnecessary to fully sympathize with Mrs. Gereth's emotions to be amused by the lengths to which she will go in single combat, and in fact one senses James's own moral reserve on her subject. But the fuss made over Milly Theale makes one irritably ask why, what is so admirable about her that cannot be named, unless it is just her bank balance? Similar doubts may be felt about the Ververs, father and daughter, in *The Golden Bowl*.

Their creator's reluctance to furnish them with identifiable traits that might let us "place" them in real life has curious consequences for the principals of the late novels. These figures, one realizes, must be accepted on faith, as ectoplasms emanating from an entranced author at his desk, in short as ghostly abstractions, pale ideas, which explains, when you come to think of it, the fever of discussion they excite in the other characters. Those by comparison are solid. They have bodies and brains, however employed. Motives are allotted to them, such as plain curiosity (the Assinghams, Henrietta Stackpole) or money greed or sexual hunger (both seem to be working, though sometimes at cross-purposes, in Kate Croy, Morton Densher, Charlotte Stant), motives that give them a foot in the actual world. And if, despite their concerted effort of analysis, the principals they keep wondering over evade definition, if, unlike furniture, they cannot be established as universals standing for a whole class of singulars, Milly and Maggie and Chad remain nonetheless ideas of a sort. That is, ideas, expelled by a majestic butler at the front door, return by another entrance and stand waiting pathetically to be dressed in words.

Before leaving James, hoist—if I am right—by his own petard, I want to ask whether his exclusion of ideas in the sense of mental concepts was connected or not with the exclusion of common factuality. The two are not *necessarily* related. Consider Thomas Love Peacock. There the ordinary stuff of life is swept away to make room for abstract speculation. That, and just that, is the joke. It tickles our funny bone to meet the denizens of *Nightmare Abbey*—young Scythrop, the heir of the house, and Flosky, who has named his eldest son Emanuel after Kant, and Listless, up from London, complaining that Dante is growing fashionable. Each has his own bats in the belfry; there is a bad smell of midnight oil in the derelict medieval structure, where practical affairs are neglected for the necromancy of "synthetical reasoning." In hearty, plain-man style (which is partly a simulation), Peacock treats the brain's sickly products as the end result of the general disease of modishness for which the remedy would be prolonged exposure to common, garden reality.

But for James, mental concepts, far from being opposed to the ordinariness of laundry lists and drains, seem themselves to have belonged to a lower category of inartistic objects, like the small article of "the commonest domestic use" manufactured by the Newsome family in *The Ambassadors*—I have always guessed that it was a brass safety pin. But safety pin or sink stopper, it could not be mentioned in the text, any more than Milly Theale's cancer (if that is what it was), or, let us say, *The Origin of Species*. I confess I do not easily see what these tabooed subjects have in common, unless that they were familiar to most people and hence bore the traces of other handling. Yet, though both were in general circulation, a safety pin is not the same as the idea of natural selection. More likely, James wished his fictions to dwell exclusively on the *piano nobile*, as he conceived it, of social intercourse—neither upstairs in the pent garrets of intellectual labor nor below in the basement and kitchens of domestic toil. And the garret and the basement have a secret sympathy between them of which the *piano nobile* is often unaware. That, at any rate, seems to be the lesson of the greatest fictions, past and present.

What is curious, though, is that ideas are still today felt to be unsightly in the novel, whereas the nether areas—the cloaca—are fully admitted to view. I suppose that the ban on ideas that even now largely prevails, above all in English-speaking countries, is a heritage from modernism in its prim anti-Victorian phase. To Virginia Woolf, for instance, it was not a question of what might be brought *into* the novel —sex, the natural functions—but of what should be kept out. In the reaction against the Victorian novel, it was natural that the discursive authors, from Dickens to Meredith and Hardy, should stand in the pillory as warning examples of what was most to be avoided. When the young Eliot complimented James on the fact that no rough bundles of concepts disfigure and coarsen his novels, he at once went on to cite Meredith ("the disciple of Carlyle") as a bad case of the opposite.

Actually Meredith with his tendency to aphorism was in his own way an experimental writer, which made him exciting to the young. This may have been why he was singled out for rapid disposal. That he went counter to the "stuffy" realist tradition, jested with the time-honored conventions of the form, even gave hints of something like the interior monologue, did not excuse him. In fact he has not lasted, except, I think, for *The Egoist*; the mock-heroic vein, which he worked and overworked, failed to undermine the old structure and became a blind alley. Brio was not enough. In any case, his way with ideas, wavering between persiflage and orotund pronouncement, was too unsteady to maintain a serious weight. His contemporaries seem to have known what he was "about," but a reader today finds it hard to determine the overall pattern of his thought.

This can never be said of Dickens, George Eliot, Hardy. Nor on the Continent of Hugo, Stendhal, Balzac, even Flaubert, of Manzoni, or any of the Russians except Chekhov, who was relatively taciturn. The talkative, outspoken novelist was evidently the norm and always had been. In America, those who have survived—chiefly Melville and Hawthorne—seldom expressed themselves on topics and issues of the day, and their utterances could be somewhat riddling on the great themes of good and evil. Nevertheless they cannot be charged with unsteadiness, lack of serious purpose. They were sermonizers like their contemporaries in the Old World; it was only that their sermon, like the Book of Revelation, required some decoding; the apocalyptic imagery, as with an allegory, called for interpretation.

In fact the nineteenth-century novel was so evidently an idea carrier that the component of overt thought in it must have been taken for granted by the reader as an ingredient as predictable as a leavening agent in bread. He came to expect it in his graver fiction, perhaps to count on it, just as he counted on the geographical and social coordinates that gave him his bearings in the opening chapter: the expanse of Egdon Heath at sundown crossed by the solitary red-dleman and his cart; the mountain heights of the Lecco district looking down on the lone homeward-bound figure of Don Abbondio. Or "A rather pretty little chaise on springs, such as bachelors, half-pay officers, staff captains, landowners with about a hundred serfs...drive about in, rolled in at the gates of the hotel of the provincial town of N." Or "About thirty years ago, Miss Maria Ward, with only seven thousand pounds, had the good fortune to captivate Sir Thomas Bertram, of Mansfield Park, in the county of Northampton." We are so much in the habit of skipping pages of introductory description and general reflections that interrupt the story that we can scarcely believe that such "blemishes" once gave pleasure, that a novel would have been felt by our ancestors to be a far poorer thing without them. They can be dismissed by the modern reader as "mere" conventions of the genre, but in the old times a novel that lacked them would have been like an opera without an overture, which of course is a convention too.

The function of geographical descriptions—naming of counties, rivers, and so forth—and social topography is to make the reader feel comfortable in the vehicle he has boarded, like passengers in a plane having landmarks below pointed out to them and receiving bulletins from the pilot on altitude and cruising speed. Yet it was not essentially different from the function performed by ideas. Both gave depth and perspective. And the analogy to air travel is illustrative. The briefings supplied by the pilot ("On your left, folks, you'll see the city of Boston and the Charles River") are a relic of earlier days of aviation —a mere outworn convention we "put up with" in a contemporary airbus. Scarcely anybody bothers any more to rise in his seat to try to make out the landmark being mentioned—you cannot see anything anyway—the plane is going too fast and the view is obstructed. Besides, who cares? The destination is the point. But if you put yourself back in fancy to the propeller plane, you will see, as with the novel, what has been lost. So intrinsic to the novelistic medium were ideas and other forms of commentary, all tending to "set" the narration in a general scheme, that it would have been impossible in former days to speak of "the novel of ideas." It would have seemed to be a tautology.

Now the expression is used with such assurance and frequency that I am surprised not to find it in my *Reader's Guide to Literary Terms*, which is otherwise reasonably current. For example, under "NOVEL," I read: "In the late nineteenth and twentieth centuries the novel, as an art form, has reached its fullest development. Concerned with their craft, novelists such as Flaubert, Henry James, Virginia Woolf, James Joyce, E. M. Forster, and Thomas Mann have used various devices to achieve new aesthetic forms within the genre." I do not know what Flaubert, who died in 1880, is doing there, but the tenor of the list is clear. If the "NOVEL OF IDEAS" does not figure as an entry (though "NOVEL OF THE SOIL" does), it may be that the authors were not sure what the term covered. I must say that it is not clear to me either, though I sense something derogatory in the usage, as if there were novels and novels of ideas and never the twain shall meet. But rather than attempt to define a term that has never been in my own vocabulary, I shall try to discover what other people mean by it.

Does it mean a novel in which the characters sit around, or pace up and down, enunciating and discussing ideas? Examples would be *The Magic Mountain*, *Point Counter Point*, in fact all of Huxley's novels, Sartre's *Les chemins de la liberté*, Malraux's *Man's Fate*. The purest cases would be Peacock—*Headlong Hall*, *Nightmare Abbey*, *Crotchet Castle*—if they could be called novels, which I doubt, since they lack a prime requisite—length—and another—involvement of the reader in the characters' fates. You might also count Flaubert's unfinished *Bouvard et Pécuchet*, where the joint heroes are busy compiling a Dictionary of Received Ideas, and Santayana's *The Last Puritan*, by now forgotten. But though the term would seem clearly to apply to the works just mentioned (*The Magic Mountain* being the one everybody remembers best, having read it at nineteen), there are not very many of them and they are rather out of style.

Solzhenitsyn's *Cancer Ward*, which belongs to our own time, roughly conforms to the type. Like *The Magic Mountain*, it takes place in a sanatorium, where patients who have come to be cured have little else to do after their treatments and medical examinations than muse and argue. Isolation is crucial to this type of novel: the characters are on an island, out on a limb, either of their own choosing—Peacock's crotchety castles, Huxley's grand country house presided over by Mr. Scogan (*Crome Yellow*)—or by force majeure, as in a hospital or a prison (Solzhenitsyn's *The First Circle*). Or the island may be moral, self-constituted by a literary clique (*Point Counter Point*), by a group of like-thinking, semipolitical bohemians (*Les chemins de la liberté*), by a cell of revolutionaries (*Man's Fate*). What is involved is always a contest of faiths. The debates on the magic mountain between Naphta and Settembrini oppose nihilistic Jesuitry to progressive atheistic humanism but also pan-Germanism to pro-Russian *entente-cordiale* doctrine, prophecies of war to firm belief in peace, repose to work, in other words, you might say, night to day. Beneath the circuslike confrontation of current creeds lies a clash between very ancient faiths. Settembrini is a monist, Naphta a dualist. Settembrini, asked to choose, exalts mind over body: "...Within the antithesis of body and mind, the body is the evil, the devilish principle, for the body is nature." It is like a game of preferences with the aim being self-definition, which no doubt is why young people are dazzled by it.

On a simpler level and without encyclopedic pretensions, *Cancer Ward* presents us with various naive faiths—from faith in Stalin to faith in the healing properties of radioactive gold to faith in the mandrake root—sometimes peacefully coexisting, sometimes at odds with each other. It is natural that in a hospital the belief in a cure, in sovereign remedies, should dominate every mind. It becomes vital to have a theory, and world theories, global diagnoses of the body politic or the human state generally, take on, as though of necessity, an importance not usually accorded them by the healthy. The pressing need to have faith, i.e., grounds for hope, gives an urgency to the abstract disputes of both *The Magic Mountain* and *Cancer Ward*. Here ideas of any and every kind become, as if by contagion, matters of life and death. It is also true that in these narratives no idea can win out over another. Nobody is convinced or persuaded. The excited debates between patients or between doctor and patient end up in the air. Hans Castorp, whose young mind has been the salient contested for by opposing forces, leaves the sanatorium and returns "down below," to the plains, which should be the level ground of sound, commonplace reality, except for the fact that there he dies as a soldier in the general reasonless catastrophe of the First World War. In *Cancer Ward*, Kostoglotov, too, leaves his sanatorium, having been let out as cured, which should be a happy ending, except for the fact that the cancer ward whose gates close behind him has been a species of sanctuary; he is slated to return to his real down-to-earth life of penal exile. One kind of death sentence, in both cases, has been exchanged for another.

It is not especially uncanny (or no more than any resemblance or twinning) that this pair of novels, so widely separated in space and time, so widely divergent in manner, should match in a number of respects. Sanatorium life is much the same, I suppose, everywhere and always. But sanatorium life, as such, did not dictate the ending; a positive conclusion would have been possible if the novel were only about sickness and recovery. The ending is imposed not by the particular case—cancer ward or tubercular clinic—but by the fact that in general the so-called novel of ideas (at least the kind I have been describing) does not allow of any resolution. Nothing decisive can happen in it; it is a seesaw. Events that do occur in it are simply incidents, sometimes diverting, as in Peacock. A real event, such as the death of Hans Castorp, is reserved for a postscript; it does not belong to the text proper. The same with Kostoglotov's reshouldering of his penal identity. We do not see it happen; in fact it may not happen "for good," since when he goes to register with the NKVD in the town outside the hospital gates, the *Komendant* speaks cheerfully of an amnesty in the offing. But Kostoglotov cannot make himself believe him—he has heard of amnesties before and nothing came of them—and the reader knows no more than he. It is left in suspension, like the arguments between the sick men, which never "get" anywhere.

If a secondary character chances to die—for instance, Quarles's child in *Point Counter Point*—that, too, is an incident, outside the work's proper concerns; the main characters go on arguing as before. When it occurs in a sanatorium, it is just an episode, figuring in the normal mortality rate; a new patient moves into the bed the next day, and the ripple of concern quickly subsides. The sanatorium is an ideal setting for the discussion novel, for time does not count there. Ideas, though some may age, are indifferent to time. Mann speaks of "the more spacious time conceptions prevalent 'up here.'" That is an effect, of course, of the routine, which makes one day like another. But there is an endlessness, an eternal regularity, in all such novels; the characters slip into their places like habitués of a corner café. The sense of eternity may be represented under other aspects. In André Gide's *The Counterfeiters*, which I might have included under this heading, Edouard, the chief character, is shown writing a novel in which a facsimile of him is writing a novel, in which, we suppose, still a third figure... The black-hatted Quaker on the Quaker Oats box holding a Quaker Oats box portraying a Quaker holding a Quaker Oats box, getting smaller and smaller in infinite regress. In *Point Counter Point* Huxley borrowed the repeating-decimal device.

Still, when the novel of ideas is spoken of, maybe another type of story is being referred to—a story that does come to some sort of resolution. That is, the missionary novel sometimes referred to as a "tract." On the surface it may look like the kind of novel I have just been trying to analyze, in that it may have the air of a panel discussion, with points of view put forward by several characters speaking in turn and each being allowed equal time. But it soon appears that one speaker is right and the others, though momentarily persuasive, are wrong. I am thinking of D. H. Lawrence.

Of course there are missionary novels that are not novels of ideas, for example, *Uncle Tom's Cabin*. It is animated by a strong conviction but, if I remember right, does not "go into" the argument for and against slavery. And there are missionary elements hiding in many tales that pass for thrillers or love stories. In fact it is hard to think of a novel that in some sense does not seek to proselytize. But what I have in mind are books like *Women in Love*, *Aaron's Rod*, *Kangaroo*,

Lady Chatterley's Lover, where reasoning occupies a large part of the narrative, exerting a leverage that seems to compel the reader's agreement. The incidents, few or many, press home like gripping illustrations the point being proved. There is something of parable in most of Lawrence's plots.

In *Kangaroo* we get a powerful example of Lawrence's method at work. The ideas, fully expounded in long conversations, far from being unresolved, are boldly lived out and tested. The Lawrence figure, Somers, finds certain already held and seductive ideas made flesh for him in the shape of the Australian working-class leader known as Kangaroo. It is an incarnation Somers had never hoped to come upon, sickened as he is by Europe. He is smitten by Kangaroo's proto-fascist movement and by the wild fresh country of which working men and their virile matey principles seem to be a natural and harmonious part. The infatuation holds for many pages; he is drawn into the movement as a sympathetic foreign observer. He is nearly converted when, rather abruptly, he is startled into closer inspection: Kangaroo, dying, asks for a declaration of Somers's love, and the sickly plea lets Somers finally see the soft, weak, flabby underside of native fascism. The Australian spell is broken; Somers and his woman leave.

Up to the end, however, an equilibrium of ideas is maintained, so that the conversations remain interesting, by no means one-sided. In Somers, a genuine intellectual process, going from curiosity to attraction to repulsion and disillusionment, is shown with considerable honesty. It is typical of Lawrence at his best that even when Kangaroo and his ideas are rejected, he is not vulgarly "seen through"; something is left for a kind of dry pity and understanding.

Lady Chatterley's Lover is surely the most biased of Lawrence's books. Yet Sir Clifford, Lady Chatterley's husband, is nonetheless given his say, not too unfairly represented by and large; it is only that he and his entire set of convictions are refuted out of hand by a quiet adversary, Mellors, whose strong point is not words but performance.

His performance is itself an argument, speaking for a view of natural life and sexuality that is hostile to the intellect. Sir Clifford is no intellectual; he is a retired country gentleman who sometimes writes poetry and short stories. But the weapons he is familiar with and falls back on as a disabled champion of a social order and mild way of life are the weapons his education has taught him to use: received notions and principles.

Lawrence's hatred of the intellect, of the "upper story" (there is maybe a class prejudice here), is strange, certainly, in a man who himself lived almost wholly for ideas. The fact that they were his own made the difference apparently; he had hammered them out for himself. They were not quite so much his own as he thought, one must add. Was he unconscious of being one of a number of writers who disliked and distrusted the intellect, who, like him, held it responsible for most of the ills of modern civilization? He showed no awareness of such a fellowship, just as he showed no awareness of a paradox underlying the whole position, that is, that without the intellect and its system-making bent neither he nor his fellow thinkers would have been able to carry out their mission of teaching at all. His insistence on blood and instinct as superior to brain was a mental construct incapable of proof except on the mental level.

Yet if his ideas, true or false, have stayed with us, if he was a novelist of ideas in my second, missionary, sense to whom we can still listen —the only one, probably—this must be because he was an artist as well as a cogent, programmatic mind, in other words, because he makes us feel as we read those novels that there is *something* in what he says. But while despising the intellect, he would not have liked the name "artist" either. For him it would have been six of one and half a dozen of the other—who could measure which was the less effete? He was unable to get along with any of his own kind, really, and could only associate, finally, with people who shared his ideas, which was bound to mean in practice people who consented to have no ideas of their own.

His life was a near-tragedy, and his self-infection, quite early, with concepts—which, when he took them for absolutes, made him quarrelsome—shared responsibility with his bad lungs. But if he had not been fevered, he might not have taken to the stump, and we might never have had these burning novels or, if you wish, tracts. Far more than the discussion novels with their eternal seesaw, they are truly novels of ideas. Without ideas none of them, after *Sons and Lovers*, could even palely exist. If you cut out Naphta and Settembrini, and the author's musings on time, *The Magic Mountain* will still hold up as a story of a sort. The equivalent cannot be argued of *Aaron's Rod*, say. I am not sure whether this makes Lawrence better or worse than Mann; at any rate it makes him special. At the same time, surprisingly, it links him with the old novelists, to whom I shall turn next. If you are going to voice explicit ideas in a novel, evidently this requires a spokesman, and I shall begin by discussing the spokesman.

—*1980*

PART TWO

18

AMERICA THE BEAUTIFUL:
THE HUMANIST IN THE BATHTUB

A VISITING EXISTENTIALIST wanted recently to be taken to dinner at a really American place. This proposal, natural enough in a tourist, disclosed a situation thoroughly unnatural. Unless the visiting lady's object was suffering, there was no way of satisfying her demand. Suki-yaki joints, chop suey joints, Italian table d'hôte places, French provincial restaurants with the menu written on a slate, Irish chophouses, and Jewish delicatessens came abundantly to mind, but these were not what the lady wanted. Schrafft's or the Automat would have answered, yet to take her there would have been to turn oneself into a tourist and to present America as a spectacle—a *New Yorker* cartoon or a savage drawing in the *New Masses*. It was the beginning of an evening of humiliations. The visitor was lively and eager; her mind lay open and orderly, like a notebook ready for impressions. It was not long, however, before she shut it up with a snap. We had no recommendations to make to her. With movies, plays, current books, it was the same story as with the restaurants. *Open City*, *Les Enfants du Paradis*, Oscar Wilde, a reprint of Henry James were *pâté de maison* to this lady who wanted the definitive flapjack. She did not believe us when we said that there were no good Hollywood movies, no good Broadway plays—only curios; she was merely confirmed in her impression that American intellectuals were "negative."

Yet the irritating thing was that we did not feel negative. We admired and liked our country; we preferred it to that imaginary America, land of the *peaux rouges* of Caldwell and Steinbeck, dumb paradise of violence and the detective story, which had excited the sensibilities of our visitor and of the up-to-date French literary world. But to found our preference, to locate it materially in some admirable object or institution, such as Chartres, say, or French café life, was for us, that night at any rate, an impossible undertaking. We heard ourselves saying that the real America was elsewhere, in the white frame houses and church spires of New England; yet we knew that we talked foolishly—we were not Granville Hicks and we looked ludicrous in his opinions. The Elevated, half a block away, interrupting us every time a train passed, gave us the lie on schedule, every eight minutes. But if the elm-shaded village green was a false or at least an insufficient address for the *genius loci* we honored, where then was it to be found? Surveyed from the vantage point of Europe, this large continent seemed suddenly deficient in objects of virtue. The Grand Canyon, Yellowstone Park, Jim Hill's mansion in St. Paul, Jefferson's Monticello, the blast furnaces of Pittsburgh, Mount Rainier, the yellow observatory at Amherst, the little-theatre movement in Cleveland, Ohio, a Greek revival house glimpsed from a car window in a lost river-town in New Jersey—these things were too small for the size of the country. Each of them, when pointed to, diminished in interest with the lady's perspective of distance. There was no sight that in itself seemed to justify her crossing of the Atlantic.

If she was interested in "conditions," that was a different matter. There are conditions everywhere; it takes no special genius to produce them. Yet would it be an act of hospitality to invite a visitor to a lynching? Unfortunately, nearly all the "sights" in America fall under the head of conditions. Hollywood, Reno, the sharecroppers' homes in the South, the mining towns of Pennsylvania, Coney Island, the Chicago stockyards, Macy's, the Dodgers, Harlem, even Congress, the forum of our liberties, are spectacles rather than sights, to use the term in the colloquial sense of "Didn't he make a holy spectacle of himself?" An Englishman of almost any political opinion can show a visitor through the Houses of Parliament with a sense of pride or at least of indulgence toward his national foibles and traditions. The American, if he has a spark of national feeling, will be humiliated by the very prospect of a foreigner's visit to Congress—these, for the most part, illiterate hacks whose fancy vests are spotted with gravy, and whose speeches, hypocritical, unctuous, and slovenly, are spotted also with the gravy of political patronage, these persons are a reflection on the democratic process rather than of it; they expose it in its underwear. In European legislation, we are told, a great deal of shady business goes on in private, behind the scenes. In America, it is just the opposite, anything good, presumably, is accomplished *in camera*, in the committee rooms.

It is so with all our institutions. For the visiting European, a trip through the United States has, almost inevitably, the character of an exposé, and the American, on his side, is tempted by love of his country to lock the inquiring tourist in his hotel room and throw away the key. His contention that the visible and material America is not the real or the only one is more difficult to sustain than was the presumption of the "other" Germany behind the Nazi steel.

To some extent a citizen of any country will feel that the tourist's view of his homeland is a false one. The French will tell you that you have to go into their homes to see what the French people are really like. The intellectuals in the Left Bank cafés are not the real French intellectuals, etc., etc. In Italy, they complain that the tourist must not judge by the *ristorantes*; there one sees only black-market types. But in neither of these cases is the native really disturbed by the tourist's view of his country. If Versailles or Giotto's bell tower in Florence do not tell the whole story, they are still not incongruous with it; you do not hear a Frenchman or an Italian object when these things are noticed by a visitor. With the American, the contradiction is more serious. He must, if he is to defend his country, repudiate its visible aspect almost entirely. He must say that its parade of phenomenology, its billboards, superhighways, even its skyscrapers, not only fail to represent the inner essence of his country but in fact contravene it. He may point, if he wishes, to certain beautiful objects, but here too he is in difficulties, for nearly everything that is beautiful and has not been produced by Nature belongs to the eighteenth century, to a past with which he has very little connection, and which his ancestors, in many or most cases, had no part in. Beacon Street and the Boston Common are very charming in the eighteenth-century manner, so are the sea captains' houses in the old Massachusetts ports, and the ruined plantations of Louisiana, but an American from Brooklyn or the Middle West or the Pacific Coast finds the style of life embodied in them as foreign as Europe; indeed, the first sensation of a westerner, coming upon Beacon Hill and the gold dome of the State House, is to feel that at last he has traveled "abroad." The American, if he is to speak the highest truth about his country, must refrain from pointing at all. The virtue of American civilization is that it is unmaterialistic.

This statement may strike a critic as whimsical or perverse. Everybody knows, it will be said, that America has the most materialistic civilization in the world, that Americans care only about money, they have no time or talent for living; look at radio, look at advertising, look at life insurance, look at the tired businessman, at the Frigidaires and the Fords. In answer, the reader is invited first to look instead into his own heart and inquire whether he personally feels himself to be represented by these things, or whether he does not, on the contrary, feel them to be irrelevant to him, a necessary evil, part of the conditions of life. Other people, he will assume, care about them very much: the man down the street, the entire population of Detroit or Scarsdale, the back-country farmer, the urban poor or the rich. But he himself accepts these objects as imposed on him by a collective "otherness" of desire, an otherness he has not met directly but whose existence he infers from the number of automobiles, Frigidaires, or television sets he sees around him. Stepping into his new Buick convertible, he knows that he would gladly do without it, but imagines that to his neighbor, who is just backing *his* out of the driveway, this car is the motor of life. More often, however, the otherness is projected farther afield, onto a different class or social group, remote and alien. Thus the rich, who would like nothing better, they think, than for life to be a perpetual fishing trip with the trout grilled by a native guide, look patronizingly upon the whole apparatus of American civilization as a cheap Christmas present to the poor, and city people see the radio and the washing machine as the farm-wife's solace.

It can be argued, of course, that the subjective view is prevaricating, possession of the Buick being nine tenths of the social law. But who has ever met, outside of advertisements, a true parishioner of this church of Mammon? A man may take pride in a car, and a housewife in her new sink or wallpaper, but pleasure in new acquisitions is universal and eternal; an Italian man with a new gold tooth, a French bibliophile with a new edition, a woman with a new baby, a philosopher with a new thought, all these people are rejoicing in progress, in man's power to enlarge and improve. Before men showed off new cars, they showed off new horses; it is alleged against modern man that he as an individual craftsman did not make the car; but his grandfather did not make the horse either. What is imputed to Americans is something quite different, an abject dependence on material possessions, an image of happiness as packaged by the manufacturer, content in a can. This view of American life is strongly urged by advertising agencies. We know the "others," of course, because we meet them every week in full force in *The New Yorker* or *The Saturday Evening Post*, those brightly colored families of dedicated consumers, waiting in unison on the porch for the dealer to deliver the new car, gobbling the new cereal ("Gee, Mom, is it good for you too?"), lining up to bank their paychecks, or fearfully anticipating the industrial accident and the insurance check that will "compensate" for it. We meet them also, more troll-like underground, in the subway placards, in the ferociously complacent One-A-Day family, and we hear their courtiers sing to them on the radio of Ivory or Supersuds. The thing, however, that repels us in these advertisements is their naive falsity to life. Who are these advertising men kidding, besides the European tourist? Between the tired, sad, gentle faces of the subway riders and the grinning Holy Families of the Ad-Mass, there exists no possibility of even a wishful identification. We take a vitamin pill with the hope of feeling (possibly) a little less tired, but the superstition of buoyant health emblazoned in the bright, ugly pictures has no more power to move us than the blood of Saint Januarius.

Familiarity has perhaps bred contempt in us Americans: until you have had a washing machine, you cannot imagine how little difference it will make to you. Europeans still believe that money brings happiness, witness the bought journalist, the bought politician, the bought general, the whole venality of European literary life, inconceivable in this country of the dollar. It is true that America produces and consumes more cars, soap, and bathtubs than any other nation, but we live among these objects rather than by them. Americans build skyscrapers; Le Corbusier worships them. Ehrenburg, our Soviet critic, fell in love with the Check-O-Mat in American railway stations, writing home paragraphs of song to this gadget—while deploring American materialism. When an American heiress wants to buy a man, she at once crosses the Atlantic. The only really materialistic people I have ever met have been Europeans.

The strongest argument for the unmaterialistic character of American life is the fact that we tolerate conditions that are, from a materialistic point of view, intolerable. What the foreigner finds most objectionable in American life is its lack of basic comfort. No nation with any sense of material well-being would endure the food we eat, the cramped apartments we live in, the noise, the traffic, the crowded subways and buses. American life, in large cities, at any rate, is a perpetual assault on the senses and the nerves; it is out of asceticism, out of unworldliness, precisely, that we bear it.

This republic was founded on an unworldly assumption, a denial of "the facts of life." It is manifestly untrue that all men are created equal; interpreted in worldly terms, this doctrine has resulted in a pseudoequality, that is, in standardization, in an equality of things rather than of persons. The inalienable rights to life, liberty, and the pursuit of happiness appear, in practice, to have become the inalienable right to a bathtub, a flush toilet, and a can of Spam. Left-wing critics of America attribute this result to the intrusion of capitalism; right-wing critics see it as the logical dead end of democracy. Capitalism, certainly, now depends on mass production, which depends on large-scale distribution of uniform goods, till the consumer today is the victim of the manufacturer who launches on him a regiment of products for which he must make house-room in his soul. The buying impulse, in its original force and purity, was not nearly so crass, however, or so meanly acquisitive as many radical critics suppose. The purchase of a bathtub was the exercise of a spiritual right. The immigrant or the poor native American bought a bathtub, not because he wanted to take a bath, but because he wanted to be in a *position* to do so. This remains true in many fields today; possessions, when they are desired, are not wanted for their own sakes but as tokens of an ideal state of freedom, fraternity, and franchise. "Keeping up with the Joneses" is a vulgarization of Jefferson's concept, but it too is a declaration of the rights of man, and decidedly unfeasible and visionary. Where for a European, a fact is a fact, for us Americans, the real, if it is relevant at all, is simply symbolic appearance. We are a nation of twenty million bathrooms, with a humanist in every tub. One such humanist I used to hear of on Cape Cod had, on growing rich, installed two toilets side by side in his marble bathroom, on the model of the two-seater of his youth. He was a clear case of Americanism, hospitable, gregarious, and impractical, a theorist of perfection. Was his dream of the conquest of poverty a vulgar dream or a noble one, a material demand or a spiritual insistence? It is hard to think of him as a happy man, and in this too he is characteristically American, for the parity of the radio, the movies, and the washing machine has made Americans sad, reminding them of another parity of which these things were to be but emblems.

The American does not enjoy his possessions because sensory enjoyment was not his object, and he lives sparely and thinly among them, in the monastic discipline of Scarsdale or the barracks of Stuyvesant Town. Only among certain groups where franchise, socially speaking, has not been achieved, do pleasure and material splendor constitute a life-object and an occupation. Among the outcasts—Jews, Negroes, Catholics, homosexuals—excluded from the communion of ascetics, the love of fabrics, gaudy show, and rich possessions still anachronistically flaunts itself. Once a norm has been reached, differing in the different classes, financial ambition itself seems to fade away. The self-made man finds, to his anger, his son uninterested in money; you have shirtsleeves to shirtsleeves in three generations. The great financial empires are a thing of the past. Some recent immigrants—movie magnates and gangsters particularly—retain their acquisitiveness, but how long is it since anyone in the general public has murmured, wonderingly, "as rich as Rockefeller"?

If the dream of American fraternity had ended simply in this, the value of humanistic and egalitarian strivings would be seriously called into question. Jefferson, the Adamses, Franklin, Madison, would be in the position of Dostoevsky's Grand Inquisitor, who, desiring to make the Kingdom of God incarnate on earth, inaugurated the kingdom of the devil. If the nature of matter is such that the earthly paradise, once realized, becomes always the paradise of the earthly, and a spiritual conquest of matter becomes an enslavement of spirit, then the atomic bomb is, as has been argued, the logical result of the Enlightenment, and the land of opportunity is, precisely, the land of death. This position, however, is a strictly materialist one, for it asserts the Fact of the bomb as the one tremendous truth: subjective attitudes are irrelevant; it does not matter what we think or feel; possession again in this case is nine tenths of the law.

It must be admitted that there is a great similarity between the nation with its new bomb and the consumer with his new Buick. In both cases, there is a disinclination to use the product, stronger naturally in the case of the bomb, but somebody has manufactured the thing, and there seems to be no way *not* to use it, especially when everybody else will be doing so. Here again the argument of the "others" is invoked to justify our own procedures: if we had not invented the bomb, the Germans would have; the Soviet Union will have it in a year, etc., etc. This is keeping up with the Joneses indeed, our national propagandists playing the role of the advertising men in persuading us of the "others"' intentions.

It seems likely at this moment that we will find no way of not using the bomb, yet those who argue theoretically that this machine is the true expression of our society leave us, in practice, with no means of opposing it. We must differentiate ourselves from the bomb if we are to avoid using it, and in private thought we do, distinguishing the bomb sharply from our daily concerns and sentiments, feeling it as an otherness that waits outside to descend on us, an otherness already destructive of normal life, since it prevents us from planning or hoping by depriving us of a future. And this inner refusal of the bomb is also a legacy of our past; it is a denial of the given, of the power of circumstances to shape us in their mold. Unfortunately, the whole asceticism of our national character, our habit of living in but not through an environment, our alienation from objects, prepare us to endure the bomb but not to confront it.

Passivity and not aggressiveness is the dominant trait of the American character. The movies, the radio, the superhighway have softened us up for the atom bomb; we have lived with them without pleasure, feeling them as a coercion on our natures, a coercion seemingly from nowhere and expressing nobody's will. The new coercion finds us without the habit of protest; we are dissident but apart.

The very "negativeness," then, of American intellectuals is not a mark of their separation from our society, but a true expression of its separation from itself. We too are dissident but inactive. Intransigent on paper, in "real life" we conform; yet we do not feel ourselves to be dishonest, for to us the real life is rustling paper and the mental life is flesh. And even in our mental life we are critical and rather unproductive; we leave it to the "others," the best sellers, to create.

The fluctuating character of American life must, in part, have been responsible for this dissociated condition. Many an immigrant arrived in this country with the most materialistic expectations, hoping, not to escape from a world in which a man was the sum of his circumstances, but to become a new sum of circumstances himself. But this hope was self-defeating; the very ease with which new circumstances were acquired left insufficient time for a man to live into them: all along a great avenue in Minneapolis the huge stone châteaux used to be dark at night, save for a single light in each kitchen, where the family still sat, Swedish style, about the stove. The pressure of democratic thought, moreover, forced a rising man often, unexpectedly, to recognize that he was *not* his position: a speeding ticket from a village constable could lay him low. Like the agitated United Nations delegates who got summonses on the Merritt Parkway, he might find the shock traumatic: a belief had been destroyed. The effect of these combined difficulties turned the new American into a nomad, who camped out in his circumstances, as it were, and was never assimilated to them. And, for the native American, the great waves of internal migration had the same result. The homelessness of the American, migrant in geography and on the map of finance, is the whole subject of the American realists of our period. European readers see in these writers only violence and brutality. They miss not only the pathos but the nomadic virtues associated with it, generosity, hospitality, equity, directness, politeness, simplicity of relations—traits which, together with a certain gentle timidity (as of very *unpracticed* nomads), comprise the American character. Unobserved also is a peculiar nakedness, a look of being shorn of everything, that is very curiously American, corresponding to the spare wooden desolation of a frontier town and the bright thinness of the American light. The American character looks always as if it had just had a rather bad haircut, which gives it, in our eyes at any rate, a greater humanity than the European, which even among its beggars has an all too professional air.

The openness of the American situation creates the pity and the terror; status is not protection; life for the European is a career; for the American, it is a hazard. Slaves and women, said Aristotle, are not fit subjects for tragedy, but kings, rather, and noble men, men, that is, not defined by circumstance but outside it and seemingly impervious. In America we have, subjectively speaking, no slaves and no women; the efforts of *PM* and the Stalinized playwrights to introduce, like the first step to servitude, a national psychology of the "little man" have been, so far, unrewarding. The little man is one who is embedded in status; things can be done for and to him generically by a central directive; his happiness flows from statistics. This conception mistakes the national passivity for abjection. Americans will not eat this humble pie; we are still nature's noblemen. Yet no tragedy results, though the protagonist is everywhere; dissociation takes the place of conflict, and the drama is mute.

This humanity, this plain and heroic accessibility, was what we would have liked to point out to the visiting Existentialist as our national glory. Modesty perhaps forbade and a lack of concrete examples—how could we point to ourselves? Had we done so she would not have been interested. To a European, the humanity of an intellectual is of no particular moment; it is the barber pole that announces his profession and the hair oil dispensed inside. Europeans, moreover, have no curiosity about American intellectuals; we are insufficiently representative of the brute. Yet this anticipated and felt disparagement was not the whole cause of our reticence. We were silent for another reason: we were waiting to be discovered. Columbus, however, passed on, and this, very likely, was the true source of our humiliation. But this experience also was peculiarly American. We all expect to be found in the murk of otherness; it looks to us very easy since *we* know we are there. Time after time, the explorers have failed to see us. We have been patient, for the happy ending is our national belief. Now, however, that the future has been shut off from us, it is necessary for us to declare ourselves, at least for the record.

What it amounts to, in verity, is that we are the poor. This humanity we would claim for ourselves is the legacy, not only of the Enlightenment, but of the thousands and thousands of European peasants and poor townspeople who came here bringing their humanity and their sufferings with them. It is the absence of a stable upper class that is responsible for much of the vulgarity of the American scene. Should we blush before the visitor for this deficiency? The ugliness of American decoration, American entertainment, American literature—is not this the visible expression of the impoverishment of the European masses, a manifestation of all the backwardness, deprivation, and want that arrived here in boatloads from Europe? The immense popularity of American movies abroad demonstrates that Europe is the unfinished negative of which America is the proof. The European traveler, viewing with distaste a movie palace or a Motorola, is only looking into the terrible concavity of his continent of hunger inverted startlingly into the convex. Our civilization, deformed as it is outwardly, is still an accomplishment; all this had to come to light.

America is indeed a revelation, though not quite the one that was planned. Given a clean slate, man, it was hoped, would write the future. Instead, he has written his past. This past, inscribed on billboards, ballparks, dance halls, is not seemly, yet its objectification is a kind of disburdenment. The past is at length outside. It does not disturb us as it does Europeans, for our relation with it is both more distant and more familiar. We cannot hate it, for to hate it would be to hate poverty, our eager ancestors, and ourselves.

If there were time, American civilization could be seen as a beginning, even a favorable one, for we have only to look around us to see what a lot of sensibility a little ease will accrue. The children surpass the fathers and Louis B. Mayer cannot be preserved intact in his descendants... Unfortunately, as things seem now, posterity is not around the corner.

—September 1947

19

MLLE. GULLIVER EN AMÉRIQUE

IN JANUARY 1947, Simone de Beauvoir, the leading French *femme savante*, alighted from an airplane at LaGuardia Field for a four-months' stay in the United States. In her own eyes, this trip had something fabulous about it, of a balloonist's expedition or a descent in a diving bell. Where to Frenchmen of an earlier generation, America was the incredible country of *les peaux rouges* and the novels of Fenimore Cooper, to Mlle. de Beauvoir America was, very simply, movieland— she came to verify for herself the existence of violence, drugstore stools, boy-meets-girl, that she had seen depicted on the screen. Her impressions, which she set down in journal form for the readers of *Les Temps modernes*, retained therefore the flavor of an eyewitness account, of confirmation of rumor, the object being not so much to assay America as to testify to its reality.

These impressions, collected into a book, made a certain stir in France; now, three years later, they are appearing in translation in Germany. The book has never been published over here; the few snatches excerpted from it in magazine articles provoked wonder and hostility.

On an American leafing through the pages of an old library copy, the book has a strange effect. It is as though an inhabitant of Lilliput or Brobdingnag, coming upon a copy of *Gulliver's Travels*, sat down to read, in a foreign tongue, of his own local customs codified by an observer of a different species: everything is at once familiar and distorted. The landmarks are there, and some of the institutions and personages—Eighth Avenue, Broadway, Hollywood, the Grand Canyon, Harvard, Yale, Vassar, literary celebrities concealed under initials; here are the drugstores and the cafeterias and the buses and the traffic lights—and yet it is all wrong, schematized, rationalized, like a scale model under glass. Peering down at himself, the American discovers that he has "no sense of *nuance*," that he is always in a good humor, that "in America the individual is nothing," that all Americans think their native town is the most beautiful town in the world, that an office girl cannot go to work in the same dress two days running, that in hotels "illicit" couples are made to swear that they are married, that it almost never happens here that a professor is also a writer, that the majority of American novelists have never been to college, that the middle class has no hold on the country's economic life and very little influence on its political destiny, that the good American citizen is never sick, that racism and reaction grow more menacing every day, that "the appearance, even, of democracy is vanishing from day to day," and that the country is witnessing "the birth of fascism."

From these pages, he discovers, in short, that his country has become, in the eyes of Existentialists, a future which is, so to speak, already a past, a gelid eternity of drugstores, jukeboxes, smiles, refrigerators, and "fascism," and that he himself is no longer an individual but a sort of Mars man, a projection of science fiction, the man of 1984. Such a futuristic vision of America was already in Mlle. de Beauvoir's head when she descended from the plane as from a spaceship, wearing metaphorical goggles: eager as a little girl to taste the rock-candy delights of this materialistic moon civilization (the orange juice, the ice creams, the jazz, the whiskeys, the martinis, and the lobster). She knows already, nevertheless, that this world is not "real," but only a half-frightening fantasy daydreamed by the Americans.

She has preserved enough of Marxism to be warned that the spun-sugar façade is a device of the "Pullman class" to mask its exploitation and cruelty: while the soda fountains spout, Truman and Marshall prepare an anti-Communist crusade that brings back memories of the Nazis, and Congress plots the ruin of the trade unions. "The collective future is in the hands of a privileged class, the Pullman class, to which are reserved the joys of large-scale enterprise and creation; the others are just wheels in a big steel world; they lack the power to conceive an individual future for themselves; they have no plan or passion, hope or nostalgia, that carries them beyond the present; they know only the unending repetition of the cycle of seasons and hours."

This image of a people from Oz or out of an expressionist ballet, a robot people obedient to a generalization, corresponds, of course, with no reality, either in the United States or anywhere else; it is the petrifaction of a fear very common in Europe today—a fear of the future. Where, in a more hopeful era, America embodied for Europe a certain millennial promise, now in the Atomic Age it embodies an evil presentiment of a millennium just at hand. To Mlle. de Beauvoir, obsessed with memories of Jules Verne, America is a symbol of a mechanical progress once dreamed of and now repudiated with horror; it is a Judgment on itself and on Europe. No friendly experience with Americans can dispel this deep-lying dread. She does not wish to know America but only to ascertain that it is there, just as she had imagined it. She shrinks from involvement in this "big steel world" and makes no attempt to see factories, workers, or political leaders. She prefers the abstraction of "Wall Street."

This recoil from American actuality has the result that might be expected, a result, in fact, so predictable that one might say she willed it. Her book is consistently misinformed in small matters as well as large. She has a gift for visual description which she uses very successfully to evoke certain American phenomena: Hollywood, the Grand Canyon, the Bronx, Chinatown, women's dresses, the stockyards, the

Bowery, Golden Gate, auto camps, Hawaiian dinners, etc. Insofar as the US is a vast tourist camp, a vacationland, a Stop-in Serv-Urself, she has caught its essence. But insofar as the United States is something more than a caricature of itself conceived by the mind of an ad man or a western Chamber of Commerce, she has a disinclination to view it. She cannot, for example, take in the names of American writers even when she has their books by her elbow: she speaks repeatedly of James Algee (Agee), of Farrel (Farrell), O'Neil (O'Neill), and of Max Twain—a strange form of compliment to authors whom she professes to like. In the same way, Greenwich Village, which she loves, she speaks of throughout as "Greeniwich," even when she comes to live there.

These are minor distortions. What is more pathetic is her credulity, which amounts to a kind of superstition. She is so eager to appear well informed that she believes anything anybody tells her, especially if it is anti-American and pretends to reveal the inner workings of the capitalist mechanism. The Fifth Avenue shops, she tells us, are "reserved for the capitalist international," and no investigative instinct tempts her to cross the barricade and see for herself. Had she done so, she might have found suburban housewives, file clerks, and stenographers swarming about the racks of Peck & Peck or Best's or Franklin Simon's, and colored girls mingling with white girls at the counters of Saks Fifth Avenue. A Spanish painter assures her that in America you have to hire a press agent to get your paintings shown. An author tells her that in America literary magazines print only favorable reviews. A student tells her that in America private colleges pay better salaries than state universities, so that the best education falls to the privileged classes, who do not want it, and so on. At Vassar, she relates, students are selected "according to their intellectual capacities, family, and fortune." Every item in this catalog is false. (Private colleges do not pay better salaries—on the contrary, with a few exceptions, they pay notoriously worse; family plays no part in the selection of students at Vassar, and fortune only to the extent that the tuition has to be paid by someone—friend, parent, or scholarship donor; you do not have to hire a press agent; some literary magazines make a positive specialty of printing unfavorable reviews.)

Yet Mlle. de Beauvoir, unsuspecting, continues volubly to pass on "the low-down" to her European readers: there is no friendship between the sexes in America; American whites are "stiff" and "cold"; American society has lost its mobility; capital is in "certain hands," and the worker's task is "carefully laid out." "True, a few accidental successes give the myth of the self-made man a certain support, but they are illusory and tangential...."

The picture of an America that consists of a small ruling class and a vast inert, regimented mass beneath it is elaborated at every opportunity. She sees the dispersion of goods on counters but draws no conclusion from it as to the structure of the economy. The American worker, to her, is invariably the French worker, a consecrated symbol of oppression. She talks a great deal of American conformity but fails to recognize a thing that Tocqueville saw long ago; that this conformity is the expression of a predominantly middle-class society; it is the price paid (as yet) for the spread of plenty. Whether the diffusion of television sets is, in itself, a good is another question; the fact is, however, that they *are* diffused; the "Pullman class," for weal or woe, does not have a corner on them, or on the levers of political power.

The outrage of the upper-class minority at the spectacle of television aerials on the shabby houses of Poverty Row, at the thought of the Frigidaires and washing machines in farmhouse and working-class kitchens, at the new cars parked in ranks outside the factories, at the very thought of installment buying, unemployment compensation, social security, trade union benefits, veterans' housing, at General Vaughan, above all at Truman the haberdasher, the symbol of this cocky equality—their outrage is perhaps the most striking phenomenon in American life today. Yet Mlle. de Beauvoir remained unaware of it, and unaware also, for all her journal tells us, of income taxes and inheritance taxes, of the expense account and how it has affected buying habits and given a peculiar rashness and transiency to the daily experience of consumption. It can be argued that certain angry elements in American business do not know their own interests, which lie in the consumers' economy; even so, this ignorance and anger are an immense political fact in America.

The society characterized by Mlle. de Beauvoir as "rigid," "frozen," "closed" is in the process of great change. The mansions are torn down and the real estate "development" takes their place: serried rows of ranch-type houses, painted in pastel colors, each with its picture window and its garden, each equipped with deep freeze, oil furnace, and automatic washer, spring up in the wilderness. Class barriers disappear or become porous; the factory worker is an economic aristocrat in comparison to the middle-class clerk; even segregation is diminishing; consumption replaces acquisition as an incentive. The America invoked by Mlle. de Beauvoir as a country of vast inequalities and dramatic contrasts is rapidly ceasing to exist.

One can guess that it is the new America, rather than the imaginary America of economic royalism, that creates in Mlle. de Beauvoir a feeling of mixed attraction and repulsion. In one half of her sensibility, she is greatly excited by the United States and precisely by its material side. She is fascinated by drugstore displays of soap and dentifrices, by the uniformly regulated traffic, by the "good citizenship" of Americans, by the anonymous camaraderie of the big cities, by jazz and expensive record players and huge collections of records, and above all—to speak frankly—by the orange juice, the martinis, and the whiskey. She speaks elatedly of "my" America, "my" New York; she has a child's greedy possessiveness toward this place which she is in the act of discovering.

Toward the end of the book, as she revises certain early judgments, she finds that she has become "an American." What she means is that she has become somewhat critical of the carnival aspects of American life which at first bewitched her; she is able to make discriminations between different kinds of jazz, different hotels, different nightclubs. Very tentatively, she pushes beyond appearance and perceives that the American is not his possessions, that the American character is not fleshly but abstract. Yet at bottom she remains disturbed by what she has seen and felt, even marginally, of the American problem. This is not one of inequity, as she would prefer to believe, but of its opposite. The problem posed by the United States is, as Tocqueville saw, the problem of equality, its consequences, and what price shall be paid for it. How is wealth to be spread without the spread of uniformity? How create a cushion of plenty without stupefaction of the soul and the senses? It is a dilemma that glares from every picture window and whistles through every breezeway.

If Americans, as Mlle. de Beauvoir thinks, are apathetic politically, it is because they can take neither side with any great conviction—how can one be *against* the abolition of poverty? And how, on the other hand, can one champion a leveling of extremes? For Europeans of egalitarian sympathies, America *is* this dilemma, relentlessly marching toward them, a future which "works," and which for that very reason they have no wish to face. Hence the desire, so very evident in Mlle. de Beauvoir's impressions and in much journalism of the European left, not to know what America is really like, to identify it with "fascism" or "reaction," not to admit, in short, that it has realized, to a considerable extent, the economic and social goals of President Franklin D. Roosevelt and of progressive thought in general.

—January 1952

20

MY CONFESSION

EVERY AGE HAS a keyhole to which its eye is pasted. Spicy court memoirs, the lives of gallant ladies, recollections of an ex-nun, a monk's confession, an atheist's repentance, true-to-life accounts of prostitution and bastardy gave our ancestors a penny peep into the forbidden room. In our own day, this type of sensational fact-fiction is being produced largely by ex-Communists. Public curiosity shows an almost prurient avidity for the details of political defloration, and the memoirs of ex-Communists have an odd resemblance to the confessions of a white slave. Two shuddering climaxes, two rendezvous with destiny, form the poles between which these narratives vibrate: the first describes the occasion when the subject was seduced by Communism; the second shows him wresting himself from the demon embrace. Variations on the form are possible. Senator McCarthy, for example, in his book, *McCarthyism, the Fight for America*, uses a tense series of flashbacks to dramatize his encounter with Communism: the country lies passive in Communism's clasp; he is given a tryst with destiny in the lonely Arizona hills, where, surrounded by "real Americans without any synthetic sheen," he attains the decision that will send him down the long marble corridors to the Senate Caucus Room to bare the shameful commerce.

The diapason of choice plays, like movie music, round today's apostle to the Gentiles: Whittaker Chambers on a park bench and, in a reprise, awake all night at a dark window, facing the void. These people, unlike ordinary beings, are shown the true course during a lightning storm of revelation, on the road to Damascus. And their decisions are lonely decisions, silhouetted against a background of public incomprehension and hostility.

I object. I have read the reminiscences of Mr. Chambers and Miss Bentley. I too have had a share in the political movements of our day, and my experience cries out against their experience. It is not the facts I balk at—I have never been an espionage agent—but the studio atmosphere of sublimity and purpose that enfolds the facts and the chief actor. When Whittaker Chambers is mounted on his tractor, or Elizabeth Bentley, alone, is meditating her decision in a white New England church, I have the sense that they are on location and that, at any moment, the director will call "Cut." It has never been like that for me; events have never waited, like extras, while I toiled to make up my mind between good and evil. In fact, I have never known these mental convulsions, which appear quite strange to me when I read about them, even when I do not question the author's sincerity.

Is it really so difficult to tell a good action from a bad one? I think one usually knows right away or a moment afterward, in a horrid flash of regret. And when one genuinely hesitates—or at least it is so in my case—it is never about anything of importance, but about perplexing trivial things, such as whether to have fish or meat for dinner, or whether to take the bus or subway to reach a certain destination, or whether to wear the beige or the green. The "great" decisions—those I can look back on pensively and say, "That was a turning point"—have been made without my awareness. Too late to do anything about it, I discover that I have chosen. And this is particularly striking when the choice has been political or historic. For me, in fact, the mark of the historic is the nonchalance with which it picks up an individual and deposits him in a trend, like a house playfully moved by a tornado.

My own experience with Communism prompts me to relate it, just because it had this inadvertence that seems to me lacking in the true confessions of reformed Communists. Like Stendhal's hero, who took part in something confused and disarrayed and insignificant that he later learned was the Battle of Waterloo, I joined the anti-Communist movement without meaning to and only found out afterward, through others, the meaning or "name" assigned to what I had done. This occurred in the late fall of 1936.

Three years before, I had graduated from college—Vassar, the same college Elizabeth Bentley had gone to—without having suffered any fracture of my political beliefs or moral frame. All through college, my official political philosophy was royalism; though I was not much interested in politics, it irritated me to be told that "you could not turn the clock back." But I did not see much prospect for kingship in the United States (unless you imported one, like the Swedes), and, *faute de mieux*, I awarded my sympathies to the Democratic Party, which I tried to look on as the party of the Southern patriciate. At the same time, I had an aversion to Republicans—an instinctive feeling that had been with me since I was a child of eight pedaling my wagon up and down our cement driveway and howling "Hurray for Cox" at the Republican neighbors who passed by. I disliked businessmen and business attitudes partly, I think, because I came from a professional (though Republican) family and had picked up a disdain for businessmen as being beneath us, in education and general culture. And the anti-Catholic prejudice against Al Smith during the 1928 election, the tinkling amusement at Mrs. Smith's vulgarity, democratized me a little in spite of myself: I was won by Smith's plebeian charm, the big coarse nose, and rubbery politician's smile.

But this same distrust of uniformity made me shrink, in 1932, from the sloppily dressed Socialist girls at college who paraded for Norman Thomas and tirelessly argued over "Cokes"; their eager fellowship and scrawled placards and heavy personalities bored me—there was something, to my mind, deeply athletic about this socialism. It was a kind of political hockey played by big, gaunt, dyspeptic girls in pants. It startled me a little, therefore, to learn that in an election poll taken of the faculty, several of my favorite teachers had voted for Thomas; in them, the socialist faith appeared rather charming, I decided—a gracious and attractive oddity, like the English Ovals they gave you when you came for tea. That was the winter Hitler was coming to power and, hearing of the anti-Jewish atrocities, I had a flurry of political indignation. I wrote a prose-poem that dealt, in a mixed-up way, with the Polish Corridor and the Jews. This poem was so unlike me that I did not know whether to be proud of it or ashamed of it when I saw it in a college magazine. At this period, we were interested in Surrealism and automatic writing, and the poem had a certain renown because it had come out of my interior without much sense or order, just the way automatic writing was supposed to do. But there my political development stopped.

The Depression was closer to home; in New York I used to see apple-sellers on the street corners, and, now and then, a bread line, but I had a very thin awareness of mass poverty. The Depression was too close to home to awaken anything but curiosity and wonder—the feelings of a child confronted with a death in the family. I was conscious of the suicides of stockbrokers and businessmen, and of the fact that some of my friends had to go on scholarships and had their dress allowances curtailed, while their mothers gaily turned to doing their own cooking. To most of us at Vassar, I think, the Depression was chiefly an upper-class phenomenon.

My real interests were literary. In a paper for my English Renaissance seminar, I noted a resemblance between the Elizabethan Puritan pundits and the school of Marxist criticism that was beginning to pontificate about proletarian literature in the *New Masses*. I disliked the modern fanatics, cold, envious little clerics, equally with the insufferable and ridiculous Gabriel Harvey—Cambridge pedant and friend of Spenser—who tried to introduce the rules of Latin quantity into English verse and vilified a true poet who had died young, in squalor and misery. I really hated absolutism and officiousness of any kind (I preferred my kings martyred) and was pleased to be able to recognize a Zeal-of-the-Land-Busy in proletarian dress. And it was through a novel that I first learned, in my senior year, about the Sacco-Vanzetti case. The discovery that two innocent men had been executed only a few years back while I, oblivious, was in boarding school gave me a disturbing shock. The case was still so near that I was tantalized by a feeling that it was not too late to do something— try still another avenue, if Governor Fuller and the Supreme Court obdurately would not be moved. An unrectified case of injustice has a terrible way of lingering, restlessly, in the social atmosphere like an unfinished equation. I went on to the Mooney case, which vexed not only my sense of equity but my sense of plausibility—how was it possible for the prosecution to lie so, in broad daylight, with the whole world watching?

When in May 1933, however, before graduation, I went down to apply for a job at the old *New Republic* offices, I was not drawn there by the magazine's editorial policy—I hardly knew what it was—but because the book review section seemed to me to possess a certain elegance and independence of thought that would be hospitable to a critical spirit like me. And I was badly taken aback when the book review editor, to whom I had been shunted—there was no job—puffed his pipe and remarked that he would give me a review if I could show him that I was either a genius or starving. "I'm not starving," I said quickly; I knew I was not a genius and I was not pleased by the suggestion that I would be taking bread from other people's mouths. I did not think this a fair criterion and in a moment I said so. In reply, he put down his pipe, shrugged, reached out for the material I had brought with me, and half-promised, after an assaying glance, to send me a book. My notice finally appeared; it was not very good, but I did not know that and was elated. Soon I was reviewing novels and biographies for both *The New Republic* and *The Nation* and preening myself on the connection. Yet, whenever I entered *The New Republic*'s waiting room, I was seized with a feeling of nervous guilt toward the shirt-sleeved editors upstairs and their busy social conscience, and, above all, toward the shabby young men who were waiting too and who had, my bones told me, a better claim than I to the book I hoped to take away with me. They looked poor, pinched, scholarly, and supercilious, and I did not know which of these qualities made me, with my clicking high heels and fall "ensemble," seem more out of place.

I cannot remember the moment when I ceased to air my old royalist convictions and stuffed them away in an inner closet as you do a dress or an ornament that you perceive strikes the wrong note. It was probably at the time when I first became aware of Communists as a distinct entity. I had known about them, certainly, in college, but it was not until I came to New York that I began to have certain people, celebrities, pointed out to me as Communists and to turn my head to look at them, wonderingly. I had no wish to be one of them, but the fact that they were there—an unreckoned factor—made my own political opinions take on a protective coloration. This process was accelerated by my marriage—a week after graduation—to an actor and playwright who was in some ways very much like me. He was the son of a Minnesota normal school administrator who had been the scapegoat in an academic scandal that had turned him out of his job and reduced him, for a time, when my husband was nine or ten, to selling artificial limbs and encyclopedia sets from door to door. My husband still brooded over his father's misfortune, like Hamlet or a character in Ibsen, and this had given his nature a sardonic twist that inclined him to behave like a paradox—to follow the mode and despise it, live in a Beekman Place apartment while lacking the money to buy groceries, play bridge with society couples and poker with the stage electricians, dress in the English style and carry a walking stick while wearing a red necktie.

He was an odd-looking man, prematurely bald, with a tense, arresting figure, a broken nose, a Standard English accent, and wry, circumflexed eyebrows. There was something about him both baleful and quizzical; whenever he stepped on the stage he had the ironic air of a symbol. This curious appearance of his disqualified him for most Broadway roles; he was too young for character parts and too bald for juveniles. Yet just this disturbing ambiguity—a Communist painter friend did a drawing of him that brought out a resemblance to Lenin —suited the portentous and equivocal atmosphere of left-wing drama. He smiled dryly at Marxist terminology, but there was social anger in him. During the years we were married, the only work he found was in productions of "social" significance. He played for the Theatre Union in *The Sailors of Cattaro*, about a mutiny in the Austrian fleet, and in *Black Pit*, about coal miners; the following year, he was in *Winterset* and Archibald MacLeish's *Panic*—the part of a blind man in both cases. He wrote revue sketches and unproduced plays, in a mocking, despairing, but nonetheless radical vein; he directed the book of a musical called *Americana* that featured the song "Brother, Can You Spare a Dime?" I suppose there was something in him of both the victim and the leader, an undertone of totalitarianism; he was very much interested in the mythic qualities of leadership and talked briskly about a Farmer-Labor party in his stage English accent. Notions of the superman and the genius flickered across his thoughts. But this led him, as it happened, away from politics, into sheer personal vitalism, and it was only in plays that he entered "at the head of a mob." In personal life he was very winning, but that is beside the point here.

The point is that we both, through our professional connections, began to take part in a left-wing life, to which we felt superior, which we laughed at, but which nevertheless was influencing us without our being aware of it. If the composition of the body changes every seven years, the composition of our minds during the seven years changed, so that though our thoughts looked the same to us, inside we had been altered, like an old car which has had part after part replaced in it under the hood.

We wore our rue with a difference; we should never have considered joining the Communist Party. We were not even fellow travelers; we did not sign petitions or join "front" groups. We were not fools, after all, and were no more deceived by the League against War and Fascism, say, than by a Chinatown bus with a carload of shills aboard. It was part of our metropolitan sophistication to know the truth about Communist fronts. We accepted the need for social reform, but we declined to draw the "logical" inference that the Communists wanted us to draw from this. We argued with the comrades backstage in the dressing rooms and at literary cocktail parties; I was attacked by a writer in the *New Masses*. We knew about Lovestoneites and Trotskyites, even while we were ignorant of the labor theory of value, the law of uneven development, the theory of permanent revolution vs. socialism in one country, and so on. "Lovestone is a Lovestone-ite!" John wrote in wax on his dressing room mirror, and on his door in the old Civic Repertory he put up a sign: "Through these portals pass some of the most beautiful tractors in the Ukraine."

The comrades shrugged and laughed, a little unwillingly. They knew we were not hostile but merely unserious, politically. The comrades who knew us best used to assure us that our sophistication was just an armor; underneath, we must care for the same things they did. They were mistaken, I am afraid. Speaking for myself, I cannot remember a single broad altruistic emotion visiting me during that period—the kind of emotion the simpler comrades, with their shining eyes and exalted faces, seemed to have in copious secretion. And yet it was true: we were not hostile. We marched in May Day parades, just for the fun of it, and sang, "Hold the Fort, for We Are Coming," and

"Bandiera Rossa," and "The Internationale," though we always bellowed "The *Socialist* International shall be the human race," instead of "The International Soviet," to pique the Communists in our squad. We took part in evening clothes in a consumers' walkout at the Waldorf to support a waiters' strike—the Communists had nothing to do with this—and we grew very excited (we did have negative feelings) when another young literary independent was arrested and booked. During a strike at a department store, John joined the sympathetic picketing and saw two of his fellow actors carried off in the Black Maria; they missed a matinee and set off a controversy about what was the *first* responsibility of a Communist playing in a proletarian drama. We went once or twice to a class for actors in Marxism, just to see what was up; we went to a debate on Freud and/or Marx, to a debate on the execution of the 104 White Guards following Kirov's assassination.

Most ex-Communists nowadays, when they write their autobiographies or testify before congressional committees, are at pains to point out that their actions were very, very bad and their motives very, very good. I would say the reverse of myself, though without the intensives. I see no reason to disavow my actions, which were perfectly all right, but my motives give me a little embarrassment, and just because I cannot disavow them: that fevered, contentious, trivial show-off in the May Day parade is still recognizably me.

We went to dances at Webster Hall and took our uptown friends. We went to parties to raise money for the sharecroppers, for the Theatre Union, for the *New Masses*. These parties generally took place in a borrowed apartment, often a sculptor's or commercial artist's studio; you paid for your drinks, which were dispensed at a long, wet table; the liquor was dreadful; the glasses were small, and there was never enough ice. Long-haired men in turtle-necked sweaters marched into the room in processions and threw their overcoats on the floor, against the wall, and sat on them; they were only artists and bit actors, but they gave these affairs a look of gangsterish menace, as if the room were guarded by the goons of the future. On couches with wrinkled slipcovers, little spiky-haired girls, like spiders, dressed in peasant blouses and carapaced with Mexican jewelry, made voracious passes at baby-faced juveniles; it was said that they "did it for the Party," as a recruiting effort. Vague, soft-faced old women with dust mops of whitish hair wandered benevolently about seeking a listener; on a sofa against a wall, like a deity, sat a bearded scion of an old Boston family, stiff as a post. All of us, generally, became very drunk; the atmosphere was horribly sordid, with cigarette burns on tables, spilled drinks, ashes everywhere, people passed out on the bed with the coats or necking, you could not be sure which. Nobody cared what happened because there was no host or hostess. The fact that a monied person had been simple enough to lend the apartment seemed to make the guests want to desecrate it, to show that they were exercising not a privilege but a right.

Obviously, I must have hated these parties, but I went to them, partly because I was ashamed of my own squeamishness, and partly because I had a curiosity about the Communist men I used to see there, not the actors or writers, but the higher-ups, impresarios and theoreticians—dark, smooth-haired owls with large white lugubrious faces and glasses. These were the spiritual directors of the Communist cultural celebrities and they moved about at these parties like so many monks or abbés in a worldly salon. I had always liked to argue with the clergy, and I used to argue with these men, who had the air, as they stood with folded arms, of listening not to a disagreement but to a confession. Whenever I became tight, I would bring up (oh, *vino veritas*) the tsar and his family. I did not see why they all had had to be killed—the tsar himself, yes, perhaps, and the tsarina, but not the young girls and the children. I knew the answer, of course (the young tsarevitch or one of his sisters might have served as a rallying point for the counterrevolutionary forces), but still I gazed hopefully into these docents' faces, seeking a trace of scruple or compassion. But I saw only a marmoreal astuteness. The question was of bourgeois origin, they said with finality.

The next morning I was always bitterly ashamed. I had let these omniscient men see the real me underneath, and the other me squirmed and gritted her teeth and muttered, Never, never, *never* again. And yet they had not convinced me—there was the paradox. The superiority I felt to the Communists I knew had, for me at any rate, good grounding; it was based on their lack of humor, their fanaticism, and the slow drip of cant that thickened their utterance like a nasal catarrh. *And yet* I was tremendously impressed by them. They made me feel petty and shallow; they had, shall I say, a daily ugliness in their life that made my pretty life tawdry. I think all of us who moved in that ambience must have felt something of the kind, even while we laughed at them. When John and I, for instance, would say of a certain actor, "He is a Party member," our voices always contained a note of respect. This respect might be mixed with pity, as when we saw some blue-eyed young profile, fresh from his fraternity and his C average, join up because a sleazy girl had persuaded him. The literary Communists I sincerely despised because I was able to judge the quality of the work they published and see their dishonesty and contradictions; even so, when I beheld them in person, at a Webster Hall dance, I was troubled and felt perhaps I had wronged them —perhaps there was something in them that my vision could not perceive, as some eyes cannot perceive color.

People sometimes say that they envied the Communists because they were so "sure." In my case, this was not exactly it; I was sure, too, intellectually speaking, as far as I went. That is, I had a clear mind and was reasonably honest, while many of the Communists I knew were pathetically fogged up. In any case, my soul was not particularly hot for certainties.

And yet in another way I did envy the Communists, or, to be more accurate, wonder whether I ought to envy them. I could not, I saw, be a Communist because I was not "made that way." Hence, to be a Communist was to possess a sort of privilege. And this privilege, like all privileges, appeared to be a source of power. Any form of idiocy or aberration can confer this distinction on its owner, at least in our age, which aspires to a "total" experience; in the Thirties it was the Communists who seemed fearsomely to be the happy few, not because they had peace or certitude but because they were a mutation—a mutation that threatened, in the words of their own anthem, to become the human race.

There was something arcane in every Communist, and the larger this area was the more we respected him. That was why the literary Communists, who operated in the open, doing the hatchet work on artists' reputations, were held in such relatively low esteem. An underground worker rated highest with us; next were the theoreticians and oracles; next were the activists, who mostly worked, we heard, on the waterfront. Last came the rank and file, whose work consisted of making speeches, distributing leaflets, attending Party and faction meetings, joining front organizations, marching in parades and demonstrations. These people we dismissed as uninteresting not so much because their work was routine but because the greater part of it was visible. In the same way, among individual comrades, we looked up to those who were close-lipped and stern about their beliefs and we disparaged the more voluble members—the forensic little actors who tried to harangue us in the dressing rooms. The idea of a double life was what impressed us: the more talkative comrades seemed to have only one life, like us; but even they, we had to remind ourselves, had a secret annex to their personality, which was signified by their Party name. It is hard not to respect somebody who has an alias.

Of fellow travelers, we had a very low opinion. People who were not willing to "go the whole way" filled us with impatient disdain. The only fellow travelers who merited our notice were those of whom it was said: the Party prefers that they remain on the outside. I think some fellow travelers circulated such stories about themselves deliberately, in order to appear more interesting. There was another type of fellow traveler who let it be known that they stayed out of the Party because of some tiny doctrinal difference with Marxism. This tiny difference magnified them enormously in their own eyes and allowed them to bear gladly the accusation of cowardice. I knew one such person very well—a spruce, ingratiating swain, the heir to a large fortune—and I think it was not cowardice but a kind of pietistic vanity. He felt he cut more of a figure if he seemed to be doing the Party's dirty work gratuitously, without compulsion, like an oblate.

In making these distinctions (which were the very distinctions the Party made), I had no idea, of course, that I was allowing myself to be influenced by the Party in the field where I was most open to suasion—the field of social snobbery. Yet in fact I was being deterred from forming any political opinions of my own, lest I find I was that despised article, a "mere" socialist or watery liberal, in the same way that a young snob coming to college and seeing who the "right" people are will strive to make no friends rather than be caught with the wrong ones.

For me, the Communist Party was *the* party, and even though I did not join it, I prided myself on knowing that it was the pinnacle. It is only now that I see the social component in my attitude. At the time, I simply supposed that I was being clear-sighted and logical. I used to do research and typing for a disgruntled middle-aged man who was a freak for that day—an anti-Communist Marxist—and I was bewildered by his anti-Party bias. While we were drinking hot tea, Russian style, from glasses during the intervals of our work, I would try to show him his mistake. "Don't you think it's rather futile," I expostulated, "to criticize the Party the way you do, from the outside? After all, it's the *only* working-class party, and if *I* were a Marxist I would join it and try to reform it." Snorting, he would raise his small deep-set blue eyes and stare at me and then try patiently to show me that there was no democracy in the Party. I listened disbelievingly. It seemed to me that it would just be a question of converting first one comrade and then another to your point of view till gradually you had achieved a majority. And when my employer assured me that they would throw you out if you tried that, my twenty-three-year-old wisdom cocked an eyebrow. I thought I knew what was the trouble: he was a pathologi-cally lazy man and his growling criticisms of the Party were simply a form of malingering, like the aches and pains he used to manufacture to avoid working on an article. A real revolutionary who was not afraid of exertion would get into the Party and fight.

The curious idea that being critical of the Party was a compelling rea-son for joining it must have been in the air, for the same argument was brought to bear on me in the summer of 1936—the summer my hus-band and I separated and that I came closest to the gravitational pull of the Communist world. Just before I went off to Reno, there was a week in June when I stayed in Southampton with the young man I was planning to marry and a little Communist organizer in an old summer house furnished with rattan and wicker and Chinese matting and mother-of-pearl and paper fans. We had come there for a pur-pose. The little organizer had just been assigned a car—a battered old Ford roadster that had been turned over to the Party for the use of some poor organizer; it may have been the very car that figured in the Hiss case. My fiancé, who had known him for years, perhaps from the peace movement, was going to teach him to drive. We were all at a pause in our lives. The following week our friend was supposed to take the car to California and do propaganda work among the migrant fruit pickers; I was to go to Reno; my fiancé, a vivacious young bachelor, was to conquer his habits of idleness and buckle down to a serious job. Those seven days, therefore, had a special, still quality, like the days of a novena you make in your childhood; a part of each of them was set aside for the Party's task. It was early in June; the musty house that belonged to my fiancé's parents still had the winter smell of mice and old wood and rust and mildew. The summer colony had not yet arrived; the red flag, meaning that it was dangerous to swim, flew daily on the beach; the roads were nearly empty. Every afternoon we would take the old car, canvas flapping, to a deserted stretch of straight road in the dunes, where the neophyte could take the wheel.

He was a large-browed, dwarfish man in his late thirties, with a deep widow's peak, a bristly short mustache, and a furry western accent—rather simple, open-natured, and cheerful, the sort of person who might have been a small-town salesman or itinerant newspaperman. There was an energetic, hopeful innocence about him that was not confined to his political convictions—he could *not* learn to drive. Every day the same thing happened; he would settle his frail yet stocky figure trustingly in the driver's seat, grip the wheel, step on the starter, and lose control of the car, which would shoot ahead in first or backward in reverse for a few perilous feet till my fiancé turned off the ignition; Ansel always mistook the gas for the brake and forgot to steer while he was shifting gears.

It was clear that he would never be able to pass the driver's test at the county seat. In the evenings, to make up to him for his oncoming disappointment (we smiled when he said he could start without a license), we encouraged him to talk about the Party and tried to take an intelligent interest. We would sit by the lamp and drink and ask questions, while he smoked his short pipe and from time to time took a long draft from his highball, like a man alone musing in a chair.

And finally one night, in the semi-dark, he knocked out his pipe and said to me: "You're very critical of the Party. Why don't you join it?" A thrill went through me, but I laughed, as when somebody has proposed to you and you are not sure whether they are serious. "I don't think I'd make very good material." "You're wrong," he said gravely. "You're just the kind of person the Party needs. You're young and idealistic and independent." I broke in: "I thought independence was just what the Party didn't want." "The Party needs criticism," he said. "But it needs it from the inside. If people like you who agree with its main objectives would come in and criticize, we wouldn't be so narrow and sectarian." "You admit the Party is narrow?" exclaimed my fiancé. "Sure, I admit it," said Ansel, grinning. "But it's partly the fault of people like Mary who won't come in and broaden us." And he confided that he himself made many of the same criticisms I did, but he made them from within the Party, and so could get himself listened to. "The big problem of the American Party," said Ansel, puffing at his pipe, "is the smallness of the membership. People say we're ruled from Moscow; I've never seen any sign of it. But let's suppose it's true, for the sake of argument. This just means that the American Party isn't big enough yet to stand on its own feet. A big, indigenous party couldn't be ruled from Moscow. The will of the members would have to rule it, just as their dues and contributions would support it." "That's where I come in, I suppose?" I said, teasing. "That's where you come in," he calmly agreed. He turned to my fiancé. "Not you," he said. "You won't have the time to give to it. But for Mary I think it would be an interesting experiment."

An interesting experiment... I let the thought wander through my mind. The subject recurred several times, by the lamplight, though with no particular urgency. Ansel, I thought (and still think), was speaking sincerely and partly in my own interest, almost as a spectator, as if he would be diverted to see how I worked out in the Party. All this gave me quite a new sense of Communism and of myself too; I had never looked upon my character in such a favorable light. And as a beneficiary of Ansel's charity, I felt somewhat ashamed of the very doubt it raised: the suspicion that he might be blind to the real facts of inner Party life. I could admire where I could not follow, and, studying Ansel, I decided that I admired the Communists and would probably be one, if I were the person he thought me. Which I was afraid I was not. For me, such a wry conclusion is always uplifting, and I had the feeling that I mounted in understanding when Sunday morning came and I watched Ansel pack his sturdy suitcase and his briefcase full of leaflets into the old roadster. He had never yet driven more than a few yards by himself, and we stood on the front steps to await what was going to happen: he would not be able to get out of the driveway, and we would have to put him on the train and return the car to the Party when we came back to New York. As we watched, the car began to move; it picked up speed and grated into second, holding to the middle of the road as it turned out of the driveway. It hesitated and went into third: Ansel was driving! Through the back window we saw his figure hunched over the wheel; the road dipped and he vanished. We had witnessed a miracle, and we turned back into the house, frightened. All day we sat waiting for the call that would tell us there had been an accident, but the day passed without a sound, and by nightfall we accepted the phenomenon and pictured the little car on the highway, traveling steadily west in one indefatigable thrust, not daring to stop for gas or refreshment, lest the will of the driver falter.

This parting glimpse of Ansel through the car's back window was, as it turned out, ultimate. Politically speaking, we reached a watershed that summer. The first Moscow trial took place in August. I knew nothing of this event because I was in Reno and did not see the New York papers. Nor did I know that the Party line had veered to the right and that all the fellow travelers would be voting, not for Browder as I was now prepared to do (if only I remembered to register), but for Roosevelt. Isolated from these developments in the mountain altitudes, I was blossoming, like a lone winter rose overlooked by the frost, into a revolutionary thinker of the pure, uncompromising strain. The detached particles of the past three years' experience suddenly "made sense," and I saw myself as a radical.

"Book Bites Mary," wrote back a surprised literary editor when I sent him, from Reno, a radiant review of a novel about the Paris Commune that ended with the heroine sitting down to read the *Communist Manifesto*. In Seattle, when I came to stay with my grandparents, I found a strike on and instantly wired *The Nation* to ask if I could cover it. Every night I was off to the Labor Temple or a longshoreman's hall while my grandparents took comfort from the fact that I seemed to be against Roosevelt, the Democrats, and the tsars of the A. F. of L.—they did not quite grasp my explanation, that I was criticizing "from the left."

Right here, I come up against a puzzle: Why didn't I take the *next step*? But it is only a puzzle if one thinks of me not as a concrete entity but as a term in a logical operation: you agree with the Communist Party; ergo, you join it. I reasoned that way but I did not behave so. There was something in me that capriciously resisted being a term in logic, and the very fact that I cannot elicit any specific reason why I did not join the Party shows that I was never really contemplating it, though I can still hear my own voice, raised very authoritatively at a cafeteria table at the Central Park Zoo, pointing out to a group of young intellectuals that if we were serious we would join the Communists.

This was in September and I was back in New York. The Spanish Civil War had begun. The pay-as-you-go parties were now all for the Loyalists, and young men were volunteering to go and fight in Spain. I read the paper every morning with tears of exaltation in my eyes, and my sympathies rained equally on Communists, Socialists, Anarchists, and the brave Catholic Basques. My heart was tense and swollen with popular-front solidarity. I applauded the Lincoln Battalion, protested nonintervention, hurried into Wanamaker's to look for cotton-lace stockings: I was boycotting silk on account of Japan in China. I was careful to smoke only union-made cigarettes; the white package with Sir Walter Raleigh's portrait came proudly out of my pocketbook to rebuke Chesterfields and Luckies.

It was a period of intense happiness; the news from the battle front was often encouraging and the practice of virtue was surprisingly easy. I moved into a one-room apartment on a crooked street in Greenwich Village and exulted in being poor and alone. I had a part-time job and read manuscripts for a publisher; the very riskiness of my situation was zestful—I had decided not to get married. The first month or so was scarifyingly lonely, but I survived this, and, starting early in November, I began to feel the first stirrings of popularity. A new set of people, rather smart and moneyed, young Communists with a little "name," progressive hosts and modernist hostesses, had discovered me. The fact that I was poor and lived in such a funny little apartment increased the interest felt: I was passed from hand to hand, as a novelty, like Gulliver among the Brobdingnagians. During those first days in November, I was chiefly conscious of what a wonderful time I was starting to have. All this while, I had remained ignorant of the fissure that was opening. Nobody, I think, had told me of the trial of Zinoviev and Kamenev—the trial of the sixteen—or of the new trial that was being prepared in Moscow, the trial of Pyatakov and Radek.

Then, one afternoon in November, I was taken to a cocktail party, in honor of Art Young, the old *Masses* cartoonist, whose book, *The Best of Art Young*, was being published that day. It was the first publisher's party I had ever been to, and my immediate sensation was one of disappointment: nearly all these people were strangers and, to me, quite unattractive. Art Young, a white-haired little kewpie, sitting in a corner, was pointed out to me, and I turned a respectful gaze on him, though I had no clear idea who he was or how he had distinguished himself. I presumed he was a veteran Communist, like a number of the stalwarts in the room, survivors of the old *Masses* and the

Liberator. Their names were whispered to me and I nodded; this seemed to be a commemorative occasion, and the young men hovered in groups around the old men, as if to catch a word for posterity. On the outskirts of certain groups I noticed a few poorly dressed young men, bolder spirits, nervously flexing their lips, framing sentences that would propel them into the conversational center, like actors with a single line to speak.

The solemnity of these proceedings made me feel terribly ill at ease. It was some time before I became aware that it was not just me who was nervous: the whole room was under a constraint. Some groups were avoiding other groups, and now and then an arrow of sarcasm would wing like a sniper's bullet from one conversation to another.

I was standing, rather bleakly, by the refreshment table, when a question was thrust at me: Did I think Trotsky was entitled to a hearing? It was a novelist friend of mine, dimple-faced, shaggy-headed, earnest, with a whole train of people, like a deputation, behind him. Trotsky? I glanced for help at a sour little man I had been talking with, but he merely shrugged. My friend made a beckoning gesture and a circle closed in. What had Trotsky done? Alas, I had to ask. A tumult of voices proffered explanations. My friend raised a hand for silence. Leaning on the table, he supplied the background, speaking very slowly, in his dragging, disconsolate voice, like a schoolteacher wearied of his subject. Trotsky, it appeared, had been accused of fostering a counterrevolutionary plot in the Soviet Union—organizing terrorist centers and conspiring with the Gestapo to murder the Soviet leaders. Sixteen old Bolsheviks had confessed and implicated him. It had been in the press since August.

I blushed; everybody seemed to be looking at me strangely. I made a violent effort to take in what had been said. The enormity of the charge dazed me, and I supposed that some sort of poll was being taken and that I was being asked to pronounce on whether Trotsky was guilty or innocent. I could tell from my friend's low, even, melancholy tone that he regarded the charges as derisory. "What do you want me to say?" I protested. "I don't know anything about it." "Trotsky denies the charges," patiently intoned my friend. "He declares it's a GPU fabrication. Do you think he's entitled to a hearing?" My mind cleared. "Why, of course." I laughed—were there people who would say that Trotsky was *not* entitled to a hearing? But my friend's voice tolled a rebuke to this levity. "She says Trotsky is entitled to his day in court."

The sour little man beside me made a peculiar, sucking noise. "You disagree?" I demanded, wonderingly. "I'm smart," he retorted. "I don't let anybody ask me. You notice, he doesn't ask me?" "Shut up, George," said my novelist friend impatiently. "I'm asking *her*. One thing more, Mary," he continued gravely. "Do you believe that Trotsky should have the right of asylum?" The right of asylum! I looked for someone to share my amusement—were we in ancient Greece or the Middle Ages? I was sure the US government would be delighted to harbor such a distinguished foreigner. But nobody smiled back. Everybody watched dispassionately, as for form's sake I assented to the phrasing: yes, Trotsky, in my opinion, was entitled to the right of asylum.

I went home with the serene feeling that all these people were slightly crazy. *Right of asylum, his day in court!*—in a few hours I had forgotten the whole thing.

Four days later I tore open an envelope addressed to me by something that called itself "Committee for the Defense of Leon Trotsky," and idly scanned the contents. "We demand for Leon Trotsky the right of a fair hearing and the right of asylum." Who were these demanders, I wondered, and, glancing down the letterhead, I discovered my own name. I sat down on my unmade studio couch, shaking. How dared they help themselves to my signature? This was the kind of thing the Communists were always being accused of pulling; apparently, Trotsky's admirers had gone to the same school. I had paid so little heed to the incident at the party that a connection was slow to establish itself. Reading over the list of signers, I recognized "names" that had been present there and remembered my novelist-friend going from person to person, methodically polling...

How were they feeling, I wondered, when they opened their mail this morning? My own feelings were crisp. In two minutes I had decided to withdraw my name and write a note of protest. Trotsky had a right to a hearing, but I had a right to my signature. For even if there had been a legitimate misunderstanding (it occurred to me that perhaps I had been the only person there not to see the import of my answers), nothing I had said committed me to Trotsky's *defense*.

The "decision" was made, but according to my habit I procrastinated. The severe letter I proposed to write got put off till the next day and then the next. Probably I was not eager to offend somebody who had been a good friend to me. Nevertheless, the letter would undoubtedly have been written, had I been left to myself. But within the next forty-eight hours the phone calls began. People whom I had not seen for months or whom I knew very slightly telephoned to advise me to get off the newly formed Committee. These calls were not precisely threatening. Indeed, the caller often sounded terribly weak and awkward, as if he did not like the mission he had been assigned. But they were peculiar. For one thing, they usually came after nightfall and sometimes quite late, when I was already in bed. Another thing, there was no real effort at persuasion: the caller stated his purpose in standardized phrases, usually plaintive in tone (the Committee was the tool of reaction, and all liberal people should dissociate themselves from its activities, which were an unwarranted intervention in the domestic affairs of the Soviet Union), and then hung up, almost immediately, before I had a proper chance to answer. Odd too—the voices were not those of my Communist friends but of the merest acquaintances. These people who admonished me to "think about it" were not people whose individual opinions could have had any weight with me. And when I did think about it, this very fact took on an ominous and yet to me absurd character: I was not being appealed to personally but impersonally warned.

Behind these phone calls there was a sense of the Party wheeling its forces into would-be disciplined formations, like a fleet or an army maneuvering. This, I later found, was true: a systematic telephone campaign was going on to dislodge members from the Committee. The phone calls generally came after dark and sometimes (especially when the recipient was elderly) in the small hours of the morning. The more prominent signers got anonymous messages and threats.

And in the morning papers and the columns of the liberal magazines I saw the results. During the first week, name after name fell off the Committee's letterhead. Prominent liberals and literary figures issued statements deploring their mistake. And a number of people protested that their names had been used without permission...

There, but for the grace of God, went I, I whispered, awestruck, to myself, hugging my guilty knowledge. Only Heaven—I plainly saw—by making me dilatory had preserved me from joining this sorry band. Here was the occasion when I should have been wrestling with my conscience or standing, floodlit, at the crossroads of choice. But in fact I was only aware that I had had a providential escape. I had been saved from having to decide about the Committee; *I* did not decide it—the Communists with their pressure tactics took the matter out of my hands. We all have an instinct that makes us side with the weak, if we do not stop to reason about it, the instinct that makes a householder shield a wounded fugitive without first conducting an inquiry into the rights and wrongs of his case. Such "decisions" are simple reflexes; they do not require courage; if they did, there would be fewer of them. When I saw what was happening, I rebounded to the defense of the Committee without a single hesitation—it was nobody's business, I felt, how I happened to be on it, and if anybody had asked me, I should have lied without a scruple.

Of course, I did not foresee the far-reaching consequences of my act—how it would change my life. I had no notion that I was now an anti-Communist, where before I had been either indifferent or pro-Communist. I did, however, soon recognize that I was in a rather awkward predicament—not a moral quandary but a social one. I knew nothing about the cause I had espoused; I had never read a word of Lenin or Trotsky, nothing of Marx but the *Communist Manifesto*, nothing of Soviet history; the very names of the old Bolsheviks who had confessed were strange and almost barbarous in my ears. As for Trotsky, the only thing that made me think that he might be innocent was the odd behavior of the Communists and the fellow-traveling liberals, who seemed to be infuriated at the idea of a free inquiry. All around me, in the fashionable Stalinist circles I was now frequenting, I began to meet with suppressed excitement and just-withheld disapproval. Jeweled lady authors turned white and shook their bracelets angrily when I came into a soiree; rising young men in publishing or advertising tightened their neckties dubiously when I urged them to examine the case for themselves; out dancing in a night-club, tall, collegiate young Party members would press me to their shirt bosoms and tell me not to be silly, honey.

And since I seemed to meet more Stalinists every day, I saw that I was going to have to get some arguments with which to defend myself. It was not enough, apparently, to say you were for a fair hearing; you had to rebut the entire case of the prosecution to get anybody to incline an ear in your direction. I began to read, headlong, the literature on the case—the pamphlets issued by Trotsky's adherents, the verbatim report of the second trial published by the Soviet Union, the "bourgeois" press, the Communist press, the radical press. To my astonishment (for I had scarcely dared think it), the trials did indeed seem to be a monstrous frame-up. The defendant, Pyatakov, flew to Oslo to "conspire" with Trotsky during a winter when, according to the authorities, no planes landed at the Oslo airfield; the defendant, Holtzmann, met Trotsky's son, Sedov, in 1936, at the Hotel Bristol in Copenhagen, which had burned down in 1912; the witness, Romm, met Trotsky in Paris at a time when numerous depositions testified that he had been in Royan, among clouds of witnesses, or on the way there from the south of France.

These were only the most glaring discrepancies—the ones that got in the newspapers. Everywhere you touched the case something crumbled. The carelessness of the case's manufacture was to me its most terrifying aspect; the slovenly disregard for credibility defied credence, in its turn. How did they dare? I think I was more shaken by finding that I was on the right side than I would have been the other way round. And yet, except for a very few people, nobody seemed to mind whether the Hotel Bristol had burned down or not, whether a real plane had landed, whether Trotsky's life and writings were congruent with the picture given of him in the trials. When confronted with the facts of the case, people's minds sheered off from it like jelly from a spoon.

Anybody who has ever tried to rectify an injustice or set a record straight comes to feel that he is going mad. And from a social point of view, he *is* crazy, for he is trying to undo something that is finished, to unravel the social fabric. That is why my liberal friends looked so grave and solemn when I would press them to come to a meeting and listen to a presentation of the facts—for them this was a Decision, too awful to be considered lightly. The Moscow trials were a historical fact and those of us who tried to undo them were uneasily felt to be crackpots, who were trying to turn the clock back. And of course the less we were listened to, the more insistent and earnest we became, even while we realized we were doing our cause harm. It is impossible to take a moderate tone under such conditions. If I admitted, though, to being a little bit hipped on the subject of Trotsky, I could sometimes gain an indulgent if flickering attention—the kind of attention that stipulates, "She's a bit off but let's hear her story." And now and then, by sheer chance, one of my hearers would be arrested by some stray point in my narrative; the disparaging smile would slowly fade from his features, leaving a look of blank consternation. He would go off and investigate for himself, and in a few days, when we met again, he would be a crackpot too.

Most of us who became anti-Communists at the time of the trials were drawn in, like me, by accident and almost unwillingly. Looking back, as on a love affair, a man could say that if he had not had lunch in a certain restaurant on a certain day, he might not have been led to ponder the facts of the Moscow trials. Or not then at any rate. And had he pondered them at a later date, other considerations would have entered and his conversion would have had a different style. On the whole, those of us who became anti-Communists during that year, 1936–1937, have remained liberals—a thing that is less true of people of our generation who were converted earlier or later. A certain doubt of orthodoxy and independence of mass opinion was riveted into our anti-Communism by the heat of that period. As soon as I make this statement, exceptions leap into my mind, but I think as a generalization it will stand. Those who became anti-Communist earlier fell into two classes: the experts and those to whom any socialist ideal was repugnant. Those whose eyes where opened later, by the Nazi–Soviet pact, or still later, by God knows what, were left bruised and full of self-hatred or self-commiseration, because they had palliated so much and truckled to a power center; to them, Communism's chief sin seems to be that it deceived *them*, and their public atonement takes on both a vindicating and a vindictive character.

We were luckier. Our anti-Communism came to us neither as the fruit of a special wisdom nor as a humiliating awakening from a prolonged deception, but as a natural event, the product of chance and propinquity. One thing followed another, and the will had little to say about it. For my part, during that year, I realized, with a certain wistfulness, that it was too late for me to become any kind of Marxist.

Marxism, I saw, from the learned young men I listened to at Committee meetings, was something you had to take up young, like ballet dancing.

So, I did not try to be a Marxist or a Trotskyite, though for the first time I read a little in the Marxist canon. But I got the name of being a Trotskyite, which meant, in the end, that I saw less of the conventional Stalinists I had been mingling with and less of conventional people generally. (My definition of a conventional person was quite broad: it included anyone who could hear of the Moscow trials and maintain an unruffled serenity.) This, then, was a break or a rupture, not very noticeable at first, that gradually widened and widened, without any conscious effort on my part, sometimes to my regret. This estrangement was not marked by any definite stages; it was a matter of tiny choices. Shortly after the Moscow trials, for instance, I changed from the *Herald Tribune* to the *Times*; soon I had stopped doing crossword puzzles, playing bridge, reading detective stories and popular novels. I did not "give up" these things; they departed from me, as it were, on tiptoe, seeing that my thoughts were elsewhere.

To change from the *Herald Tribune* to the *Times*, is not, I am aware, as serious a step as breaking with international Communism when you have been its agent; and it occurs to me that Mr. Chambers and Miss Bentley might well protest the comparison, pointing out that they were profoundly dedicated people, while I was a mere trifler, that their decisions partook of the sublime, where mine descended to the ridiculous—as Mr. Chambers says, he was ready to give his life for his beliefs. Fortunately (though I could argue the point, for we all give our lives for our beliefs, piecemeal or whole), I have a surprise witness to call for my side, who did literally die for his political views.

I am referring to Trotsky, the small, frail, pertinacious old man who wore whiskers, wrinkles, glasses, shock of grizzled hair, like a gleeful disguise for the erect young student, the dangerous revolutionary within him. Nothing could be more alien to the convulsed and tormented moonscapes of the true confessions of ex-Communists than Trotsky's populous, matter-of-fact recollections set out in *My Life*. I have just been rereading this volume, and though I no longer subscribe to its views, which have certainly an authoritarian and doctrinaire cast that troubles me today, nevertheless I experience a sense of recognition here that I cannot find in the pages of our own repentant "revolutionaries." The old man remained unregenerate; he never admitted that he had sinned. That is probably why nobody seems to care for, or feel apologetic to, his memory. It is an interesting point—and relevant, I think, to my story—that many people today actually have the impression that Trotsky died a natural death.

In a certain sense, this is perfectly true. I do not mean that he lived by violence and therefore might reasonably be expected to die by violence. He was a man of words primarily, a pamphleteer and orator. He was armed, as he said, with a pen and peppered his enemies with a fusillade of articles. Hear the concluding passages of his autobiography: "Since my exile, I have more than once read musings in the newspapers on the subject of the 'tragedy' that has befallen me. I know no *personal* tragedy. I know the change of two chapters of revolution. One American paper which published an article of mine accompanied it with a profound note to the effect that in spite of the blows the author had suffered, he had, as evidenced by his article, preserved his clarity of reason. I can only express my astonishment at the Philistine attempt to establish a connection between the power of reasoning and a government post, between mental balance and the present situation. I do not know, and never have known, of any such connection. In prison, with a book or pen in my hand, I experienced the same sense of deep satisfaction that I did at mass-meetings of the revolution. I felt the mechanics of power as an inescapable burden, rather than as a spiritual satisfaction."

This was not a man of violence. Nevertheless, one can say that he died a natural death—a death that was in keeping with the open manner of his life. There was nothing arcane in Trotsky; that was his charm. Like an ordinary person he was hospitably open to hazard and accident. In his autobiography, he cannot date the moment when he became a socialist.

One factor in his losing out in the power struggle at the time of Lenin's death was his delay in getting the telegram that should have called him home from the Caucasus, where he was convalescent, to appear at Lenin's funeral—*had* he got the telegram, the outcome perhaps would have been different. Or again, perhaps not. It may be that the whims of chance are really the importunities of design. But if there is a Design, it aims, in real lives, like the reader's or mine or Trotsky's, to look natural and fortuitous; that is how it gets us into its web.

Trotsky himself, looking at his life in retrospect, was struck, as most of us are on such occasions, by the role chance had played in it. He tells how one day, during Lenin's last illness, he went duck shooting with an old hunter in a canoe on the River Dubna, walked through a bog in felt boots—only a hundred steps—and contracted influenza. This was the reason he was ordered to Sukhu for the cure, missed Lenin's funeral, and had to stay in bed during the struggle for primacy that raged that autumn and winter. "I cannot help noting," he says, "how obligingly the accidental helps the historical law. Broadly speaking, the entire historical process is a refraction of historical law through the accidental. In the language of biology, one might say that the historical law is realized through the natural selection of accidents." And with a touch of quizzical gaiety he sums up the problem as a Marxian: "One can foresee the consequences of a revolution or a war, but it is impossible to foresee the consequences of an autumn shooting-trip for wild ducks." This shrug before the unforeseen implies an acceptance of consequences that is a far cry from penance and prophecy. Such, it concedes, is life. *Bravo*, old sport, I say, even though the hall is empty.

—Fall 1953

21

UP THE LADDER
FROM *CHARM* TO *VOGUE*

"WILL YOU WEAR a star in your hair at night...or a little embroidered black veiling hat?...Will you wear a close little choker of pearls or a medal on a long narrow velvet ribbon?...Will you serve a lunch, in the garden, of *prosciutto* and melon and a wonderful green salad...or sit in the St. Regis' pale-pink roof and eat *truite bleue*?"

It is the "Make Up Your Mind" issue: *Vogue*'s editresses are gently pressing the reader, in the vise of these velvet alternatives, to choose the looks that will "add up" to *her* look, the thing that is hers alone. "Will you make the point of your room a witty screen of drawings cadged from your artist friends...or spend your all on a magnificent carpet of flowers that decorates and almost furnishes the room itself?"

Twenty years ago, when *Vogue* was on the sewing room table of nearly every respectable upper-middle-class American house, these Sapphic overtures to the subscriber, this flattery, these shared securities of *prosciutto* and *wonderful* and *witty* had no place in fashion's realm. *Vogue*, in those days before *Mademoiselle* and *Glamour* and *Charm* and *Seventeen*, was an almost forbidding monitor enforcing the discipline of Paris. An iron conception of the mode governed its semimonthly rulings. Fashion was distinguished from dress; the woman of fashion, by definition, was a woman of a certain income whose clothes spoke the idiom of luxury and bon ton; there was no compromise with this principle. Furs, jewels, sumptuous materials, fine leathers, line, cut, atelier workmanship, were the very fabric of fashion; taste, indeed, was insisted on, but taste without money had a starved and middle-class pathos. The tastefully dressed little woman could not be a woman of style.

To its provincial subscribers *Vogue* of that epoch was cruel, rather in the manner of an upper servant. Its sole concession to their existence was a pattern department, *Vogue's Designs for Dressmaking*, the relic of an earlier period when no American woman bought clothes in a shop. And these patterns, hard to cut out as they were, fraught with tears for the amateur, who was safer with the trusty Butterick, had an economical and serviceable look that set them off from the designer fashions: even in the sketches they resembled maternity dresses.

As for the columns of etiquette, the bridal advice, the social notes from New York, Philadelphia, San Francisco—all these pointedly declined acquaintance with the woman-from-outside who was probably their principal devotee. Yet the magazine was read eagerly and without affront. Provincial women with moderate incomes pored over it to pick up "hints," carried it with them to the family dressmaker, copied, approximated, with a sense, almost, of pilferage. The fashion ideas they lifted made the pulse of the Singer race in nervous daring and defiance (What would *Vogue* say if it knew?).

This paradoxical relation between magazine and audience had a certain moral beauty, at least on the subscribers' side—the beauty of unrequited love and of unflinching service to an ideal that is arbitrary, unsociable, and rejecting, like Kierkegaard's God and Kafka's Castle. Lanvin, Paquin, Chanel, Worth, Vionnet, Alix—these stars of the Paris firmament were worshiped and charted in their courses by reverent worshipers who would come no closer to their deities than to copy, say, the characteristic fagoting that Vionnet used in her dress yoke or treasure a bottle of Chanel's Number Two on the bureau, next to father's or husband's photograph.

Like its competitor, *Harper's Bazaar*, and following the French dressmaking tradition, *Vogue* centered about the mature woman, the *femme du monde*, the sophisticated young matron with her clubs, her charities, and her cardcase. The jewels, the rich fabrics, the furs and plumes, the exquisite corseting, the jabots and fringe, implied a sexual as well as a material opulence, something preening, flavorsome, and well satisfied. For the *jeune fille* (so defined) there was a page or two of party frocks, cut usually along princess lines, in pastel taffetas, with round necks. In this Racinean world, where stepmother Phèdre and grandmother Athalie queened it, the actual habits of the American young girl, who smoked and wore lipstick, were excised from consideration. Reality was inferior to style.

Covertly, the assumptions of this period remain in force. Despite social change, fashion is still luxurious. It is possible to dress prettily on a working girl's or business wife's income, but to dress handsomely is another matter, requiring, as before, time, care, and money. Fashion is a craft, not an industrial, conception, exemplifying to perfection the labor theory of value. The toil of many hands is the sine qua non of fashion. The hand of the weaver, the cutter, the fitter, the needleworker must be seen in the finished product in a hundred little details, and fashion knowledge, professionally, consists in the recognition and appraisal of the *work* that has gone into a costume. In gores and gussets and seams, in the polish of leather and its softness, the signature of painstaking labor must be legible to the discerning, or the woman is not fashionably dressed. The hand-knit sweater is superior to the machine-knit, not because it is more perfect, but on the contrary because its slight imperfections reveal it to be *hand*-knit. The Oriental pearl is preferred to the fine cultured pearl because the marine labor of a dark diver secured it, a prize wrested from the depths, and the woman who wears Oriental pearls believes that they show variations in temperature or that they change color with her skin or get sick when they are put away in the safe—in short, that they are alive, whereas cultured pearls, mass-stimulated in mass beds of oysters, are not. This sense of the accrued labor of others as a complement to one's personality, as *tribute* in a double sense, is intrinsic to the fashionable imagination, which desires to *feel* that labor next to its skin, in the hidden stitching of its underwear—hence the passion for handmade lingerie even among women whose outer clothing comes off the budget rack.

In spite of these facts, which are known to most women, if only in the form of a sudden anguish or hopelessness ("Why can't *I* look like that?"), a rhetoric of fashion as democracy, as an inherent right or manufacturer's guarantee, has swept over the style world and created a new fashion public, a new fashion prose, and a whole hierarchy of new fashion magazines. *Mademoiselle*, *Glamour*, *Charm*—respectively "the magazine for smart young women," "for the girl with the job," "the magazine for the BG (Business Girl)"—offer to the girl without means, the lonely heart, and the drudge, participation in the events of fashion, a sense of belonging, en masse and yet separately, individually, of being designed for, shopped for, read for, predicted for, cherished. The attention and care and consideration lavished on the woman of leisure by lady's maid, coiffeur, *vendeuse*, bootmaker, jeweler, are now at the disposal of the masses through the various Shophounds, Mlles. Wearybones, beauty editors, culture advisers, male and female confidants. The impersonally conceived Well-Dressed Woman of the old *Vogue* ("What the Well-Dressed Woman Will Wear") is tutoyered, so to speak, as *You* ("Will you wear a star in your hair?..."); and a tone of mixed homage and familiarity: "For you who are young and pretty," "For you who have more taste than money," gives the pronoun a custom air.

The idea of a custom approach to ready-made, popular-priced merchandise was first developed by *Mademoiselle*, a Street and Smith publication launched during the Depression, which differed from *Vogue* and the *Bazaar*, on the one hand, and from *McCall's* and *Pictorial Review*, expressions of the housewife, on the other. Before the Depression, there had been, roughly speaking, only three types of women's apparel: the custom dress, the better dress, and the budget or basement dress. Out of the Depression came the college shop and out of this the whole institutionalized fiction of the "debutante" shop and the "young-timers'" floor. These departments, which from the very outset were swarming with middle-aged shoppers, introduced a new category of merchandise: the "young" dress, followed by the "young" hat, the "young" shoe, the "young" petticoat, and so on. The "young" dress was a budget dress with status, an ephemeral sort of dress, very often—a dress that excited comment and did not stand up very well. Its popularity proved the existence of a new buying public of high school and college girls, secretaries and office workers, whose dress requirements were very different from those of the busy housewife or matron. What these buyers demanded, for obvious vocational reasons, was not a durable dress or a dress for special occasions, even, but the kind of dress that would provoke compliments from co-workers, fellow students, bosses—a dress that could be discarded after a few months or transformed by accessories into the simulation of a new dress. To this public, with its craving for popularity, its personality problems, and limited income, *Mademoiselle* addressed itself as "your" magazine, the magazine styled for *you*, individually.

Unlike the older magazines, whose editresses were matrons who wore (and still wear) their hats at their desks as though at a committee meeting at the Colony Club, *Mademoiselle* was staffed by young women of no social pretensions, college graduates and business types, live wires and prom queens, middle-class girls peppy or sultry, fond of fun and phonograph records. Its tone was gamely collegiate, a form of compliment perhaps, since its average reader, one would have guessed, was either beyond college or below it, a secretary or a high school student. It printed fiction—generally concerned then with the problems of adolescence—job hints and news, beauty advice, and pages of popular-priced fashions photographed in Burpee-cataloged hues against glamorous backgrounds. Its models were windswept and cute.

Fashion as fun became *Mademoiselle*'s identifying byword, a natural corollary to the youth theme. *Fun* with food, *tricks* with spices, herbal *magic*, Hawaiian pineapple, Hawaiian ham, Hawaiian bathing trunks, Hollywood playclothes, cruise news, casserole cookery, Bar-B-Q sauce reflect the dream mentality of a civilization of office conscripts to whom the day off, the two weeks basking in the sun during February or August, represent not only youth but an effortless, will-less slack season (*slacks*, *loafers*, hostess *pajamas*), quite different from the dynamic good time of the 1920s.

In the *Mademoiselle* play world, everything is romp-diminutive or make-believe. The beau is a "cute brute," the husband a "sahib," or "himself," or "the little fellow." The ready-mix cake "turns out *terrific*." Zircons are "almost indistinguishable from diamonds." "Little tricks of combination, flavor and garnishment help the bride and enchant the groom...who need never know!" Brides wearing thirty-five-dollar dresses are shown being toasted in champagne by ushers in ascots and striped trousers.

Work may be fun also. "I meet headline people on the Hill every day." Husband-and-wife *teams* do "the exciting things" together. And the work-fun of a reader-surrogate named Joan, *Mademoiselle*'s Everygirl, is to be continually photographed backstage at "exciting" events, "meeting summer halfway on a Caribbean island," meeting Maurice Evans in his dressing room, or gapily watching a chorus rehearsal. The word *meet*, in the sense of "coming into contact with or proximity of" is a denotation of holiday achievement. Resort news is eternal, like hotel-folder sunshine.

The strain of keeping up this bright deception is marked by the grotesquerie of adverbs ("Serve piping hot with a dish of wildly hot mustard nearby"), by the repeated exclamation point, like a jerky, convulsive party smile, and by garish photographic effects. The typical *Mademoiselle* model with her adolescent, adenoidal face, snub nose, low forehead, and perpetually parted lips is immature in an almost painful fashion—on the plane, in the Parisian street, or the tropic hotel she appears out of place and ill at ease, and the photography which strives to "naturalize" her in exotic or expensive surroundings only isolates her still further. Against the marble columns or the balustrades, with fishing rod, sailboat, or native basket, she stands in a molar eternity, waving, gesticulating, like the figures in home movies of the vacation trip.

Another magazine, *Seventeen*, which from its recipes and correspondence column appears to be really directed to teenagers and their problems, strikes, by contrast with *Mademoiselle*, a grave and decorous note. Poorly gotten out and cheaply written, it has nevertheless an authentic small-town air; more than half its circulation is in towns under twenty-five thousand. It is not, strictly speaking, a fashion magazine (though it carries pages of fashions, gifts, and designs for knitting and dressmaking), but rather a home magazine on the order of *Woman's Home Companion*. How to make things at home, simple dishes to surprise the family with, games to play at parties, nonalcoholic punches for after skating, candies, popcorn balls, how to understand your parents, how to stop a family quarrel, movies of social import, the management of high school proms, stories about friendships with boys, crushes on teachers, a department of poems and stories written by teenagers—all this imparts in a rather homiletic vein the daily lesson of growth and character-building.

Pleasures here are wholesome, groupy ("Get your gang together") projects, requiring everybody's cooperation. Thoughtfulness is the motto. The difficulty of being both good and popular, and the tension between the two aims (the great crux of choice for adolescence), are the staple matter of the fiction; every boy hero or girl heroine has a bitter pill to swallow in the ending. The same old-fashioned moral principles are brought to bear on fashion and cooking. The little cook in *Seventeen* is not encouraged, à la *Mademoiselle*, to think she can make "high drama" out of a Drake's Cake and a pudding mix; she starts her party biscuits or her cake with fresh eggs, fresh butter, and sifted flour. Her first grown-up jewelry is not an "important-looking" chunk of glass but a modest gold safety pin or, if she is lucky and has an uncle who can give it to her for graduation, a simple gold wristwatch.

And in *Seventeen*, surprisingly, the fashions, while inexpensive, have a more mundane look than *Mademoiselle*'s dresses, which tend to be junky—short-waisted, cute, with too many tucks, pleats, belts, and collars for the money. The *Seventeen* date dress is not very different from the "young fashions" in *Harper's Bazaar*. It has been chosen to give its wearer a little air of style and maturity, on the same principle that an actor playing a drunk tries, not to stagger, but to walk straight. The artifice of youth in the *Mademoiselle* fashions betrays the very thing it is meant to cover—cheapness—and the little short bobbing jackets and boleros and dirndls become a sort of class uniform of the office worker, an assent to permanent juniority as a form of second-class citizenship, on the drugstore stool.

In the upper fashion world, the notion of fashion as fun acquires a delicate savor. The *amusing*, the *witty*, the *delicious* ("a deliciously oversized stole") evoke a pastoral atmosphere, a Louis Seize scene where the queen is in the dairy and pauperdom is Arcadia. The whim, piquant or costly, defines the personality: try (*Harper's Bazaar*) having everything slipcovered in pale Irish linen, including the typewriter and the birdcage; and "just for the fun of it, black with one white glove." The idea of spending as thrift, lately coined by *Vogue*, implies the pastoral opposite of thrift as the gayest extravagance. "There is the good handbag. The pairs of good shoes. . . . The wealth-to-spare look of rich and lean clothes together." A "timeless" gold cross made from old family stones, and seventy-dollar shoes are proposed under the heading "Economical Extravagances." "And upkeep, extravagantly good, is the ultimate economy. Examples: having your books with fine bindings oiled by an expert every year or having your wooden shoe-trees made to order. . . . And purely for pleasure: flowers, silver, and the price of keeping it polished; an Afghan hound, the collection, from stamps to butterflies, to Coalport cabbages, that you, or we, skimp for rather than do without."

The fabrication here of a democratic snobbery, a snobbery for everyone, is *Vogue*'s answer to the tumbrils of Truman. The trend of the times is resolutely reckoned with: today "the smaller collectors who have only one Giorgione" buy at Knoedler's Gallery, just as Mellon used to do. As John Jacob Astor III said, "A man who has a million dollars is as well off as if he were rich." (What a *delicious* sow's ear, my dear, where did you *get* it?) The *small* collection, the *little* evening imply the intimate and the choice, as well as the tiniest pinch of necessity. *Little* hats, *little* furs, *tiny* waists—*Vogue* and the *Bazaar* are wriggling with them; in the old days hats were *small*. And as some images of size contract or cuddle ("Exciting too the tight skull of a hat with no hair showing"; "the sharp, small, polished head"), others stretch to wrap and protect: *enormous, huge, immense*—"a colossal muff," "vast" sleeves; how to have enormous eyes. By these semantic devices the reader is made to feel small, frail, and valuable. The vocabulary has become extremely tactile and sensuous, the caress of fine fabrics and workmanship being replaced by the caress of prose.

The erotic element always present in fashion, the kiss of loving labor on the body, is now overtly expressed by language. Belts *hug* or *clasp*; necklines *plunge*; jerseys *bind*. The word *exciting* tingles everywhere.

"An outrageous amount of S.A." is promised by a new makeup; a bow is a "shameless piece of flattery." A dress is no longer low-cut but *bare*. The diction is full of movement: "hair swept all to one side and just one enormous earring on the bare side." A waist rises from a skirt "like the stem of a flower." Images from sport and machinery (*team, spark*) give this murmurous romanticism a down-to-business, American twang and heighten the kinetic effect. "First a small shopping expedition.... Then give your mind a good going-over, stiffen it with some well-starched prose; apply a gloss of poetry, two coats at least."

The bugaboo of getting in a rut, of letting your mind, your figure, or your wardrobe become habit-ridden and middle-aged, is conjured up with a terrible seriousness by all fashion magazines and most vividly of all by *Harper's Bazaar*, which sees culture as a vital agent in the general toning-up process, tries to observe unifying trends and to relate a revival of interest in Scott Fitzgerald to Carol Channing and the cloche hat, and is the victim of its own orderliness in collating a mode to a movement.

Literature and the arts, in the middle and upper fashion magazines, are offered as a tonic to the flabby personality, a tonic frequently scented with the musky odor of Tabu or My Sin. The fiction published by *Harper's Bazaar* (*Vogue* does not print stories), to be conned by suburban ladies under the drier, belongs almost exclusively to the mannerist or decadent school of American writing. Truman Capote, Edita Morris, Jane Bowles, Paul Bowles, Eudora Welty, Jean Stafford, Carson McCullers—what these writers have in common, beyond a lack of matter and a consequent leukemia of treatment (taken by the *Bazaar* editors to be the very essence of art), is a potpourri of *fleurs de mal*, a preoccupation with the décor of sorrow, sexual aberration, insanity, and cruelty, a tasteful arrangement of the bric-a-brac of pathology around the whatnot of a central symbol. This fashionable genre of literary story is published in good faith by the *Bazaar*, with a positive glow, in fact, of high-minded, disinterested evangelism. The editors, to do them justice, are as honestly elated by the discovery of a new decadent talent as by the announcement of a new silhouette, a new coiffure, a new young designer.

For both *Vogue* and *Harper's Bazaar*, the regular discovery of younger and younger authors, of newer and newer painters, is a rather recent development and a concession to democratic principle. Society people do not read, and are not interested (ask a modern dealer) in any painters later than the Impressionists. (The theatre is the only branch of art much cared for by people of wealth; like canasta, it does away with the bother of talk after dinner.) A society person who is enthusiastic about modern painting or Truman Capote is already half a traitor to his class: it is middle-class people who, quite mistakenly, imagine that a lively pursuit of the latest in reading and painting will advance their status in the world. It is for them and for their financial inferiors, students of interior decorating or the dance, bookstore clerks, models, assistant buyers, and advertising copywriters, that photographs of Picasso drawing with a ray of light, reproductions of paintings by de Kooning or Baziotes, stories by Carson McCullers, Peggy Bennett, or Speed Lamkin have moment. For all those engaged in competition for status, the surge of a new name forward anywhere, in any field, in astrophysics even, or medicine, is of intense personal reference and concern. Any movement in the social body, any displacement, is felt at once by every mobile member of the organism as relating to his own case, and the inside knowledge of these distant events gives poise and assurance—hence the relevance of the yearly awards given by *Mademoiselle* and other fashion magazines for achievement in science, medicine, human relations, and the like.

A writer for *Mademoiselle* expresses the position of those on the lower rung of the ladder very clearly when she tells about how exciting it is to live in Washington, and adduces as an example the fact that her husband, Bob, once rode on a plane with the US special representative to Israel and another time "bumped into Henry Wallace and

General Vaughan coming out of the White House the day Wallace had his farewell row with the President." Here the sense of being close to important events (itself vicarious) passes from the husband to the author to the reader. It is three removes off. What she likes about a certain Washington couple, she continues, is "that they always have interesting people around them, kicking around interesting ideas." And of her friends, in general, "What really roots them to the spot is that the work they do has intrinsic, social meaning." The concluding phrase, with its queer use of the comma, suggests that the intrinsic and the social are distinct and antithetical properties. But from the context it is plain that work that has intrinsic, comma, social meaning is work that is close to the big, busy, important things.

What has happened, in the course of twenty years, is that culture and even political liberalism have been converted by the mass-fashion mind, with its competitive bias, into a sort of Beaux Arts Ball. "A literary and artistic renaissance is what they're talking about over coffee at the Francis Scott Key, Martinis at the Press Club.... The Phillips Gallery...pace-sets with frequent shows of important contemporary artists, photographers.... At Whyte's Bookshop and Gallery...the important draw is...." The idea that it's smart to be in step, to be liberal or avant-garde, is conveyed through the name-dropping of a Leo Lerman in *Mademoiselle*. To allude negligently to Kafka, Yeats, Proust, Stendhal, or Saint John of the Cross in a tone of of-course-you-know-them is canonical procedure for *Mademoiselle* contributors, whatever the topic in hand, while the minor name here (Capote, Büchner, Tennessee Williams, Vidal) has the cachet of the little evening, the little hat, the little fur. The conception of a mass initiate involves an assembly-line production of minority objects of virtu, and is producing a new conformity altogether dominated by the mode, in which late Beethoven, boogie-woogie, the UN, Büchner, Capote, FEPC, and *The Cocktail Party* are all equally important names to be spent. Contrary to the practice in high society, the recherché is more prized than the known great, and Shakespeare is a virtually worthless counter, which Mrs. Astor never was.

The conspicuous mass display of the bibelots of a curio culture is the promotional secret of *Flair*, the new Cowles magazine, with its first-naming of the New Bohemians, "Carson," "Truman," and "Tennessee," and its splashy collage of democrats and decadents— Margaret Mead and Salvador Dali, Simone de Beauvoir and Mme. de Pompadour, Jean Genet and W. H. Auden, Thomas Jefferson and Angus Wilson, Barbara Ward and Franco Spain, Leonor Fini and the Middleburg Hunt, Cocteau and Mauriac. As an instrument of mass snobbery, this remarkable magazine, dedicated simply to the personal cult of its editress, to the fetishism of the flower (Fleur Cowles, *Flair*, a single rose), outdistances all its competitors in the audacity of its conception. It is a leap into the Orwellian future, a magazine without contest or point of view beyond its proclamation of itself, 120 pages of sheer presentation, a journalistic mirage. The principle of the peep show or illusion utilized in the cutouts, where the eye is led inward to a false perspective of depth, is the trick of the entire enterprise. The articles, in fact, seem meant not to be read but inhaled like a whiff of scent from the mystic rose at the center (flair, through Old French, from *fragrare*, to emit an odor: an instinctive power of discriminating or discerning). Nobody, one imagines, has read them, not even their authors: grammatical sentences are arranged around a vanishing point of meaning. Yet already, in the very first, quite androgyne number, an ectoplasmic feminine you is materialized, to whom a fashion editor's voice speaks in tones of assured divination: "Fashion is Personal.... Seven silhouettes chosen from wide possibilities, not because they are extreme high fashion, but because they are silhouettes you might claim.... " There follow seven dresses in the current high fashion.

The cynicism and effrontery of this surpass anything previously tried out in journalism. And yet *Vogue* immediately fell into line with its own warm defense of the reader against fashion's tyranny. "Ignore the exquisite exaggerations of fashion drawings" when trying to determine the weight that is right for you; study yourself, know your self, wear what is timelessly yours. "Copy courageous Mrs. Carroll Carstairs, who wears the same beanies every year regardless of the milliners; or Pauline Potter, who carries the same custom-made suede handbag suspended from a jeweler's gold chain." To an experienced reader, this doctrine is merely a 1950 adaptation of the old adage about knowing your own type, a text that generally prefaces the suggestion that the reader should go out and spend a great deal of money on some item of quality merchandise. But beyond the attempt to push quality goods during a buying recession like the recent one, or to dodge responsibility for an unpopular mode (this year's sheaths and cloches are widely unbecoming), there appears to be some periodic feminine compulsion on the editresses' part to strike a suffragette attitude toward the merchants whose products are their livelihood, to ally themselves in a gush with their readers, who are seen temporarily as their "real" friends.

And as one descends to a lower level of the fashion structure, to *Glamour* (Condé Nast) and *Charm* (Street and Smith), one finds a more genuine solicitude for the reader and her problems. The pain of being a BG (Business Girl), the envy of superiors, self-consciousness, awkwardness, loneliness, sexual fears, timid friendliness to the Boss, endless evenings with the mirror and the tweezers, desperate Saturday social strivings ("Give a party and ask *everyone* you know"), the struggle to achieve any identity in the dead cubbyhole of office life, this mass misery, as of a perpetual humiliating menstrual period, is patently present to the editors, who strive against it with good advice, cheeriness, forced volubility, a psychiatric nurse's briskness, so that the reiterated "Be natural," "Be yourself," "Smile," "Your good points are you too" (*Mademoiselle*), have a therapeutic justification.

A characteristic running feature in *Glamour* and *Charm* is a newsy letter from the editors, datelined London, Paris, New York, or Rome, a letter back home full of gossip and family jokes, the sort of letter one writes to a shut-in. The vicarious here is carried to its furthest extreme: the editors live out for the readers a junketing, busy life in which the readers, admittedly, will share only by mail—quite a different thing from the *Mademoiselle* Everygirl projection. The delegation of experience from reader to editor is channeled through a committee of typical (*Charm*) or outstanding (*Glamour*) business girls—the Charm Advisory Committee, the Glamour Career Counselors—selected from all over the country, who are polled from time to time on problems of special interest and who not only keep the editors in touch with the desires of the readers but pass on, through the editors, their own superior know-how to the lowest members of the caste.

A publication of Street and Smith, *Charm* has a more vulgar tone than *Glamour*, which belongs to the *Vogue* chain. Its circulation, considerably smaller than *Glamour*'s, larger than *Mademoiselle*'s, seems drawn preponderantly from the West and the South, backward fashion areas, while *Glamour*'s public is eastern or urban, the differences being sharpest in the vicinity of New York, Philadelphia, Boston, and Los Angeles. *Glamour*'s dresses are more expensive than *Charm*'s. It is conscious of Paris, Italy, and London, and will illustrate, in the front of the magazine, the work of Italian craftsmen and French designers for their own sake, as objects of beauty and wonder. As in the old *Vogue,* the cultivation of taste, the development of a fashion sensibility which impersonally delights in the finely made and the rare, are, at least in part, the editorial purpose.

A letter from *Glamour*'s editor to the readers in last year's Christmas number, suggesting that the American girl lives too much on dreams and illusions and proposing impersonal goals, has the gently remonstrative seriousness of a young woman dean exhorting her alumnae. Maturity and dignity are valued. Photographs of secretaries of well-known persons, photographs of successful women who began as secretaries, a history of the secretarial profession emphasize the dignity of office work and give it status through history and a tradition. Serenity in work ("Why I Like My Job"—a contest) and at home are stressed to the point where this itself becomes an aristocratic illusion: an article called "These Gracious Customs" showing the cocktail party with hunt-breakfast silver; the inevitable wedding pictures with champagne, striped trousers, and a butler. Yet the general attitude of *Glamour* is sensible, without much side, and in its own terms idealistic, the eye being directed less downward toward the immediate bargain counter than inward toward self-examination and outward toward the great cities and fine artisans of the world.

With *Charm*, on the other hand, the nadir of the personal is reached: the Business Girl is greeted at her lowest common denominator. The editor becomes "Your Ed," the fun-fabulous-wonderful-sensational shriek ("Learn to make one fabulous dish.... Give your earrings a new locale.... Carry an umbrella as a costume adjunct.... DARE TO DO IT"), addressed to the insecure and the maladroit, echoes in a national hollowness of social failure and fear. A presumption of previous failure in the reader, failure with men, with friends, failure in schoolwork, is the foundation of the average feature: "This Little Girl Never Had Any Fun," "Stood Up."

A lead article on "Smiles" in the January issue points to the Roosevelt smile, the Mona Lisa smile, the Betty Grable smile, the Jolson smile, the Dietrich smile: "...People in the public eye have never underestimated the power of a smile: it's odd that *you* have so often overlooked it.... Though smiling is nicer as a *spontaneous* thing, you might, just in the nature of an experiment, start smiling as a *conscious* thing. Smile at your family...your husband...your employer...your young man. Smile deliberately at some point in an argument...at a break in the conversation.... Smile a while in front of your mirror."

The article finishes characteristically with some hints about dentifrices and the art of toothbrushing. In another feature by the same author, the natural attractions of the bride-to-be are so despaired of that she is advised to apply a lip-coloring base before going to bed, spray the room with "fragrance," and even "steal" a sachet under the pillow.

A preoccupation with deodorants and "personal hygiene" becomes more and more noticeable as the economic scale is descended. Social failure is ascribed to a lack of "fastidiousness," a lower-middle-class fear that first reveals itself in *Mademoiselle*, where the likelihood of giving "offense" is associated with the male sex. "It's the rare man... who isn't considerably more attractive when he uses some [toilet water or cologne]." "A consistently fastidious, scrubby male is mighty nice to have around the house.... If he doesn't mind tomorrow's garlic and you do, get him a bottle of the leaf-fresh mouth wash that *all* men love on first gargle. If he uses a deodorant—and more men could— keep his brand on hand. If he doesn't, put a squeeze-spray version where he'll see it—it will appeal to a man's mechanical instinct."

The bridal number of *Charm* carries a feature ("His and Hers") on bathroom etiquette, showing pictures of a man and woman gargling, shaving, creaming, brushing teeth, putting powder between the toes against athlete's foot, using a deodorant (male); the bathroom is called the *lavabo*. In the same number, a marriage article, "The Importance of Not Being Prudish," contains the following advice: "You'll also be a silly prude if you squeak like a mouse when he, thoughtlessly, walks into the bedroom without knocking and finds you standing in your bra and panties. Don't make like September Morn. Respecting your natural modesty, he'll probably say he's sorry, walk backward through the door.... (He *should* have knocked...)." And another feature, "Beauty Steps to the Altar," includes two "Secret Steps"; crayons to color your gray hair give a "natural, plausible performance.... And remember there are very good preparations that make a secret of scars and blemishes."

Thus, at the lowest fashion level, a most painful illusionism becomes the only recipe for success. Admiration and compliments provide momentarily the sense of well-being which, for the woman of fashion of the upper level, is an exhalation of the stuffs and stays that hold her superb and erect as in a vase of workmanship. For the reader of *Charm* it is her very self that is the artifact, an artifact which must be maintained, night and day, in the close quarters of marriage, brought to higher sparkle for party evenings with the gang ("Your quips were a tearing success; his gags killed 'em"), at the office, in the subway ("Smile"). The continued tribute to be extorted from others, which the *Charm* policy promises its untouchables, if only they will follow directions, is laid down as an American right, to be fought for, creamed for, depilated and massaged for—more than that, as duty, with ostracism threatened for slackers. Every woman, says *Glamour* categorically, can be 50 percent more beautiful. It is the rigorous language of the factory in which new production goals are set yearly, which must not only be met but exceeded. "Mirror, mirror on the wall...?" begs the reader. "You," answers the editor, "if you did your exercises, were the prettiest girl in the Republic."

—July–August 1950

22

LETTER FROM PORTUGAL

"THE HAPPIEST MONTH of my life—an idyll," said a German refugee publisher in New York, kissing his fingertips to Portugal, when he heard that my husband and I were coming here last winter. "You probably think we have a dictatorship. Ho, ho, ho!" roared Portugal's vice-chieftain of propaganda, when I went to see him in his office on our third day in Lisbon. I had to confess that this was what we Americans had been given to understand—"a benevolent dictatorship," I hurriedly qualified, this being the formula that had been current among the passengers on the *Vulcania* as the ship glided up the Tagus. We were expecting an idyll and apprehending a dictatorship. These two notions had fused, for the time being, in a resolve not to be insular: democracy was not necessarily suited to *all* countries, we assured each other, gripping our travel books. "Salazar is a very good man, very wise for his people," said an old Portuguese-American, brown-skinned as an Arab, who was identifying the approaching sights of pink-and-white Lisbon for us from the deck. "He must be *wonderful*," sighed a lady in a tricorne, who came from Manchester, Vermont. The old man went on to relate eagerly, in broken English, how terrible conditions had been in Portugal in 1928, when António de Oliveira Salazar, born a poor peasant, left his post in economics at the University of Coimbra to serve his country, first as minister of finance and then as premier, saving, always saving, till the national debt was paid; and how he had sacrificed his personal life to the Estado Novo—never married, lived very simply and austerely, stayed up late at night, working, always working. "What's that?" I kept asking, pointing to orange-roofed white buildings, gleaming new, that were spread out on the green hills of Lisbon's suburbs. "Housing project," the old man invariably answered, simply and proudly. This was the first thing I found out about the Estado Novo; whenever you point to anything, the answer is "Housing project." After a few days, I learned to frame the question the other way around. "Housing project?" I would cautiously inquire. "*Sim, Senhora.*"

Most visitors to Portugal have come here to see something old, but the Portuguese are full of zeal to show you something new—Economic Homes, syndicate apartments, the *auto-estrada*, the airport, the stadium, the modernistic shrine of Our Lady of Fátima, that twentieth-century vision who came to warn against Communism. And in Lisbon signs of progress are not far to seek. Walking through the streets the first evening, I felt as though I had made an appointment in Samarra. The shop windows glittered with radios, pressure cookers, electric mixers, automobile hubcaps, washing machines, gas ranges, soda water siphons, mechanical iceboxes, grills, electric razors, soap flakes, plastics, hot water bottles. In the delicacy shops, Tootsie Rolls and Ritz crackers rested on beds of red velvet, like holy images. There was a din of horns honking. Everybody, at first glance, appeared to have a new car; it was several days before I realized that what I had been noticing, actually, was that every car was new. In the Rossio, the yellow principal square, the coffeehouses, which look like New York cafeterias, were dense with men in overcoats, reading the newspaper and having their shoes shined. Outside, electric signs were advertising TWA and Philips electrical products. Movie palaces, playing French and American films, disgorged crowds into the teashops of the Avenida da Liberdade. From the open doors of taverns near the waterfront you could hear the radio playing the fado. The liquor store windows were full of Haig & Haig. In the center of the pale-green Praça de Comércio—the famous Black Horse Square, on the harbor—there was a parking lot. And everywhere, in every quarter, there were windows and windows of shoes for sale. Lisbon, as every tourist knows, has a law forbidding the people to go barefoot; the shoe, I perceived, was a talisman of Portuguese progress, the fulfillment of a prophecy, a miracle, like the wonder-working relics in the churches, meant to be venerated through glass. I had never seen so many shoes displayed anywhere: oxfords, brogues, sandals, loafers, slippers, mules, pumps, play shoes, beach shoes, baby shoes—all in the latest American-style models, perforated, fringed, crepe- or wedge-soled.

This "little America" aspect of Lisbon contrasts rather naively with the rest of Portugal, like a figure out of drawing in a primitive painting. Yet just this naiveté comes to seem, after a time, typically Portuguese. This small country, with its variety of climates and mixture of racial strains, is an assiduous copyist, mimic, and borrower. Any sizable Portuguese town looks like a superstitious bride's finery—something old, something new, something borrowed, and something blue. Portugal has its "little Versailles," in the pink palace of Queluz (with a miniature Dutch canal added); its Balmoral, in the Scottish-baronial Pena Palace. It has its "little Switzerland," in the merry northern province of the Minho; its bit of Africa, in the southern Algarve. The Miguelite wars were a small-scale version of the Carlist wars in Spain; the present government's politics were borrowed from Charles Maurras, the originator of "integral nationalism." Portugal got its characteristic *azulejos* (painted tiles) from the Arabs and then subjected them to a Dutch influence. Its painters copied the Flemish, and its furniture makers the English and the French. "*Style renaissance française, travail portugais... Style anglais, travail portugais,*" drone the guides as they conduct you through the palaces. "They can copy anything," say the resident foreigners, speaking of the "little" dressmakers and the shoemakers. "But you must be sure to give them a model." This appears to have been true of nearly all the crafts throughout Portuguese history. Even the Manueline architecture, done in the Age of Discoveries and uniquely Portuguese, with its stone ropes and knots and anchors, seems not so much a true architectural style as an innocent imitation of real life, too literally conceived. It is only in the far north, in the Minho and the "lost" province of Trás-os-Montes (Beyond the Mountains), that you find a pure architecture—the Portuguese baroque, done in granite and severe white plaster, and decorated with gold—that is not like anything else in the world.

This persistent copying of foreign models, this literal translation from one medium to another, produces an effect of monkey humor—a slight absurdity that at its best is charming, like a child's recitation, and at its worst grotesque. The Portuguese genius, in fact, ranges between the charming and the grotesque: on the one hand, a miniature barnyard exquisitely worked in marzipan, a statue of Saint Anthony wearing a British officer's sash, pink-faced baroque angels in buskins and powdered periwigs, Saint Anne sitting in a Queen Anne chair; on the other, the horrors of late Manueline realism, the gross "cute" ceramics of lifelike cabbages and wrinkled spinach leaves, the votive offerings in the shrines and chapels, where one sees arms, legs, and ears painstakingly executed in mortuary greenish-white wax.

Lisbon itself is almost wholly charming—a model city of nearly a million people and an incalculable number of dogs. These multitudinous dogs—in muzzles, as prescribed by law—are forever underfoot, like stray bits of torn fur scattered on the streets; they are and must always have been one of the charms and absurdities of Lisbon. (The rational French, under Junot, during Napoleon's occupation, killed ten thousand of them.) The Portuguese love animals. In the country, the donkeys and oxen look better nourished, often, than their owners. In Lisbon, pet shops abound, full of lovebirds, parrots, parakeets, hens, and puppies, and along the narrow slum streets, hung with clean, bright washing, birdcages swing in the sun. Every day is wash-day in Lisbon. The Portuguese are famous for their cleanliness; no matter where you go, in city or suburb or country, you see laundry festooning the scene—spread out on cactus plants, flapping in back yards, hanging from windows. The smallest, muddiest rivulet has its band of women pounding clothes on flat rocks. "You can eat off their floors," the foreigners say, and this is very nearly true. But I have been in Portuguese restaurants where I would rather eat off the floor than off the plate before me. The Portuguese are very erratic and confound generalization.

But the cleanness of Lisbon *is* dazzling. In January, the steep stone streets are washed several times daily by sudden tropical showers, and Nature is assisted by street cleaners with brooms made of twigs. The Portuguese have a green thumb. Lisbon, in winter, is brilliant with orange calendulas, blooming everywhere, together with geraniums and succulents; oranges and lemons dangle from trees in the walled gardens like bright Christmas balls, the oranges matching the orange sails of the little fishing boats on the blue Tagus. The seasons at this time of year are all awry. Autumn is present in the calendulas and oranges; spring in the first wicker baskets of camellias that come down from the nearby mountains to the florist shops; summer lingers in a few exhausted petunias; winter—last January, at least—came for a day in a fall of snow, which brought the population, marveling, out into the streets to touch it. As the new year gets under way, everything is growing, all at once; even the old tile roofs have windfall crops of grass and yellow mustard, which, if you look down from a window, over the rooftops to the Tagus, make the whole city seem fertile—a sort of semitropical paradise that combines the exuberance of the south, with the huge palms in the public squares, the oranges and the monumental statuary, and the neatness and precision of the north, seen in the absence of dirt and litter, the perfectly kept public gardens and belvederes, the black-and-white mosaic patterns (ships and ropes and anchors) of the sidewalks, and the bright tiles of so many house fronts, painted in green-and-white diamonds or pink roses or solid Dutch blues and yellows. Lisbon is a city built on hills, like San Francisco, and it is full of beautiful prospects, of which every advantage has been taken. It is designed, so to speak, for a strolling tourist, at sunset, to ensconce himself in a belvedere and gaze out over the Tagus, down to the pink-and-white dome of the Basilica of Estrela, or across a ravine of buff and pink and gold buildings to the old fortress of São Jorge.

Lisbon is a planned city. It sprang from the despotic imagination of the Marquis of Pombal, who rebuilt it in the eighteenth century, after the great earthquake. It was planned, I should think, for pleasure and efficient administration, and this is what makes it seem like a toy city. It is full of ingenious contrivances—underpasses and cable cars and a tall outdoor elevator tower that has a view and a restaurant on top of it. The ferryboats chugging back and forth across the harbor, the little blue train that sets forth, on time, for Estoril, half an hour away, and the yellow open streetcars all seem part of the toy mechanism; the very fragrance of fresh coffee that drifts like a golden haze over the city seems to have come from a doll's electric stove. The eighteenth-century taste for curios and for a ruin, rightly placed, still animates the twentieth-century administrators. Lisbon has recently created one of the wonders of the world—the Estufa Fria, which is a sort of reverse hothouse, a large, shady terrarium for trees and plants that like coolness and moisture. Full of grottoes, streams, and bridges in a green, subaqueous light, it is in the height of early romantic feeling, a cultivated jungle popular with lovers and with French governesses on holiday. Lisbon also has a romantic ruin—an old Carmelite convent, just off the Chiado, the fashionable shopping street.

Above the cathedral there is an old quarter, called the Alfama, that escaped the earthquake and preserves the sights and smells of the

Middle Ages. The Lisbonese are proud of the Alfama, which resembles the worst pages of Victor Hugo. Rags, smells, and emaciation teem here; the narrow, cobbled streets, where the leaning houses almost meet overhead, are dirty and full of verminous-looking dogs; every orange in the stalls has been felt a hundred times by skinny hands; there are cripples, and one-eyed men, and every species of deformity. Yet the Portuguese are eager to show the Alfama, as a bit of local color. The tourist is directed to visit it at night to hear the fado sung in the taverns, and is assured that it is perfectly safe; you will never get a knife in your back nowadays in the Alfama, they say, though before Salazar you risked your life in broad daylight every day, right on the Avenida. Before Salazar, they say, a rich man never went out without wondering whether he would come home.

I wondered myself, I must confess, the Sunday morning we picked our way through the Alfama after Mass at the cathedral. I was afraid, and at the same time repelled by the vivid poverty. But everybody assured me that the people in the Alfama were a special breed, that they *liked* their way of life and would not live respectably if you made them. In fact, the government had considered cleaning up the district in the course of a slum-clearance program and had been compelled to desist, hastily, by the outcry of the populace. In the Estado Novo there is a whole repertory of such tales—of slum dwellers who refuse to be moved from their hovels, of men who refuse to work. "Is there unemployment?" I asked the propaganda man. There was seasonal unemployment in agriculture, he said, but no real unemployment—any man who wanted to could get work. "But what about the people in the Alfama?" I inquired. He shrugged and replied, "They don't want. A few work; others don't want." And to illustrate the government's plight he told me a "personal experience"—of a well-dressed man who asked him for money one day in a café, saying that he could not get work, and how he, the government official, promised the man a job but the man failed to turn up for the appointment, and how again he saw the man begging and beckoned him over to his table and again got a hard-luck story and again promised him work, and again discovered him begging. The plot of the story was familiar; I had heard it on occasion in my own country. No doubt these experiences really do befall people who, as it were, act as lightning rods for them; it is a case of serendipity.

"Still," I murmured, when the propaganda man had finished, "many of the people look very poor." "Oh, Alfama!" he said genially, and started to explain again that the Alfama was an institution. "Not the Alfama," I interrupted. "Other places." I had not intended to be-devil the propaganda chieftain, a big, dark, rubicund, jolly fat man, pronounced by foreigners to be more civilized and indulgent than his predecessors. But without my wishing it, it began to happen. The Portuguese, as I have since learned, are very sensitive, and certain words offend them; one of these words is "poor." "Portugal is a poor country," they will begin by telling you, with an air of self-deprecation. But they do not like *you* to say it. "Poor?" they will reply, as the propaganda man did now, contemplating the word with a kind of majestic wonder, as if it were susceptible of many different meanings. "Where did you see poor people?" The answer was, nearly everywhere, but I simply named the Rua de São Bento, a main street in a working-class quarter. There I had seen half-naked children, and women, like shapeless rummage bundles, buttoned into two or three torn sweaters, their feet tied up in rags and stuffed into men's shoes of odd pairs, or into gaping old felt bedroom slippers; some of the younger women wore once-fancy mules on raw, chapped, bare feet. I tried to describe this. When I had finished, he leaned back in his chair, lit a cigarette, and gave a long, tolerant laugh. "You don't understand," he said. "These women are very saving. They have good clothes, but they don't wear them. They keep them for Sunday or a special occasion. If you meet them on Sunday or a holiday, you will see they have a nice dress, nice shoes, pocketbook, stockings. You would not know them for the same person. Our women are not like yours; they save, save, save. You cannot get them out of it."

I smiled dubiously. The strange thing was that I had not been especially conscious of poverty in Lisbon until I spoke of it in the propaganda man's office. In this bureaucratic setting, all the sorry sights I had beheld, almost without seeing them, came out as if they had been recorded on a photographic plate that was only now immersed in a solution. Not to see, in fact, is a part of the Portuguese idyll, a sort of trick of the dazzling light and brilliant weather. It is easy for the foreigner in Lisbon, bewitched by the fruit and flowers and the myriad cakes and cheeses and sausages in the glittering shop windows, to miss the signs of poverty or to assimilate them to the picturesque. Oporto is different. There, gray misery is very evident; the Oporto equivalent of the Alfama is a scene of such purulent horror that the tourist flees, with his handkerchief to his nose, under the gaze of the mustached Mmes. Defarges along the riverbank. But Oporto, a dirty, foggy industrial city and the classic hotbed of Portuguese radicalism and rebellion, is under a cloud, both literally and figuratively, and nothing has been done to make it charming or colorful—while Lisbon has been beautified by government fiat. Visitors see the pink and pistachio and buff and yellow washes of the houses gleaming in the Lisbon sun and take this as evidence of individual prosperity and initiative, whereas the fact is that Lisbon houseowners are compelled by law to repaint every five years, and in the government-subsidized housing projects the range of colors is prescribed by the authorities.

The visitor's first impression is that the people of Lisbon are extraordinarily well dressed, on the whole; outside the Alfama and some of the poorer working-class sections, practically every man you see, not counting the lottery-ticket sellers and the street cleaners and the policemen and the laborers repairing the streets, is wearing a business suit, a clean shirt, and a necktie. It is a little time before you get to realize that the suit on the man next to you in the streetcar is terribly frayed and patched and mended, the surface of the shoes worn and cracked, the briefcase ragged and made of simulated leather, and the hand holding it seamed and cracked, too, like red leatherette. The laundry garlanding the streets is so fetching at first glance that you do not notice that many of the articles hung out are, literally, shreds and tatters of garments—scarecrow shirts and underwear. And there is something about Lisbon, not only the government's enterprise but the pride and politeness of the people, that makes you, politely, not want to notice.

Portugal has a misleading reputation for being an inexpensive country to live in. From our point of view, food and wine and rent and laundry and tobacco *are* cheap. There are a number of hotels and *pensãos* where you can get a room and three meals, with wine, for two dollars and forty-five cents a day, plus a 10 percent service charge, plus, in most places, a 3 percent tax if you are a tourist. At a restaurant, you can have an excellent meal—a shrimp omelet to start, then a golden *bacalhau* (dried cod, done with egg yolks, black olives, sauté potatoes, and onions), a tender beefsteak, a salad, white-mountain or Azeitão cheese, a superb peeled and sugared orange, and black coffee —for a dollar and seventy-five cents, which includes a bottle of good wine. (This is the ideal meal; you can eat less and pay less, or you can eat a worse meal and pay more in a luxury restaurant.) Taxis and trolleys are cheap by our standards, and buses and trains very reasonable. In general, any product or service that has human labor as its chief component is not at all costly. But if you want to buy something imported (a pressure cooker, an electric stove, a radio) or something made in a modern factory, it is often quite expensive by any standards. Cars are very expensive, and gasoline costs around seventy cents a gallon. Kleenex is about seventy-five cents a small box. I had to buy a one-piece bathing suit with a skirt, as decreed by the authorities, to take to the Algarve coast; this, quite ugly and made of inferior wool in a Portuguese factory, cost twelve dollars. If, however, I had had the suit made up by a seamstress, in cotton, it would have cost five dollars, or even less. My husband had a pair of shoes made for him by a shoemaker in Potimão; they squeak, like all Portuguese shoes, but they cost only eight dollars and fifty cents. A factory-made shoe of comparable quality but ugly design costs ten dollars.

Thus even the most slow-witted foreigner begins to wonder, as I did, who buys the things in the Chiado—the refrigerators and electric mixers and washing machines. A maid's monthly salary, one learns, is from two hundred to four hundred escudos, or from seven to fourteen dollars, plus room and board. Construction workers get about twenty escudos (seventy cents) a day take-home pay, with no pay for days when rain halts work; workers in the sardine canneries get about the same, and are frequently laid off for a day or more, depending upon the catch of fish. "How do they live on it?" foreigners ask one another. The answer is that nobody seems to know. Most economic questions dissolve into mystery in Portugal. The Portuguese themselves, except those in the poorer classes, have no curiosity about such matters. "Who buys the things in the Chiado?" In the early days of my stay in Portugal, this question harried me. In a country where labor was the cheapest of all commodities, who was buying the labor-saving devices? And who was munching the Tootsie Rolls? Not the *marquesas*, surely, gliding by, with eyes like black diamonds, in their Rolls-Royces. After a while, I gave up asking these questions, as most Americans do who stay on here, because I never got a satisfactory answer. "Foreigners," some Portuguese say, vaguely, and some think it may be the parvenus—the people who made money on Portuguese wolfram during the war. ("Wolfram" is one of those ready answers, along with "Housing project," that come like responses in a litany. "Wolfram?" you learn to ask, pointing to a fur piece or a stream of traffic on the *auto-estrada*, and your companion nods.) After my curiosity had shrunk, from constant thwarting, I finally met an actual consumer—a high government official, who had given his wife a pressure cooker, which she had used, or had her cook use, once or twice, to see how it worked; it was evidently a toy.

Certainly there is new money in Portugal. They did well on wolfram, and on refugees, during the war. The Oppositionists say that many of these gains found their way into the pockets of the government bureaucrats, and that these bureaucrats continue to profit, through bribery, on every business transaction. A surprising thing about Portugal, which is admired as a model state by laissez-faire conservatives abroad, is that it does not have a free economy. Prices, wages, and the profit margin are mostly fixed by law. "Why, it's Communism!" lamented an American who is in the chemical business here. He also had a low opinion of the Caixa de Previdência, the Portuguese social security system, which exacts from the employer an amount equal to 15 percent of the worker's wages, adds to it 2 percent from the worker, and invests the whole in a fund for sickness, disability, old age, widows' pensions, and burial allowances; there is no unemployment insurance. The chemicals man was objecting not so much to the tax itself as to what he called the "socialist" use the government was making of the Caixa de Previdência fund—investing it in public housing, which competes with private industry. "It's the economic principle behind it that's all wrong!" he said excitedly, adding that there had been scandals in the administration of the funds.

But this man is a foreigner. Portuguese businessmen do not worry about principle; they look at the facts. Except for the 2 percent levy on wages, there is no income tax in Portugal. The rich do not forget that they were saved, as they say, from anarchy; it is Salazar or worse, they declare. "You never had it better," the government tells them, in effect, and doubtless this is true. If the margin of profit is fixed (as it is even for the small retailer; the customer can send in a complaint if he is overcharged in a shop), most wages are fixed, also. Strikes are forbidden; agitators are run out of the syndicates, which might be described as government company unions; Communists are outlawed. It is true that there is a heavy duty on imports, which is tantamount to a tax on the rich—the only people who can afford cars and French neckties and foreign gadgets, Chesterfields and Yardley's —but to some this has marked social advantages, for it preserves class distinctions. A Chesterfield cigarette is a badge of class; the Portuguese make a queer, characteristic little grimace—the lower lip thrust out in pouting dismay— when they see a foreigner smoking one of the domestic Dianas or Suaves. The same with gin; the English in residence drink Portuguese gin, but the Portuguese middle class serves Gordon's. Coca-Cola is not permitted to enter the country—for moral aesthetic reasons, I was given to understand by the propaganda man, although I have since heard that the Coca-Cola case was "mishandled"; pressure was applied too heavily and at the wrong spot. At any rate, other foreign companies that compete with Portuguese manufacturers have been able to come to terms with the government; Lux, for instance, made in Portugal and not very sudsy, can be bought, at considerable cost, by ladies with nylons to wash.

A number of taxes assume the form of licenses. Cigarette lighters are licensed. Cars, naturally, are licensed, and so are bicycles and dogs; every parrot, croaking in its cage, is licensed; every donkey toiling up a mountain road. There is the 3 percent tourism tax, which is taken from the tourist in most hotels and *pensãos* and in luxury restaurants. And there are hosts of regulations, conducive to a disciplined atmosphere. You have to have a permit to buy a typewriter ribbon. Hotel rates are regulated, and the hotel and boardinghouse keepers are required to serve a third of a liter of wine (the *vinho da casa*) with every lunch or dinner. Road menders—poor men who work from sunrise to sundown for a tiny wage as part of the Portuguese PWA—salute every passing car; it is a rule, one is told. Every newspaper must be approved, daily, by the censor. Political parties are proscribed, except Salazar's National Union, which calls itself not a party but an "organ" of the people. Workers syndicates are bound "to abstain from all ideological discussions and to concentrate on the defense of the material and moral interests of their members, on the technical improvement of their trade, and on the creation of the frame of mind necessary for social peace." Factories with more than twenty employees must conduct adult-education courses for the illiterate. Every landowner is assessed for the number of hands his property can theoretically employ, and in periods of agricultural crisis or general unemployment he is required to take on workers up to that capacity. The assessments, I have heard, are often unjust, and fall hardest on the small landowner, who cannot afford to bribe the proper officials. For such a landowner, they put mechanization out of the question; there is no point in buying a tractor if you are obliged to employ extra field hands, whose labor you must contrive a use for.

This is corporativism; everybody, except the housewives, is organized, or "integrated," in some fashion, even the priests. To be expelled from a syndicate means literal outlawry for a worker; if anybody is to hire him, he must change his name or get his record expunged. Agricultural workers are incorporated into Houses of the People, which are syndicates of a sort; employers are incorporated into *gremios*, or guilds; lawyers, doctors, engineers, and other professional people are incorporated into *ordens*, or societies. Youth is mobilized into the Mocidade Portuguesa—a semimilitary youth movement—but membership in it is not compulsory. There are five kinds of police—municipal and national—plus a National Guard, a Fiscal Guard, and the volunteer Portuguese Legion. "Two persons, one policeman" is the sardonic comment of the lower-class Portuguese on the omnipresent police, who are also referred to as "Salazar's friends." The size of the Regular Army is under a security blanket at present, although there can be no real secrecy, since the figures are known to NATO, and it is typical of Portugal that nobody can explain why this regulation was imposed. "Perhaps the army is afraid the Russians will find out," one Portuguese suggested to me hopefully. In any case, there are sour-looking soldiers and their barracks everywhere, most noticeably in the provincial towns. Many of the big convents, from which Christ's volunteers were driven out half a century ago, now house army conscripts.

But all such hardships and annoyances do not worry government officials or the well-to-do Portuguese and foreigners living in villas in the resort towns of Sintra, Estoril, and Praia da Rocha. "I adore Salazar" is the cry of the English lady-in-exile, with a blue chiffon scarf at her throat. "*Dictature? Pas du tout. C'est ridicule,*" the chief male dancer of the Portuguese ballet said to me. This young man adored Salazar, too, while holding *les choses portugaises* in a certain wry contempt. He read only French books, and disliked port and the fado and cooking with oil. This is typical of the sophisticated Portuguese. "Manueline —it's simply futurism, the parvenu art of commerce," I was told by a Portuguese art historian who was also in the cotton business. People of standing complain about the servants, about the food, about the Portuguese character, but not about the corporate state. The more vexed such critics are with the Portuguese people, the more they applaud the strong hand the government takes with them. Most of the few kind words I have heard about the Portuguese character have come from Oppositionists—people who have been in prison or are living on the edge of disaster. There are many exiles in Portugal, including some famous kings and pretenders, and the Portuguese of the upper classes have developed an air of living in exile themselves; there is a tendency among them to look upon the people of the lower classes as natives, in the colonial sense of the term—to berate them, bewail them, smile over their idiosyncrasies, boast of their devotion.

And, indeed, there is something at once maddening and endearing about the Portuguese people—"*le peuple portugais, le vrai peuple,*" as the upper classes and the intelligentsia call them, to distinguish them from the middle classes, whom all the other classes unite in abominating. This maddening quality—a sort of bizarre inefficiency, lumpishness, and illogicality—is encountered chiefly in the men and overgrown boys, the *rapazes* of the hotels and shops and boarding-houses. The women and children are angels, most people agree. But the word *rapaz*, meaning "boy," comes for the foreigner to be a word of horror, combining, in the Anglo-Saxon mind, the worst features of "rascal" and "rapscallion" and evoking a picture of a tepid, scowling, scurfy, lazy, lying youth who cannot get anything right and who will soon grow into a man with the same characteristics—his sole source of drowsy interest his football club. (There are charming boys and men, too, of course—sensitive, courteous, but somewhat frail and pensive, as though their virtues had attenuated them.) The Spanish call the Portuguese *estúpido*, and the Portuguese men say it of one another, furiously, leaning out of their cars to bellow it at a pedestrian, at a policeman, at another driver: "*Estúpido, estúpido, estúpido!*"

"*Fantástico!*" our intelligent young Portuguese driver kept saying, with a grin, whenever we struck on some instance of illogicality during a ten-day trip through the north. "Fontaschtic," he would sigh. It was his favorite word, in Portuguese and English, the sign that he had become an onlooker, like the foreigners he drove. "Fontaschtic," we would agree, as the road menders stopped work to salute. This fantastically, or freakishness, as of a piebald horse or a flower curiously streaked, runs irrepressibly through the Portuguese character. Doubtless it is partly the result of the conjunction of an illiterate peasant people and modern machinery. (Critics, biologically minded, trace it to hereditary syphilis, brought back during the Age of Discoveries, and there are certainly many freaks of nature in Portugal—hunchbacks and mustached women, recalling the Middle Ages. In the course of our ten days in the north, we saw three women bearded like prophets.) What is strange about Portugal, on the whole, is the unevenness of its development. The terraced farms in the mountains, with their rock walls like rows of teeth, are masterpieces of masonry; a plowed field in Portugal is more beautiful than a garden elsewhere.

Many of the mechanical contrivances one sees are extremely inventive. Yet there are eerie zigzags and contradictions. For instance, practically all of Portugal is electrified, including the most primitive villages, but the lights are always going out, even in the big hotels, often several times in an evening, and the boy who goes to fix them does not understand electricity. Though this happens with almost predictable regularity, nobody thinks to provide candles. Only once in my three-months' stay here have candles been on hand when the fuses blew, and that was in a hotel run by an Englishman. In Praia da Rocha, the lights went out every Sunday morning all over the town; it was explained that the authorities were "washing" the electricity. In the same town, at the principal hotel, which was filled with foreigners of all nationalities, there was nobody on the staff who spoke any language other than Portuguese, and there was no railway timetable; an adventurous old Swiss gentleman with a beard, who spoke eight languages and had once made an ascent in a balloon over Moscow, nearly lost his reason trying to discover how to get a train to nearby Loulé. An Englishman at the hotel was dying from a heart condition; the ambulance taking him to Lisbon ran out of gas on a hill, the hand brake did not work, and the two orderlies stood by as the vehicle, with the stretcher in it, slipped jerkily back down to level ground.

On the comical side, there is the turkey walk from Estoril. Once every fortnight or so, the turkeys for the Lisbon market are walked in from there by a turkeyherd; driving along the *auto-estrada*, you can sometimes see them—the turkeyherd sleeping under a tree with his flock beside him. It is a fifteen-mile walk, and the turkey is a tough, seasoned veteran by the time you look him in the eye, still alive and ready to be poked, in the Lisbon market.

Most Americans shun Lisbon and huddle together in a sort of stockade in Estoril, which is an ugly little beach resort, with a casino, and houses painted blue and cream, like so many filling stations. The

American wives in Estoril hate Portugal and complain that there is nothing to do here. There is some justice in the charge. Lisbon has a delightful rococo opera house in which a German and an Italian company appeared last season, but the National Theatre did one play for dreary months on end—a Portuguese adaptation of a Spanish or Italian comedy laid in England in 1850. The movies are rather wearying, with many intermissions, and a great deal of cutting by the censor; when "The Seven Deadly Sins," a French picture, opened in Lisbon, only four deadly sins were left in it. There is very little artistic life—though not for lack of "intellectuals," as a man in the government wryly explained to me. Foreign books, chiefly, are read by the avant-garde—Sartre and Camus and Baudelaire and Rimbaud and Tolstoy. The most recent Portuguese literary renaissance was in the nineteenth century. Portuguese painting continues in its derivative course; last spring, in a tiny gallery, there was an abstract show for which all the local painters obligingly became abstractionists.

In time, most of the resident foreigners become disaffected and moody. Some take to drink, driven loco by the Portuguese peculiarities. As in the tropics, trifles begin to get on their nerves. I, for instance, cannot bear the way the Portuguese answer the telephone. "*Não está*," they usually growl, and hang up. You can never tell whether the person you have asked for is out or whether you have the wrong number. One American girl, whose husband is here on business, has become obsessed by the Portuguese men's habit of spitting. I told her one day that I had heard that some Oppositionists had been tortured. "What did they do to them?" she asked sharply. "Prevent them from spitting?" All winter, the Portuguese nose runs; most of the children one sees on the street have colds. The men seldom use handkerchiefs, except in the highest reaches of society. The American girl told me the other day that she nearly burst into tears of affection when she saw a very poor, ragged old man on the cable car get out a handkerchief and blow his nose. She gave him ten escudos.

It is the beggars who rasp the nerves of most foreigners—the shawled women with babies in their arms, and the old men, and the children whining, "Gimme an escudo, mister." The English tell you never to give to children; it gets them into bad habits. But it is hard to resist the children, either because they are so pretty or, on the contrary, because they are so wretched looking, with cold, thin, raw legs, and running noses and sores. In the Algarve, the children have caught on to the English moral disapproval of begging, and offer to sell you things instead—necklaces of seashells, and small shell dangles meant to be worn on the lapel. One little boy, on the beach, tried to sell my husband his homework.

Whether you give or not, the beggars will not leave you alone. As soon as a foreigner goes outdoors, he is surrounded, as if by a swarm of mosquitoes, and he begins to grow angry at the Portuguese. "There are plenty of rich people in Portugal!" cried an exacerbated old lady from Iowa in a hotel in the north. "Why don't they take care of their own poor?" This indignant question echoes through the hotels and *pensãos*. The old American ladies and retired couples who arrive in Portugal—from upstate New York, largely, and the Middle West—are not especially well-to-do; they come because they have read in a magazine that Portugal is cheap. And the rich in Portugal are said to be the richest in Europe. As you watch them in the hotels—silent, like sharks, endlessly masticating, with their medicines before them—you form a new conception of what cold selfishness can be. Strangely, it is not the peasants on their donkeys, with their umbrellas, or the white-collar workers in the cafés, with their newspapers, or the working-class women, with their baskets on their heads, who look foreign to American eyes; it is the moneyed classes who appear to be of a different breed. The lowering, heavy darkness of the moneyed classes seems to be as much a state of mind or soul as a physical appearance. The thick skin, the somnolent, heavy-lidded gaze are perhaps a kind of protection against fellow feeling. The difference between rich and poor is so extreme in Portugal that it seems to have formed a carapace over the rich, making them torpid and incurious. A gentle Portuguese lady, herself engaged in charity, explained to me, rather apologetically, that there is very little charity in Portugal. "It is not that they are bad," she said of the wealthy. "They simply do not think. They have never been trained to think. In America and England, at Christmas, your children are taught to make packages and send toys to poor children. Here they are not taught things like that."

The Caixa de Previdência is the fruit of official thought on the subject of the underprivileged; so are Economic Homes, and the various limited-rent housing projects, and the National Federation for Joy in Work, which is a workers' vacation plan. Among the official class, there is a good deal of social consciousness. There are breezy young bureaucrats—half playboy, half hard-driving worker—who remind you of enlightened young businessmen in America. They are "selling" Portugal to the tourist trade and fighting for appropriations to build hotels and clean up slums. There are other officials of a different type—stodgy, sincere, devoted, of lower social origins, fathers of growing families, who make you think of the Soviet officials of the early Thirties, before the great trials and the purges. This is a government of "new men." Portugal is called a fascist state by the Oppositionists, but the term seems a little out-of-date, for fascism as we knew it expired with Hitler and Mussolini. General Franco's regime already appears superannuated beside the Estado Novo. The quality of Portugal is modern. It is a semitotalitarian state, with certain positive aspects. It is possible for an official here to believe in the value of his work, to think that he is furthering the cause of progress as it is generally understood in the world by combating illiteracy, improving health and hygiene, building dams and roads, rehousing the underprivileged, reforming the school curriculum (less "book learning," more training in citizenship; less "strictly intellectual culture," more physical education).

Except for the question of dictatorship, on which they are stiff and sensitive, many of the officials I have met here (and this is a troubling fact) do not differ greatly in their views from many progressive American school superintendents. The functionaries of Salazar talk like practical idealists; they have no patience with "sentimentality." Salazar's own rhetoric belongs to an older school: "Although with delays, with possible wanderings from detail which the difficult times explain, we still stride along the same road, with our spirit faithful to the everlasting truth.... For every arm a hoe, for every family a home, for every mouth its bread." Yet even Salazar, in his most exalted vein, engages in the bureaucratic self-criticism that is characteristic of the modern totalitarian state. He complains that corporativism is slowing down, that the people are relaxing, and urges the pursuit of "our corporative crusade"; he bewails the "lack of indoctrination of the Portuguese people." This self-criticism is prevalent in the ranks of the franker officials all along the line, among whom it wears the mask of tolerance. One thing they tolerate is the Opposition, which, as they point out, was allowed to run candidates during the most recent election, in 1953—the first "free" election since the military coup in 1926. This election had a little of the flavor of a Soviet election. The Oppositionists were permitted to run candidates, but they were not permitted to organize as political parties. Their newspaper, the *Republica*, was allowed more freedom than previously, but it was still under censorship; it could "criticize but not defame," as my propaganda informant put it. The campaign was a rather improvised affair; without funds, without organization, the old parliamentarians and Socialists who had been in jail or exile off and on were restored to life in a state of slight confusion, somewhat like old Dr. Manette in *A Tale of Two Cities*. In many districts, they were not able to arrange a slate of candidates. Nevertheless, they did very well, considering; in the districts where they had candidates they polled up to 25 percent of the vote. Indeed, in a country in which the government was in a position (to say the least) to take economic reprisals against every citizen through his syndicate or *gremio* or *orden*, in which mass arrests and long detentions on mere suspicion were a thing of the very recent past (1948 is the latest I have heard of), this was remarkable. But it was also sad for the veteran parliamentarians and Socialists, since it represented probably a better showing than they would ever again be able to make in their lifetimes. Since the election, the censorship has tightened again. The real standard of living, say the Oppositionists, is lower than it has ever been: the rich have been getting richer throughout Salazar's regime and the poor steadily poorer, in real wages, despite housing projects and social benefits. Moreover, they point out, the intensification of the corporativist program makes the state steadily more powerful: two bureaucracies—the ordinary state servants and the functionaries of the corporative society—have the people in double harness. And the Oppositionist leaders themselves, a handful of persons—notably Dr. Francisco Cunha Leal, engineer and former professor at Coimbra; Dr. António Sérgio, humanist, critic, and educational theorist; and Dr. Egas Moniz, neurologist and Nobel Prize winner—are in their sixties, seventies, and eighties. For Dr. Sérgio, a charming old man with an engraving of Kant in his study, it is a cross that the government does not trouble to arrest him anymore but confines itself to persecuting his associates in various petty ways.

"Ah, António Sérgio!" said the press chief of Salazar's National Union, smiling broadly. "He is a little pink. We let these people talk unless they go too far." This official was a live wire, in his early thirties, who had been to America and conferred with John L. Lewis. He was proud to tell me that he knew very well the difference between a Communist and an old-style socialist intellectual. The Communists were jailed, of course, whenever the government could catch them, but even in dealing with *them*, he declared, the state showed moderation; the most dangerous Communists got only five years. Were we in America any more tolerant? he demanded. I replied that in the

Algarve I had heard of some people being arrested as Communists who were simply attending a funeral service for an old parliamentarian. Yes, that had happened, he acknowledged, but it had been a mistake, and such mistakes were rare. In the case I mentioned, the innocent bystanders had been released after two days' interrogation, and the more suspicious ones had been held for only a month and a half. The press chief spoke with a cocky frankness of what he called the small mistakes and shortcomings of the government. If he could have his way, he said, he would push the social security program much further and take the equivalent of 25 percent of each worker's wage from the employer for the Caixa de Previdência. And he would break up the big estates in the Alentejo—the great central dust bowl of Portugal. He aired these daring views coolly, rather like an insouciant young Marxist; he belonged, evidently, to the left, or "Bolshevik," wing of Salazar's National Union. For some reason—a kind of delicacy, I suppose—I never mentioned Salazar during our conversation. But as the press chief was guiding me out through a conference room hung with pictures of dignitaries, he suddenly whirled around and, with a violent jab of his short arm, pointed to a photograph of Salazar. "Do you know who that is?" he shouted, in a completely new voice, as though an angry public-address system had been switched on. "Dr. António de Oliveira *Salazar*!"

Here, apparently, was a case of political dual personality, a special mutation of our period. Another example was provided by a bilious-looking official of the Casa dos Pescadores who, with his colleague (officials here often come in pairs, like FBI men), was explaining to me matter-of-factly how corporativism works in fish. All at once, abruptly interrupting his colleague, he leaned over, fastened his yellowed eyeballs on me, and said, in a soft, menacing purr, "Have you ever heard of a man called *Salazar*?" In Portugal, Salazar's name, like God's, is usually spoken in a special manner—not exactly fearful, but dutiful, as if the voice were in a Sunday suit. There are dozens of stories about him, illustrating his economical habits, his modesty, his late and lonely vigils, his reluctance to wield power; they all sound apocryphal, like the stories that used to be told about Stalin. Some of them have a sort of gingerly humor—one, for instance, that I heard from a Portuguese chauffeur who drives for some English friends of mine. According to this story, Salazar, while driving in his Packard, encountered a Volkswagen on the road, got out, and asked its driver what it was. "It is the People's Car," said the driver, translating the German name into Portuguese. "And what is that?" he continued, pointing to Salazar's Packard. "That," said Salazar, "is *my* car," and he got in and drove away.

—*February 1955*

23

THE HOME PROGRAM

I CONFESS THAT when I went to Vietnam early last February I was looking for material damaging to the American interest and that I found it, though often by accident or in the process of being briefed by an official. Finding it is no job; the Americans do not dissemble what they are up to. They do not seem to feel the need, except through verbiage; e.g., napalm has become "Incinderjell," which makes it sound like Jell-O. And defoliants are referred to as weed-killers—something you use in your driveway. The resort to euphemism denotes, no doubt, a guilty conscience or—the same thing nowadays—a twinge in the public-relations nerve. Yet what is most surprising to a new arrival in Saigon is the general unawareness, almost innocence, of how what "we" are doing could look to an outsider.

At the airport in Bangkok, the war greeted the Air France passengers in the form of a strong smell of gasoline, which made us sniff as we breakfasted at a long table, like a delegation, with the Air France flag—our banner—planted in the middle. Outside, huge Esso tanks were visible behind lattice screens, where US bombers, factory-new, were aligned as if in a salesroom. On the field itself, a few yards from our Boeing 707, US cargo planes were warming up for takeoff; US helicopters flitted about among the swallows, while US military trucks made deliveries. The openness of the thing was amazing (the fact that the US was using Thailand as a base for bombing North Vietnam was not officially admitted at the time); you would have thought they would try to camouflage it, I said to a German correspondent, so that the tourists would not see. As the 707 flew on toward Saigon, the tourists, bound for Tokyo or Manila, were able to watch a South Vietnamese hillside burning while consuming a "cool drink" served by the hostess. From above, the bright flames looked like a summer forest fire; you could not believe that bombers had just left. At Saigon, the airfield was dense with military aircraft; in the "civil" side, where we landed, a passenger jetliner was loading GIs for Rest and Recreation in Hawaii. The American presence was overpowering, and, although one had read about it and was aware, as they say, that there was a war on, the sight and sound of that massed American might, casually disposed on foreign soil, like a corporal having his shoes shined, took one's breath away. "They don't try to hide it!" I kept saying to myself, as though the display of naked power and muscle ought to have worn some cover of modesty. But within a few hours I had lost this sense of incredulous surprise, and, seeing the word "hide" on a note pad in my hotel room the next morning, I no longer knew what I had meant by it (as when a fragment of a dream, written down on waking, becomes indecipherable) or why I should have been pained, as an American, by this high degree of visibility.

As we drove into downtown Saigon, through a traffic jam, I had the fresh shock of being in what looked like an American city, a very shoddy West Coast one, with a Chinatown and a slant-eyed Asiatic minority. Not only military vehicles of every description, but Chevrolets, Chryslers, Mercedes-Benz, Volkswagens, Triumphs, and white men everywhere in sport shirts and drip-dry pants. The civilian takeover is even more astonishing than the military. To an American, Saigon today is less exotic than Florence or the Place de la Concorde. New office buildings of cheap modern design, teeming with teased, puffed secretaries and their Washington bosses, are surrounded by sandbags and guarded by MPs; new, jerry-built villas in pastel tones, to rent to Americans, are under construction or already beginning to peel and discolor. Even removing the sandbags and the machine guns and restoring the trees that have been chopped down to widen the road to the airport, the mind cannot excavate what Saigon must have been like "before." Now it resembles a gigantic PX. All those white men seem to be carrying brown paper shopping bags, full of whiskey and other goodies; rows of ballpoints gleam in the breast pockets of their checked shirts. In front of his villa, a leathery oldster, in visored cap, unpacks his golf clubs from his station wagon, while his cotton-haired wife, in a flowered print dress, glasses slung round her neck, stands by, watching, her hands on her hips. As in the American vacationland, dress is strictly informal; nobody but an Asian wears a tie or a white shirt. The Vietnamese old men and boys, in wide, conical hats, pedaling their Cyclos (the modern version of the rickshaw) in and out of the traffic pattern, the Vietnamese women in high heels and filmy *ao dais* of pink, lavender, heliotrope, the signs and welcome banners in Vietnamese actually contribute to the Stateside impression by the addition of "local" color, as though you were back in a Chinese restaurant in San Francisco or in a Japanese sukiyaki place, under swaying paper lanterns, being served by women in kimonos while you sit on mats and play at using chopsticks.

Perhaps most of all Saigon is like a stewing Los Angeles, shading into Hollywood, Venice Beach, and Watts. The native stall markets are still in business, along Le Loi and Nguyen Hue Streets, but the merchandise is, for Asia, exotic. There is hardly anything native to buy, except flowers and edibles and firecrackers at Tet time and—oh yes—souvenir dolls. Street vendors and children are offering trays of American cigarettes and racks on racks of Johnnie Walker, Haig & Haig, Black & White (which are either black market, stolen from the PX, or spurious, depending on the price); billboards outside car agencies advertise Triumphs, Thunderbirds, MGs, Corvettes, "For Delivery Here or Stateside, Payment on Easy Terms"; nonwhites, the less-affluent ones, are mounted on Hondas and Lambrettas. There are photo-copying services, film-developing services, Western tailoring and dry-cleaning services, radio and TV repair shops, air conditioners, Olivetti typewriters, comic books, *Time, Life*, and *Newsweek*, airmail paper—you name it, they have it. Toys for Vietnamese children (there are practically no American kids or wives in Vietnam) include US-style jackknives, pistols, and simulated-leather belts, with holsters—I did not see any cowboy suits or Indian war feathers. Pharmaceuti-cals are booming; young Vietnamese women of the upper crust are enrolling in the School of Pharmacy in order to open drugstores; and a huge billboard all along the top of a building in the central market-place shows a smiling Negro—maybe a long-ago Senegalese soldier—with very white teeth advertising a toothpaste called Hynos.

If Saigon by day is like a PX, at night, with flares overhead, it is like a World's Fair or Exposition in some hick American city. There are Chinese restaurants, innumerable French restaurants (not surprising), but also La Dolce Vita, Le Guillaume Tell, the Paprika (a Spanish restaurant on a rooftop, serving paella and sangría). The national cui-sine no American wants to sample is the Vietnamese. In February, a German circus was in town. "French" wine is made in Cholon, the local Chinatown. In the nightclubs, if it were not for the bar girls, you would think you were on a cruise ship: a chanteuse from Singapore sings old French, Italian, and American favorites into the microphone; an Italian magician palms the watch of a middle-aged Vietnamese customer; the band strikes up "Happy Birthday to You," as a cake is brought in. The "vice" in Saigon—at least what I was able to observe of it—has a pepless *Playboy* flavor.

As for virtue, I went to church one Sunday in the cathedral (a medley of Gothic, Romanesque, and vaguely Moorish) on John F. Kennedy Square, hoping to hear the Mass in Vietnamese. Instead, an Irish-American priest preached a sermon on the hemline to a large male white congregation of soldiers, construction workers, newspaper correspondents; in the pews were also a few female secretaries from the embassy and other US agencies and a quotient of middle-class Vietnamese of both sexes. I had happened, it turned out, on the "American" Mass, said at noon. Earlier services *were* in Vietnamese. The married men present, the celebrant began, did not have to be told that for a woman the yearly rise or fall in skirt lengths was a "traumatic experience," and he likened the contemporary style centers—New York, Chicago, San Francisco—to the ancient "style centers" of the Church—Rome, Antioch, Jerusalem. His point seemed to be that the various rites of the Church (Latin, Coptic, Armenian, Maronite—he went into it very thoroughly) were only *modes* of worship. What the Sunday-dressed Vietnamese, whose hemline remains undisturbed by changes emanating from the "style centers" and who were hearing the Latin Mass in American, were able to make of the sermon, it was impossible to tell. Just as it was impossible to tell what some very small Vietnamese children I saw in a home for ARVN war orphans were getting out of an American adult TV program they were watching at bedtime, the littlest ones mother-naked. Maybe TV, too, is catholic, and the words do not matter.

Saigon has a smog problem, like New York and Los Angeles, a municipal garbage problem, a traffic problem, power failures, inflation, juvenile delinquency. In short, it meets most of the criteria of a modern Western city. The young soldiers do not like Saigon and its clip joints and high prices. Everybody is trying to sell them something or buy something from them. Six-year-old boys, cute as pins, are plucking at them: "You come see my sister. She Number One fuck." To help the GI resist the temptations of merchants—and soak up his buying power—diamonds and minks are offered him in the PX, tax free. (There were no minks the day I went there, but I did see a case of diamond rings, the prices ranging up to 900-odd dollars.) Unfortunately, the PX presents its own temptation—that of resale. The GI is gypped by taxi drivers and warned against Cyclo men (probably VC), and he may wind up in a Vietnamese jail, like some of his buddies, for doing what everybody else does—illegal currency transactions. If he walks in the center after nightfall, he has to pick his way among whole families who are cooking their unsanitary meal or sleeping, right on the street, in the filth. When he rides in from the airport, he has to cross a bend of the river, bordered by shanties, that he has named, with rich American humor, Cholera Creek.

To the servicemen, Saigon stinks. They would rather be in base camp, which is clean. And the JUSPAO press officer has a rote speech for arriving correspondents: "Get out of Saigon. That's my advice to you. Go out into the field." As though the air were purer there, where the fighting is.

That is true in a way. The Americanization process smells better out there, to Americans, even when perfumed by napalm. Out there, too, there is an enemy a man can respect. For many of the soldiers in the field and especially the younger officers, the Vietcong is the only Vietnamese worthy of notice. "If we only had them fighting on our side, instead of the goddamned Arvin [Army of the Vietnamese Republic], we'd *win* this war" is a sentiment the newspapermen like to quote. I never heard it said in those words, but I found that you could judge an American by his attitude toward the Vietcong. If he called them "Charlie" (cf. John Steinbeck), he was either an infatuated civilian, a low-grade primitive in uniform, or a fatuous military mouthpiece. Decent soldiers and officers called them "the VC." The same code of honor applied in South Vietnamese circles; with the Vietnamese, who are ironic, it was almost a pet name for the enemy. Most of the American military will praise the fighting qualities of the VC, and the more intellectual (who are not necessarily the best) praise them for their "motivation." In this half of the century Americans have become very incurious, but the Vietcong has awakened the curiosity of the men who are fighting them. From within the perimeter of the camp, behind the barbed wire and the sandbags, they study their habits, half-amused, half-admiring; a gingerly relationship is established with the unseen enemy, who is probably carefully fashioning a booby trap a few hundred yards away. This relation does not seem to extend to the North Vietnamese troops, but in that case contact is rarer. The military are justly nervous of the VC, but unless they have been wounded out on a patrol or have had the next man killed by a mine or a mortar, they do not show hatred or picture the black-pajama saboteur as a "monster," a word heard in Saigon offices.

In the field, moreover, the war is not questioned; it is just a fact. The job has to be finished—that is the attitude. In Saigon, the idea that the war can ever be finished appears fantastic: the Americans will be there forever, one feels; if they go, the economy will collapse. What postwar aid program could be conceived—or passed by Congress—that would keep the air in the balloon? And if the Americans go, the middle-class Saigonese think, the Vietcong will surely come back, in two years, five years, ten, as they come back to a "pacified" hamlet at Tet time, to leave, as it were, a calling card, a reminder—we are still here. But, at the same time, in Saigon the worth of the American presence, that is, of the war, seems very dubious, since the actual results, in uglification, moral and physical, are evident to all. The American soldier, bumping along in a jeep or a military truck, resents seeing all those Asiatics at the wheels of new Cadillacs. He knows about corruption, often firsthand, having contributed his bit to it, graft, theft of AID and military supplies from the port. He thinks it is disgusting that the local employees steal from the PX and then stage a strike when the manageress makes them line up to be searched on leaving the building. And he has heard that these "apes," as some men call them, are salting away the profits in Switzerland or in France, where De Gaulle, who is pro-VC, has just run the army out.

Of course, all wars have had their profiteers, but it has not usually been so manifest, so inescapable. The absence of the austerity that normally accompanies war, of civilian sacrifices, rationing, shortages, blackouts (compare wartime London or even wartime New York, twenty-five years ago) makes this war seem singularly immoral and unheroic to those who are likely to die in it—for what? So that the Saigonese and other civilians can live high off the hog? The fact that the soldier or officer is living pretty high off the hog himself does not reconcile him to the glut of Saigon; rather the contrary. Furthermore, an atmosphere of sacrifice is heady; that—and danger—is what used to make wartime capitals gay. Saigon is not gay. The peculiar thing is that with all those young soldiers wandering about, all those young journalists news-chasing, Saigon seems so middle-aged—inert, listless, bored. That, I suppose, is because everyone's principal interest there is money, the only currency that is circulating, like the stale air moved by ceiling fans and air conditioners in hotels and offices.

The war, they say, is not going to be won in Saigon, nor on the battlefield, but in the villages and hamlets. This idea, by now trite (it was first discovered in Diem's time and has been rebaptized under a number of names—New Life Hamlets, Rural Construction, Counter Insurgency, Nation-Building, Revolutionary Development, the Hearts and Minds Program), is the main source of inspiration for the various teams of missionaries, military and civilian, who think they are engaged in a crusade. Not just a crusade against Communism, but something *positive*. Back in the Fifties and early Sixties, the war was presented as an investment: the taxpayer was persuaded that if he stopped Communism *now* in Vietnam, he would not have to keep stopping it in Thailand, Burma, etc. That was the domino theory, which our leading statesmen today, quite comically, are busy repudiating before congressional committees—suddenly nobody will admit to ever having been an advocate of it. The notion of a costly investment that will save money in the end has a natural appeal to a nation of homeowners, but now the assertion of an American "interest" in Vietnam has begun to look too speculative as the stake increases

("When is it going to pay off?") and also too squalid as the war daily becomes more savage and destructive. Hence the "other" war, proclaimed by President Johnson in Honolulu, which is simultaneously pictured as a strategy for winning War Number One and as a top priority in itself. Indeed, in Vietnam, there are moments when the "other" war, for hearts and minds, seems to be viewed as the sole reason for the American presence, and it is certainly more congenial to American officials, brimming with public spirit, than the war they are launching from the skies. Americans do not like to be negative, and the "other" war is constructive.

To see it, of course, you have to get out of Saigon, but, before you go, you will have to be briefed, in one of those new office buildings, on what you are going to see. In the field, you will be briefed again, by a military man, in a district or province headquarters, and frequently all you will see of New Life Hamlets, Constructed Hamlets, Consolidated Hamlets are the charts and graphs and maps and symbols that some ardent colonel or brisk bureaucrat is demonstrating to you with a pointer, and the mimeographed handout, full of statistics, that you take away with you, together with a supplement on Vietcong Terror. On paper and in chart form, it all sounds commendable, especially if you are able to ignore the sounds of bombing from B-52s that are shaking the windows and making the charts rattle. The briefing official is enthusiastic, as he points out the progress that has been made, when, for example, the activities organized under AID were reorganized under OCO (Office of Civil Operations). You stare at the chart on the office wall which to you has no semblance of logic or sequence ("Why," you wonder, "should Youth Affairs be grouped under Urban Development?"), and the official rubs his hands with pleasure: "First we organized it *vertically*. Now we've organized it *horizontally!*" He does not say that one of the main reasons for the creation of OCO was to provide a cover for certain CIA operations. Out in the field, you learn from some disgruntled officer that the AID representatives, who are perhaps now OCO representatives without knowing it, have not been paid for six months.

In a Saigon "backgrounder," you are told about public health measures undertaken by Free World Forces. Again a glowing progress report. In 1965, there were 180 medical people from the "Free World" in Vietnam treating patients; in 1966, there were 700—quite a little escalation, almost four times as many. The troop commitment, of course, not mentioned by the briefer, jumped from 60,000 to 400,000 —more than six and a half times as many. That the multiplication of troops implied an obvious escalation in the number of civilian patients requiring treatment is not mentioned either. Under questioning, the official, slightly irritated, estimates that the civilian casualties comprise between 7½ and 15 percent of the surgical patients treated in hospitals. He had "not been interested particularly, until all the furor," in what percentage of the patients were war casualties. And naturally he was not interested in what percentage of civilian casualties never reached a hospital at all.

Nor would there have been any point in asking him what happens to the Vietcong wounded—a troubling question I never heard raised in nearly a month in Vietnam. A very few are in hospitals—some have been seen recently by a journalist in Can Tho—and the mother of a Marine killed in action has made public in a Texas newspaper a letter from her boy telling how he felt when ordered to go back to the battlefield and shoot wounded VC in the head (prompt denial from the Marine Corps). But American officials on the spot are not concerned by the discrepancy between estimated VC wounded and estimated VC in hospitals: 225 being treated in US medical facilities in one week in May, whereas at the end of April an estimated 30,000 to 35,000 had been wounded in action since the first of the year.

But—to return to the "backgrounder"—the treatment of war victims, it turned out, was not one of the medical "bull's-eyes" aimed at in the "other" war. Rather, a peacetime-type program, "beefing up" the medical school, improvement of hospital facilities, donation of drugs and antibiotics (which, as I learned from another source, are in turn *sold* by the local nurses to the patients for whom they have been prescribed), the control of epidemic diseases, such as plague and cholera, education of the population in good health procedures. American and allied workers, you hear, are teaching the Vietnamese in the government villages to boil their water, and the children are learning dental hygiene. Toothbrushes are distributed, and the children are shown how to use them. If the children get the habit, the parents will copy them, a former social worker explains, projecting from experience with first-generation immigrants back home. There is a campaign on to vaccinate and immunize as much of the population as can be got to cooperate; easy subjects are refugees and forced evacuees, who can be lined up for shots while going through the screening process and being issued an identity card—a political health certificate.

All this is not simply on paper. In the field, you are actually able to see medical teams at work, setting up temporary dispensaries under the trees in the hamlets for the weekly or biweekly "sick call"—distributing medicines, tapping, listening, sterilizing, bandaging; the most common diagnosis is suspected tuberculosis. In Tay Ninh Province, I watched a Philcag (Filipino) medical team at work in a Buddhist hamlet. One doctor was examining a very thin old man, who was stripped to the waist; probably tubercular, the doctor told me, writing something on a card which he gave to the old man. "What happens next?" I wanted to know. Well, the old man would go to the province hospital for an x-ray (that was the purpose of the card), and if the diagnosis was positive, then treatment should follow. I was impressed. But (as I later learned at a briefing) there are only sixty civilian hospitals in South Vietnam—for nearly 16 million people—so that the old man's total benefit, most likely, from the open-air consultation was to have learned, gratis, that he might be tubercular.

Across the road, some dentist's chairs were set up, and teeth were being pulled, very efficiently, from women and children of all ages. I asked about the toothbrushes I had heard about in Saigon. The Filipino major laughed. "Yes, we have distributed them. They use them as toys." Then he reached into his pocket—he was a kindly young man with children of his own—and took out some money for all the children who had gathered round, to buy popsicles (the local equivalent) from the popsicle man. Later I watched the Filipino general, a very handsome tall man with a cropped head, resembling Yul Brynner, distribute Tet gifts and candy to children in a Cao Dai orphanage and be photographed with his arm around a little blind girl. A few hours earlier, he had posed distributing food in a Catholic hamlet— "Free World" surplus items, such as canned cooked beets. The photography, I was told, would help sell the Philcag operation to the Assembly in Manila, where some leftist elements were trying to block funds for it. Actually, I could not see that the general was doing any harm, whatever his purposes might be, politically—unless not doing more is harm, in which case we are all guilty—and he was more efficient than other Civic Action leaders. His troops had just chopped down a large section of jungle (we proceeded through it in convoy, wearing bulletproof vests and bristling with rifles and machine guns, because of the vc), which was going to be turned into a hamlet for resettling refugees. They had also built a school, which we stopped to inspect, finding, to the general's surprise, that it had been taken over by the local district chief for his office headquarters.

The Filipino team, possibly because they were Asians, seemed to be on quite good terms with the population. Elsewhere—at Go Cong, in the delta—I saw mistrustful patients and heard stories of rivalry between the Vietnamese doctor, a gynecologist, and the Spanish and American medical teams; my companion and I were told that we were the first "outsiders," including the resident doctors, to be allowed by the Vietnamese into *his* wing—the maternity, which was far the cleanest and most modern in the hospital and contained one patient.

Similar jealousies existed of the German medical staff at Hué. In the rather squalid surgical wing of the Go Cong hospital, there were two badly burned children. Were they war casualties, I asked the official who was showing us through. Yes, he conceded, as a matter of fact they were. How many of the patients were war-wounded, I wanted to know. "About four" of the children, he reckoned. And one old man, he added, after reflection.

The Filipinos were fairly dispassionate about their role in pacification; this may have been because they had no troops fighting in the war (those leftist elements in the Assembly!) and therefore did not have to act like saviors of the Vietnamese people. The Americans, on the contrary, are zealots—above all, the blueprinters in the Saigon offices—although occasionally in the field, too, you meet a true believer—a sandy, crew-cut, keen-eyed army colonel who talks to you about "the nuts and bolts" of the program, which, he is glad to say, is finally getting the "grass-roots" support it needs. It is impossible to find out from such a man what he is doing, concretely; an aide steps forward to state, "We sterilize the area prior to the insertion of the RD teams," whose task, says the colonel, is to find out "the aspirations of the people." He cannot tell you whether there has been any land reform in his area—that is a strictly Vietnamese pigeon—in fact he has no idea of *how* the land in the area is owned. He is strong on co-ordination: all his Vietnamese counterparts, the colonel who "wears two hats" as province chief, the mayor, a deposed general, are "very fine sound men," and the marine general in the area is "one of the finest men and officers" he has ever met. For another army zealot every Vietnamese officer he deals with is "an outstanding individual."

These springy, zesty, burning-eyed warriors, military and civilian, engaged in AID or Combined Action (essentially pacification) stir far-away memories of American college presidents of the fund-raising type; their diction is peppery with oxymoron ("When peace breaks out," "Then the commodities started to hit the beach"), like a college president's address to an alumni dinner. They see themselves in fact as educators, spreading the American way of life, a new *propaganda fide*. When I asked an OCO man in Saigon what his groups actually did in a Vietnamese village to prepare—his word—the people for elections, he answered curtly, "We teach them Civics 101."

The American taxpayer who thinks that aid means direct help to the needy has missed the idea. Aid's first target is economic stability within the present system, i.e., political stability for the present ruling groups. Loans are extended, under the counterpart-fund arrangement, to finance Vietnamese imports of American capital equipment (thus AIDing, with the other hand, American industry). Second, aid is *education*. Distribution of canned goods (instill new food habits), distribution of seeds, fertilizer, chewing gum and candy (the Vietnamese complain that the GIs fire candy at their children, like a spray of bullets), lessons in sanitation, hog raising, and crop rotation. The program is designed, not just to make Americans popular, but to shake up the Vietnamese, as in some "stimulating" freshman course where the student learns to question the "prejudices" implanted in him by his parents. "We're trying to wean them away from the old barter economy and show them a market economy. Then they'll really *go*."

"We're teaching them free enterprise," explains a breathless JUSPAO official in the grim town of Phu Cuong. He is speaking of the "refugees" from the Iron Triangle, who were forcibly cleared out of their hamlets, which were then burned and leveled, during Operation Cedar Falls ("Clear and Hold"). They had just been transferred into a camp, hastily constructed by the ARVN with tin roofs painted red and white, to make the form, as seen from the air, of a giant Red Cross—1,651 women, 3,754 children, 582 men, mostly old, who had been kindly allowed to bring some of their furniture and pots and pans and their pigs and chickens and sacks of their hoarded rice; their water cattle had been transported for them, on barges, and were now sickening on a dry, stubbly, sandy plain. "We've got a captive audience!" the official continued excitedly. "This is our big chance!"

To teach them free enterprise and, presumably, when they were "ready" for it, Civics 101; for the present, the government had to consider them "hostile civilians." These wives and children and old fathers of men thought to be at large with the Vietcong had been rice farmers only a few weeks before. Now they were going to have to pitch in and learn to be vegetable farmers; the area selected for their eventual resettlement was not suitable for rice growing, unfortunately. Opportunity was beckoning for these poor peasants, thanks to the uprooting process they had just undergone. They would have the chance to buy and build their own homes on a pattern and of materials already picked out for them; the government was allowing them 1,700 piasters toward the purchase price. To get a new house free, even though in the abstract that might seem only fair, would be unfair to them as human beings, it was explained to me: investing their own labor and their own money would make them feel that the house was really *theirs*. "The Lord helps those who help themselves"—the social worker's Great Commandment—is interpreted in war-pounded Vietnam, and with relentless priggery, as "The US helps those who help themselves."

In the camp, a schoolroom had been set up. Interviews with the parents revealed that more than anything else they wanted education for their children; they had not had a school for five years. I remarked that this seemed queer, since Communists were usually strong on education. The official insisted. "Not for five years." But in fact another American, a young one, who had actually been working in the camp, told me that strangely enough the small children there knew their multiplication tables and possibly their primer—he could not account for this. And in one of the razed villages, he related, the Americans had found, from captured exercise books, that someone had been teaching the past participle in English, using Latin models—defectors spoke of a high school teacher, a Ph.D. from Hanoi.

Perhaps the parents, in the interviews, told the Americans what they thought they wanted to hear. All over Vietnam, wherever peace has broken out, if only in the form of a respite, marine and army officers are proud to show the schoolhouses their men are building or rebuilding for the hamlets they are patroling, rifle on shoulder. At Rach Kien, in the delta (a Pentagon pilot project of a few months before), I saw the little schoolhouse Steinbeck wrote about, back in January, and the blue school desks he had seen the soldiers painting. They were still sitting outside, in the sun; the school was not yet rebuilt more than a month later—they were waiting for materials. In this hamlet, everything seemed to have halted, as in "The Sleeping Beauty," the enchanted day Steinbeck left; nothing had advanced. Indeed, the picture he sketched, of a ghost town coming back to civic life, made the officers who had entertained him smile—"He used his imagination." In other hamlets, I saw schoolhouses actually finished and one in operation. "The school is dirty," the colonel in charge barked at the alarmed Revolutionary Development director, who claimed to have been the first to translate Pearl Buck into Vietnamese. It was an instance of American tactlessness, though the belligerent colonel was right. A young Vietnamese social worker said sadly that he wished the Americans would stop building schools. "They don't realize—we have no teachers for them."

Yet the little cream schoolhouse is essential to the American dream of what we are doing in Vietnam, and it is essential for the soldiers to believe that in *Vietcong* hamlets no schooling is permitted. In Rach Kien I again expressed doubts, as a captain, with a professionally shocked face, pointed out the evidence that the school had been used as "Charlie's" headquarters. "So you really think that the children here got no lessons, *nothing*, under the vc?" "Oh, indoctrination courses!" he answered with a savvy wave of his pipe. In other words, vc Civics 101.

If you ask a junior officer what he thinks our war aims are in

Vietnam, he usually replies without hesitation: "To punish aggression." It is unkind to try to draw him into a discussion of what constitutes aggression and what is defense (the Bay of Pigs, Santo Domingo, Goa?), for he really has no further ideas on the subject. He has been indoctrinated, just as much as the North Vietnamese POW, who tells the interrogation team he is fighting to "liberate the native soil from the American aggressors"—maybe more. Only, the young American does not know it; he probably imagines that he is *thinking* when he produces that formula. And yet he does believe in something profoundly, though he may not be able to find the words for it: free enterprise. A parcel that to the American mind wraps up for delivery hospitals, sanitation, roads, harbors, schools, air travel, Jack Daniel's, convertibles, Stim-U-Dents. That is the moral C ration in his survival kit. The American troops are not exactly conscious of bombing, shelling, and defoliating to defend free enterprise (which they cannot imagine as being under serious attack), but they plan to come out of the war with their values intact. Which means that they must spread them, until everyone is convinced, by demonstration, that the American way is better, just as American seed strains are better and American pigs are better. Their conviction is sometimes baldly stated. North of Da Nang, at a marine base, there is an ice cream plant on which is printed in large official letters the words: "ICE-CREAM PLANT: ARVN MORALE BUILDER." Or it may wear a humanitarian disguise, e.g., Operation Concern, in which a proud little town in Kansas airlifted 110 pregnant sows to a humble little town in Vietnam.

Occasionally the profit motive is undisguised. Flying to Hué in a big C-130, I heard the pilot and the co-pilot discussing their personal war aim, which was to make a killing, as soon as the war was over, in Vietnamese real estate. From the air, while keeping an eye out for VC below, they had surveyed the possibilities and had decided on Nha Trang—"beautiful sand beaches"—better than Cam Ranh Bay—a "desert." They disagreed as to the kind of development that would make the most money: the pilot wanted to build a high-class hotel and villas, while the co-pilot thought that the future lay with low-cost housing. I found this conversation hallucinating, but the next day, in Hué, I met a marine colonel who was back in uniform after retirement; having fought the Japanese, he had made his killing as a "developer" in Okinawa and invested the profits in a frozen-shrimp (from Japan) import business supplying restaurants in San Diego. War, a cheap form of mass tourism, opens the mind to business opportunities.

All these developers were Californians. In fact, the majority of the Americans I met in the field in Vietnam were WASPs from Southern California; most of the rest were from the rural South. In nearly a month I met *one* Jewish boy in the services (a nice young naval officer from Pittsburgh), two Boston Irish, and a captain from Connecticut. Given the demographic shift toward the Pacific in the United States, this Californian ascendancy gave me the peculiar feeling that I was seeing the future of our country as if on a movie screen. Nobody has yet dared make a war movie about Vietnam, but the prevailing unreality, as experienced in base camps and headquarters, is eerily like a movie, a contest between good and evil that is heading toward a happy ending, when men with names like "Colonel Culpepper," "Colonel Derryberry," "Captain Stanhope" will vanquish Victor Charlie. The state that has a movie actor for governor and a movie actor for US senator seemed to be running the show.

No doubt the very extensive press and television coverage of the war has made the participants very conscious of "exposure," that is, of role playing. Aside from the usual networks, Italian television, Mexican television, the BBC, CBC were all filming the "other" war during the month of February, and the former Italian chief of staff, General Liuzzi, was covering it as a commentator for the *Corriere della Sera*. The effect of all this attention on the generals, colonels, and lesser officers was to put a premium on "sincerity."

Nobody likes to be a villain, least of all a WASP officer, who feels he is playing the heavy in Vietnam through some awful mistake in type-casting. He *knows* he is good at heart, because everything in his home environment—his TV set, his paper, his Frigidaire, the President of the United States—has promised him that, whatever shortcomings he may have as an individual, collectively he is good. The "other" war is giving him the chance to clear up the momentary misunderstanding created by those bombs, which, through no fault of his, are happening to hit civilians. He has *warned* them to get away, dropped leaflets saying he was coming and urging "Charlie" to defect, to join the other side; lately, in pacified areas, he has even taken the precaution of having his targets cleared by the village chief before shelling or bombing, so that now the press officer giving the daily briefing is able to reel out: "Operation Blockhouse. Twenty-nine civilians reported wounded today. Two are in 'poor' condition. Target had been approved by the district chief." Small thanks he gets, our military hero, for that scrupulous restraint. But in the work of pacification, his real self comes out, clear and true. Digging wells for the natives (too bad if the water comes up brackish), repairing roads ("Just a jungle trail before we came," says the captain, though his colonel, in another part of the forest, has just been saying that the engineers had uncovered a fine stone roadbed built eighty years ago by the French), building a house for the widow of a Vietcong (so far unreconciled; it takes time).

American officers in the field can become very sentimental when they think of the good they are doing and the hard row they have to hoe with the natives, who have been brainwashed by the Vietcong. A marine general in charge of logistics in I-Corps district was deeply moved when he spoke of his marines: moving in to help rebuild some refugee housing with scrap lumber and sheet tin (the normal materials were cardboard boxes and flattened beer cans); working in their off-hours to build desks for a school; giving their Christmas money for a new high school; planning a new marketplace. The Marine Corps had donated a children's hospital, and in that hospital, right up the road ("Your ve-hickels will conduct you"—he pronounced it like "nickels"), was a little girl who had been wounded during a marine assault. "We're nursing her back to health," he intoned—and paused, like a preacher accustomed, at this point, to hearing an "Amen"; his PIO (Information Officer) nodded three times. In the hospital, I asked to see the little girl. "Oh, she's gone home," said the PIO. "Nursed her back to health." In reality the little girl was still there, but it was true, her wounds were nearly healed.

A young marine doctor, blue-eyed, very good-looking, went from bed to bed, pointing out what was the matter with each child and showing what was being done to cure it. There was only the one war casualty; the rest were suffering from malnutrition (the basic complaint everywhere), skin diseases, worms; one had a serious heart condition; two had been badly burned by a stove, and one, in the contagious section, had the plague. The doctor showed us the tapeworm, in a bottle, he had extracted from one infant. A rickety baby was crying, and a middle-aged corpsman picked it up and gave it its bottle. They were plainly doing a good job, under makeshift conditions and without laboratory facilities. The children who were well enough to sit up appeared content; some even laughed, shyly. No amusements were provided for them, but perhaps it was sufficient amusement to be visited by tiptoeing journalists. And it could not be denied that it was a break for these children to be in a marine hospital, clean, well fed, and one to a bed. They were benefiting from the war, at least for the duration of their stay; the doctor was not sanguine, for the malnutrition cases, about what would happen when the patients went home. "We keep them as long as we can," he said, frowning. "But we can't keep them forever. They have to go back to their parents."

Compared to what they were used to, this short taste of the American way of life no doubt was delicious for Vietnamese children. John Morgan, in the London *Sunday Times*, described another little Vietnamese girl up near the DMZ—do they have one to a battalion?—who had been wounded by marine bullets ("A casualty of war," that general repeated solemnly. "A casualty of war.") and whom he saw carried in one night to a drinking party in sick bay, her legs bandaged, a spotlight playing on her, while the marines pressed candy and dollar bills into her hands and had their pictures taken with her; she had more dolls than Macy's, they told him—"that girl is real spoiled." To spoil a child you have injured and send her back to her parents, with her dolls as souvenirs, is pharisee virtue, whitening the sepulcher, like "treating" malnutrition in a hospital ward. The young doctor, being a doctor, was possibly conscious of the fakery—from a responsible medical point of view—of the "miracle" cures he was effecting; that was why he frowned. Meanwhile, however, the Marine Corps brass could show the "Before" and "After" to a captive audience. In fact two. The studio audience of children, smiling and laughing and clapping, and the broader audience of their parents, who, when allowed to visit, could not fail to be awed by the "other" side of American technology. And beyond that still a third audience—the journalists and their readers back home, who would recognize the Man in White and his corpsmen, having brought them up, gone to school with them, seen them on TV, in soap opera. I felt this myself, a relieved recognition of the familiar face of America. These are the American boys we know at once, even in an Asian context, bubbling an Asian baby. We do not recognize them, helmeted, in a bomber aiming cans of napalm at a thatched village. We have a credibility gap.

Leaving the hospital, I jolted southward in a jeep, hanging on, swallowing dust; the roads, like practically everything in Vietnam, have been battered, gouged, scarred, torn up by the weight of US matériel. We passed marines' laundry, yards and yards of dark-green battle cloth, hanging outside native huts like a kind of currency displayed by the fortunate washwoman. Down the road was a refugee camp, which did not form part of the itinerary. This, I realized, must be "home" to some of the children we had just seen; the government daily allowance for a camp family was ten piasters (six cents) a day—sometimes twenty if there were two adults in the family. Somebody had put a streamer, in English, over the entrance: "REFUGEES FROM COMMUNISM."

This was a bit too much. The children's hospital had told the story the Americans were anxious to get over. Why put in the commercial? And who was the hard sell aimed at? Not the refugees, who could not read English and who, if they were like all the other refugees, had fled, some from the Vietcong and some from the Americans and some because their houses had been bombed or shelled. Not the journalists, who knew better. Whoever carefully lettered that streamer, crafty marine or civilian, had applied all his animal cunning to selling himself.

—April 1967

24

PHILIP RAHV
(1908–1973)

SO HE'S GONE, that dear phenomenon. If no two people are alike, he was less like anybody else than anybody. A powerful intellect, a massive, overpowering personality and yet shy, curious, susceptible, confiding. All his life he was sternly faithful to Marxism, for him both a tool of analysis and a wondrous cosmogony, but he loved Henry James and every kind of rich, shimmery, soft texture in literature and in the stuff of experience. He was a resolute modernist, which made him in these recent days old-fashioned. It was as though he came into being with the steam engine: for him, literature began with Dostoevsky and stopped with Joyce, Proust, and Eliot; politics began with Marx and Engels and stopped with Lenin. He was not interested in Shakespeare, the classics, Greek city-states, and he despised most contemporary writing and contemporary political groups, being grumblingly out of sorts with fashion, except where he felt it belonged, on the backs of good-looking women and girls.

This did not overtake him with age or represent a hardening of his mental arteries. He was always that way. It helped him be a Trotskyite (he was a great admirer of the Old Man, though never an inscribed adherent) when Stalinism was chic. Whatever was "in" he threw out with a snort. Late in his life, serendipity introduced him to the word "swingers," which summed up everything he was against.

With sardonic relish he adopted it as his personal shorthand. If he came down from Boston to New York and went to a literary party and you asked him, "Well, how was it?" he would answer, "Nothing but swingers!" and give his short soft bark of a laugh.

Yet he had a gift for discovering young writers. I think of Saul Bellow, Elizabeth Hardwick, Jarrell, Berryman, Malamud. There were many others. He was quickly aware of Bob Silvers, editor of *The New York Review of Books*, and became his close friend—counselor, too, sometimes. To the end of his life, he remained a friend of young people. It was middle-aged and old swingers he held in aversion; young ones, on the whole, he did not mind.

He had a marvelous sensitivity to verbal phrasing and structure. What art dealers call "quality" in painting he would recognize instantly in literature, even of a kind that, in principle, ought to have been foreign to him. I remember when I first knew him, back in the mid-Thirties, at a time when he was an intransigent (I thought), pontificating young Marxist, and I read a short review he had done of *Tender Is the Night*—the tenderness of the review, despite its critical stance, startled me. I would not have suspected in Rahv that power of sympathetic insight into a writer glamorized by rich Americans on the Riviera. Fitzgerald, I must add, was "out" then and not only for the disagreeable crowd at the *New Masses*.

That review was delicately, almost poetically written, and this too was a surprise. I would have expected him to write as he talked, pungently, harshly, drivingly, in a heavy Russian accent. It was as though another person had written the review. But as those who knew him discovered, there were two persons in Rahv, but solidly married to each other in a longstanding union—no quarrels. It would be simplifying to say that one was political, masculine, and aggressive, one feminine, artistic, and dreamy, but those contrasts were part of it.

Perhaps there were more than two, the third being an unreconstructed child with a child's capacity for wonder and amazement.

Philip marveled constantly at the strangeness of life and the world. Recounting some story, seizing on some item in a newspaper, he would be transported, positively enraptured, with glee and offended disbelief. His black eyes with their large almost bulging whites would roll, and he would shake his head over and over, have a fit of chuckling, nudge you, if you were a man, squeeze your arm, if you were a woman—as though together you and he were watching a circus parade of human behavior, marvelous monstrosities and curious animals, pass through your village.

His own childhood in the Russian Ukraine had stayed fast in his mind. He used to tell me how his grandmother (his parents were Jewish shopkeepers living in the midst of a peasant population) ran into the shop one day saying, "The tsar has fallen," and to him it was as if she had said, "The sky has fallen"; he hid behind the counter. Then, when the Civil War began, he remembered staying in the shop for weeks, it seemed, with the blinds pulled down, as Red and White troops took and retook the village. His parents were early Zionists, and, after the Civil War, they emigrated to Palestine, where in the little furniture factory his father opened he got to know those strange people—Arabs. Just before or after this, he went to America, alone, to live with his older brother. There, in Providence, Rhode Island, already quite a big boy, he went to grade school still dressed as an old-fashioned European schoolboy, in long black trousers and black stockings, looking like a somber little man among the American kids. Starting to work early, as a junior advertising copywriter for a small firm out in Oregon, he had no time for college and got his education, alone, in public libraries. In the Depression, he migrated to New York. Standing in breadlines and sleeping on park benches, he became a Marxist.

This education—Russia, the Revolution, Palestine, books read in libraries, hunger—shaped him. He read several languages: Russian, German (his family on its way to Palestine had spent a year or two in Austria), probably some Hebrew, and French, which he picked up by himself. He had a masterly sense of English and was a masterful copy editor—the best, I am told by friends, they ever knew. American literature became a specialty with him; he had come to it curious and exploratory like a pioneer. Hawthorne, Melville, James, these were the main sources that fed his imagination. His insights, never random but tending to crystallize in theory, led him to make a series of highly original formulations, including the now famous distinction between redskins and palefaces among our literary men. He himself, being essentially a European, was neither.

Though he knew America intimately, he remained an outsider. He never assimilated, not to the downtown milieu of New York Jewish intellectuals he moved in during his early days, not to the university, although in time he occupied a professor's chair. When he lived in the country, which he did for long stretches, he was an obstinate city man and would hold forth darkly on the theme of "rural idiocy." He never learned to swim. This metaphorically summed up his situation: he would immerse his body in the alien element (I have nice pictures of him in bathing trunks by the waterside) but declined or perhaps feared to move with it. His resistance to swimming with the tide, his mistrust of currents, were his strength.

Remaining outside the American framework, his mind had a wider perspective, and at three critical junctures in our national intellectual life, its reflections were decisive. First, at the time of the Moscow trials, when he and William Phillips broke with the Communists and "stole" *Partisan Review*, which they had edited as an organ of the John Reed Club. Second, during the war, when he broke with his former collaborators Dwight Macdonald and Clement Greenberg on the issue of whether the war against Hitler should be supported by American radicals or not. We had all been affirming the negative, but Rahv in a long meditative article moved toward the opposite position: I remember the last sentence, with which I did not agree at the time but which struck on my mind nevertheless and reverberated: "And yet in a certain sense it is our war." Third, in the McCarthy time, when so many of his old friends of the anti-Stalinist left were either defending McCarthy or "postponing judgment," Rahv, alone in his immediate, *PR* circle, came out, in print, with an unequivocal condemnation and contemptuous dismissal. On Vietnam, so far as I remember, he did not pronounce at any length but maybe he did and his characteristic voice is lost to my recollection, having mingled with so many others.

The words "radical" and "modern" had a wonderful charm for Philip; when he spoke them, his sometimes grating tone softened, became reverent, loving, as though touching prayer beads. He was also much attached to the word "ideas." "He has no ideas," he would declare, dismissing some literary claimant; to be void of ideas was, for him, the worst disaster that could befall an intellectual. He found this deficiency frequent, almost endemic, among us. That may be why he did not wish to assimilate. I said, just now, that he was unlike anybody but now I remember that I have seen someone like him—on the screen. Like the younger Rahv anyway: Serge Bondarchuk, the director of *War and Peace*, playing the part of Pierre. An uncanny resemblance in every sense and unsettling to preconceived notions. I had always pictured Pierre as blond, pink, very tall, and fat; nor could I picture Philip as harboring Pierre's ingenuous, embarrassed, puzzled, placid soul—they were almost opposites, I should have thought. And yet that swarthy Russian actor was showing us a different interior Philip and a different exterior Pierre. Saying good-bye to my old friend, I am moved by that and remember his tenderness for Tolstoy (see the very Rahvian and beautiful essay "The Green Twig and the Black Trunk") and Tolstoy's sense of Pierre as the onlooker, the eternal civilian, as out of place at the Battle of Borodino in his white hat and green swallowtail coat as the dark "little man" in his long dark East European clothes eyeing the teacher from his grammar school desk in Providence.

—February 17, 1974

25

F. W. DUPEE
(1904–1979)

JAUNTY, WRY, RUEFUL. Flash of kingfisher blue eyes. Edmund Wilson liked to say there was something French about him. A person of courage and irony. Much self-irony. Voice ironical with a sort of slide in it. Wrote particularly well about elegant, dandyish writers—James, Nabokov, Malraux—if anyone as elephantine as James can be thought of as a dandy or fop. He himself had a quality of elegance, but mixed, very appealingly, with innocence, the Joliet, Illinois, of his youth. Though he had the normal quota of parents, there was a sense of the orphan about him—he and his sister as two orphans in the big wide world. Was always like the boyish hero of a *Bildungsroman*.

Unsuitable, often comic things were always happening to him, as when he worked as an organizer for the Communist Party on the waterfront while being literary editor of the *New Masses*. Or his being on the protective picket line for the students at Columbia in 1968, the day he got a new and expensive set of the finest porcelain teeth—example of rueful courage, since he expected to be hit by a night stick. On that occasion he stood up against his respectable friends of the faculty. Wrote about it—including the teeth, I think—for *The New York Review of Books*.

There was something permanently subversive about him, and he was attracted to the modern literature he taught so well—Proust,

Joyce, Mann, Kafka, etc.—by the sense that it was subversive of established values and forms. Yet he was never a bohemian; he was too much attracted to style for that. Hence he was continually finding himself in incongruous positions. He was a lightning rod for the absurd and the incongruous. Or you could say that the dryness of his mind—he was very intelligent—accorded strangely with a wild streak in him, with curiosity and with an impressionable soul.

It was through him I came to Bard College to teach, and I think he was more at home at a place like Bard than he was later at Columbia —for one thing, Bard was more amusing, more incorrigible, like himself. Yet he was not, and never could have been, a cult figure. In his own way, he was an upholder of order and legitimacy, or, let's say, a wry sympathizer with their efforts to stay in place. Not vain, unprejudiced, fair-minded.

—March 8, 1979

26

THE VERY UNFORGETTABLE
MISS BRAYTON

IN THE LAST quarter of her life, Alice Brayton's garden in Portsmouth, on the island of Rhode Island, became a social magnet for visitors to Newport, "society's summer capital," a fifteen-minute drive away. I was first brought to see it in 1949, when I had moved to a farmhouse on Union Street, Portsmouth, and already, on that first afternoon, I had the sense of being taken to a delightful little circus with its own P. T. Barnum in the form of a small white-haired spinster ("I'm not an old maid, I'm a spinster"), the owner, the impresario, and a principal exhibit of the show.

Officially the property was famous for its topiary work, the "Green Animals" she had decided to name it for at about the time I met her. Before that, it had no name, not pretending to be an estate; the address was simply "Cory's Lane, Portsmouth"—an address it shared with the Priory, a boys' school run by "black" Benedictines across the country road. The land sloped down to Narragansett Bay, which made for very mild winters allowing her to grow figs, virtually unheard of elsewhere in that part of the world, and bamboo for staking. The topiary collection stood on an elevation like a grassy platform behind the large white frame house, and several of the privet animals—the giraffe, the camel, the ostrich, the elephant, the horse and the rider—besides being raised on clipped green pedestals, were

unusually tall in their own right, so that the impression on one coming from Cory's Lane was of a sheared family of Mesozoic creatures
—dinosaurs, pterodactyls.

That impression remained even though the greater number of
the animals belonged to the classic repertory—a swan, a pair of peacocks, a unicorn, a bear, a boar, a cock, a she-wolf (copied from the
Roman bronze of Romulus and Remus's foster parent); there were
also baskets with handles, tall tubular forms resembling tops, and
(the greatest hit) a policeman at the entry with a night stick and a
metal star on his bristly green chest.

The general assumption was that the animals were a collaboration
between Alice Brayton's fancy and the clippers of a family of Portuguese gardeners who worked and lived on the place. But sometimes
she would disown her own part in the creation. "Folk art," she said
dryly when in that humor. "It all came out of Joe's head." At other
times she insisted that the topiary was as old as herself; in that version
she was just the curator, maintaining it "as it was"—this despite the
fact that there were accessions to the collection, including, if I'm not
mistaken, the policeman, who could hardly have been "in restora-
tion" when I first saw the garden.

It was the same with the inside of the house: she could never decide
whether she preferred to have us think that wallpapers, draperies,
and so on were "original," i.e., more than 150 years old (the age of
the house varied too, according to her mood), or testimony to her
prowess as a decorator. Was it better to have had "ancestors" or to be
a genius in one's own right—self-made? I don't think Miss Brayton
was ever able to settle her mind on that point, which nevertheless was
the pivot of her existence. The truth was she had created something
indisputably her own—her gingery self, her evolving animals, her
continually revised mythology of wallpapers, draperies, carpets, bell-
pulls—and never knew whether to be proud of that or ashamed.

Alice Brayton did not come from Portsmouth. She was a Fall River woman, from one of the ruling mill families; Lizzie Borden she claimed as a cousin or cousin once removed. The Fall River gentry—Hazards and Durfees, Bordens and Braytons (there was also a "Satan" Drayton)—were plain people, largely undisturbed by their wealth. In Fall River, I was told, husbands and wives were seated side by side at dinners, on the ground that at least they would have something to talk about. Practical, hard-headed people; the main business block was called "Granite Block" and looked it. Another Brayton I knew, a granitic young lawyer with an office in the block, gave me his matter-of-fact prescription for surviving the "wild" late-starting (6:30 PM) cocktail parties of a Westport Harbor hostess: "I have my supper first."

In fact, as I now know, the Portsmouth house was not a family property but a purchase Alice Brayton's father made. It was normal for well-off Fall River people to have summer houses near the seashore, which was how, I suppose, "Green Animals" started out. But the vicinity of Newport, for Miss Brayton later a strategic height to be scaled with rope ladders, was a little "different." Usually Fall River men did not take their wives and children so far; they went (and still did in my time) to Westport Harbor, Sakonnet, à la rigueur to Little Compton. I would love to have seen the inside of Alice Brayton's "real house" in Fall River; if I remember the outside right, it was gray, stone, square, without frills—no gazebo on the lawn, not so much as an arbor. But she had not lived there for many years when it was pointed out to me, on Cliff Street, naturally—she herself never spoke of it, as though it were a divorced relation.*

Now, ten years after her death, I learn from a book on eastern public gardens that her father, Thomas Brayton of the Union Cotton Manufacturing Co., Fall River, bought the Portsmouth house in 1872 and that the topiary dates from 1893. According to this authority, he

---

* In fact, her nephew tells me, I was shown the wrong house, the property of some other Braytons. Her own had been torn down.

had seen topiary work in a botanical garden in the Azores and hired a gardener, Joseph Carreiro, a native of the Azores, to make something like it for him on Narragansett Bay. But *is* there a botanical garden in the steep volcanic Azores, mainly noted for the growing of pineapples? And what was a Massachusetts mill owner doing in the Azores anyway—hiring Portuguese labor to sweat? I feel very skeptical about that part of the tale. It sounds like a typical Alice Brayton invention, very much in her narrative vein, and has the virtue of providing her animals with ancestors.

Miss Brayton was a fabulist. I do not think she lied about other people (she was mischievous but not malicious), nor to obtain advantage or get herself out of a scrape. She was a pure spinner of tales and myths centering on herself and her life story. She lied constantly, inveterately; it was almost one of her charms. You discovered to your amazement that you could not trust anything she told you pertaining to herself or to anything she owned.

And did she sometimes catch herself lying? If so, what an awful experience. She professed to hate liars, and I believed her. As she grew older, she grew more class-obsessed, and it distressed me to hear her talk more and more wildly after her second martini on themes of class and race—I felt ashamed for her. One of her phobic convictions on the subject of "them"—Portuguese, Catholics, Irish, the whole race of millhands—was that they lied. When the fit was on her, she liked to explain that the difference between "us" and "them" boiled down to the fact that "we" never told a lie. As an observant little party, she knew better. It is a puzzle to me where she got her obstinate delusion of being a truth-teller either as an individual *or* as a representative of her class. I wonder whether for her it may not have figured as a synonym for outspokenness, the habit of speaking her mind. Maybe she honestly did more of that than the lesser breeds—she could afford it.

But to leave general speculation and get down to brass tacks: *Did* she plant the pair of Turkish oaks that stood at the head of the garden, by the water lily pool? She maintained that she grew them from two acorns that she had buried at the spot when she was a little girl. Oaks are slow growers, yet here the two were, nodding as she told their story, ninety or a hundred feet tall. Years ago, alas, when I looked them up in a tree book with the thought of planting a pair of my own, I found reference only to a "turkey oak" (*Quercus laevis*), a small Southern variety whose popular name is said to derive from the wild turkeys attracted to the sweet acorn—no resemblance to the ones on Cory's Lane.

But wait. Hers, I now discover, trying an older book, must have been *Quercus cerris*, also known as "turkey oak," a fast grower that was brought to England from the Turkish peninsula and became fashionable with nurserymen in late Victorian times. So Miss Brayton stands vindicated; even the dates tally. If the trees had reached their full height when she was seventy years old, she could well have been eight when she planted them. There is just one bothersome note: in today's descriptive flier, issued by the Newport Preservation Society, no Turkish oaks are listed, and in the spot where they ought to be, bordering on the lily pool, is "White oak, *Quercus alba*," a common native article, of which in the diagram there do appear to be two.

And what about the stair carpet she tacked up the front stairs, "for Mother," because Father would not let Mother have one? "Drugget," said Miss Brayton, with a droll little sniff to show she was speaking figuratively, drugget being a lowly cotton material, brown or dun colored, that one read about in old novels where the characters are struggling to make ends meet. With the memory of tears in her old gray-blue eyes, she drew a word picture of herself on her knees on the bare treads, with hammer and carpet tacks hastening to finish the loving task before Father came home. It was her notion that I, though in less cruel circumstances, might use a strip of tan canvas (from Wilmarth's in Newport) for our front stairs in the old Coggeshall house on Union Street. I obeyed, and there is still a runner of tan duck (no, not the same one) on the front and back stairs of my house in Maine—people often ask me how I came to think of the idea.

Concede her her mother's stair carpet and the Little Dorrit figure kneeling with tacks in its mouth while Father thunders, concede her the Turkish oaks of Victorian taste, but what of her claim to have run welfare for the city of Fall River during the Depression? The city was bankrupt; unemployment figures stood at 50,000—half the population; Roosevelt had not yet moved in with the Civilian Conservation Corps and Public Works Administration or perhaps he had not yet taken office. In the background was a history of strikes and labor violence. Into the crisis stepped Alice Brayton, enlisted by a desperate mayor to run a relief program. It was not clear how the city happened to turn to her. She had had no previous experience; her education had stopped with Fall River High School, where they gave Greek and Latin but scarcely economics or urban administration. Yet for her, embarking on the story, apparently it went without saying that her city should have called her in its hour of need. And matter-of-factly (as she told it) she put up the money, out of her own pocket, to tide over the initial crisis. How much that amounted to she did not say— only that every cent was repaid.

I forget all the unique features of the relief plan she ran. The main outlines were that it was cheap and gave value. She cited her first decision: every man on relief should receive a pair of shoes. To ensure good quality (cheaper in the long run), she checked on where the men in her family got their shoes and ordered the same, with the choice of low shoes like her brother's or high like her father's. Next she bought shirts: every unemployed man had the choice of work shirt or dress shirt of Father's or Brother's brand. That was her picture of democracy in action—every man jack wearing Father's shoes.

For groceries she issued food stamps redeemable at the family grocer's. In fact, she claimed to have invented the food stamp idea. The mayor of a big English city—Manchester or Leeds—came to Fall River, she well remembered, to study how her methods worked. As with any public-spirited action, criticism was inevitable. But upholding her hand throughout was the Catholic bishop of Fall River—Bishop Cassidy, I think it was—who became a friend and steady admirer, figuring in more than one of her narratives.

Naturally, she was antibureaucratic. From a small office in City Hall she administered the program single-handed, receiving all complaints personally. And complaints were what Alice Brayton knew how to handle. She liked to tell the story of the man who objected because his groceries weren't being delivered. Your average welfare administrator would have used the rough side of his tongue on him, giving fresh grounds for complaint. Not Alice Brayton; she agreed to delivery and *outsmarted* him. She hired a boy to follow the complainer from the office and observe his goings and comings. That done, the same little boy was detailed to wait in a doorway opposite the man's house till he had gone out for the day, then quickly deliver the bags of food to his doorstep, making sure to leave them in the sun. Soon the man was back in Miss Brayton's office asking to have the special service discontinued...

The anecdote, of course, is a story against the poor, of the classical coal-in-the-bathtub type but with retribution added. Miss Brayton was a prankish moralist. Most of the fables she related of human wickedness showed people getting what they asked for, in perfect justice. The Christmas party she gave every year was a neat illustration of a morality play. Neighbors and relatives, old and young, arriving by tradition in mid-morning, found the tall spruce tree by the back door hung with brightly wrapped presents and beside it in the snow little Miss Brayton, wearing a hat and muffler and stamping her feet to keep warm. There were no names on the presents, and when you began to unwrap the one she had pulled down for you, you knew—or if it was your first time somebody explained—that what you got now didn't matter, you would be able to exchange it inside. That was the point of this Christmas.

Inside, in the dining room, the long table had been converted into an exchange, and the guests, having taken off their outdoor things and been given a glass of hot mulled wine and a biscuit, circled slowly around the table, on which were laid out bolts of tweed and silk, cars and tracks for electric trains, paint boxes, gloves, golf balls, scarves, sweaters, stockings, bottles of sherry and claret, flower vases, books, games, perhaps a chess set of little ivory men, delicate batiste place mats, a French cheese, a piece of old lace... Some years there was a lazy Susan in the middle to hold more presents, and once a whole electric train was whirring around on a sort of trestle. You turned in your door present and chose from the table the thing you wanted most. Some chose fast and some kept circling, undecided, fingering, looking at a label.

The exchange was a character test. Whatever you took, or failed to take, you gave yourself away. Children, inclined to grab without second thoughts, came off better than their elders, inhibited by an awareness of our hostess's watching eyes. But there was one year when a ferrety youth earned, I thought, Miss Brayton's eternal contempt (not to mention that of his brothers and sister) by picking *something for his mother, to help her in her cooking*, rather than the top or kite his natural heart should have craved.

The table was full of traps for hypocrites. One year she set out her bait almost too crudely. A single small flower—let's say an unseasonal hyacinth—stood in a small container between a large box of Louis Sherry chocolates and a Nuits St. Georges. "Food for the soul," Miss Brayton, behind us like a tempter, could not forbear hinting. Whereupon the silly man next to me in line leapt forward with abandon to claim the *spiritual* remembrance.

As usual, that year I picked the most expensive thing on the table. Those traps of hers held no terror for me. Being a hypocrite about my wants was never one of my faults. Hence I greatly enjoyed those Christmas mornings, though for some of her guests (and I fear she intended it) they must have been quite an ordeal. To covetous children who, intoxicated by the display, chafed at being limited to *one* present, to adults who felt they had taken a present that was much too big or else not big enough, the exchange "taught a lesson," and "learning your lesson" was maybe not in the Christmas spirit. Was it our Redeemer or our Judge whose birth we were celebrating?

Possibly Christmas brought out an ambivalent imp in Miss Brayton. The giving of gifts was a provocation to naughtiness. With many generous people, the pleasures of bestowing have their counterpart in the joy of withholding, or at any rate in a barely controllable reluctance to part with something one has. The coexistence of the two in Miss Brayton was never more marked than in her Christmas morning reception of the monks from the Priory across Cory's Lane. Every year an invitation went out, though relations were never what they had been with Bishop Cassidy of Fall River and were strained almost to the breaking point sometimes by a boundary dispute. But Christmas was Christmas, and the monks always came—last, after the guests had gone and after the servants had received their gifts.

The once-groaning exchange table must have been down to the hardcore remains when the Prior, by appointment, knocked. There were never witnesses to what happened next, but doubtless it varied from year to year. Sometimes it seems to have been a decidedly convivial party. Then there was the dreadful time referred to only in reminiscence: "Yes [musing], that was the year I gave the Father Prior bubble bath." Often, I suspect, the exchange-table procedure was followed normally, albeit with diminished stocks. But I remember hearing of a time that was still close to the telling when she was boasting of it, like a bantam cock. That was the wicked Christmas when the monks were shown to a sumptuously laden table: wines and cordials, fruit pastes, cheeses, liqueur chocolates, Turkish delight, nuts—everything calculated to speak to the Friar Tuck in a "black" Benedictine. Then, having allowed the poor men a full minute of contemplation, she barked, "Well, you're monks, aren't you? You've renounced all that," and marched them out of the room. And there was another year, I think, when in the same taunting spirit she gave them all *books*. Religious books, irreligious books, books on the Index, the story did not specify. But they might have been books written by herself and published at her own expense.

Rather surprisingly, Miss Brayton was an author, a historian, and not a bad one. Her books—*George Berkeley in Apulia, George Berkeley in Newport, Scrabbletown*—were handsomely produced, well written, and carefully proofread. She is thought to have got her start as a garden club chronicler. She had been attracted to Berkeley for the obvious reason that the idealist philosopher had spent three years in "Whitehall," a house in Middletown, near Newport and the rocks called Purgatory and Paradise. But I am not sure to what extent she had looked into his philosophical writings. After Bishop Berkeley came *Scrabbletown*, a biting analysis of records found in a trunk in a Massachusetts town between Fall River and New Bedford; this is the most personal and the best, in my view, of her books. There were the makings of an intellectual in Miss Brayton, I always thought. That she did not use her mind more fully, direct it to more interesting ends, was her own doing and represented a choice in life.

It must have had to do with "Father." During my years in Portsmouth, it was my firm conviction that she had made a devil's pact with him. It partly concerned the house. She wanted the house and garden, and in order to get them she had to wed herself to him, stay with him, turning into a spinster, while her sisters left home (one went to Bryn Mawr) and made their own lives. She loved her mother and she may have put it to herself that she stayed to protect her, interpose her small figure between her and the tyrant, fight her battles for her, including the Battle of the Stair Carpet.

But her mother died, and Alice stayed on with him, doubtless thinking that, having made the loving sacrifice, now at least she should get the good out of it—the house and old Joe's topiary. There must have been a large share of the money too, to judge by her *train de vie*—winters at the Colony Club, a well-paid pair of nice servants, Joe and Bertha (Bertha must have been French Canadian but Miss Brayton called her French, pretending that that was why she cooked so well), gardener and gardener's helpers, the cost of publishing her books, donations to the Preservation Society, membership in Bailey's Beach, furs, and couturier clothes from Bergdorf. She had the usual charities and subscriptions of a society woman. Yet the strange thing was that when you saw her, winters, in New York in her long mink coat and smart small gray hat on her way to a wedding or a matinée, she looked like an old rural body—liver-spotted hands under the white gloves, weathered cheeks, strawy white disobedient hair rearing up beneath the hat brim. Toil had left its signature on her.

She emphatically did not belong, and much of that emphasis was her own. She capitalized on her homely traits, on the Scrabbletown in her. The Lizzie Borden connection, for instance, which may once have been an embarrassment ("Not a cousin," her nephew firmly told me). Now she plumed herself on it; someone had sent her a record that she delighted in putting on the phonograph: "Oh, you *can't* chop your *mama up* in *Massachu*setts, *Not* even if it's done as a *surprise....*" She was proud of her Yankee cunning. In dealing with the New York maids at the Colony Club, she boasted, she always got her room made up before anyone else's; that was simply because she always left her door ajar and an open box of chocolates on her dresser ("Never fails to lure 'em"). Her laconic wit put you in mind of a sharp rustic having the last word.

My favorite illustration of that is a true story that took place in Portsmouth one Sunday morning when I brought an old White Russian, Serge Cheremetev, to see her and her garden. Both of these old people were what they claimed to be—he was a former governor of Galicia under the tsar, his uncle invented boeuf Stroganoff—yet there was something spurious somewhere about both of them, and each felt it in the other. Ignoring her topiary, Cheremetev, dressed in an ancient suit of coffee-colored silk and carrying a stick, began to talk of the roses on his former estate in Grasse; she countered with a terse dismissal of roses, having only a few "pernettys" to show. Her rows of espaliered fruit trees, so exciting at the time to Americans, said little to him. Still less did her gourds. If he tapped her Sensitive Plant lightly with his cane, he did not stay to witness the quivering response. I was dying with shame for both of them: *she* was boasting more than usual, and in Cheremetev's hoarse rasping voice, a repeated "honored lady" crackled like gunfire.

Since things were not going well in the garden, I suggested that she show him the house. He glanced at the library, somewhat overstocked with detective stories, that lined the walls of the billiard room; he was a rare book dealer in Washington and she was a member of the Hroswitha Society, but no common chord was struck. In the front parlor, he peered at a Piranesi on the wall. Just below it on a table stood a small bronze statue that echoed a detail in the engraving; the arrangement was one of Miss Brayton's witty visual puns, and underneath the statue or beside it was a rare edition of Piranesi plates—I forget which —that had belonged to the tsar. Cheremetev, by invitation, examined the flyleaf, which stated in the imperial handwriting that the book had been the property of Nicholas II of Russia. "Ah, dear lady," he croaked, "I see you have the book of my godfather, the tsar." Miss Brayton started, as if for once taken aback; her blue eyes took in her dark-eyed visitor with his Tartar cheekbones. Then she let out a sort of cackle: "You've got the blood. I've got the book." Mr. Cheremetev bowed. She had won. Yet if I had had only her word for the story, I would not have believed it.

She had come a long way up from the cotton mills to be able to meet the tsar's godson in single combat in her front parlor, and he of course had come a long way down. On her side, it was the privet animals—the legacy of her pact with the devil—that had put her in a position to score. First of all, they had put her on the social map, marked Cory's Lane as an outlying bastion of Newport, which was still *the* society to get into while the summer lasted. But first Father had to die for her to emerge as a debutante on the Newport scene. That happened in 1939. She was sixty-one years old.

Despite the late start, when I met her ten years later, she had made it. Her social strategy, as carefully worked out as a Napoleonic battle plan, was based on reaching the child that she counted on finding in every Newport dowager and tycoon.

After Father was gone, she started giving her lawn parties, featuring a big rented merry-go-round near the gate on the Priory side and a clambake on the beach below the railroad tracks, with well-stocked bars dotted about in between. These parties were an instant success; old-time leaders like the Misses Wetmore were teetering down the slope in their heels and long dresses to view the oddity of the clambake.

It was the child in Miss Brayton who knew that to succeed you must make a party an adventure or a treat. Even an ordinary afternoon visit to her garden, ending with a tray of strong martinis, obeyed a canonical rule of children's parties: each guest must get a present to take home. In the summer it was flowers from the garden, which she picked as you walked along and unexpectedly handed you on the front porch as you left, or fruit (her white clingstone peaches, a variety no longer to be found in catalogs, a basket of figs, or her slipskin grapes, Delaware or Catawba). Then—aside from the clipped animal and geometric figures, appealing to the scissors artist in all of us—she had funny plants like that Sensitive Plant, which quails when you strike it, carnivores like the flycatcher and pitcher plants, freaks like the parrot tulip (new then), and the tropical-looking bamboo.

With these arts and wiles, she swiftly conquered the territory she had designs on, designs perhaps dating back to her maiden visit to Bellevue Avenue with the Fall River or Tiverton Garden Club, where the society bug may have first bitten her—why not in Mrs. Arthur Curtiss James's blue garden, whose grass was once said to be dyed? It was at about the same time that she had got her start as a writer, too, in her local *Garden Club Bulletin*. Father's death, when it finally came, had had a double effect, opening the gate of ivory as well as the gate of horn. It had not only set her free to pursue her social ambition. It was what had allowed her to become an author. The first of her Berkeley books, *George Berkeley in Apulia*, came out in 1946; Thomas Brayton had been dead seven years, some of which she must have used for travel and self-education. After that came *George Berkeley in Newport* (1954) and after that *Scrabbletown*, which peculiarly has no date but which I know came out toward the end of my years on Union Street—1949–1954. Following that, her publications were of less interest, probably because she was no longer interested herself. The two paths that had been opened up to her by her father's death, though she may not have thought so, were divergent. She could not take both even if suddenly having so much more money seemed to promise it. She chose society—the Chilton Club, the Colony, opera seats, Joe's chauffeur's uniforms.

She could not have maintained "Green Animals" and herself in the Bellevue Avenue orbit and continued to be a scholarly historian with a lively pen for the simple reason that she had run out of local material—after Berkeley, what? There were only Governor Arnold's burying ground and the so-called Viking tower. If she was determined to stay put at the place where she had arrived, she could not move on mentally. That she should become a *social* historian in the line of Henry James and Edith Wharton was out of the question. To do that would have required a real break, and probably she was not up to it because she had stayed with Father too long, bargaining for freedom. Who sups with the devil must bring a long spoon.

Though she claimed off and on to be a Quaker I think she had no particular religion. She was a natural rebel (that was the great thing about her), naturally independent in her views, and what she worshiped was a kind of intelligence that, given her self-imposed limitations, had to be visual and aesthetic. Once I heard her enunciate almost fiercely the principle she lived for, standing by her mantelpiece, chin out, like one willing to be counted. "Taste!" she cried, virtually shouting. "T-A-S-T-E." She spelled it out as if we might fail to understand her and then struck her small chest. "I have it. T-A-S-T-E." She stared at us all belligerently. "Yes, Miss Brayton. Of course you have." We laughed. "Obviously you have." The proof was all around us, in the flames leaping in the fireplace, in the shaker of unbeatable martinis, in the sandwiches of thin-cut soft white bread, thick white meat of chicken, and "Bertha's mayonnaise." But it was tasteless of her to say so. Once the word was pronounced, you had lost the thing it was meant to designate: an eye, an ear. It was embarrassing and sad, as if poor little Psyche had spilled the hot wax of her taper on a sleeping Cupid. Wishing she wouldn't, we hastily left.

She was ninety-four when she died in 1972, leaving "Green Animals" to the Preservation Society of Newport County. I was no longer living in the US and had not seen her or had news of her for more than ten years. Her relatives, probably forgetting about me or thinking I would not be interested, did not send me an announcement of decease or an obituary notice from the paper. But I see from *The Great Public Gardens of the Eastern United States* that she left no endowment and the garden depends for its maintenance on gate receipts and profits from the gift shop. Does this mean she was living on capital at the end, like the grasshopper in the fable? Or expressing in that spare legacy her Yankee faith in the self-help principle? "Green Animals," like a relief client, should learn to be self-supporting. Somehow the end and final secret of her story must lie laconically in the willing of her property. If she intended "to live on," she may have hoped to be planted, warts and all, like a tiny rugged Turkish acorn up by the lily pool, and turn by force of character into an indomitable tree.

—*December 1983*

27

NOTES OF A RESIDENT
OF THE WATERGATE

THIS HAS BEEN the week of the so-called Brezhnev recess. Senator Ervin's panel, in order not to embarrass Nixon before his Soviet guest, voted to suspend the Watergate hearings during the state visit. Otherwise we might have had the treat of seeing the first secretary of the Party among the foreign spectators in the Senate Caucus Room, seated in the first row with his translator and his bodyguards while John Dean testified to whatever he is going to testify—despite leaks, no one yet can be sure. A functionary from the State Department (or maybe General Haig?) could have briefed the Brezhnev party on the curious and to them perhaps Swiftian workings of democracy. Instead, Washington has been waiting irritably for Brezhnev to go home, so that traffic can be restored to normal and Dean can at last be heard. On the personal side, I ought to be grateful for the postponement. For the first time since I have been here, I have leisure to look around at the physical setting of the Watergate break-in and to think a little about the moral setting or "ecology" out of which it emerged.

I get an appreciative chuckle whenever I tell people I am staying at the Watergate Hotel. Even before the break-in, the ten-acre aggregate comprising three cooperatives, the hotel, and two office buildings began to tickle the public fancy because the Mitchells lived here—in the cooperative known as Watergate East—at the time when Martha, looking out of the window of her husband's office downtown at the Justice Department, watched "the very liberal Communists, the worst kind" demonstrating in the street below.

Now the Mitchell tenure here and that of Maurice Stans are only vaguely recalled; what tourists come to look at and be photographed in front of are the office building, where the Democratic National Committee had its headquarters on the sixth floor, and the more plebeian red-roofed Howard Johnson Motor Lodge, opposite, where the listening post of the wiretappers was situated. Tourists also roam through the hotel lobby, buy Watergate joke material, including bugs, at the newsstand, and take a peep at the Watergate Terrace Restaurant overlooking the outdoor swimming pool (restricted to cooperative residents; there is an indoor swimming pool, with sauna, for hotel guests), where McCord and his men are supposed to have had a lobster dinner before the break-in.

As the hotel literature puts it, "The Watergate Complex, one of the most distinctive private real estate developments in the nation, offers a way of life that is complete in every respect . . . for you, the visitor, as well as for those who reside and/or work in this pace-setting community." Designed by an Italian architect, the whole complex, with the exception of the office buildings, bristles with rows of stony teeth, which are a sort of coping around the balconies opening off nearly every room. The impression is of an updated medieval fortress, quite extensive, and between Watergate East and Watergate South there is what looks like a Bridge of Sighs, topped by an American flag. Those uniform gray-white teeth projecting from the curious swollen shapes, elliptical, wedgelike, semicircular, of the building units, suggest a sea animal—a whale, somebody said, but also something sharkish. To assure privacy, balconies are separated from each other by what seem to be cement fins. Maybe the marine imagery is meant to be in harmony with the Potomac setting. The teeth, on close inspection, turn out to be made of tiny stones pressed into cement, giving a scaly effect.

Even though it is summer and not always too hot, almost nobody appears on the balconies, which are the main architectural feature; empty garden furniture stares out from them on the landscaped grounds. Once I saw a single figure, a fat woman in a pink wrapper, wander ghostlike behind her toothy parapet. Yet at some point in time, as the Ervin Committee witnesses express it, somebody must have used *my* balcony, for when I arrived, ten days ago, two empty beer cans (Budweiser) were lying there; this morning, finally, they were gone—the window washer had come by. On a few of the co-operative balconies, there are some ill-tended, long-suffering flowering plants. The cells of this "community" are not neighborly; no voices call across the outdoor expanse, and the rooms are effectively soundproofed.

The sense of being in a high-security castellated fort or series of forts is added to by lower-level passages, known as Malls, which constitute a labyrinth. The whole place, in fact, is a maze, marked here and there by highly misleading signs directing you to "Les Champs," "Mall," "Restaurant," "Arcade." When you try to follow them, you either go round in circles or end up against a blank, no-entry wall. It is as if there were a war on, and the red, green, and blue directional arrows had been turned to point the wrong way in order to confuse the enemy expected to invade at sunrise. Every day, so far, I have got lost in this eerie complex, hoping to find an espresso bar that was rumored to exist somewhere in the vicinity of "Les Champs." Once I found myself in "Peacock Alley," and another time standing on the verge of the forbidden swimming pool. Yesterday, though, I reached the goal, following the instructions of a porter: "You just keep goin' around."

This Kafkian quest for the espresso bar had an economic motive. I was comparison-shopping the breakfasts available. The People's

Drugstore, in a "popular" region of the Mall near the hotel, is the cheapest, offering fruit juice, toasted English muffin, grape jelly, and coffee for sixty cents; the Howard Johnson, across from the famed office building, is the best value, giving you the same but with a better muffin and a *choice* of grape jelly or marmalade for eighty cents; the hotel Terrace Restaurant calls this—with an inferior muffin but more copious marmalade—a Continental breakfast and charges two dollars and fifty cents. The espresso bar, which doubles as a hot-dog stand, does not serve breakfast, it turns out, but is a fairly good value for a sandwich- or salad-and-coffee lunch. It too has a "popular" clientele, and it was there I heard a young girl, yesterday, say to her friend, "Senator Ervin? I heard him on the radio. He's real sharp."

The main attraction, though, of the Watergate complex was intended, evidently, to be the shopping, ranging from low-cost, lower-level (the People's Drugstore and a Safeway, where Senator Brooke, they say, can be seen with a shopping bag full of groceries), to unarmed robbery in "Les Champs." There are Pierre Cardin, Gucci, Yves St. Laurent, Enzo Boutique for men, located in the "exclusive" end, and Saks and more moderate shoe and dress shops along the arcade. But you can buy almost any kind of goods and services, short of guns or a suit of armor, in these labyrinthine ways: wigs, pottery and china, jewelry, antiques, Uruguayan handicrafts, patchwork, Swedish everything, Oriental everything, flowers, liquor (including Watergate brands of scotch and bourbon, now much in demand by souvenir hunters), insurance, air tickets, and hotel reservations. In the Mall, there are an optician and a US post office; a bookstore, the Savile, has gone out of business and a cheese shop is moving into the space. On the street level there are a bank and a building and loan association. As the hotel flier indicates, the idea has been to make Watergate as nearly as possible self-sustaining. As though it were under siege.

This, I suppose, is the Watergate mentality, in a more general sense: a compound of money, the isolation or insulation it can buy, and fear.

Though conceived as a cosmopolitan center, the result is rather pathetically suburban and middle-American. What it boils down to is not very different from any of the so-called shopping malls along US highways. Except that they can usually support at least a paperback bookstore.

The hotel employment policy seems to be somehow meaningful and to imply a curious notion of classification, like that distinguishing the Malls from the Arcade and "Les Champs." Downstairs, in front, the help is mainly Spanish-speaking—one imagines a staff of brown-uniformed Cuban defectors, potential recruits for CREEP and the CIA. In the Terrace Restaurant, again Spanish-speaking, but in red uniforms and with a few Southeast Asians and East Europeans added— more CIA material? Upstairs, the chambermaids and maintenance men, who constitute the core of the hotel invisible from below, are nearly all black; I think of Ralph Ellison and his invisible man. Probably there is a key to employment policy here that eludes me; maybe it is artistic—a matter of subtle color blends and contrasts, designed to please the eye.

A French friend, in town for a picture story on the hearings, says he thinks that the Americans are using Watergate to cleanse themselves of guilt for Vietnam. As he says this, a light goes on in my mind. Yes, he is right; if it had not been for Vietnam, the scandal of the break-in might have soon dropped from notice like previous scandals—a tempest in a teapot.

I had assumed it was just luck, a happy coincidence of independent factors—the zeal of *The Washington Post* in tracking down the story, Judge Sirica's determination to be told the truth, the early leaks coming from the Justice Department and the FBI—that had brought about disclosure and led to what is now spoken of as a turning point in the nation's history or at least of Richard Nixon's place in it. None of these factors singly would have sufficed, but all of them converging,

369

plus Senator Ervin, did it, and many editorialists took pride in this as showing that the American system—the judiciary, the press, the Congress—worked to curb the arrogant power of the executive. No doubt this is true (though we have not yet seen the end), but without another factor—Vietnam—the pursuit of truth, I now feel, might have been less vigorous and public interest slight.

Because of Vietnam, the country suddenly wants to be "*clean*," as my French friend said. Watergate is the scrubbing brush, sometimes painful to the skin, since it is not easy on the national touchiness to have all those cosmetics scrubbed away. Watergate hurts many simple patriots, to the point where they don't want to hear about it. This is understandable when you think of Nixon's "landslide"—the millions of voters who must to some degree have identified themselves with the image he presented on the TV screen. What is surprising is the turnabout: the vast numbers that now watch the rapid erosion of that image without too much complaint. Most of those viewers participated with Richard Nixon and with LBJ before him in the crime of Vietnam.

It is worth examining the fact that those most prominent now in the pursuit of truth about Watergate (i.e., about the character-potentialities of the President; what may he still be capable of?) were not, to say the least, among the leading opponents of the war in Vietnam. I do not know Judge Sirica's voting record but I do not recall seeing his name on any peace manifesto; the same for Archibald Cox. Of the senators on the Ervin Committee I wonder how many took a stand against the war. Well, on the McGovern-Hatfield amendment cutting off funds for Indochina after December 31, 1971—scarcely the acid test—two, Montoya and Inouye, voted Yes. We know the position of Goldwater, who is now calling for the truth, and I believe he means it. Judge Sirica, most of the senators of the committee, and Goldwater must be fairly representative of that almost consistent majority that answered "Approve" when asked by pollsters for their opinion of US policy in Vietnam.

The innocent in that crime, if anybody can be considered so, i.e., the liberals and radicals who spoke out and demonstrated, have been taking rather a back seat in the Watergate investigation. As far as the Congress goes, this is being ascribed to a Democratic Party strategy of letting the Republicans carry the ball, to avoid giving any appearance of narrow partisanship: let his own party call for Nixon's impeachment or go to him and demand that he resign. No doubt that strategy is operating, but there is something deeper involved that has compelled conservatives of both parties to play leading roles in the investigation and compels ordinary lifelong Republicans to demand the truth almost more loudly than the rest of us—possibly because they had had no suspicion of it before.

One can say that Watergate is a good test to determine who is really a conservative and who just pretends to be: Goldwater passes the test; Senator Ervin passes with honors; Agnew fails; William Buckley gets a D. But are there, then, as many true conservatives in the country as poll results on Watergate (58 percent think Nixon was in on it, after if not before) by this criterion would seem to show? I wonder, having found it difficult in my private, pre-Watergate experience to meet more than one or two, though I have gone out with a Diogenes lantern.

It might be safer to conclude that 58 percent of the nation still has some common sense left and can be trusted to serve on a jury. But I will go further and say that a considerable percent of that percent (reducing the figure to allow for those who think Nixon guilty but regard it as "just politics," who are in other words apolitical and don't care) has a conscience. On which Vietnam has weighed. Despite all rationalization. Napalm, defoliants, area bombing, Lazy Dogs, antipersonnel missiles, these means to achieve an end presumed to be virtuous have cost this country much secret pain.

Watergate too has been justified before the Senate Committee as a means to achieve a similar though not identical end: the defeat of subversion through the reelection of Nixon. Watergate too is advanced technology enlisted in the service of patriotism. Of course the means of Watergate are much less repellent than napalm and cluster bombs. Wiretapping doesn't "hurt anybody." That may be why the emerging truth of Watergate could be faced day after day by such a large part of the US population. It did not seem, at the beginning, too heavy a load for the national conscience to shoulder, and confession would have been good for the White House collective soul. Yet confession did not come; Nixon did not make "a clean breast" in his much-awaited April 30 television appearance. He sacrificed Haldeman, Ehrlichman, Kleindienst, Dean to the gods of retribution but failed to appease them. The guilty secrets remained unadmitted and in fact increased and multiplied, or, rather, first suspicion, then knowledge of them did.

It was no longer just the little sin of wiretapping but lying, perjury, bribery, burglary, obstruction of justice, misuse of funds, fraud, extortion, forgery. The discovered guilt spread till it embraced nearly every common crime short of rape and murder. Suspicion fell heavily on Agnew's fund-raising dinner and reached out to San Clemente to touch not only the shrouded financing of the purchase but Nixon's office chair, his lamp, his septic tank, bought with public money, to enhance his security and aid him in the transaction of the national business. Certainly this kind of petty profit-taking—charging off personal expenses to the company—is SOP among certain categories of American businessmen, and Nixon may have been incapable of distinguishing the nation from a company of which he was chairman of the board.

It is quite likely that he was unaware of any wrongdoing in many of the shady operations that have come to light: wiretapping of rival firms is common in business, and donations to public officials are as much taken for granted as fixing a parking ticket. Except in the matters of burglary and subornation of perjury, he and his aides did not make any great departure from the prevailing business ethic. Startled by the public outcry, he may have waked up to the existence of another world, with other standards than those he and his associates were accustomed to.

In any case, unable to face the louder and louder music, he found no way of "containing" the Watergate scandal. Meanwhile every fresh disclosure, far from exhausting the public capacity for shock, whetted the appetite for more and worse revelations, as if the desire for truth was unslakable, had no limits, although in normal circumstances this is seldom the case: "Don't tell me any more" is a common plea, except in crises of sexual jealousy.

The public's ability to absorb more shocks than it was originally prepared for can be explained by the residue of guilt left over from Vietnam, guilt unadmitted by the majority and therefore all the more in need of relief. There has been much talk about atonement in the Senate Committee's proceedings, some of it hypocritical on the part of both senators and witnesses. Senator Baker's insistent questions about motive suggest that he is playing a TV role of spiritual surgeon and counselor, and only once, I feel, did his pious probing elicit a truthful answer: when Herbert Porter told him, "I did not do it [perjury] for money for power... for position. My vanity was appealed to. They said I was talked about in high councils... that I was an honest man."

Porter said he had recognized, looking back, a weakness in himself he had not been conscious of. This simple, direct, and rather touching answer, however, did not seem to be what Senator Baker had been after when he talked musingly of "atonement"; if I recall right, he quickly dropped the subject. As for Jeb Stuart Magruder, I myself was less saddened by the evidence that Williams College had been unable to teach him ethics (it would have been a tough job) than by the grammar it had left him with: "Mitchell told he and I" would be a fair sample. The senators' readiness to be moved and edified by Magruder's repentant posture led them to overlook the fact that he did not admit to a single weakness or character flaw, but only to "mistakes." Mistakes made from an excess of good motives, naturally. The idea that these hearings ought to be morally *improving* (i.e., ought to show a profit) made most of the senators easy marks for Magruder.

Yet behind all the facile moralizing, I think, there is some notion of a genuine need for atonement and purification. Obviously, identification of the guilty in Watergate and associated crimes will not "make up" for Vietnam or wash it away, but I do not blame anybody for the wish and even think it a good thing. You cannot undo Vietnam, but that is true of most offenses, certainly all those involving murder, where no restitution is possible. You can't bring back the dead, and with many other wrongs, when contrition arrives it is generally too late.

Atonement is directed not toward the victims but toward the crime, that is, toward the injury inflicted by the crime—on God or on the fragile social tissue holding living beings together. Some degree of repair here is possible, or at least the attempt is salutary and may benefit the criminal, if nobody else. Ever since my mind and emotions became centered on Vietnam, I have been thinking about the problem of purgation and atonement. Perhaps this is due, a little, to living in France throughout this period, where so many of the early churches, abbeys, and hospitals you visit are memorials of some horrible blood crime committed by a high-placed person, king, duke, or noble. This is particularly true of Normandy and the Plantagenet country, where there was an unusual degree of violence. These religious buildings were blood money exacted by God, i.e., by the conscience, never by the Church. In other words, they were not a punishment but a self-punishment and served a double purpose: of symbolically washing away the blood the murderer had shed and of making that blood, so to speak, indelible, crying out to Heaven for as long as the abbey-church or Old Men's Hospice would stand.

374

Modern people, by contrast, have no way of dealing with guilt, which is probably why they so seldom acknowledge it. I used to wonder about public men like McNamara, who, apparently seeing the error of his ways, left LBJ's government. When anybody has done anything as bad as what they did, there ought to be some possibility of redemption. McNamara, in my opinion, would have been better off had he retired to a monastery rather than to the World Bank. McGeorge Bundy, if in any way penitent, scarcely demonstrated it by his switch to the Ford Foundation. The old recourse of philanthropy used by big-scale public sinners like Carnegie, Frick, and Rockefeller to signify, if not atonement, repayment of a slight debt to humanity is now just another tax writeoff. Reparations are paid, if at all, by governments, never by an individual war criminal.

It is hard to see Nixon abdicating like Charles V to seek peace in a little house attached to a monastery or its Quakerish equivalent, but with LBJ one could just barely picture some Texan Thebaid, where he might have dotted the land with anchorites' cells for himself and his cronies. If the various Watergate inquiries, trials, civil suits, and grand jury hearings are, as I feel, steps toward purgation, cathartic efforts, on the part of the country as a whole, direct expiation is being suggested, though, only to those pale or pink-faced young men, wearing earnest glasses, who have appeared before the Ervin Committee. It is as if they were expected, through typecasting, like little oblates, to expiate all the nation's sins against its own conception of itself. "Mr. Porter," declared Senator Ervin, "you give the appearance of a man who was brought up in a good home." "Yes, Senator, I was." The thought, certainly, would not occur to anybody about John Mitchell, who looks as if he were brought up in a reformatory. The burden of repentance is being offered to the *young* Republicans or to those among them, like Porter and Hugh Sloan, who have a quality of innocence.

Yet what are they supposed to do, exactly, to redeem themselves and their country? This is not clear. The free admission of wrongdoing is a first step, but where are they meant to go from there? They have been trained in American business life, and that, presumably, is what they will return to, as they try to "reinstate themselves" in society. But the society itself is corrupted, as their testimony before the Senate interrogators demonstrates. They do not belong in jail, but the good home of which Senator Ervin spoke—and we all knew what he meant—is situated almost in another century.

Metaphorically speaking, it is America, the "old" parental America. Senator Ervin still believes in it and has his eleven-year-old yellow-haired grandson acting as a Senate page-boy in the Caucus Room to offer as proof. This house, he feels, with a little elbow grease can be cleaned and restored to at least a semipristine condition. That is why he is stubbornly convinced that the hearings will arrive at their destination—the truth. "But if it doesn't come out that way?" I said to him. "If they fail? Just take it as a hypothesis." "I refuse to entertain the thought," was his answer, as though the thought was a felon seeking entry into his mental premises. He is becoming a folk hero because of that stout, old-fashioned attitude. I hope he is right, but if he is right and nothing then happens—a strong possibility—then we are worse off than we were before. If we know, that is, and don't act, can find no frame for action, Nixon and his sly firm, *knowing* that *we* know and won't do anything, will have nothing more to fear.

—*June 24, 1973*

28

THE MORAL CERTAINTIES
OF JOHN D. EHRLICHMAN

A "DUMB, SHOCKING, irredeemable type of thing," John Ehrlichman called it this week in his testimony. This view of the Watergate break-in has been endorsed by all the hard-liner witnesses before the Senate Committee. You keep hearing it loudly proclaimed, too, in conversation whenever you meet a Nixon loyalist. It is the one thing the Ehrlichmans and Mitchells and Mardians feel strongly about—the *stupidity* of the break-in. They and their allies throughout the land do not mince words in condemning the perpetrators and sound truly outraged, as if an injury to their brains had been sustained.

Haldeman felt the same way, Ehrlichman told the senators. On June 18, the day after the break-in (an earlier, unrevealed one had taken place in May), they were talking it over on the telephone. "Both of us wondered why in the world anybody would want to break in there." From where they sat, they could see nothing in Democratic headquarters to warrant the effort: the Democratic Party was just a shambles. And John Mitchell, in a civil deposition, when asked whether he had ever contemplated any form of surveillance of the Democrats, answered dryly: "No, sir, I can't imagine a less productive activity than that."

The idea that Watergate was a folly ("an unauthorized adventure by some boys with hundred-dollar bills in their pockets...James

Bond..." gurgled white-haired Richard Moore) has never been examined on its merits by the opposition, which has assumed, perhaps through sheer aversion to the Watergate dismissers, that there was something useful to the Republicans to be learned at Democratic headquarters. It was natural to do so in the first heat of argument, for to agree that it was "dumb" implied that the break-in could not be taken seriously, that being of course the White House attitude. The gravity of a violation of the law tends to be weighed in terms of the end product. If I steal a loaf of stale bread, I may expect more lenient treatment than if I stole a Cadillac. To Mitchell and his boys, the files and telephone conversations on the sixth floor of the Watergate office building were a loaf of stale bread, so what was all the fuss about? "A ridiculous caper blown up out of all proportions." Mitchell a year later was still standing by that early press statement. It was not just CREEP that could not contain its amusement. Those bungling Cubans wearing surgical gloves! For months journalists and newscasters referred to it as the Watergate caper.

This helps to explain why the Democrats were able to do so little with the issue during the McGovern campaign. It was only when the original crime was compounded by a series of felonies and found to have been linked with other crimes—the dirty tricks department, which included the forgery of letters sent through the US mails—that the gravity of Watergate became apparent.

Though the break-in, when they heard of it, struck them as loony, Haldeman and Ehrlichman nevertheless were worried. There was "a lot of concern," Ehrlichman acknowledged, that the trail would lead to the White House. Unfair, but the opposition would play it that way. "The fact that the Democrats were going to exploit it was the most important thing." Facing up to that contingency led to a number of hasty countermeasures and efforts to cover the trail that in Ehrlichman's estimation (so he let us understand) were just as idiotic as the original break-in. But nobody consulted him, naturally. When he heard that Acting FBI Director Pat Gray had gone ahead and destroyed the "politically sensitive" papers in Hunt's White House safe, he was "just nonplussed," he declared with feeling. What a dumb, shocking thing to do. Who would have thought that that was how the bonehead would interpret the instruction given him by Dean in Ehrlichman's own presence, which was to make sure nobody saw them? Gray was to take them for safekeeping, that was all.

In the same way, he still remembers his shock and surprise when he heard about the burglary at Ellsberg's psychiatrist's office. Not that it was *wrong*: he is sure (or, as he says, "shurr") that the President has the constitutional power to burglarize in the interests of national security and sure that in these circumstances a doctor–patient relationship should come under that head—no doubt of that at all. But it was so *unnecessary*. Anybody who had practiced law knew there were smarter ways of getting a patient's dossier—perfectly legal ways: working through another doctor, conning a nurse or a nurse's aide... For their part, former Attorney General Mitchell and former Assistant Attorney General Mardian would not *think* of paying blackmail: it never worked; the ante just kept going up. And Mitchell knew better, he said, than to try to put a fix on a federal judge: "absolutely nonproductive."

In fact, the burglary of Dr. Fielding's office proved to be nonproductive too. When Hunt and Liddy broke in, presumably wearing their CIA-provided disguises, the Ellsberg file was not there. No doubt the doctor, having already been visited by the FBI, took the obvious precaution of removing the file from the premises.

The two Watergate break-ins, the cover-up activities, the Plumbers' activities (at least the ones known to the public) turned out, in the long or short run, to be totally useless in accomplishing their objects, and sarcastic men like Mitchell and Ehrlichman looked back dourly from the witness chair on the disagreeable shocks and surprises they had had on learning (usually, they claimed, from the newspapers) of the clownish, pointless actions of their associates and hirelings. A continual embarrassment. Listening to Ehrlichman, one was led to wonder whether there could be such a thing as an intelligent crime, a crime, that is, worth committing in the eyes of an intelligent person. The answer, probably, is no, though not from a point of view to which Ehrlichman would be attracted.

Perhaps he cannot help his face, but he looks like somebody of a deeply criminal nature, out of a medieval fresco: the upward sneering curl of the the left-hand side of the mouth matched, on the bias, by the upward lift of the right eyebrow, above which there is a barely discernible scar; the aggressive tilted nose that cameramen say has been growing all week, the sinister (literally) thrust of the jaw. Everything about his features and body movements is canted, tilted, slanting, sloping, askew. The arms swing loosely; the left hand with a big seal ring, like a brass knuckle, moves in a sweeping gesture. The broad head is too round—pygmyish. There is a horrible concessive little smile, like a tight parenthesis, when somebody else makes a joke.

A deformed personality, one would say, so much so that it gives one a start to hear him use the phrase "I am morally certain" in a sentence, to indicate "I am practically sure" that something or other did not happen. To Ehrlichman, most of the crimes under discussion—perjury, obstruction of justice, breaking and entering—appeared profoundly stupid and childish, above all avoidable, as legal ways of obtaining the desired result always exist. There is no reason not to believe that this is indeed his feeling, and there was no evidence on hand that he had personally committed any of them. The only crimes he could respect would be crimes wearing the mask of legality (or embodied into the statutes by an administration with a "mandate") and crimes that are not traceable. When he put a big "E" for "Approve" on the Krogh-Young memo recommending a covert operation against the Ellsberg psychiatrist, he added, "As long as it's not traceable."

Confronted with the memo by the committee, he gladly identified his handwriting; the proviso only meant, of course, that the Plumbers should not present their "calling cards" at the doctor's office.

In handling the Watergate matter, his technique is utter disassociation. In his own mind, there is not the faintest connection between him and the actions performed by other characters in the story. Ulasewicz? He was "a facility that came with the office." Kalmbach? He had given Herb no assurances; the eye-searching (he smiled) of course never took place. He would remember it if it had. The Houdini-like power of self-extrication was so extraordinary that he actually shifted the scene of that compromising dialogue: where Kalmbach had placed it in Washington, Ehrlichman wafted it to California on a magic carpet, and none of the senators or committee counsel noticed the landing bump.

The motive for this transfer was not obvious. Perhaps it was to avoid a perjury citation. Since he denied the content of the conversation, by referring it to another place—Kalmbach's office at Newport Beach, where they met on some different occasion—he avoided a direct lie.

In many ways his testimony with its repeated failures to recall and its little triumphant quibbles ("Did you bug that conversation?" "No, Senator, I did not." "What did you do?" "I recorded it.") was very like Mitchell's. In the Caucus Room people were arguing whether he or Mitchell was more purely evil. It is hard to decide which of the two should be awarded that particular apple. Mitchell was sour, old, rancid, terse. Ehrlichman was resilient, extremely loquacious, limber as his eyebrow; he thought very fast, deflecting a question almost before it reached him, impatiently interrupting. His thinking process was a massive motor response to a set of stimuli; no instant for reflection intervened. Tilting back and forth in his chair he resembled one of those old snap-back dolls with a very low center of gravity. In this sense, he was stupid and lumpishly unaware of it.

The difference between him and Mitchell came down to the difference between the randy insolence of power and a surly nihilism proceeding from defeat. Mitchell is finished, a gloomy discard, but unless Ehrlichman's energetic confidence was simulated, he has no doubts about his future. He and Haldeman *are* the future, his outthrust jaw proclaimed: Watergate was a minor interruption. He is a Christian Scientist, which should not be overlooked in estimating his sense of superiority to mere matter in the form of evidence. But he is also a political animal and must estimate that Nixon's decision to tough it out with the Senate Committee and the special prosecutor is a winning decision. If the court blocks him and the Congress continues its petty harassment, he can govern by plebiscite, going straight to the nation for a vote of confidence in the presidency—yes or no. One could almost see the thought shaped in Ehrlichman's broad skull. Hence his insistence on the President's constitutional power to suspend the Constitution (for that is what his arguments amounted to), which sounded bizarre, nearly crazy, in the setting of the Caucus Room. One watched Senator Ervin follow the elated, voluble reasoning, somber eyes forward, palm to cheek, almost motionless, like a Statue of Desponding Liberty.

Ehrlichman's arrogant sureness of himself, the grandiose doctrine he was enunciating of presidential powers, half-cracked or not, seemed portentous as the week went on. When all the senators rose and raised their right hands to vote Aye on sending the case of the White House subpoenas to the courts to compel Nixon to honor them, the room was completely silent except for the whizzing of the cameras. We were respecting what all felt to be a historic moment—the kind that used to be painted and hung, in reproduction, in schoolrooms: Washington Crossing the Delaware. It looked as though a collision course had been set, and everyone remembered Ehrlichman's raised right hand as he took the oath on Tuesday with a gesture one newspaper had compared to a fascist salute.

He lost no opportunity to patronize, bully, and affront the senators, as well as Majority Counsel Dash. The performance seemed carefully deliberated, like his opening statement, the "high school civics lesson" which he had evidently rehearsed before a mirror, while shaving perhaps. Yet it did not look, at least to me, as if he were aiming—over the heads of the committee and the hostile crowd—at an unseen TV audience. Nixon's devoted adherents are not watching the hearings anyway, and as a media-conscious man, Ehrlichman must be aware of the national popularity of the show and of Senator Sam as a folk hero. But his behavior with the courteous old legislator was so contumacious that the hearing room grew turbulent; there was a general incensed feeling that the senators should not take this lying down. I slipped into one of the reveries of the impotent and imagined the chairman signaling to the sergeants-at-arms: "Arrest that man." The sneering devil, like Iago (I daydreamed), would be hustled out, preferably in chains, down to the old prison below the House of Representatives where persons in contempt of Congress used to be held. That was what he deserved, to be kicked back several eras into the antique history of the Republic. Many agreed with the thought.

On Thursday, Senator Ervin, very much in his TV character, reminded the witness of the parable of the Good Samaritan. "I read the Bible. I don't quote it," Ehrlichman muttered, very loudly, back. He can hardly have expected applause from the national TV audience for that.

If his performance was designed for an audience, its purpose at times seemed to be to frighten and overawe it, at times to disregard it utterly—itself a terror technique. He did not mind looking like a hangman. Senator Weicker, his most doughty antagonist (Ervin to our dismay appeared stricken or on the verge of an apoplectic seizure), faced him with remarks he had made about Pat Gray, a friend of Weicker's, during the Senate confirmation hearings for the post of FBI director. Gray, then acting director, an honest cop, though weak, had talked too much while being examined by the Senate and had just lost the administration's backing. Ehrlichman was talking to Dean: "I think we ought to let him hang there. Let him twist slowly, slowly in the wind." Ehrlichman, in the witness chair, bared his teeth in brief amusement. "That was my metaphor."

Under friendly questioning, he treated himself as a highly responsible, firm-jawed civil servant, concerned with national security, relations with Congress, and general updating of administrative processes. He had stepped in to give the senators an inside view of how the shop was run. When the questioning would ramble on to Watergate or other uncomfortable topics, he would still be the preoccupied executive, excusing himself for not having knowledge of matters outside his immediate field or too minor to claim his attention, saying blandly over and over, "I'm not your best witness on that." This did not work with Pat Gray's friend from Connecticut. "I am not your man," Ehrlichman told Weicker, when Weicker demanded a responsive answer to a question involving the Pentagon Papers. "*You're* the man," Weicker thundered, like a school-play Jehovah descending from a cloud. "You're a *good* witness." Unfortunately, by this time Senator Ervin, tired of using the gavel to quell the hissing and bursts of applause, had announced that persons expressing approval or disapproval would be removed from the hearing room.

Ehrlichman's bold maneuvers to pose as a nonwitness to what was virtually a nonhappening bearing the name of Watergate had an effect, similar to the Mitchell effect, of making the proceedings seem perfectly senseless, like the break-in they were meant to be probing into. If you got to the bottom of Watergate, there would be nothing, a mirage. At the same time, though, his disparagement of Watergate and all the futile nonproductive activity leading up to it and away from it began to raise, for the first time, a fundamental question: Did Watergate make sense or not? If the burglars had not been caught, would it have paid off?

Magruder had testified that Mitchell had been disgusted by the meager fruits of the first break-in, and this, he said, became the reason for the second. But the first break-in's failure to deliver did not lie so much in mechanical ineptitude (one of the original bugs did not work) as in the nature of the project. What was to be gained from tapping Larry O'Brien's telephone and hearing his secretary make appointments with her hairdresser? The risk of detection had to be measured against the off-chance of learning something compromising. If, unlikely as that seemed, the Democratic Party had a secret strategy, they were not going to be discussing it on the telephone. O'Brien knew about taps.

The dirty-tricks department, by comparison, looked like a good investment. It was active, where the Liddy operation was passive. If the Democrats had nothing worth overhearing, Liddy's men had nothing to deliver, whereas the dirty tricksters could intervene positively in the Democrats' affairs, writing false letters, disrupting the candidates' schedules, hiring blatant homosexuals and pseudo-homosexuals to lead their demonstrations, pressing explosives on veterans-against-the-war-in-Vietnam groups... It almost seems as though the Mitchell-Haldeman-Ehrlichman thesis was right: Watergate *was* stupid.

One arrives then at a mystery. Someone higher than Magruder must have approved it, and what could have been the object, if not "intelligence," of which there was so little to be gathered? Perhaps Watergate responded to a soul need of the Nixon circle rather than to an immediate utilitarian goal? A need for total control of the environment. The model may be found in the Eastern bloc countries. Listening devices installed in offices, hotels, homes, embassies serve no directly profitable purpose but simply go on recording, like an endlessly playing phonograph, furnishing employment to a vast labor force of translators and file clerks who are the only visible beneficiaries. The very purposelessness is part of the point. The citizen can find no graspable, identifiable reason for a bug to be in his house, but he guesses it is there and feels unnerved and apprehensive, to the point where he may fear to go to bed lest he talk some nonsense in his sleep.

Now we come upon this same seeming purposelessness in the White House monitoring system. The Nixon crowd, whenever they approached the President, have been under hidden surveillance. He has been under surveillance himself, like an older person setting an example. True, only Haldeman and a few others were supposed to know, but the Polish UB does not *tell* you that they have installed microphones in your apartment. At the White House an uneasy feeling got around, evidently. Dean had told of holding a Dictaphone up to the receiver when talking to Ehrlichman from Camp David. A Boy Scout improvisation. The hearings brought to light considerable evidence of regular taping of each other by Nixon's mistrustful associates—a contagion, doubtless, from the top.

This week we heard Ehrlichman tell about sounding out Judge Byrne, who was presiding at the Ellsberg trial—on a presidential offer to head the FBI. And what did they do when they met? At Ehrlichman's suggestion, they took a walk in a park. Just as you would do in Warsaw or Belgrade, and just as John Dean and Kalmbach did when they met in Washington to arrange the hush money payments. But what were these men so suspicious of when they sought the privacy of the outdoors? Indoors, they could scarcely have feared that Senator Sam would have planted a wheezy tape recorder in a drawer or be listening on an aerial attached to an ancient parked car.

In the White House and at San Clemente it must have been their own people they mistrusted—with reason—either each other or a parallel apparatus in government, FBI or CIA. For men working under these conditions the desire to extend surveillance to the opposition party would be almost automatic. No immediate gain may have been anticipated; any gleanings would have been treated as a windfall.

The Ellsberg-Fielding burglary, to which the hearings keep coming back, as though by a homing instinct, offers some illumination when set beside Watergate. There were the same personnel—Hunt and Liddy —the same failure to obtain results, the same effort to involve the CIA, apparently as a "cover," the same evident lack of sense, if the pretended aim—to protect national security—is taken as serious. The real aim, to smear Ellsberg in the press—clearly stated in the Krogh-Young memo ("How quickly do we advance to bring about a change in Ellsberg's image?") but never admitted by Ehrlichman—itself belonged more to dreamland than to current US real life.

Everybody knew that Ellsberg had been going to a psychiatrist, so how could the usual details—Oedipal murder fantasies, desire to dethrone Authority—in a doctor's file have hurt him with the press? Ehrlichman, disavowing the smear intention, was not called upon to explain. Reverting, as always, to national security, he did testify lingeringly and with emphasis to the President's intense "interest in the case." "The President was really putting the pressure on us." His own self-protective interest here, obviously, was to show himself as a mere wondering instrument of the overriding presidential will. But in his enthusiasm to make it graphic he became indiscreet. Senator Weicker: "Are you telling me you did the break-in to satisfy the President of the United States?" Ehrlichman rapidly retreated: "No." Yet for once it had sounded as if John D. Ehrlichman had been telling something like the truth.

Whoever approved Watergate may not have been conscious of any particular compelling reason for spying on the Democrats and have acted only at the behest of an ungovernable urge. The pathology suggests Nixon.

—July 29, 1973

Sources

The essays in this volume are reprinted from the following collections by Mary McCarthy:

"Introduction to *Theatre Chronicles*," "Class Angles and a Wilder Classic," "Shaw and Chekhov," "Eugene O'Neill—Dry Ice," "A Streetcar Called Success," "A New Word," "The American Realist Playwrights," and "Elizabethan Revivals" from *Mary McCarthy's Theatre Chronicles 1937–1962* (Farrar, Straus and Company, 1963).

"A Bolt from the Blue," "Burroughs's *Naked Lunch*," "J.D. Salinger's Closed Circuit," "On *Madame Bovary*," and "Hanging by a Thread" from Mary McCarthy, *The Writing on the Wall and Other Literary Essays* (Harcourt Brace Jovanovich, 1970).

"On Rereading a Favorite Book," "Acts of Love," "Philip Rahv (1908–1973)," "F.W. Dupee (1904–1979)," and "The Very Unforgettable Miss Brayton" from Mary McCarthy, *Occasional Prose* (Harcourt Brace Jovanovich, 1985).

"The Fact in Fiction," "America the Beautiful: The Humanist in the Bathtub," "Mlle. Gulliver en Amérique," "My Confession," "Up the Ladder from *Charm* to *Vogue*," and "Letter from Portugal" from Mary McCarthy, *On the Contrary* (Farrar, Straus and Cudahy, 1961).

"*Ideas and the Novel*: Lecture I" from Mary McCarthy, *Ideas and the Novel* (Harcourt Brace Jovanovich, 1980).

"The Home Program" from Mary McCarthy, *The Seventeenth Degree* (Harcourt Brace Jovanovich, 1974).

"Notes of a Resident of the Watergate" and "The Moral Certainties of John D. Ehrlichman" from Mary McCarthy, *The Mask of State: Watergate Portraits* (Harcourt Brace Jovanovich, 1974).